AF835708

161984.
T34

PROPERTY AND PROTECTION

Property and Protection

Legal Rights and Restrictions

Essays in Honour of
BRIAN W. HARVEY

Edited by
F. MEISEL and P. J. COOK

•HART•
PUBLISHING
OXFORD – PORTLAND OREGON
2000

Hart Publishing
Oxford and Portland, Oregon

Published in North America (US and Canada) by
Hart Publishing c/o
International Specialized Book Services
5804 NE Hassalo Street
Portland, Oregon
97213-3644
USA

Distributed in the Netherlands, Belgium and Luxembourg by
Intersentia, Churchillaan 108
B2900 Schoten
Antwerpen
Belgium

© The contributors severally 2000

The contributors severally have asserted their right under the Copyright, Designs and Patents Act 1988, to be identified as the authors of this work

Hart Publishing is a specialist legal publisher based in Oxford, England. To order further copies of this book or to request a list of other publications please write to:

Hart Publishing Ltd, Salter's Boatyard, Folly Bridge,
Abingdon Road, Oxford OX1 4LB
Telephone: +44 (0)1865 245533 or Fax: +44 (0)1865 794882
e-mail: mail@hartpub.co.uk
WEBSITE: http//www.hartpub.co.uk

British Library Cataloguing in Publication Data
Data Available
ISBN 1–84113–063–X (cloth)

Typeset by Hope Services (Abingdon) Ltd.
Printed and bound in Great Britain on acid-free paper by
Biddles Ltd, www.biddles.co.uk

BRIAN WILBERFORCE HARVEY

Brian Harvey's wide range of interests are well represented in this fine collection of essays on "Property and Protection". the editors, Frank Meisel and Peter Cook (long time colleagues at the University of Birmingham) have marshalled a set of papers that are at once eclectic and appropriate to the man they honour.

Brian has always combined scholarship with a very practical turn of mind. I think I can claim to have noticed that when I sat on the Electoral Board of the Faculty that recommended his appointment in 1973 to the Chair of Property Law that he was to hold for 22 years. In 1973, Brian was returning after a ten year absence to the University that had given him his first academic post. In between times he had, like many budding academic lawyers, played a part in the development of one of the new law schools of the newly independent countries of Africa—in his case, the Nigerian Law School. And, as with other seasoned "Africa hands", he went on to Queen's University, Belfast, progressing rapidly through the ranks of Lecturer, Senior Lecturer and Professor.

His travels did not end when he returned to Birmingham in 1973. He later assisted Queen's University, Belfast, as adviser to their Institute of Professional Studies and as a member of the Committee on Legal Education in Northern Ireland, chaired by Sir Arthur Armitage. He was also an external examiner at various overseas Universities, including Hong Kong, Malaysia, Nairobi and the West Indies. He spent a year in the mid-1980s as a Visiting Professor at the National University of Singapore and spoke at Commonwealth Law Conferences in Hong Kong and Jamaica.

But, after 1973, the University of Birmingham became very firmly Brian's base. He did his stint as Dean of the Faculty of Law (1982-85) and, like an earlier long serving Birmingham Law Professor (Owen Hood Phillips) he served as Pro-Vice-Chancellor of the University (1986–91).

During Brian's two decades and more as Professor of Property Law, he not only taught effectively and wrote regularly on property law topics. Books and articles poured from his pen on a much wider range of legal matters. One subject area he developed, in which I took a special interest when I was Director General of Fair Trading, was consumer protection. The first edition of his book "The Law of Consumer Protection and Fair Trading" was published by Butterworths in 1978 and quickly established itself as a leading textbook as the subject took off in the syllabus of many Law Schools. Now in its 5th edition, the work is now shared with Deborah Parry, a contributor to this Festschrift.

The practical dimension to Brian's work rested on the very firm basis of his admission as a Solicitor of the Supreme Court in 1961, full-time practice as a solicitor in the early 1960s and continuous part-time practice from 1973 to 1987. The University of Birmingham benefitted greatly from his agreeing to take on the part-time role of being in charge of the University's Legal Office 1990-1999. The creation of this Office came about following the large amount of legal advice and drafting which Brian himself undertook in earlier years, dealing among other things with the constitution of the University Senate and student discipline. But in addition, Brian put his legal knowledge and experience at the service of the community at large through his willingness to act as part-time chairman of Greater Birmingham Social Security Appeals, Medical Appeals and Disability Appeal Tribunals from 1982 to 1999. He has heard Consumer Credit appeals (for the Department of Trade and Industry) against decisions of the Director General of Fair Trading since 1990.

No one who knows Brian for more than a very short time will be unaware of his deep love of music. He had made music by way of solo broadcast recitals and through singing with various choirs, most notably the Choir of Worcester Cathedral and the University Choral Society. For some years he played violin in the University Orchestra.

In his career as a lawyer, Brian created many links: between scholarship and legal practice, between teaching and writing, and between all of these and judicial work as a member of various appeal tribunals. But even his music is not isolated, cut off from his legal career. He is the legal adviser of the British Violin Making Association and author of "Violin Fraud—Deception, Fraud, Theft and the Law" and "The Violin Family and its Makers in the British Isles—An Illustrated History and Directory". Brian is very much a "joined up" modern man. He is well rounded, at home in the library, the lecture room, on the Bench, and in the concert hall. His friends and colleagues have done him proud in this volume and he is deserving of that.

Gordon Borrie
March 2000

Contents

Table of Cases

Australia

Canada

European Commission and Court of Human Rights

European Court of First Instance and Court of Justice

New Zealand

South Africa

United Kingdom

Supplementary Benefits Commission and Department of Health and Social Security

United Nations Human Rights Committee

United States of America

Notes on Contributors

LORD BORRIE QC

TIM KAYE is a Lecturer in Law at the University of Birmingham and Consultant to the Education Team at Martineau Johnson Solicitors.

PETER COOK is a Lecturer in Law at the University of Birmingham.

CARLA J SHAPREAU is an attorney with the law firm of Giancarlo & Gnazzo, PC, in San Francisco, California. An art law and intellectual property litigator, as well as a violin maker, she co-authored the second edition of *Violin Fraud, Deception, Forgery and Law Suits in England and America* with Brian Harvey.

FRANK MEISEL is a Senior Lecturer in Law at the University of Birmingham.

DAVID FELDMAN is a Legal Adviser to the Joint Select Committee on Human Rights, Houses of Parliament, and Professor of Law at the University of Birmingham.

JONATHAN HARRIS is a Reader in Law at the University of Nottingham.

JEREMY MCBRIDE is a Reader in International Human Rights at the University of Birmingham.

DEBORAH L PARRY is a Lecturer in Law at the University of Hull and co-author of *The Law of Consumer Protection and Fair Trading* (with Brian W Harvey) and *Consumer and Trading Law, Text, Cases and Materials* (with CJ Miller and Brian W Harvey).

DAVID SALTER is a Senior Lecturer in Law at the University of Birmingham.

JOHN STEVENS is a Senior Lecturer in Law at the University of Birmingham.

MP THOMPSON is Professor of Law at the University of Leicester

NICK WIKELEY is a Professor of Law at the University of Southampton.

JCW WYLIE is a Professor in Law at the University of Cardiff

NORMAN PALMER is a Barrister and Professor of Commercial Law at University College, London

Introduction

If Brian Harvey is described as an eclectic in two of the contributions to this work, then it is in the best possible taste–denoting an intellectual 'cherry-picker', someone who is selective yet compound, broad rather than exclusive, multiple and yet clearly faceted. In an age where there is a tendency to pigeon-hole and, perhaps, for legal academics (along with practitioners) to be driven to narrower and yet even more narrow specialisms, Brian stands out as a polymath–learned, engaging and academically versatile.

The multifaceted nature of Brian's work has posed a challenge for us, the editors of this collection of essays. We have tried to reflect both his many interests and the several areas of the law to which Brian has made such a distinctive and distinguished contribution. To that end we have assembled contributions from authors working in the fields of property law (both real and personal) and consumer protection, and from other colleagues whose main interests lie in more disparate areas such as tax law, social security and last, but by no means least, in auctions law.

Nevertheless, composite themes do emerge from the range of issues addressed. The general focus of the book is on the nature and extent of property rights. The nature of property rights is concerned not only with what it means to own property–in the sense of establishing what rights an owner has and what significance such ownership carries with it–but also with the circumstances under which (and the extent to which) others may acquire rights in and over such property.

One incident of ownership is the right of disposition. The rights of a purchaser (broadly defined) may come into conflict with claims to protection made, for example, by virtue of the existence of equitable rights in the property. The judges may be regarded here as exhibiting a certain "fumbling in the formulation of the principles to be applied", to employ the phrase used by one of the contributors. Limitations on dispositive powers may also find expression in the context of revenue law and the 'chess match' between taxpayer and Inland Revenue is given fresh analysis. Equally, the position of a purchaser of goods gives rise to special concerns and considerations when he or she is a 'consumer' and accordingly consumer protection issues are examined, especially in the light of European Community initiatives. Auction sales throw up peculiar problems for buyers and the issue of disputed bids is subjected to scrutiny.

In the opening chapter, Norman Palmer explores, largely through the medium of modern commonwealth judicial developments, the characteristics and extent of possessory titles in the context of the rights of a finder of a chattel.

In a painstaking analysis, he examines relativity of title and the role of bailment in resolving questions of title to personal property. David Feldman then questions the extent to which public law principles and values might encroach upon private law rights, and argues that the demarcation lines between public and private landholding should remain distinct. He maintains that the different interests which public and private landholding serve must be respected and that it is neither necessary nor desirable to reconceptualise property rights as being intrinsically limited by public rights and freedoms. This debate is particularly relevant in the post- Human Rights Act era. Also with an eye to Human Rights, Tim Kaye examines the nature of property rights to argue that the right to education (the New Labour 'talisman') is indeed in the nature of a proprietory right (rather than a merely contractual one) with implications for admissions, exclusions and special need provision in our schools. International human rights provides the perspective for Jeremy McBride's analysis of the burgeoning jurisprudence on compensation or restitution claims in respect of expropriation of property under former 'iron-curtain' regimes. Finally, in the 'property' rather than 'protection' field, Peter Cook looks at the nature of property rights as revealed by an historical study of the English Game laws and argues that the Game Law system, as essentially in operation between the seminal Game Acts of 1671 and 1831, was based on a statutory suppression of the notion of common law property rights rather than, as Blackstone and other later writers were to maintain, on political and social power based on the continued and effective application of aspects of the royal prerogative to this area.

The dominant property theme then expands more into how property law strives to balance the rights of the owner (or more pertinently a purchaser from the legal owner) with the competing claims for protection by holders of rights of occupation. The law has long attempted to grapple with this major problem. The specific problem of the non-owning spouse is treated by John Wylie, who has taken a comparative approach contrasting the solutions offered in Irish law with those achieved in England and Wales. The Republic of Ireland's frontal attack on the issue by the Family Protection Act–despite leaving difficulties of construction with which the Irish courts have had to contend–may be regarded as contrasting favourably with the 'fumblings' of the lawmakers in England and Wales. The problem is not, of course, confined to the spouse (deserted or otherwise); other cohabitees are similarly affected. The problems associated with dispositions by the owner are exposed by the incidence of mortgage possession actions which may result not only in the dispossession of the mortgagor but also in the loss of a roof over the head of a mere occupier. The exponential increase in mortgage re-possessions, the high water mark of which was reached in 1991, brought the question of balance into sharp relief. Mark Thompson examines the impact of legislative and judicial intervention in favour of these occupiers in a contribution which shows that the old aphorism that the mortgagee is entitled to possession 'as soon as the ink is dry on the mortgage deed' is rendered somewhat diluted. The impact of *Cheltenham and Gloucester Building Society* v.

Norgan may prove to be decisive in helping to secure the interests of the hard-pressed mortgagor and render the so-called 'right to possession' merely a remedy in the hands of the mortgagee. With a wider sweep, John Stevens then calls for a resurgence of equity's willingness to temper conveyancing needs with doctrines designed to protect holders of informal rights in the land. Such a 'moral dimension' in the conveyancing machinery was formerly manifested in the doctrine of notice. The abolition of the doctrine in favour of a registration system may create efficiency and certainty but is achieved at the cost of notions of justice and fairness. Similarly, with 'justice considerations' in mind, co-ownership–and especially inchoate co-ownership rights–can pose a difficulty in relation to the definition and valuation of jointly held capital for social security (or, more specifically, income support) purposes. Nick Wikeley shows how the courts have struggled to interpret and apply complex regulations and how, to a greater or lesser extent, the resulting decisions may prove a lottery for benefits claimants. Brian Harvey, as a former chairman of the supplementary benefit appeal tribunal, will perhaps appreciate the need for the blunt axe approach involved in treating co-owners as having equal shares but, surely, the trusts of land reform campaigner in him would recoil from that.

Brian's interest in consumer protection matters is reflected in the contributions of Deborah Parry and Jonathan Harris. Deborah Parry assesses the impact of European Community initiatives on consumer protection in the UK. She notes that the results over the last quarter century have been something of a 'curate's egg' with some palpable gains but also some losses. Sometimes consumer interests may appear to be sacrificed on the altar of free movement, and the Community's rules on origin marking may be an instance of this. Jonathan Harris looks at the impact of the United Kingdom's accession to the Brussels Convention (on jurisdiction and judgments) and the Rome Convention (on applicable contract law), both of which have specific provisions designed to protect consumer buyers under private international law. In particular the consumer enjoys the advantage of litigating in the 'home courts' and is entitled to the protection, to a considerable extent, of his or her own laws. In the gamble of litigation these are powerful chips.

Tax is, of course, one of Benjamin Franklin's certainties. What is also an inevitable fact of life is that wealth owners will seek to avoid tax. However, the dividing line between avoidance and evasion may be difficult to draw and David Salter, specifically re-visiting issues addressed by Brian Harvey in a public lecture in the Faculty of Law, Queen's University, Belfast over thirty years ago, asks how far avoidance may be attacked by appeals to moral considerations. Any attempt , he argues, to attack avoidance schemes by the deceptive simplicity of a general anti-avoidance provision founders on the rock of uncertainty, an uncertainty which is a product of the size and Byzantine complexity of the tax system itself. In relation to Auctions Law, there are also tax problems–especially in relation to VAT–but Frank Meisel's contribution, the penultimate essay in this festschrift, looks rather at the particular problem of rival claims to the status of the highest (and therefore the successful) bidder at auction. Brian Harvey's work in auctions, and the law and practice relating to them, brings together a number of the many facets of his interests: auctions involve the sale of a wide range of personal and real property, including art, antiquity, musical instruments and reversionary interests in land. The transaction gives rise to particular problems for buyers, not least that they are deemed not to be consumers under the Unfair Contract Terms Act 1977, while auctioneers find themselves subject to a plethora of consumer protection statutory offences including those under the Trade Descriptions Act. Finally, as a reflection of Brian's passion for music and musical instruments, Carla Shapreau writes on violin fraud, the subject of their joint work covering deception and forgery in this area in both England and America. As readers of Lord Borrie's biographical note will be aware, Brian has not only been concerned with writing about the law relating to violin fraud, he has written also a handsome book on violin making. And, ever marrying the theory with practice (not that anyone would suggest that he has practiced the art of instrument deception!) he has mastered the techniques of both making and playing that instrument

As editors of this volume we owe a considerable debt of gratitude to the contributors. Their patience in the preparation of final copy has been enormously appreciated, and we are certain that Brian will enjoy thoroughly their wide-ranging and thoughtful contributions. Particular thanks must also be directed towards Denise Lees, who was responsible for preparing the copy in a format to be sent to the publishers (somehow finding time from her demanding Common Professional Examination Course duties in order to assist fully in the process). It is not necessary for us, as editors, to speak of our respect and deep affection for Brian Harvey; that goes without saying. The ready willingness of the contributors in making their papers available in such good time and with such a sense of goodwill speaks volumes in itself. We should, however, record formally our deep appreciation of the continual encouragement and help of Richard Hart and Hannah Young at Hart Publications. They helped turn a nice idea into a splendid reality. Primarily, however, it is firmly hoped that Brian himself will be able to look on this collection of essays as a mark of the esteem in which he was held throughout his university career, and equally of the genuine and fond attachment that all of those involved in this work (along with many others) have for him.

Frank Meisel
Peter Cook

1

Bad Apples and Blighted Windfalls: Finding, Bailment and the Fruits of Crime

NORMAN PALMER*

A. INTRODUCTION

DESPITE THE enactment of the Treasure Act 1996,[1] there remains in England and Wales[2] a wide range of objects which fall subject to the old common law of finders,[3] with all its contradictions and flaws.[4] At common law, the right to a discovered object depends mainly on priority in possession: the party first in possession is said to have title against anyone except the true owner.[5] This rule has at least one exception, in that possession gained by trespass may be ineffective against the occupier on whose land the trespass occurred,[6] though the

* Professor of Commercial Law, University College London; Barrister; Chairman, Ministerial Advisory Panel on the Illicit Trade in Cultural Objects.

1 The Act came into force on 24 September 1997. For discussion of the pre-existing law and the need for reform see R. Bland "Treasure Trove and the Case for Reform" (1996) 1 *Art Antiquity and Law* 11; C. Cheesman "Religious Offerings and the Intention to Recover in the Law of Treasure Trove" (1996) 1 *Art Antiquity and Law* 27; N.E. Palmer "Treasure Trove and Title to Discovered Antiquities" in Palmer and McKendrick (eds.) *Interests in Goods* (1st edn., 1993), ch. 12, p. 305. For analysis of the Act itself see N.E. Palmer "The Treasure Act 1996" in *Title To Finds and Discovered Antiquities*, Institute of Art and Law Seminars, 3 October 1995 (2nd edn.).

2 Scotland is governed by a different legal regime: see D. Carey Miller "Treasure Trove in Scots Law" in *Title to Finds and Discovered Antiquities*, above.

3 For a modern example, see *The Times*, *Daily Telegraph*, 7 August 1998 and leader items therein (discovery in Cornwall of slate tablet inscribed with the name "Artognov", an early version of "Arthur").

4 As to some of these, see Law Reform Committee, 18th Report, *Conversion and Detinue*, Cmnd 4774 (1971) Appendix I; R. v. *Hancock* [1990] 2 Q.B. 242 at 251–252 *per* Auld J., C.A., for the court; N.E. Palmer "Title to Discovered Antiquities after the *Waverley* Decision," in *Title to Finds and Discovered Antiquities*, Institute of Art and Law Seminars, 3 October 1995 (2nd edn.) and N. Bamforth, "Finding and Possession in English Property Law" in *Title to Finds and Discovered Antiquities*, Institute of Art and Law seminars, 3 October 1995 (2nd edn.).

5 E.g., *Parker* v. *British Airways Board* [1982] 1 Q.B. 1004 at 1019, 1021, *per* Eveleigh L.J.

6 In this and subsequent references to an "occupier", it will be assumed that the occupier is in possession of the relevant land. It should be noted, however, that occupation does not necessarily denote possession, and that for our present purposes possession of land is the critical factor. For a modern analysis of the conceptual interrelation of ownership, title, possession and occupancy of

occupier had no possession of the object itself.[7] In that event the finder appears to defer to two rivals: the true owner and the party against whom he trespassed.[8] Moreover, a finder may later abandon his possession,[9] or he may voluntarily subordinate it to that of a third party, for example by leasing the object for a fixed term, or by creating a lien over it.[10] In such circumstances, parties other than the true owner may again have a right of possession superior to that of the finder. But the search for title is essentially a search for the first possessor.

This essay explores the strength of that title and tests the proposition that, subject only to the interest of the owner, the finder's right is universal. In so doing, it seeks to evaluate the role of bailment as an alternative means of resolving questions of title to discovered objects. It takes, as its starting point, a recent Australian decision. The facts of that decision raise critical questions about title to personal property, only some of which are answered by the decision itself.

B. THE *FLACK* DECISION

In *Flack* v. *Chairperson, National Crime Authority and Another*[11] the police took possession of a briefcase containing Aus. $433,000 in Aus. $50 notes. They had found the hoard while conducting a search at the home of the applicant, Mrs Flack, who rented the premises on a residential weekly tenancy from the Department of Housing. The police suspected that Mrs Flack's son (who had a key to the residence but did not live there) was involved in drug-dealing. The case was concealed behind some other bags at the back of a cupboard in the hall and Mrs Flack denied all knowledge of the money. The search was conducted

land, see *Mabo and Others* v. *The State of Queensland (No. 2)* (1991–1992) 175 C.L.R. 1 at 188, 206–211, 212–214, *per* Toohey J.

[7] *Parker* v. *British Airways Board* [1982] 1 Q.B. 1004 at 1009, 1010, 1017, *per* Donaldson L.J.; *Webb* v. *Ireland and the Attorney General* [1988] I.R. 353 at 379–380 *per* Finlay C.J.; *Waverley Borough Council* v. *Fletcher* [1995] 4 All E.R. 756 at 766–767 *per* Auld L.J.; and see Palmer *Bailment* (2nd edn., 1991) ch. 23, pp. 1457–1459. The trespass rule, if sound, appears to apply regardless of whether the trespass which precipitates the find is to land, to another chattel, or even (semble) to the person.

[8] As to the superior claim of the latter over the finder, see *Parker* v. *British Airways Board* [1982] 1 Q.B. 1004 at 1009, 1017, *per* Donaldson L.J.; *Byrne* v. *Hoare* [1965] Qd. R. 135 at 168 *per* Hart J. (dissenting, but not on this point). In theory, there may be a third person to whom the trespassing finder defers, namely, any one else who was already in possession of the chattel at the time of the finder's taking into possession. But in practice, the reducing into possession in such circumstances is likely to constitute a simultaneous trespass against the possessor. Cf. note 38 below.

[9] As to this, see generally A.H. Hudson, "Abandonment" in Palmer and McKendrick, eds, *Interests in Goods* (2nd edn., 1998), ch. 23, p. 595; *Re Jigrose Pty Ltd* [1994] 1 Qd. R. 382; *Keene* v. *Carter* (1994) 12 W.A.R. 20.

[10] Such a lien would be unlikely to bind the owner: see Palmer, *Bailment* (2nd edn., 1991) ch. 26, pp. 1656 *et seq*; *Pegasus Leasing Ltd* v. *Cofini* (1991) unreported, 13 November, Sup. Ct. N.S.W., Eq. Div.

[11] (1997) 150 A.L.R. 153 (Fed. Ct., Australia, Hill J.), upheld, sub. nom. *Chairman, National Crime Authority and Another* v. *Flack* (1998) 156 A.L.R. 501 (Fed. Ct. on appeal from a single judge of the F.C.A.) Application for special leave to appeal was dismissed by the High Court of Australia on 14 May 1999. And see further note 171 below.

under a warrant and the removal of the briefcase and its contents by the police was lawful. But no charges were brought and the police eventually conceded that there was no "current operational necessity" for the money to be retained. Even so, they refused to return the money, and Mrs Flack sued on the strength of her possessory title. She succeeded on the ground that hers was the prior and superior possession and that this gave her an enduring right to the find.

The first instance decision of Hill J. (upheld by a full Federal Court) confirms that an occupier of land can possess a concealed object without being aware of the presence of that object within the bounds of her land or indeed of its very existence.[12] It also confirms that proof of possession suffices to establish the finder's right without proof of ownership,[13] that the possessor can at common law recover damages scaled to the full value of the chattel,[14] that the *Parker* principle of "manifest intention" applies to above-ground finds in Australia,[15] that the necessary manifestation of intention will almost invariably (if not always) exist where the premises are a private residence[16] and that the intention need not extend to the specific object.[17] Along with that comes specific recognition that the acceptance of the obligation of a bailee towards an object is not a prerequisite to the acquisition of a possessory title as occupier of the land where it was found.[18]

> "It is a characteristic of possession that the possessor be in a position to exercise control over that which is possessed and assert a general right to do so. In public premises, such as a shop or airport lounge, the owner/occupier of the premises is *a fortiori* not in a position to exercise control over goods which may happen to come on to the premises. The owner/occupier may, in a particular case, accept that control and in that case will have possession of the goods. The nature of the premises raises no inference in such a case as to the ability to exercise control. In a particular case, even where the public has access to the premises, the owner/occupier may be able to demonstrate the ability to control goods on the premises and may assert a right to do so . . . that would be a question of fact.
>
> It is different in a private house or other non-public area. Ordinarily the owner/occupier in such a case asserts control, not only over the property, but all that is within it. It will be irrelevant that the owner/occupier is aware of the existence of the

12 (1997) 150 A.L.R. 153 at 157, 161, 162; cf. at 164–165.

13 *Ibid.*, at 156.

14 *Ibid.*, at 157; see *The Winkfield* [1902] P. 42, not cited, but the principle clearly followed. Cf. the doubts expressed by Hutley J.A. in *Maynegrain Pty Ltd* v. *Compafina Bank* [1982] 2 N.S.W.L.R. 141 at 155–156, on appeal without reference to this point (1984) 58 A.L.J.R. 389, P.C. Hutley J.A.'s misgivings are not generally shared by English or Australian courts: see Palmer, *Bailment* (2nd edn., 191) ch. 4 especially at 313–314; *Doodeward* v. *Spence* (1908) 6 C.L.R. 406 at 418 *per* Higgins J. (dissenting, but not on this point). The rule in *The Winkfield* has been upheld on at least two recent occasions by New Zealand courts: see *Gardiner* v. *Metcalf* [1994] 2 N.Z.L.R. 8; *Trailways Transport Ltd* v. *Thomas* [1996] 2 N.Z.L.R. 443.

15 (1997) 150 A.L.R. 153 at 159–160, 161, 162–163. As to this, see further p. 5 below.

16 *Ibid.*, at 162–163.

17 *Ibid.*, at 162.

18 *Ibid.*, at 164, apparently doubting *Grafstein* v. *Holme and Freeman* (1957) 12 D.L.R. (2d) 727 at 734 *per* Le Bel J.A. on this point. Cf. at 165 and the views of Foster J. on appeal: below, pp. 9–10.

article in or on the property. The ability to exclude others from the property includes the ability to exclude others from all goods which are in or on it. In such a case the nature of the premises and the rights inherent in the owner/occupier of such premises of themselves raise an inference as to the ability to exercise control over goods in or on the premises or perhaps a presumption . . .

[W]here the goods in question are found in a private residence a finder cannot assert a better title than the owner/occupier on the basis that the owner/occupier had no knowledge of the existence of the goods and, they not belonging to the owner/occupier, he or she had not accepted an obligation to keep them safe. The owner/occupier does not need to prove that he or she is the owner of the chattels, nor to prove who the owner is. That is the crux of the present case."[19]

These propositions were broadly endorsed on appeal. In common with Hill J., the majority judges[20] held that neither a mere unawareness of the presence of chattels within the bounds of her land, nor the existence of key-holders whom the occupier licences to enter the land in her absence, prevents an occupier from getting possession. Nor did it matter that the briefcase had been deliberately deposited rather than lost,[21] or that the householder had not for twelve or thirteen years been up into that part of the cupboard where the find was located.[22] The test was that articulated in *Parker* v. *British Airways Board*[23] and applied by Hill J., viz whether at the critical time[24] the occupier had a manifest intention to exercise control over the property and all things which might be within it.[25] To fulfil that intention it was not necessary to show a specific intention to assert control over the briefcase and its contents. Here "the position immediately prior to discovery was that [Mrs Flack] had possession and intended to exercise control of both. . ."[26] Nothing in her conversation with the police at the time of discovery contradicted or disclaimed possession. Her contributions to that conversation were readily explicable as "statements of alarm".[27]

The general conclusion was assisted by a presumption that a householder intends to exercise exclusive control over everything within the private domes-

[19] (1997) 150 A.L.R. 153 at 162–163.

[20] Heerey and Tamberlin JJ: see (1998) 156 A.L.R. 501 at 510–12, 515–17. The dissenting judge, Foster J., did not dissent from these propositions: see (1998) 156 A.L.R. 501 at 505–6.

[21] (1998) 156 A.L.R. 501 at 511 *per* Heerey J. ("the authorities do not deny a possessory right to an occupier where the article in question has been hidden or deliberately placed on the premises") citing *Johnson* v. *Pickering* [1907] 2 K.B. 437 at 444–445 and *Re Cohen* [1953] Ch 88. See also *Tamworth Industries Ltd* v. *Attorney General* [1991] 3 N.Z.L.R. 616 at 619–620 (point accepted by both sides); and further below.

[22] (1998) 156 A.L.R. 501 at 515 *per* Tamberlin J: "It is not necessary to actually access all areas of the house in order to retain a general control."

[23] [1982] Q.B. 1004 at 1018, 1019 *per* Donaldson L.J., 1020 per Eveleigh L.J., 1021 *per* Sir David Cairns. The lengthiest citation of these judgments is by Heerey J. (1998) 156 A.L.R. 501 at 510–11.

[24] Identified by Tamberlin J. as immediately before the discovery of the money by the police: *ibid.* at 514.

[25] See esp. the judgment of Donaldson L.J. in *Parker* v. *British Airways Board*, note 23 above.

[26] (1998) 156 A.L.R. 501 at 516 *per* Tamberlin J.

[27] *Ibid.* at 515 *per* Tamberlin J.

tic premises which she occupies. This was a rebuttable presumption of fact,[28] described by Tamberlin J. as designed to assist in the development of a coherent doctrine of possession and a useful way of resolving disputes where there might otherwise be a hiatus in the possessory chain.[29] In his view, it is reasonable to infer that a householder "intends to extend the protection of his house to everything contained therein."[30] Rebutting this presumed intent might be easier where the goods are an inherently illegal substance and it is accordingly improbable that the householder would have intended to afford the protection of his house to them. But that was not the position here.[31]

C. THE MANIFEST INTENTION TEST: UP BUT NOT DOWN?

In a recent decision of the English Court of Appeal,[32] a distinction was drawn between objects in the land and objects on the land. Possession of the former adheres to the occupier without proof of intention and irrespective of whether he knows of the object.[33] Possession of the latter accrues to the occupier only if he manifests an intention to exercise control over the land and over things which may be on it.[34] In the author's note on *Waverley* the logic of this distinction was

[28] And possibly also a legal fiction: (1998) 156 A.L.R. 501 at 514 *per* Tamberlin J. See further *ibid.* at 506 *per* Foster J. (dissenting, but not on this point) who refers to "very strong" but rebuttable presumption of fact and expressly denies a presumption of law (which, in Foster J.'s view, the judgment of Hill J. came close to adopting).

[29] *Ibid.*, at 514–515. Cf. at 511 *per* Heerey J. who thought that it accorded with "common sense" that "the occupier of a private home will ordinarily manifest the necessary intention to control chattels therein."

[30] *Ibid.*, at 515.

[31] In the present situation, Tamberlin J. thought that the householder's intent would probably have been to take the briefcase and contents to the police and to claim it if no further or better claim to possession emerged: *ibid.*, at 516.

[32] *Waverley Borough Council* v. *Fletcher* [1995] 4 All E.R. 756, C.A.

[33] Pollock and Wright, *Possession in the Common Law* (1888) p. 41: "The possession of land carries with it in general, by our law, possession of everything which is attached to or under that land, and, in the absence of a better title elsewhere, the right to possess it also. And it makes no difference that the possessor is not aware of the thing's existence . . . It is free to anyone who requires a specific intention as part of a *de facto* possession to treat this as a positive rule of law. But it seems preferable to say that the legal possession rests on a real *de facto* possession constituted by the occupier's general power and intent to exclude unauthorised interference".

[34] In *Parker* v. *British Airways Board* [1982] 1 Q.B. 1004, the Court of Appeal had upheld the "general principle" stated in *South Staffordshire Water Co.* v. *Sharman* [1896] 2 Q.B. 44 at 47 *per* Lord Russell of Killowen C.J., that "where a person has possession of house or land, with a manifest intention to exercise control over it and the things which may be upon or in it" then, "if something is found on that land, whether by an employee of the owner or by a stranger, the presumption is that the possession of that thing is in the owner of the *locus in quo*." See especially at 1013–1014 *per* Donaldson L.J. and at 1019–1020 *per* Eveleigh L.J., both of whom emphasised that the owner's intention to exercise control over anything which might be on the premises must be "manifest" if he is to gain possession. In *Waverley Borough Council* v. *Fletcher* [1995] 4 All E.R. 756, the Court of Appeal refused to regard Lord Russell C.J.'s statement of principle, or its approval in *Parker*, as compelling the conclusion that objects in or under the land were in the possession of the occupier only if he manifested an attention to exercise control over the land and things in or under it. See especially at 764, *per* Auld L.J.: "where an article is found in or attached to land, as between the owner or lawful possessor

criticised,[35] and one might be forgiven a suspicion that it was fashioned purely to make room for the unsatisfactory decision in *Bridges* v. *Hawkesworth*.[36] In a dissenting judgment in the Queensland Supreme Court, Full Court, Hart J. went so far as to favour the contrary proposition, that the presumption that an occupier intends to exclude outsiders from things under the surface[37] extends to things on the ground, giving the occupier possession of them, regardless of positive awareness or proof of intention.[38] Similar sentiments appear in the judgment of Wells J. in another Australian case, *Minigall* v. *McCammon*.[39]

The judgments in *Flack* case little, if any, light on this point. We have already seen that one of the principal authorities relied on by the finder in *Waverley*

of the land and the finder of the article, the owner or lawful possessor of the land has the better title."

35 Palmer "Title to Antiquarian Finds: Perpetuating the Impenetrable" (1996) 1 *Art Antiquity and Law* 157 at 159–161. Cf. *Tamworth Industries Ltd* v. *Attorney General* [1991] 3 N.Z.L.R. 616 at 621 *per* Eichelbaum C.J., who appears to approve the distinction.

36 (1851) 5 Jur. 1079; 21 L.J.(Q.B.) 75: see below.

37 Such a presumption was evidently grounded on the general principle stated by Lord Russell of Killowen C.J. in *South Staffordshire Water Co.* v. *Sharman* [1896] 2 Q.B. 44 at 47; for the subsequent treatment of this principle by the English Court of Appeal, see above and p. 7 below.

38 *Byrne* v. *Hoare* [1965] Qd. R. 135 at 168: "In the absence of evidence to the contrary the possessor [of land] is presumed to intend to exclude and this in my view puts him in possession of things on the land just as much as it does of things in the land, and just as ignorance of the existence of things in the land does not mean there is no possession in the possessor of the land, ignorance of things on the land does not do so either. This gives the possessor of the land possession of all chattels on the land, not in the possession of someone else . . ." Hart J. thought (contrary to the majority but agreeing with Goodhart (1928) 3 C.L.J. 195 at 207) that *Bridges* v. *Hawkesworth* (1851) 15 Jur. 1079, 21 L.J.(Q.B.) 75 was wrongly decided and should not be followed. From its context, the quoted passage appears to be directed to finds gained by trespass or other wrong, but there is little if any reason to suppose that Hart J. did intend to limit it thus. What the passage does illustrate is that claims based on prior possession and claims based on trespass, far from involving distinct arguments in favour of occupiers of land, may often be intimately related: for if the occupier's state of mind in relation to the land and/or chattels on the land is sufficient to render the finder's taking of the specific chattel trespassory, the occupier probably has possession of that chattel, or can at least be presumed to have possession.

39 [1970] S.A.S.R. 82 at 93, Chamberlain J. (at 90) concurring: "In my opinion, a person who is in possession and occupation of a piece of land, or a building or other structure erected on land, is, speaking generally, in possession of everything that is attached to, embedded in or lying on every part of the land, building or structure, and that is not demonstrably and presently in the possession of anyone else. It seems to me that that principle must prevail whether or not the land, building or structure is customarily used by licensees, or invitees. [In this case] the owner of the wallet remained in possession of it after he had put it down, and was attending to the business that brought him to the T.A.B. office, but as soon as he left the office and went on his way, leaving the wallet behind him, it seems to me that it then fell into the possession of the T.A.B. . . . It follows . . . that when the defendant took up the wallet as he was leaving, and straightaway joined his companions in the hotel with the wallet in his pocket, he committed the tort of trespass to goods, because the wallet was taken out of the possession of the T.A.B.: in those circumstances, the general principles with respect to a loser and finder had no application because the goods had been in the possession of the T.A.B. and therefore had not been 'lost' in any appropriate sense." Wells J., while not citing *South Staffordshire Water Company* v. *Sharman* [1896] 2 Q.B. 44 (see note 34 above), clearly favoured a broad principle of occupiers' entitlement much in line with such modern authority as *Parker* and *Waverley*. Bray C.J. admitted that *Bridges* v. *Hawkesworth* was a "much battered" decision, but did not share Wells J.'s apparent (but not explicit) disapproval of it in these proceedings; the case had been approved in both *Hannah* v. *Peel* [1945] 1 K.B. 509 and *Corporation of the City of London* v. *Appleyard* [1863] 2 All E.R. 834 and its validity had not really been argued before the present court.

Borough Council v. *Fletcher*,[40] in support of his argument that the manifest intention test governed objects both in and on the land, was the judgment of Lord Russell of Killowen C.J. in *South Staffordshire Water Co.* v. *Sharman*.[41] Lord Russell C.J. favoured a general presumption that a person in possession of a house or land "with a manifest intention to exercise control over it and the things which may be upon or in it" has possession of objects "found on that land."[42] In *Waverley*,[43] Auld L.J. (for the Court) rejected the requirement of manifest intention in relation to things in the land. In *Flack*, (where *Waverley* was not cited) Hill J. did not confront this discrepancy directly, perhaps because it was unnecessary to the decision: if the briefcase stored at the back of the cupboard were merely on the land there could be little doubt that the test of manifest intention applied. Hill J. did, however, cite the relevant passage in *Sharman* and he approved the decision in general terms, declaring that the principle stated by Lord Russell C.J. was not limited to chattels below the soil.[44] He doubted whether Donaldson L.J. had been correct in *Parker* v. *British Airways Board*[45] to analyse *Sharman* as a decision where the objects were part of the realty[46] and he noted the inconclusive discussion by Dixon J. in *Willey* v. *Synan*[47] of the possible inconsistency between *Sharman* and *Bridges* v. *Hawkesworth*.

Hill J. was less concerned with the vertical range of the manifest intention test (*viz*, whether it covers subterranean objects) than with the specific focus of the occupier's intention where the test applies. His preoccupation was with the respondents' more limited submission that where chattels have not been embedded in the land, so as to form part of the land, "the owner of the land will only have a right superior to the finder, where there is a manifest intention on the part of the owner to exercise control over the specific chattel":[48] a proposition which predicated knowledge of the exact thing. Hill J. did not doubt that unawareness of the existence or presence of the specific chattel was no barrier to possession. The reasoning in *Sharman* could not be confined to chattels which were embedded in the soil and to impose any such restriction would run counter to *Parker*.[49] In Hill J.'s words:

> "When Donaldson L.J. spoke of intention to exercise control "over the building and the thing" he must, therefore, have meant that the control which it was intended

[40] [1995] 4 All E.R. 756.

[41] [1896] 2 Q.B. 44.

[42] *Ibid.*, at 47.

[43] [1995] 4 All E.R. 756 especially at 763–765.

[44] (1997) 150 A.L.R. 153 at 158, 160–161; and see at 164–165.

[45] [1982] 1 Q.B. 1004 at 1013.

[46] Though he accepted that both ownership and possession of chattels "affixed to the realty" would follow the ownership and possession of the realty and said that "[t]hat was the case" in *Elwes* v. *Brigg Gas Co. Ltd* (1886) 33 Ch. D. 562: (1997) 150 A.L.R. 150 at 160. But Hill J. almost immediately refers to the alternative view recognised by Chitty J. in *Elwes*, *viz*, that the boat was still a chattel at the time of the find: *ibid.*

[47] (1936) 57 C.L.R. 200 at 217.

[48] (1997) 150 A.L.R. 153 at 161; and see at 159.

[49] *Ibid.*, at 161.

would be exercised over the building extended generally to things in it, irrespective of knowledge of the existence of the things in question. Put in another way, it is the general manifestation of intention to exercise control over chattels and building which is important, not any specific manifestation of intention to exercise control over a specific chattel in the building. So, where the manifest intention in that sense existed, the right of the owner/occupier of the premises would prevail over the rights of the finder, whether or not, in respect of the particular chattel there was any knowledge of its existence."[50]

Hill J. did take issue, however, with the suggestion by Donaldson L.J. in *Parker* that *Sharman* might be explained as a case where the rings in the mud formed part of the realty. That was one of the grounds favoured by Chitty J. in *Elwes*[51] for holding that the prehistoric boat belonged to the tenant for life. Hill J. pointed out that in *Sharman* Lord Russell C.J. made no reference to *Elwes* (despite its citation to him) and stated a test which applied to things above as well as things below the ground.[52] The true position, of course, is that lost objects can fall into three classes:[53] those which become part of the soil, those which are within the soil but do not form part of it and retain their identity as chattels, and those which are merely on the soil. Objects within the first class cease on integration with the land to be chattels and are the outright property of the owner of the land, whose prior possession of the object (and, *a fortiori*, whose intent to exercise control) are irrelevant. What remains unclear from the judgement of Hill J. is whether in Australia (in contrast to England) the manifest intention test applies to chattels in the second class. If anything, Hill J. appears to favour a broader application of the test,[54] but the immateriality

[50] (1997) 150 A.L.R. 153 at 161.

[51] Above note 46.

[52] (1997) 150 A.L.R. 153 at 160–161.

[53] Cf. the somewhat similar three-fold classification recognised in the "fixtures" cases: *Elitestone Ltd.* v. *Morris* [1997] 2 All E.R. 513; *Melluish (Inspector of Taxes)* v. *BMI (No. 3) Ltd* [1995] 4 All E.R. 453.

[54] Hill J. observes, (1997) 150 A.L.R. 153 at 162–163 that: ". . . the rights of an owner/occupier of premises where goods are found will prevail over the rights of a finder, irrespective of knowledge of the existence of the goods on the part of the owner/occupier and irrespective of an acceptance on the part of the owner/occupier of the obligation to exercise dominion over the goods so long as it can be shown that the owner/occupier manifested an intention to exercise control over the premises in which the goods are and all items in those premises. Such manifestation of intention will be presumed where the premises are residential premises of which the owner/occupier has exclusive possession." This draws no clear distinction between above-ground and below-ground objects, thus implying that one rule governs both. Cf. Hill J.'s observation in (1997) 150 A.L.R. 153 at 162 that: ". . . the outcome of the cases, although not . . . always the reasoning explicit in them, leads to the conclusion that . . . the right of the owner/occupier depends upon the intention, express or implied, by circumstance to exclude others from the premises and things in it rather than intention to exercise dominion over the particular item." But these remarks seem more closely directed to the meaning of intention (must it encompass the specific object?) than to the full range of geographical circumstances in which it must be proved. At 164 Hill J. cites without disapproval a statement by Le Bel J.A. in *Graftstein* v. *Holme and Freeman* (1957) 12 D.L.R. (2d) 727 at 734 which applies the same test to chattels above and below the soil, while appearing to disapprove a remark by the same judge that possessory title may depend on the existence of a responsibility on the part of the land-owner as bailee of the chattel owner. Cf. on the finder's duties the judgment of Donaldson L.J. in *Parker* v.

of the point (and the non-citation of *Waverley*) weaken this aspect of the decision.

No greater guidance can be gleaned from the decision of the appeal court in *Flack*, where again *Waverley Borough Council* v. *Fletcher*[55] was not cited. Whereas, as Tamberlin J. remarked,[56] there was no dispute that the "manifest intention" test applied to determine possession of the find, we are left in the dark as to whether this was because (a) the find was above-ground and qualified as one found "on" the land within the narrow scope allowed to the manifest intention test as favoured in *Waverley*, or (b) the find was within the land and in Australia (in contrast to England) the manifest intention test applies to things both on and in the land. Certainly there is nothing in *Flack* (whether at first instance or on appeal) which decisively discountenances the wider application of the manifest intention test which was disapproved in *Waverley*.[57]

D. OCCUPATION, POSSESSION AND BAILMENT

A further curiosity of the appeal decision in *Flack* is a recurrent judicial reference to the location of goods "within the protection of the occupier's house" in the context of her possession. The improbability of the householder's extending her protection to illegal substances led Tamberlin J. to remark that the normal presumption of intent to exercise control would be rebutted in the case of such commodities.[58] Foster J. applied the concept to further extremes, refusing to

British Airways Board [1982] Q.B. 1004 at 1017, approved by Hill J. (1997) 150 A.L.R. 153 at 160. Elsewhere, however, Hill J. appears to accept that had Mrs Flack known of the presence of the bag in her home, she would have owed an obligation as bailee of its owner to safeguard and control it, and the bag "would thus be in her possession": *ibid.*, at 164, 165. Indeed, Hill J. even suggests that this line of reasoning may have become applicable when Mrs Flack briefly became aware of the existence of the bag before the police took it away. It may be questioned, however, whether she would (as Hill J. believed) have been a "voluntary bailee" in these circumstances; and it is something of an inversion of normal reasoning to say that a person is in possession because she is a bailee. For a case where a very fleeting relationship with the chattel was (apparently) sufficient to give a lessee of land a superior possessory title, see *The Times*, 21 August 1998. There, the leaseholder of land on which a lake was situated succeeded in an application under the Police (Property) Act 1897 in recovering a £20,000 statue of the Hindu goddess Shakti-Gayatri, which had been abandoned in the lake by four Asian people (currently untraced) a year previously. It appears that the police took custody of the statue almost immediately after its abandonment and that the award to the leaseholder was based on the possession which she gained through its deposit on her land. Parties who failed to secure the object for themselves in the proceedings before magistrates at Great Yarmouth included a woman who saw the statue being dumped and who telephoned the police, the Norfolk and Norwich Asian Society and a man who claimed that he was the god Shiva reincarnate and that Shakti-Gayatri was therefore his wife. Despite a national appeal, the true owner could not be traced.

[55] [1995] 4 All E.R. 756, C.A. See "Title to Antiquarian Finds: Perpetuating the Impenetrable" (1996) 1 *Art Antiquity and Law* 157.

[56] (1998) 156 A.L.R. 501 at 514.

[57] In *Flack* (1998) 156 A.L.R. 501 at 514 Tamberlin J. refers to control of everything "in" a private house, but this may simply mean beneath the roof and within the four walls. For what it is worth, he also cites without apparent disapproval *Bridges* v. *Hawkesworth* (1851) 15 Jur. 1079 (1851) 21 L.J. (Q.B.) 75, as does Foster J. (dissenting): (1998) 156 A.L.R. 501 at 505.

[58] *Ibid.*, at 516.

accept that the present householder had the briefcase and contents within the protection of her house, when she would have refused to let them into her house if requested to do so. In his view, possession remained with the depositor who had violated his or her licence to enter the premises and concealed that fact.[59]

Foster J.'s analysis comes close to hinting that possession and bailment are one in this context. He inquires rhetorically whether the householder should be "entitled or obliged, by the presumption relied on, to assume possession" of the goods, when she reacted with such horror to their discovery and clearly would not have tolerated their presence. To answer in the affirmative would be in Foster J.'s view "to impose upon her possession of unwanted goods".[60] It may be answered that, without actual or constructive knowledge, the mere fact that she had possession of the goods would not have imposed on the householder any serious obligation in regard to them, other than to refrain from deliberate or perhaps reckless damage. It is not the possession of goods which carries significant duties but consent to possession[61] and Hill J. had already rejected at first instance the view that acceptance of the obligation of a bailee towards a chattel is necessary to the acquisition of possessory title as occupier of the land where it was found.[62] The point is important in Australia because both Federal and State legal systems, having no legislation explicitly aimed at the public ownership or custody of discovered antiquities, are more heavily reliant on common law to allocate title to such objects.

E. PROJECTING THE TITLE BEYOND POSSESSION

i) General

Perhaps the most important question raised by *Flack* is the durability of the finder's interest. Given that the finder's title derives from possession, can it survive a loss of possession? Does finding confer a right to possession which outlives possession itself?[63]

[59] *Ibid.*, at 507. Cf. the judgment of Hill J. at first instance: note 54 above.

[60] *Ibid.*, at 507. In similar vein, Foster J. found unhelpful Hill J.'s own "rhetorical question" at first instance, *viz*, whether a visitor to the premises could lawfully have taken the briefcase and money away without Mrs Flack's consent? That question suggested a presumption of law in favour of the householder, which is a false analysis. Rather, the essential question was whether the householder could prove a right to possession.

[61] See *Neuwith* v. *Over Darwen Co-operative Society Ltd* (1894) 63 L.J.(Q.B.) 290 (involuntary bailment); *AVX Ltd* v. *EGM Solders Ltd* (1982) *The Times* 7 July (bailment by concealment); and generally Palmer, *Bailment* (2nd edn., 1991) chs. 6, 12. Conversely, the supposed duty of an occupier of land to take lost chattels into his possession, take reasonable steps to reunite them with their owners and care for them meanwhile (as to which see *Parker* v. *British Airways Board* [1982] Q.B. 1004 at 1007, 1008, *per* Donaldson L.J.) seems to arise regardless of whether an occupier was originally in possession of the chattel before its discovery.

[62] (1997) 150 A.L.R. 153 at 164; and see note 54 above.

[63] See generally Palmer, *Bailment* (2nd edn., 1991) ch. 23, pp. 1422–1431.

The consequences of an affirmative answer to this question are plain. If the finder who is currently out of possession nevertheless has the right to immediate possession of the chattel, he can probably sue for conversion[64] and regain possession from a later possessor. But if the finder's title depends on possession alone, it might be vanquished when possession is lost. The succeeding possessor might argue that, since the finder has no possession and relies only on a right to possession, he must prove that right.[65] To an extent, this defence may be circular, since it brings one back to the very nature of the finder's right.

A superficial reading of older authorities might suggest that the finder's right is enduring. In *Armory* v. *Delamirie*,[66] for example, Pratt C.J. described the finder as having "such a property as will enable him to keep it against all but the rightful owner"; a description which has been cited as far afield as India[67] and Queensland,[68] and which, construed literally, would grant the finder superiority over (say) an innocent second finder, or a thief from the innocent finder's bailee. It is highly unlikely, however, that Pratt C.J. had in mind the case where a finder, having lost possession, seeks to recover the chattel from someone who did not directly divest him of it.

Stronger support for the universality of the finder's right might be coaxed from Pollock and Wright,[69] who seem to recognise a difference between direct incursions on possession and other, less immediate, forms of usurpation of the possessor's interest, while accepting that both classes of conduct are remediable at the possessor's behest. In their view, "possession confers more than a personal right to be protected against wrongdoers; it confers a qualified right to possess, a right in the nature of property which is valid against everyone who cannot

64 The qualification stems from the occasionally stated, but questionable, requirement that, to ground conversion, a right of possession must stem from a proprietary right: see *International Factors Ltd* v. *Rodriguez* [1979] 1 Q.B. 351, *per* the majority, and further below. But cf. now *MCC Proceeds Inc.* v. *Lehman Bros International (Europe)* [1998] 4 All E.R. 675, C.A., noted by the author (1999) 4 *Art Antiquity and Law* 69, where the court's approval of the judgment of Buckley L.J. in *International Factors Ltd* v. *Rodriguez*, above, suggests an abandonment of the need for an immediate right of possession to be accompanied by a proprietary interest in order to ground conversion. See also *Lipkin Gorman* v. *Karpnale Ltd* [1991] 2 A.C. 548 at 587 *per* Lord Goff of Chieveley.

65 See, e.g., *Leake* v. *Loveday* (1842) 4 M. & G. 972; *Butler* v. *Hobson* (1838) 4 Bing NC 290; *Gadsden* v. *Barrow* (1854) 9 Ex 514; *Richards* v. *Jenkins* (1887) 18 Q.B.D. 451, C.A.; *Henry Berry & Co. Pty Ltd* v. *Rushton* [1937] St R Qd 109; *Casey Interiors Pty Ltd (in liquidation)* v. *Specialised Roofing Systems Pty Ltd* (1993) unreported, 15 October (Sup. Ct. South Australia, Anderson J.); Pollock and Wright, *Possession in the Common Law* (1888) p. 91. See generally Palmer "Possessory Title" in Palmer and McKendrick, eds. *Interests in Goods*, (2nd edn. 1998) ch. 3 at 65 and cf. *Chabbra Corpn. Pte. Ltd.* v. *Jag Shakti (owner of The Jag Shakti)* [1986] A.C. 337, PC. An argument along these lines was invoked by counsel for the police (Piddington K.C.) in *Russell* v. *Wilson* (1923) 33 C.L.R. 538 at 540 but proved unavailing: see further as to this decision below pp. 15 note 84, 16 *et seq*.

66 (1722) 1 Strange 505.

67 *Mussammat Sundar* v. *Mussammat Parbati* (1889) 16 Ind. App. 186 at 193.

68 *Byrne* v. *Hoare* [1965] Qd. R. 135 at 140 *per* Stable J. ("an ancient rule which has not been affected by the passage of time"), 152 *per* Gibbs J., 175–176 *per* Hart J. See also, as to New Zealand, *Tamworth Industries Ltd* v. *Attorney General* [1991] 3 N.Z.L.R. 616 at 621 *per* Eichelbaum C.J.

69 *Possession in the Common Law* (1888) p. 93; *Perpetual Trustees and National Executors of Tasmania* v. *Perkins and others* [1989] Aust. Torts Reports 80–295, 69, 198.

show a better and prior right."[70] The acknowledgement that the possessor has something more than a mere right to sue "wrongdoers" contributes much to the conviction that possession creates a right larger than the possessory period.

In fact, the solution to this question depends, at least in part, on the identity of the party against whom the finder seeks to assert his right and the relationship between them.

ii) Wrongdoer as finder's bailee

If the finder bails the chattel to another, the estoppel which applies at common law between bailor and bailee will prevent the recipient from pleading that the finder is not the owner.[71] That interpretation appears in at least one case where a finder surrendered goods to police at their request[72] and underpins the first instance decision of Blayney J. in *Webb* v. *Ireland and the Attorney General*,[73] a decision which was reversed by the Supreme Court of Ireland on the interpretation of the terms by which the finder gave up possession.[74] A similar analysis might also have been (but was not) applied in *Parker* v. *British Airways Board*,[75] where the finder handed the find to an official who promised to return it if the owner were not traced,[76] and in *Bridges* v. *Hawkesworth*,[77] where the finder appears to have delivered the find to the shopkeeper on like terms.[78] It seems also to afford an explanation for *Armory* v. *Delamirie*[79] itself, where the jeweller may well have received possession of the jewel as the bailee of the finder. All these decisions might have been decided purely on the basis of the bailee's estoppel, rendering the identity of the claimant as finder, rather than as bailor, irrelevant. On that analysis, any prior possession by the occupier would have become immaterial had the terms of the bailment by the finder obliged the occupier, regardless of that question, to return the object to the finder in the event of the non-appearance of the owner of the chattel. Rights derived from

70 *Possession in the Common Law* (1888) p. 93. See also *Cottee Dairy Products Ltd* v. *Minad Pty Ltd and another* (1997) unreported, 5 August, Supreme Court of New South Wales, Eq. Div., *per* McLelland J: "Possession of a chattel is both presumptive evidence of ownership and a source of transmissible title". The decision appears to accept that a mere immediate right of possession over a chattel, conferred by a party in possession and unconsummated by physical delivery, can be a source of title superior to that of, and enforceable against, a third person, even when that person later gains possession. See the analysis of the case in [1998] Building Law Monthly (February) 1, and further below.

71 Section 8 of the Torts (Interference with Goods) Act 1977 will reverse the position only if the true owner is identifiable, which is of course improbable in cases of this kind.

72 *Bird* v. *Fort Frances* [1949] 2 D.L.R. 791 at 800 *per* McRuer C.J.

73 [1988] I.R. 353 at 363–4.

74 [1988] I.R. 373 esp. at 376–7 *per* Finlay C.J.

75 [1982] 1 Q.B. 1004.

76 *Ibid.*, at 1007, 1008, *per* Donaldson L.J.; see also at 1005.

77 (1851) 15 Jur. 1079, (1851) 21 L.J.(Q.B.) 75.

78 There are indeed faint hints of such an analysis in the judgment of Patteson J.: see (1851) 15 Jur. 1079 at 1082, (1851) 21 L.J.(Q.B.) 75 at 78.

79 (1722) 1 Strange 505.

any prior possessory title in the occupier would then have been given up, as part of the agreement and supervening estoppel which accompanied the delivery of the chattel to that occupier by the finder. Only if there were no surrender on such terms would the identity of the first possessor be an issue.

Bailment may also afford a solution to those cases where the owner of a receptacle delivers it to another under a bailment or sale, while being unaware of goods secreted therein, which the recipient then discovers and seeks to retain;[80] or where land is sold or leased and the purchaser or lessee discovers chattels concealed thereunder;[81] or where an owner of land claims possessory

[80] See generally *Durfee* v. *Jones* 11 R.I. 588; 23 Am. Rep. 528 (1877) (Rhode Island); *Merry* v. *Green* (1841) 7 M. & W. 623; *Cartwright* v. *Green* (1803) 8 Ves. 405; *Thomas* v. *Greenslade* (1954) *The Times*, 6 November. Of these four decisions, only two involved civil actions for the recovery of the secreted articles. In *Durfee*, coincidentally a decision of Durfee C.J., the owner of an iron safe failed in his action to recover US$165 worth of bank bills, which had been found within a crack in the inner lining of the safe, by the defendant, to whom the owner had bailed the safe with instructions to sell. The owner of the safe was not the owner of the bills but claimed that he was entitled to the money "by the right of prior possession": *ibid.* (Am. Rep.) at 529. The judgment of Durfee C.J. somewhat evades the issue by denying that the plaintiff's possession of the safe gave him possession of the money, "except unwittingly," and holding that such possession "if possession it can be called, does not of itself confer a right": *ibid.* Durfee C.J. then proceeds to award the money according to the general principle that the finder of a lost object has a good title against all but the true owner, and supports his decision by reference to the reasoning in *Bridges* v. *Hawkesworth* (1851) 15 Jur. 1079, 21 L.J.(Q.B.) 75, *viz.* that the disputed items were never intentionally deposited with, or otherwise within the custody of, the defendant. Cf. the judgments of Tamberlin J. and Foster J. (dissenting) in the *Flack* decision, above, pp. 9–10. Durfee C.J. also relies on the fact that the defendant himself was in possession and that it is therefore for the claimant "to prove his better right": *ibid.* For criticism of the decision, see Palmer, *Bailment* (2nd edn., 1991), pp. 1430, 1431. *Merry* v. *Green* (an action in trespass, for assault and false imprisonment) has little to contribute on the immediate issue, involving as it did the purchase at auction of a "secretary" containing (in a secret compartment) money and other property belonging to the owner of the desk. Both at 630 *arguendo* and at 631 (by implication) Parke B. denied that there was a bailment of the secret contents to the purchaser, a conclusion which is attributed variously to the absence of intention in the owner to "part with the property" (i.e., semble, deliver it into the purchaser's possession), the absence of intention on the purchaser's part to receive possession, the ignorance of both parties of the presence of the secret items and the lack of any delivery such as to give lawful possession to the purchaser. Aside from the fact that the concepts of bailment and possession were being analysed in the context of the purchaser's criminal liability, it may be questioned whether, on the evidence, the purchaser was not sufficiently willing to take possession of whatever was in the desk as to become, on modern principles, a bailee of the contents from the moment of purchase and delivery (it being known at the time of purchase that there was a drawer which could not be opened). Moreover, it seems legitimate to conclude that, even if the purchaser was not a true (i.e. voluntary) bailee of the secret contents *ab initio*, the bailment by concealment or involuntary bailment which arose on the delivery of the desk to him was sufficient, in the circumstances, to impose on him an estoppel against the owner's title to the contents, and became converted to a (voluntary) bailment when the purchaser became aware of those contents and decided to keep them. A similar analysis could be applied to the briefly reported *Thomas* v. *Greenslade*, where the buyer of old iron boxes for £1 was held not entitled to retain 1,452 National Savings Certificates concealed at the bottom of the boxes. The boxes had been sold, and the certificates were claimed, by the administrators of the deceased owner of the boxes; their claim was upheld by Gerrard J. on the ground that they never intended to sell or otherwise part with the contents. *Cartwright* v. *Green* adds nothing on the foregoing, or other relevant, points. See, as to this decision, Crossley Vaines, *Personal Property* (5th edn., 1973) 421.

[81] See generally D.C. Hoath, "Some Conveyancing Implications of Finding Disputes" (1990) 54 *Conveyancer* 348; N. Bamforth, "Finding and Possession in English Property Law" in *Title to Finds and Discovered Antiquities*, Institute of Art and Law Seminars, 3 October 1995 (2nd edn.).

title to things discovered before he came into possession of the land.[82] To a greater or lesser degree, these cases might lend themselves to an analysis based on the implied acceptance of possession by the secondary possessor on behalf of the original possessor (finder). Such a construction may appear fanciful, but no more so than (for example) the implied licence given to an honest finder by the owner, which gives the honest finder immunity from an action in trespass.[83]

Bailment may also afford an explanation of *Flack* itself. There, it will be recalled, the money was taken lawfully from the claimant under a search warrant. By the time proceedings were issued, the claimant had neither possession nor residual legal ownership of the money. That did not deter Hill J. from awarding Mrs Flack the money on grounds of a superior right derived from her earlier possession. He proceeded on an analogy between an originally wrongful dispossessor (such as a thief) and a lawful dispossessor (such as a police officer) who fails to return the chattel once the lawful limits of his own possession have been exceeded. Someone who visited Mrs Flack at her home while the briefcase was there could not have taken it away without incurring liability to her, and the police should be in no better position. Despite the warrant, they were

[82] *Hannah* v. *Peel* [1945] K.B. 509. In this case, the owner of requisitioned premises, who had not gone into possession of them before the requisition, was held not entitled to a brooch found in a crack of a wall by a serving soldier billeted there. Instead, title was held to lie with the finder, who appears to have been regarded (of the two contestants) as the party first in possession (a conclusion justly questioned by Hart J. in *Byrne* v. *Hoare* [1965] Qd. R. 135 at 170). It is questionable whether the owner might have been treated as akin to a bailor of both premises and things concealed therein, and therefore as having a prior title by reason of the occupier's estoppel in relation to chattels. It is worth noting that a tenant bears a similar prohibition on denying the landlord's title to that borne by the bailee, and that a person can be the bailor of a current possessor without having had possession of the goods prior to the possessor's entry into possession: *Belvoir Finance Co. Ltd* v. *Stapleton* [1971] 1 Q.B. 210; *Johnson Matthey & Co. Ltd* v. *Constantine Terminals Ltd* [1976] 2 Lloyd's Rep. 215; *Transcontainer Express Ltd* v. *Custodian Security Ltd* [1988] 1 Lloyd's Rep. 128. But there are at least two difficulties with this analysis. First, the decisions on non-possessing bailors generally involve chattels which were owned (albeit not possessed) by the putative bailor before possession was assumed by the putative bailee, whereas in our example ownership of the brooch may well have lain with someone whose ownership of the premises was anterior to that of the current owner: cf. *Moffatt* v. *Kazana* [1969] Q.B. 152 and D.C. Hoath (1990) 54 *Conveyancer* 348. Secondly, a bailee's estoppel by attornment has been held, on very different facts, to be peculiar to the immediate parties to the relationship of attornor and attornee, and not to affect the proprietary interests of third parties: *Re Goldcorp Exchange Ltd* [1995] 1 A.C. 74 at 92–95 per Lord Mustill; and see W.J. Swadling "The Proprietary Effect of a Hire of Goods" in Palmer and McKendrick (eds.) *Interests in Goods* (2nd edn., 1998) ch. 20 at 521. Even so, the estoppel which gives a bailor the immediate right of possession against a bailee is almost certainly sufficiently effective against third parties to enable the bailor to sue them in conversion for an unauthorised interference which impairs the bailor's right (cf. *MCC Proceeds Inc* v. *Lehman Brothers International* [1998] 4 All ER 675, C.A.) and it might not be wholly implausible to imply or otherwise identify an estoppel between the owner and the possessor of the land, in relation to things concealed therein, by which the possessor undertakes to surrender found objects and deliver them into the land-owner's immediate possession.

[83] See e.g. *Isaack* v. *Clark* (1615) 2 Bulst 306; *Minigall* v. *McCammon* [1970] S.A.S.R. 82 at 84–87 *per* Bray C.J. and 92–93 *per* Wells J. and the decisions discussed therein. Wells J. thought that the implied licence might require a finder of an object in a place of public resort such as a shop to deliver the object to the proprietor of the premises. The effect of this limitation on the implied licence on the finder/occupier relationship might be to confer on the occupier a right of possession superior to that of the finder. See also *Hays* v. *Fries* (1988) 49 S.A.S.R. 184.

"clearly not entitled to possession of the goods, once the needs of the search warrant have been spent . . ."[84]

There is more than a hint of a bailment relationship in this reasoning, and similar hints can be glimpsed in earlier case-law. In *Byrne* v. *Hoare*,[85] Hart J. (dissenting, but not on this point) said that "if a private person found a valuable chattel in a public street and handed it to a police office and if after inquiries the owner could not be found that person would I think have a valid claim to the chattel." In *Bird* v. *Fort Frances*,[86] McRuer C.J. held that when the police officer "was unable to ascertain who the true owner was, in the absence of any other claim, he ought to have returned the money to the custody from which it came." There seems to be no proper distinction between this case and *Flack* on the basis of the lack of a warrant in *Bird*, because McRuer C.J. went on to say that even with a warrant, assuming no conviction had occurred and the true owner had not emerged, the police would have been obliged to return the find "to the custody from which it was taken."[87] While McRuer C.J. does not say so expressly, the perceived obligation again appears to be based on a view of the police as

[84] See (1997) 150 A.L.R. 153 at 162; and see further at 156–157 citing *Russell* v. *Wilson* (1923) 33 C.L.R. 538 at 546–547 *per* Isaacs and Rich JJ.: "If Mrs Flack does . . . have possessory title, then the fact that that title has been interrupted by the seizure of the bag under the warrant will not provide to the respondents a defence . . . The powers of the Australian Federal Police to search for and seize goods and impliedly to retain them for a reasonable period do not authorise continued detention beyond the time necessary for the investigation or subsequent prosecution. Once the right to retain has expired, what Isaacs and Rich JJ. referred to [see (1923) 33 C.L.R. 538 at 547] as the "superior right" of the police no longer exists and a refusal to return the goods to the person having at the time of the seizure the possessory title will be wrongful." Remarks by Eichelbaum C.J. in *Tamworth Industries Ltd* v. *Attorney-General* [1991] 3 N.Z.L.R. 616 at 620 are presumably to similar effect. The appeal decision in *Flack* gives only perfunctory treatment to the possible projection of Mrs Flack's possessory right beyond the span of her possession. The only judge to consider the matter in any detail was Heerey J., who concentrated on the limited entitlement of the crime authority rather than on the positive rights of the householder, holding that both at common law (*Ghani* v. *Jones* [1970] 1 Q.B. 693 at 709, C.A. per Lord Denning M.R., who thought that "as soon as the case is over, or it is decided not to go on with it, the article should be returned") and by Commonwealth statute (Crimes Act 1914, s.3ZV, introduced by the Crimes (Search Warrants and Powers of Arrest) Amendment Act 1994 (Cth.) (not in force at the relevant time but conforming in Heerey J.'s view to the relevant common law)) the money had to be returned to the householder unless forfeited or forfeitable to the Commonwealth, and no power of forfeiture arose merely because the chattels were inherently suspicious. It followed, in Heerey J.'s view, that the power of the crime authority to retain the briefcase and money "ceased once it was conceded that those goods are not required for the purposes of further investigation or prosecution": (1998) 156 A.L.R. 501 at 512. Such a conclusion conformed to the policy of not extending the executive power to enter private property and seize goods "which is a substantial interference with ordinary liberties": *ibid*. As to the dismissal by the High Court of the application for special leave to appeal, see note 171 below.

[85] [1965] Qd. R. 135 at 156. Cf., on the facts, *Hannah* v. *Peel* [1945] 1 K.B. 509, where the finder delivered the chattel to the police, who, having later delivered it to the landowner, interpleaded. And see *Ghani* v. *Jones* [1970] 1 Q.B. 693 at 709, C.A., *per* Lord Denning M.R; notes 82, 84 above.

[86] [1949] 2 D.L.R. 791 at 800 (Ontario High Court).

[87] *Ibid*., at 801. Cf. *Tamworth Industries Ltd* v. *Attorney General Ltd* [1991] 3 N.Z.L.R. 616 at 620 *per* Eichelbaum C.J. (police searching with warrant and finding money could have, once charges dismissed, no higher right than that of finder, and are subordinate to occupier if latter has prior possession).

bailees. Police officers have been cast as bailees before[88] and it may be plausible to regard the law-enforcement agency in *Flack* in similar terms.[89]

At first sight *Russell* v. *Wilson*[90] seems to afford strong support for a similar analysis, again fortified by an analogy with wrongful dispossession. It will be recalled that Hill J. relied on this decision in *Flack*.[91] The police took possession from Wilson of money alleged to have been received by him from "subscribers" in pursuance of betting operations allegedly prohibited by statute.[92] Wilson was convicted but sued in detinue to recover that part of the money which the police had not returned. The police argued, *inter alia*, that he had neither property nor possession at the time of their refusal to return, that their earlier dispossession of him was lawful (being by warrant), that any possessory title he may formerly have had had ended, and that he therefore lacked sufficient right to recover. The High Court of Australia assumed that the dispossession was lawful as within the terms of the warrant, but upheld the claim.

[88] See for example, *Sutcliffe* v. *Chief Constable of West Yorkshire* [1996] R.T.R. 86, C.A. (where the plaintiff's car was incinerated by vandals two months after the police took possession of it under s. 19 of the Police and Criminal Evidence Act 1984 on suspicion that the plaintiff was rebuilding it with stolen parts, and it was common ground that the police were in possession of the car at the time of its destruction by vandals and as bailees owed a duty of care, though the duty was held not to have been broken); *Goldie-Scot* v. *Chief Constable of Kent* (1995) unreported, 22 November, C.A. (where the plaintiff's caravan, having been stolen from his home, was recovered by the police and shortly afterwards stolen from a fire station next to the police station, where the police had deposited it, and there was held to be a triable issue as to whether the police were bailees and owed a duty of care in bailment). But a duty of care may not arise on the part of the police where its imposition would offend the general rule of public policy that claims in negligence do not lie against the police so far as concerns their function in the investigation and suppression of crime: see generally *Hill* v. *Chief Constable of Yorkshire* [1989] 1 A.C. 53, [1988] 2 All E.R. 238, H.L., and, for recognition of the application of this principle to cases of alleged bailment, *Goldie-Scot* v. *Chief Constable of Kent* (1995) unreported, 22 November, C.A.; *Laing, Henry Ltd* v. *Kent Constabulary* (1993) unreported, 13 December (Judge Simpson); *Lervold* v. *Chief Constable of Kent* (1994) unreported, 9th November, C.A. Cf. now the Human Rights Act 1998, Sched. 1 Part 1 Article 6(1) and Part II Article 1, which may affect the common law immunity. Cf also *Rivers* v. *Cutting* [1982] 1 W.L.R. 1146, C.A. (unsuccessful assertion of liability on police for negligence of garage instructed by police to remove broken down vehicle); *Mazullah Khan* v. *McNamara* (1911) 13 W.A.R. 151 (police liable as bailees of camels taken into custody). Cf. also the cases involving individual police officers as finders (and possibly bailees) of chattels: *Byrne* v. *Hoare* [1965] Qd R 135; *Crinion* v. *Minister for Justice* [1959] Ir Jur 15.

[89] On balance, it appears that the fact that the police might be legally obliged to take possession does not count against their characterisation as bailees: *R* v. *Uxbridge Justices, ex parte Commissioner of Police of the Metropolis* [1981] 3 All E.R. 129 at 133 *per* Lord Denning M.R.; *Kelly* v. *Attorney General* [1978] N.Z. Recent Law 94; and see generally Palmer, Bailment (2nd edn, 1991) 1478 note 36. Cf. *Property Life Insurance Co. Ltd* v. *Edgar* (1980) unreported, 15 March, Sup. Ct. New Zealand (discussed in Palmer, *Bailment* (2nd edn. 1991) 691–694: receiver); *W* v. *Essex County Council* [1998] 2 All E.R. 111 C.A. (fostering agreement) reversed in part without reference to this point [2000] 2 All E.R. 237, H.L. Cf. note 8 above.

[90] (1923) 33 C.L.R. 539 (High Ct. Aust.).

[91] (1997) 150 A.L.R. 153 at 156–157; see note 84, above. Neither of the majority members of the appeal court in *Flack* considered *Russell* v. *Wilson*, and the dissenting judge distinguished it on the ground that the claimant there was indisputably in possession of the contested money before it was seized under warrant: (1998) 156 A.L.R. 501 at 507 *per* Foster J. We later observe that most members of the High Court in *Russell* v. *Wilson* held that the claimant had property in the money and not merely possession: see below.

[92] Gaming and Betting Act 1912 (N.S.W.) s. 40.

The judgment of Isaacs and Rich JJ. comes closest to recognising that mere possession confers an enduring (albeit qualified) title. First, they appear to equate the originally lawful dispossessor whose power of dispossession has ceased by the time of the claim with the originally unlawful dispossessor. So much is reasonably plain from the citation of authorities like *Jeffries* v. *Great Western Railway Co.*,[93] *The Winkfield*,[94] *Glenwood Lumber Co.* v. *Phillips Ltd*[95] and *Eastern Construction Co. Ltd.* v. *National Trust Co. Ltd. and Schmidt*.[96] Secondly, they appear to adopt the wider and literal version of Pratt C.J.'s "all the world" observation in *Armory* v. *Delamirie* cited above,[97] concluding that Wilson had by his possession "a real 'title' to the property, just as lawful and just as powerful as if it were the absolute title, except as against the absolute owner, or any person claiming to hold it by virtue of the absolute owner's authority."[98] Thirdly, they observe that while a possessory title yields to any superior right (*scil*, here the power of the police to divest the defendant) it does so only to the extent of that superior right and revives once those limits are reached. Once the criminal proceedings authorised by the relevant Act were terminated, the police powers of seizure and retention were exhausted,[99] the police ceased to have any title in themselves, and Wilson's position "reverted to that immediately before the seizure" giving him "an instant right as against [the police] to possession."[100]

The remaining judges detected a more powerful right in Wilson and one which made the success of his action for detinue less remarkable. According to Knox C.J. and Higgins, Gavan Duffy and Starke JJ., Wilson obtained both property in the money, and possession of it, when it was first delivered to him by the punters. The seizure by the police deprived him only of possession and he became entitled to resume possession when the criminal proceedings (including his appeal) were over. As Higgins J. expressed the matter, "[t]he money . . . belonged to" Wilson[101] and "[t]he right to possession as against outsiders having no title remained in [Wilson] subject to the temporary right of possession given to the police until conviction, and to the Court until the conviction was affirmed."[102] Nothing in section 48 of the Gaming and Betting Act 1912 (N.S.W.) obstructed the passing of property to Wilson, for that provision merely gave the punters a right to recover their deposits from him, and did not debar the original transmission of property to him.[103] Knox C.J. thought he

93 (1856) 5 E & B 802 at 805 *per* Lord Campbell.

94 [1902] P. 42 at 55 *per* Collins M.R.

95 [1904] A.C. 405 at 410 *per* Lord Davey.

96 [1914] A.C. 197 at 209–211 *per* Lord Atkinson.

97 Above, p. 11.

98 (1923) 33 C.L.R. 538 at 547.

99 *Ibid.*, at 548–549.

100 *Ibid.*, at 549. The judgments of Isaacs and Rich JJ. appear to have been approved by Eichelbaum C.J. in *Tamworth Industries Ltd* v. *Attorney General* [1991] 3 N.Z.L.R. 616 at 627.

101 (1923) 33 C.L.R. 538 at 550.

102 *Ibid.*, at 551.

103 Section 48(1) deemed money or other valuable things received contrary to the Act "to have been received to the use of the person from whom it was received." Section 48(2) provided that such money or other valuable things "may be recovered accordingly."

could detect in section 48 an assumption that property would pass to the illegal operator,[104] while Starke J. did not doubt that the Act "recognises the transaction and the acquisition of property in the goods by the respondent, and then creates a statutory right in the former owners to recover them."[105] Any other construction would make section 48 "meaningless".[106] Nor did public policy compel a refusal to recognise such property.

Russell v. *Wilson* is not therefore as positive an authority for the revival of the finder's mere right of possession as its citation in *Flack* might suggest. And in other respects the bailment-by-finder analysis has its shortcomings. On facts like those in *Flack* it can appear casuistic, and it may not avail the finder where the wrongdoer is someone other than his bailee. If the wrongdoer is a subsidiary possessor (e.g. someone in possession with the consent of the finder's original bailee) the finder may be protected in one of numerous ways: by the discovery of direct rights against the subsidiary possessor under a sub-bailment; by joining the original bailee as a party to the claim against the wrongdoer;[107] by direct action against the original bailee if the surrender of possession was unauthorised; or through a direct enforcement of the bailee's rights against the subordinate possessor, if the bailee can be persuaded to co-operate by suing the wrongdoer, either in bailment if the subsidiary possession was consented to, or under the rule that "possession counts as title" if it was not. In certain cases the court may be persuaded that the finder retained possession throughout the first bailment. That was accepted in *Bird* v. *Fort Frances*, where the son who found the money was held to have retained possession notwithstanding a delivery of custody to his mother. The Court held that possession, once taken, will not be lost "so long as the power of resuming effective control remains."[108] But such an analysis stretches seams and may cause unfair difficulty for a subsidiary possessor who deals with the goods on the authority of the first bailee, by exposing him to liability for conduct occurring without the consent of the finder. In other cases the court may apply a simpler rule that a person deriving possession from the finder's bailee can have no greater right than the finder's bailee himself: again, *Bird* v. *Fort Frances* may favour such a rule. But if none of these devices lends itself to the problem, the stark question again arises.

A case where appellate judges followed a similar path of division to that in *Russell* v. *Wilson* is *Perpetual Trustees & National Executors of Tasmania Ltd &*

[104] (1923) 33 C.L.R. 538 at 543.

[105] *Ibid.*, at 554.

[106] *Ibid.* See, to similar effect as the majority reasoning in *Russell* v. *Wilson*, *R* v. *Collis* [1990] 2 N.Z.L.R. 287 and *Gordon* v. *Chief Commissioner of Metropolitan Police* [1910] 2 K.B. 1080, examined in *Tamworth Industries Ltd* v. *Attorney General* [1991] 3 N.Z.L.R. 616 at 625–628 *per* Eichelbaum C.J.

[107] *Bird* v. *Fort Frances* [1949] 2 D.L.R. 791 at 800 *per* McRuer C.J.; *sed quaere*. Cf. however *Bristol and West of England Bank* v. *Midland Railway Company* [1891] 2 Q.B. 653 at 661–662, C.A., per Lindley LJ., and at 664 *per* Fry L.J.; *The Future Express* [1993] 2 Lloyd's Rep. 452 at 549, C.A. *per* Lloyd L.J.

[108] [1949] 2 D.L.R. 791 at 800 *per* McRuer C.J.

Another v. *Perkins and Others.*[109] There, only one of the three members of the Supreme Court of Tasmania (Full Court) gave detailed consideration to the possessory title of the claimants on the premise that ownership could not be shown.[110]

iii) Wrongdoer not finder's bailee

If someone other than the owner dispossesses the finder, the finder's right can be vindicated on the strength of his possession at the time of the wrong. At common law, in the absence of the owner, possession counts as title.[111] Although opinion is divided, it seems that the finder who has gained possession by theft or trespass may yet recover from a third party who divests him without his authority.[112] So much appears to have been recognised by Isaacs and Rich JJ. in *Russell* v. *Wilson*[113] when they drew their analogy between the unlawful usurper and the party who seeks merely to exploit the ambiguity of the finder's position, to enlarge an originally lawful but limited possession in himself.

A harder case arises where a thief who has stolen the object from the finder, or a bailee who has wrongfully retained it against the finder, sells or pledges it to a third party. The thief or bailee plainly commits conversion against the finder, but does the buyer or pledgee? If the court is prepared to regard the finder's unlawfully terminated possession as persisting for this purpose, and is prepared to treat lightly the controversial rule that a right to possession must be accompanied by some proprietary interest to ground conversion,[114] the buyer or pledgee may be liable in conversion to the finder.

[109] (1989) Aust. Torts Reports 80–295, 69, 198 (Supreme Court of Tasmania, Full Court).

[110] Below, pp. 24 *et seq.*

[111] *The Winkfield* [1902] P. 42, C.A.; *O'Sullivan* v. *Williams* [1992] 3 All E.R. 385, C.A.; *Doodeward* v. *Spence* (1908) 6 C.L.R. 406 at 418 per Higgins J. (dissenting, but not on this point).

[112] See e.g. *Parker* v. *British Airways Board* [1982] 1 Q.B. 1004 at 1010 *per* Donaldson L.J.: "[The dishonest finder] probably has some title, albeit a frail one because of the need to avoid a free-for-all" (and see further at 1017); *Daniel* v. *Rogers* [1918] 2 K.B. 228 at 234 *per* Scrutton L.J.: "[M]ere possession is enough to entitle a person to sue in trover, and . . . he need not show the manner in which possession was obtained"; *Tamworth Industries Ltd* v. *Attorney General* [1991] 3 N.Z.L.R. 616 at 621, 627, *per* Eichelbaum C.J. Cf. *R* v. *Kelly and another* [1998] 3 All E.R. 741 at 744 *per* Rose L.J.; *Bird* v. *Fort Frances* [1949] 2 D.L.R. 791 at 799 *per* McRuer C.J.: "[W]here A enters upon the land of B and takes possession of and removes chattels to which B asserts no legal rights, and A is wrongfully dispossessed of those chattels, he may bring an action to recover the same." Cf. also *Thackwell* v. *Barclays Bank plc* [1986] 1 All E.R. 676 at 689 *per* Hutchison J.

[113] (1923) 33 C.L.R. 538 at 546; and see further at 547–549. See also *Flack* v. *Chairperson, National Crime Authority* (1997) 150 A.L.R. 153 at 165 *per* Hill J. Cf. *Perpetual Trustees and National Executors of Tasmania Ltd and Another* v. *Perkins and Others* (1989) Aust. Torts Reports 80–295, 69,198 at 69, 202 *per* Green C.J.

[114] *International Factors Ltd* v. *Rodriguez* [1979] Q.B. 351; for criticism, see Palmer "Possessory Title" in Palmer and McKendrick, *Interests in Goods* (2nd edn., 1998, Lloyd's of London Press) ch. 3 at 73. It is suggested earlier in this paper (above, note 64) that the requirement of a proprietary right has been impliedly disapproved by reason of the approval given in *MCC Proceeds Inc* v. *Lehman Bros International (Europe)* [1998] 4 All E.R. 675, C.A., to passages from the judgment of Buckley L.J. in *International Factors Ltd* v. *Rodriguez*, above.

Certainly, it is no defence that the buyer or pledgee acquires in good faith, unaware of the finder's interest. Since the thief or bailee lacks title, the buyer or pledgee from him normally gets none: *nemo dat quod non habet*. Subject to the statutory exceptions,[115] good faith in acquisition is immaterial to liability in conversion.[116] The question is, rather, whether the finder is a proper person to sue.

To the objection that the finder lacked possession at the time of acquisition by the buyer or pledgee, and so lacks title to sue, it may be answered (i) that the finder still had an immediate right of possession against the thief or bailee, and (ii) that this surviving right of possession is a sufficient title to enable the finder to sue third parties. In the case of a thief or other wrongful dispossessor, this argument could perhaps be fortified by treating the wrongful dispossessor as akin to a bailee of the finder.[117]

More difficult still is the situation where the finder simply loses possession. For example, goods rescued from a river and stored on the bank may break loose and float away,[118] or a tortoise found in the street and thereafter cloistered in the finder's garden may escape. In each case the object may attract a second finder who reduces it into his possession. The second finder has no relationship with the first finder, has not divested the first finder of possession, and can be made to yield the chattel under the bailment rule only if one adopts a highly synthetic and possibly circular notion of bailment.[119] The difficulty can be averted if possession is deemed to have been retained by the first finder,[120] or if the original assumption of possession is deemed to import ownership,[121] but this is not always so. In many cases it is impossible to avoid the stark question: does the finder's right survive the loss of possession?

iv) A free-standing title

There is virtually no authority. Some judgments imply that the two foregoing bases of protection are exhaustive only where the claimant formerly in possession was a wrongful taker and not a "true" (i.e. "innocent") finder.[122] Those

[115] Sale of Goods Act 1979 ss. 21, 23–5; Factors Act 1889 ss. 2, 8, 9.

[116] *MCC Proceeds Inc* v. *Lehman Bros International (Europe)* [1998] 4 All E.R. 675, C.A., at 685–66 *per* Mummery L.J. 699 *per* Hobhouse L.J.

[117] For the effect of this, see p. 12 and note 82 above.

[118] As in *Deaderick* v. *Oulds* 5 S.W. 487 (1877) (Sup. Ct. Tennessee); below p. 22.

[119] Cf. the "implied licence" theory: note 83 above.

[120] Cf. *McFadyen* v. *Wineti* (1909) 11 G.L.R. 345 (Sup. Ct., New Zealand, Chapman J.), discussed below.

[121] Cf. *Deaderick* v. *Oulds*, above; *McFadyen* v. *Wineti*, above.

[122] E.g., *Byrne* v. *Hoare* [1965] Qd. E. 135 at 144 *per* Stable J., speaking of the rights of the finder against a person to whom the chattel had been delivered pursuant to an order of the court under s. 39 of the Justices Acts 1886 to 1958 (Queensland), similar to the (English) Police (Property) Act 1897: "Previous possession of goods now in the hands of another does not raise a presumption of present title in the previous owner or possessor, unless the person who has received them from him has done so as a wrongdoer, or as an agent or bailee of the previous owner or possessor." Cf. Gibbs J. at 152

decisions which are factually close to the problem either evade it by reliance on an elastic version of possession, or (probably) involve an original possession which both confers and is thereafter underpinned by ownership. In the first category is *Bird* v. *Fort Frances*, in the second are *McFadyen* v. *Wineti*,[123] *Deaderick* v. *Oulds*[124] and (on the majority view) *Russell* v. *Wilson*.[125]

Both *McFadyen* and *Deaderick* concerned title to logs found beside watercourses. In *McFadyen* the respondent Wineti (a native of New Zealand) found a totara log, partly submerged below the waterline and partly buried by silt, straddling the bed and foreshore of the Wanganui River. The log had clearly floated downstream from an unknown starting point. Wineti marked it with his initials in a manner visible to passers-by, intending to use it to build a whare on his return from the Christchurch Exhibition, where he was to be employed. During Wineti's absence McFadyen (who appears at the time of the find to have been Wineti's employer)[126] cut up the log into posts, despite having his attention drawn to the initials. He left the posts stacked on the beach, from which location Wineti removed them on his return. In an action for conversion brought by McFadyen, the Stipendiary Magistrate found for Wineti. On appeal, Chapman J. (citing *Bridges* v. *Hawkesworth*)[127] held that any interest which McFadyen held in the land at the time the log first came to rest alongside it was insufficient to confer on him possession of the log: "There was never such a possession of things merely in doubtful contact with the land as to put them into legal possession even of its owner".[128] That being so, the question was whether Wineti took and sufficiently retained an original legal possession over the log when he found it and cut it with his marks.[129] In holding that Wineti "had done enough to take [original] possession of the log", Chapman J. relied on the respect given to such marks among the natives of the district, the intention of Wineti in making them, the nature of the subject matter and the practical limits on making the log an object of possession and control: "He took possession in the only way in which at the moment he could take it".[130] The judge then held that Wineti had not abandoned the log by his departure to Christchurch or his prolonged

"If however the plaintiff proves that as finder he acquired a good title to a chattel as against all but the true owner, he thereby proves that he is entitled to the chattel." And see the judgment of Hart J. in *Byrne* v. *Hoare* (above note 122, below p. 27); *Irving* v. *National Provincial Bank Ltd* [1962] 2 Q.B. 73, cited by Gibbs J. in *Byrne* v. *Hoare* above at 151–152.

[123] (1909) 11 G.L.R. 345 (Sup. Ct. New Zealand, Chapman J.; Maori got possession and semble ownership of hitherto ownerless totara log by marking it with personal marks). Cf. *Hays* v. *Fries* (1988) 49 S.A.S.R. 184 (owner mistakenly leaving bag in taxi retained possession for purposes of criminal law).

[124] 5 S.W. 487 (1887) (Sup. Ct. Tennessee).

[125] (1923) 33 CLR. 538; above, pp. 16–18. See also *Perpetual Trustees & National Executors of Tasmania Ltd and Another* v. *Perkins and Others* (1989) Aust. Torts Reports 80–295, 69,198; below p. 24.

[126] (1909) 11 G.L.R. 345 at 346. Nothing appears to have turned on this point.

[127] (1851) 21 L.J.(Q.B.) 75, 15 Jur. 1079 (1851); above, p. 6.

[128] (1909) 11 G.L.R. 345 at 346. Cf. the case of the Hindu idol, above, note 54.

[129] *Ibid.*, at 346, 347.

[130] *Ibid.*, at 348.

absence there.[131] In so determining, he spoke plainly of Wineti as someone whose taking of possession had conferred on him ownership of the log,[132] a conclusion assisted by its previous ownerless status.[133]

In *Deaderick*, the claimant was an occupier on whose land a walnut log came to rest. Possession of the log had previously been taken on behalf of the defendant Oulds by his employees while searching for logs which Oulds had earlier cut, marked and sent downstream. The employees released the log from a drift in a mountain gorge where it had become entangled and set it adrift downstream to Oulds's boom, which later broke, causing the log to float to a stream on Deaderick's land. Deaderick warned Oulds not to take it, Oulds disobeyed the instruction and Deaderick sued for replevin. Lurton J. treated the log as lost and Oulds as its finder. That gave Oulds a sufficient title, not only to sue if anyone had taken the log directly from him, but to prevent Deaderick from getting the "relevant superior" title necessary for him to succeed in an action for replevin against Oulds. In the judge's words, Oulds had "the superior right . . . growing out of his prior possession and earlier finding of the log."[134] The right of possession which he got through his original assumption of possession "was not lost by the log subsequently drifting upon the land of [Deaderick], and [Oulds] had a right to take and hold this log against all but the true owner, or one having a superior right of possession to that of the finder of lost property."[135]

In *Flack* itself, none of the judges betrays much awareness of the conceptual problem but Hill J. at first instance, by contributing several general statements of principle which suggest the proficiency of a right of possession to ground an action for recovery, does signal the presence of a surviving right. Chief among these statements of principle is the remark that:

> possession is . . . not just evidence in support of ownership, it confers what the law refers to as a 'possessory title', which is as good as an absolute title of ownership, as against all the world except the true owner: see *Russell* v. *Walker* (1923) 33 C.L.R. 538 at 546. If Mrs Flack does . . . have possessory title then the fact that that title has been interrupted by the seizure of the bag under the warrant will not provide to the respondents a defence.[136]

Support for the independent or free-standing quality of a finder's right might similarly be culled from the recent remark by McLelland J. in *Cottee Dairy*

131 (1909) 11 G.L.R. 345 at 348.

132 *Ibid.*, at 348; and see at 347: "The question here really is whether the acts of Wineti constituted a sufficient possession to turn into a chattel in the sense of a thing capable of being regarded as property that which was before a moveable thing which was not property."

133 *Ibid.*, at 347.

134 5 S.W. (1887) 487 at 488. It is possible that Lurton J. did not regard the acts of Oulds's employees as conferring outright ownership on Oulds, because of a suggestion in evidence that the log had first been cut and lost by one Wilson. Oulds, on the other hand, alleged that the log was one originally cut by him, a point which the judge did not find necessary to decide. Certainly the log had been cut from the tree and had not become entrapped in the gorge in its natural state. On the other hand, it may have been abandoned by an earlier owner, whether Wilson or otherwise.

135 *Ibid.*, at 488.

136 (1997) 150 A.L.R. 153 at 156. Cf., as to the appeal court, above note 84.

Products Pty. Ltd v. *Minad Pty Ltd and Another*[137] that "possession of a chattel is both presumptive evidence of ownership and a source of transmissible title,"[138] and from the observation by Jordan C.J. in *Gatward* v. *Alley*[139] that:

> . . . *de facto* possession of a chose in possession is *prima facie* evidence of ownership, and also of itself creates a legal right to possess which is enforceable against anyone who cannot prove that he has a superior right to possess: any person who interferes with this legal right, without being able to prove a superior right, is therefore a wrongdoer.

More than a century ago, Oliver Wendell Holmes Jr. was prepared to hazard an opinion, albeit guardedly. In his view:

> It is conceivable that the common law should go so far as to deal with possession in the same way as a title, and should hold that, when it has once been acquired, rights are acquired which continue to prevail against all the world but one, until something has happened sufficient to divest ownership.[140]

What other support exists? In cases of possession of land there are judicial statements which appear to favour a surviving right in the original possessor. In *Mabo and Others* v. *The State of Queensland (No. 2)*,[141] Toohey J. took "the better understanding" to be that "if no other factors come into play, then, regardless of the length of time, as between mere possessors prior possession is a better right. Possession is protected against subsequent possession by a *prima facie* right of entry".[142] On one reading, this principle may be confined to the original possessor's rights against an immediate dispossessor in an action for ejectment. But it could also be read as aiding the original possessor's action against a third party: for example, where he seeks to vindicate his title against a person who dispossesses the original possessor's own lawful possessor, or where the original dispossession was lawful and the possession thus gained is later vacated by the dispossessor, leaving a third party to take possession. In either case the possessor may be deemed to retain a possessory reversion in the land sufficient to grant him superiority over later possessors, and his right may not be confined to cases where he was unlawfully ejected by the party currently in possession. If that be possible with land it might be possible with chattels.

137 (1997) unreported 25 August, N.S.W. Sup. Ct., Eq. Div.; see above note 70.

138 This principle appears to have influenced Neasey J. in *Perpetual Trustees & National Executors of Tasmania Ltd and Another* v. *Perkins and Others* (1989) Aust. Torts Reports 80–295, 69,198 at 69,205, into holding that the prior possessors' former possession raised no presumption that theirs was a better title than that of the current possessors. Neasey J. held that this principle was not stultified by the contention that the current possessors' possession was derivative from the prior possessors (cf. the position of the fixtures in the *Cottee* case, above, note 137) because it was not, on the facts, thus derivative: "With respect, I do not think that is a correct view, because the [current possessors'] possession was not derived from [the prior possessors who] . . . were merely prior possessors for this purpose."

139 (1940) 40 S.R. (N.S.W.) 174 at 180.

140 *The Common Law* (1881) p. 238.

141 (1991–1992) 174 C.L.R. 1 at 208–211. Toohey J. also spoke of a presumption that possession has been lawfully acquired: *ibid.*, at 210.

142 *Ibid.*, at 210 and see the cases cited by him at 210, note 93 of his judgment.

Further (albeit diffident) endorsement of the enduring right of a non-owning possessor emerges from the judgment of Green C.J. of the Supreme Court of Tasmania in *Perpetual Trustees and National Executors of Tasmania Ltd and Another* v. *Perkins and Others*.[143] In this curious family tale, two family portraits (one painted by the colonial artist Benjamin Duterreau and the other by an unknown artist) were owned by the grandson of the subjects (Allan Perkins). Allan died in 1949 and his wife Nora (who inherited them) died in 1964. At the time of Nora's death she was living in the family home at Hobart with her three daughters, Elizabeth, Joan and Muriel. By her will, Nora bequeathed all her "household furniture and effects" to her daughters in equal shares. The daughters remained in possession of the portraits from Nora's death until 1967, when they moved to a smaller house and delivered the paintings to their brother Bill, on terms which both his sister Elizabeth and he recalled as being those of an entrustment "on long loan". In 1975 Bill also moved house and delivered the paintings to his brother David in circumstances which, though vague, were found not to constitute a gift. As with the earlier delivery to Bill, the transfer appears to have been prompted by a shortage of space. David and his wife Beryl had the works restored and valued, and in 1985, a year after David's death, his son Tim sold the Duterreau to the Art Galley Board of South Australia ("the Board"). Tim did so in the belief that repeated words of gift spoken to him by his father over the preceding years had made him (Tim) the owner of both works. The Duterreau was delivered to the Board and the unattributed work was packed up ready for despatch to New South Wales, when its despatch was halted by action on the part of solicitors acting for Elizabeth and the executor for Joan, who were the plaintiffs in this action. The defendants were the widow and son of David, and the Board.

Neasey and Wright JJ. (differing from the trial judge) held that, on all the evidence, the sisters were the owners of the works and could recover on the strength of their full title.[144] Green C.J. preferred to uphold the claim on the ground that ownership was in any event irrelevant. The action was in detinue and conversion and in neither case was proof of ownership essential.[145] A "possessory title derived from the fact of possession" was enough to qualify the holder to sue in these torts, and such title was amply established in the plaintiffs, who had possession of the works from Nora's death in 1964 to the delivery from Bill to David in 1975. The bailment to Bill in 1967, being gratuitous and entitling the sisters to recall the paintings at will, had not suspended their possession, which was lawful

143 (1989) Aust. Torts Reports 80–295, 69,198 (Sup. Ct. Tasmania, Full Court).

144 Neasey and Wright JJ. relied *inter alia* on the provisions of Nora's will: see above.

145 *Ibid.*, at 69,201. And see *Winkworth* v. *Christie, Manson & Woods Ltd* [1980] 1 Ch. 496 at 499 *per* Slade J. (detinue and conversion); *Lipkin Gorman* v. *Karpnale Ltd* [1991] 2 A.C. 548 at 587 per Lord Goff of Chieveley; *MCC Proceeds Inc* v. *Lehman Bros International (Europe)* [1998] 4 All E.R. 675, C.A., noted by Palmer (1999) 4 *Art Antiquity and Law* 69 (conversion). Cf. *Jarvis* v. *Williams* [1955] 1 W.L.R. 71, C.A. (detinue); *International Factors Ltd* v. *Rodriguez* [1979] Q.B. 351, C.A. (conversion); *Harris* v. *Lombard New Zealand Ltd* [1974] 2 N.Z.L.R. 161 (proprietary interest needed for detinue but not for conversion).

in its inception and now enabled them to recover the paintings from anyone (*viz*, the defendants) who did not have a superior right of possession. Wright J. agreed with this analysis, while simultaneously concurring with the judgment of Neasey J., who (as we have seen)[146] based his decision for the plaintiffs squarely on ownership rather than on possession or the right to possess.

Green C.J.'s analysis is not without difficulty, even if one accepts the proposition that a bailor to a bailee at will under a gratuitous bailment retains possession during the bailment.[147] But it is within the difficulty that the importance (if any) of his analysis lies. It is at least arguable that the plaintiffs' possession had come to an end at the latest in 1975 when Bill delivered the paintings to David, so that by the time of the alleged wrongs in 1985 the plaintiffs had only (at most) a right to possession stemming from (at most) their prior possession. It is true that the language of Green C.J.'s preference for a title derived from possession might suggest that he regarded the sisters' possession as enduring even after the delivery to David, a view for which there is oblique support elsewhere in his judgment.[148] It is also true that Bill testified that, at the moment of that delivery, David agreed with him that the paintings "belong to the girls",[149] which may have created a sub-bailment at will or (more probably) a direct substitutional bailment at will between the sisters and David, and thereby have sustained their notional possession.[150] Moreover, if Bill's delivery to David, being unauthorised, was a deviation from Bill's own gratuitous bailment,[151] the sisters' immediate right of possession (and thus in Green C.J.'s view, their possession) presumably survived. But at no point does Green C.J. explicitly hold that the sisters' possession survived the delivery from Bill to David and was therefore sustained until the delivery by Tim to the Board of the Duterreau, or until the date of the demand for return of the unattributed work. It is submitted, therefore, that Green CJ.'s reasoning on this point can be read as authority for the view that an initial period of possession in A (in this case, the eleven years from 1964–75) which is unaccompanied by ownership and followed without A's consent by another period of possession in B (in this case, the ten years from 1975–85) confers on A sufficient possessory title to sue in conversion or (outside England) detinue, to remedy a deprivation of the subject chattel: either on the part of B, or on the part of a third party C, where B and C lack A's authority so to act and can show no right of possession superior to that of A. In short, Green C.J. appears to accept that the mere fact of a past possession can generate a present right of possession sufficient to compel a future restoration of possession

146 Above.

147 At 69,203 of the judgment Green C.J. relied on *United States of America and Republic of France* v. *Dollfuss Mieg et Cie SA and Bank of England* [1952] AC 582 at 611, *per* Lord Porter. But cf. Paton, *Bailment in the Common Law* (1952), Preface and pp. 6–9; Palmer, *Bailment* (2nd edn., 1991) 108, where the proposition is contested.

148 (1989) Aust. Torts Reports 80–295 at 69,203.

149 *Ibid*., at 69,202.

150 The theoretical possibility of this analysis in the context of finding is considered above, p. 18.

151 Cf. *Mitchell* v. *Ealing London Borough Council* [1979] Q.B. 1.

though the possessor never owned the chattel. In Green C.J.'s own words, the plaintiffs "had title by possession" which "was not extinguished by the delivery of the paintings to Bill". The defendants were unable to impeach that title by showing any superior right of possession and nothing in the transactions involving Bill gave them any such superior right. Although the Chief Justice did not say so, the case appears in this respect to have been treated as one of *nemo dat quod non habet*:[152] since Bill's right was subordinate to that of the plaintiffs, he could give no right superior to that of the plaintiffs. Such an analysis treats rights of possession as proprietary, capable of transmission against third parties.[153]

That interpretation of *Perkins* may well be fortified by reference to the authorities on which Green C.J. relied. Both the passage from Pollock and Wright cited earlier in this article,[154] and the observations of Jordan C.J. in *Gatward* v. *Alley*,[155] to which he referred[156] appear to recognise this enduring quality in an erstwhile and lawful possession.[157]

v) The Trespassing Finder

Even if the title of the non-trespassing finder has some enduring quality of the type at which Holmes hinted, there remains the question of the trespassing finder. So far as can be seen, only one modern judge has directly considered this issue, and that was in the course of a dissenting judgment where other grounds

[152] But cf. Neasey J. at (1989) Aust. Torts Reports 69, 205.

[153] At (1989) Aust. Torts Reports 80–295, 69,203, Green C.J. further remarked that persons in the position of the defendants "have no more right to assert any rights arising out of their possession than did the jeweller to whom the chimney sweep's boy had given the jewel in *Armory* v. *Delamirie* (1722) 1 Strange 505." There is a possible distinction between the two cases in that the jeweller in *Armory* was almost certainly a direct bailee from the chimney sweep's boy and therefore estopped from denying his title (see above, p. 12) whereas there was almost certainly no direct bailment between the plaintiffs and their brother David or the defendants in *Perkins*. David was probably in possession without the plaintiffs' authority (the sister Elizabeth claimed that the transfer to him occurred without her knowledge: see (1989) Aust. Torts Reports 80–295 at 69, 200 per Green C.J.) and both he and (after his death) his wife Beryl and son Tim were probably at most sub-bailees of the plaintiffs. It is uncertain whether a sub-bailee bears the same estoppel as against his head bailor as a direct bailee bears as against his immediate bailor, though tentative authority to that effect can be cited: *The Hamburg Star* [1994] 2 Lloyd's Rep. 399 at 404–405 *per* Clarke J. See also (1989) Aust. Torts Reports 80–295 at 69,205 where Neasey J. observes that the defendants' possession was not derived from the sisters and that the sisters "were merely prior possessors" for this purpose, thereby suggesting that the parties to the litigation were not bailors and bailees respectively. But the quoted remark by Green C.J. might be seen as an example of the equation between an initially-lawful possession on terms which have since been exceeded and an initially-unlawful possession: see above, pp. 16–17.

[154] *Possession in the Common Law* (1888) p. 93; above, pp. 11–12.

[155] (1940) 40 SR (N.S.W.) 174 at 180; above p. 23.

[156] The material part of Jordan C.J.'s judgment is set out above p. 23.

[157] These two passages were cited both by Green C.J. and by Neasey J.: see (1989) Aust. Torts Reports 80–295 at 69,201–69,202 and 69,205 respectively.

were adduced for the judge's conclusion. In *Byrne* v. *Hoare*[158] Hart J. characterised the possession of the trespassing finder as a naked bare possession incapable of conferring any right which survived beyond the duration of possession itself. That analysis (which would still presumably permit the trespassing finder to recover the chattel from his own bailee, or from someone who took it from him without his authority) enabled the judge to hold that, once the finder was deprived of the find by a court order, he lost all right to retain or recover it. On a wider plane, such reasoning would disable the trespassing finder from, for example, recovering the chattel if he lost it and it were found by a second finder, or from suing a person who stole it from his bailee.[159]

There is support for this view of the fragility of a wrongfully assumed possession in both *Buckley* v. *Gross*[160] and *Parker* v. *British Airways Board*,[161] where Donaldson L.J. cited *Buckley* v. *Gross* in support of his speculation that "a subsequent honest taker [from the unlawful possessor] is likely to have a superior title."[162] Assuming this to be correct, however, at least three further questions arise. First, does Hart J.'s conclusion mean that a *non*-trespassing finder does get an enduring title? Secondly, does the occupier who is the victim of trespass get a title which is not only superior to that of the trespasser but sufficient, for example, to enable him to recover the chattel from a secondary finder, or from someone who derives or takes possession from the wrongdoer? And thirdly, what of an occupier who had possession at the time of the find; does his right endure against (say) the bailee of the non-trespassing finder?[163]

Hart J.'s judgment suggests (but no more) an affirmative answer to the first and second questions.[164] As to the second, it is tempting to view the right of the occupier against the trespassing finder as a modern example of restitution for unjust enrichment, an analysis which arguably conforms with occasional suggestions that the occupier's right derives from the old maxim, no man shall profit from his own wrong.[165] But a right based on unjust enrichment is harder

158 [1965] Qd. R. 135 at 161, 168, 170, 173, 174.

159 Unless (say) his bailee was unrewarded and the court accepted the view (favoured by Green C.J. in the Perkins case, see above pp. 24–5) that the bailor under a gratuitous bailment of this nature remains in personal possession of the chattel.

160 (1863) 3 B & S 566 at 572 *per* Cockburn C.J.; cf. at 572 *per* Crompton J. See G. Battersby and A.D. Preston (1975) 38 M.L.R. 77 at 80.

161 [1982] 1 Q.B. 1004.

162 *Ibid*., at 1010.

163 The rights of the occupier in possession who is the victim of a trespassing finder are presumably governed by the answer to question 2; the occupier can hardly be in a weaker position where he had possession of the object at the time of the trespass.

164 As to the first, see above pp. 10 *et seq*.

165 E.g., *Parker* v. *British Airways Board* [1982] 1 Q.B. 1002 at 1009 *per* Donaldson L.J. Considerable reliance appears to have been placed on this principle by judges considering a question which is, in certain respects at least, the converse of that under discussion, *viz*., whether the transmission of property in goods to an incoming owner confers on that owner, in the absence of an assignment, the right to sue for unredressed "antecedent" wrongs, inflicted on the goods before property passed to him. As to this see generally *Goodman* v. *Boycott* (1862) 2 B & S 1; *Bristol and West England Bank* v. *Midland Railway Company* [1891] 2 Q.B. 653, C.A.; *London Joint Stock Bank Ltd* v. *British Amsterdam Maritime Agency Ltd* (1910) 16 Com. Cas. 102; *Hannam and*

to justify where relief is sought not against the wrongdoer but against some ulterior party who has acquired a later possession. Such a party may have committed no wrong against the owner and his enrichment can only with difficulty be said to be at the owner's expense. As to the third question, it may be thought that an affirmative answer to the second question would make sense only if a similarly enduring right were detected in an occupier who had possession at the time of the find. But these are no more than the thinnest of speculations in an area where the secondary rights which derive from a find are seldom acknowledge, much less explained.

F. CONCLUSION

Modern Commonwealth authority raises some important questions for students of possessory title in all common law jurisdictions. It is remarkable, for example, that whereas in England judges have resisted pressure to extend the "manifest intention" rule to below-soil finds,[166] the judicial bias in Australia has, if anything, curved in the opposite direction, towards applying some automatic or presumptive rule of ownership to things on the ground.[167] So much is plain, perhaps, from the fact that *Bridges* v. *Hawkesworth* has been disapproved by almost as many judges in Australia over the past 40 years as have approved it.[168] The challenge to *Bridges* v. *Hawkesworth* alone is worthy of

Another v. *Arp and Another* (1928) 30 Lloyds L. Rep. 306, C.A.; *Margarine Union G.m.b.H.* v. *Cambay Prince Steamship Co. Ltd* [1969] 1 Q.B. 219; *The Future Express* [1993] 2 Lloyd's Rep. 542, C.A. The view is occasionally taken that, to allow the wrongdoer to evade liability to the new owner on the ground that he lacked the necessary title at the time of the wrong, would be to enable the wrongdoer to benefit from his own wrong: see, eg *Goodman* v. *Boycott*, above, at 7, *per* Wightman J.; *Bristol and West of England Bank* v. *Midland Railway Company*, above, at 663, 664, *per* Lindley and Fry L.JJ. Cf. *Williams* v. *Attorney General* [1990] 1 N.Z.L.R. 1; *Rosenberg* v. *Seattle Art Museum Knoedler-Modarco Inc. Third Party* 70 F. Supp. 2d 1163 (1999) (US District Court Western District of Washington); later proceedings 2000 U.S. Dist. LEXIS 2000.

166 As in *Waverley Borough Council* v. *Fletcher* [1995] 4 All E.R. 756; above, p. 5.

167 Above pp. 4–8. But see, *per* contra, *Re Jigrose Pty Ltd* [1994] 1 Qd.R. 382 at 387, where Kiefel J. applied the "manifest intention" test as stated in *Parker* to bales of hay left on farmland and discovered by the incoming purchaser.

168 It was disapproved by Wells J. (Chamberlain J. concurring) in *Minigall* v. *McCammon* (note 39 above) and by Hart J. in *Byrne* v. *Hoare* (note 38 above); it was approved by Stable J. in *Byrne* v. *Hoare* [1965] Qd. R. 135 at 139 (cf. Gibbs J., who did not specifically refer to the decision) and by Bray C.J. (perhaps reluctantly) in *Minigall* v. *McCammon* (note 39 above). In *Flack*, both parties appear to have disavowed reliance on *Bridges* v. *Hawkesworth*—see (1997) 150 A.L.R. 153 at 158—and probably the most that can be said of the judgment of Hill J. is that it is neutral on the point. On appeal, Tamberlin J. cited the decision only on the question of the time at which possession needs to be shown (see note 24 above), while Foster J. appears to have based his remarks about the need for goods to be within the protection of the occupier's house (above, pp. 8–9) on a passage in Patteson J.'s judgment: see (1998) 156 A.L.R. 501 at 516, and 505–6, respectively. *Bridges* v. *Hawkesworth* was cited in passing by McClemens J. in the faintly bizarre New South Wales decision in *Ranger* v. *Giffin* (1968) 87 W.N. (N.S.W.) 531 at 538, but the find in that case was clearly below ground and nothing turned on the validity of the older decision. In *Tamworth Industries Ltd* v. *Attorney General* [1991] 3 N.Z.L.R. 616 at 619, 621, Eichelbaum C.J. referred to *Bridges* v. *Hawkesworth* as one of a line of "classic authorities."

reflection, though in England the decision itself (for all its incoherence) is unlikely to receive its *quietus* at any level below the House of Lords.[169] No less at odds with modern English law is the apparent approval by Hill J. in *Flack* of an extension of the "manifest intention" test to below-ground cases. But it is perhaps in their acknowledgement of the possible continuance of possessory title beyond the term of possession itself that decisions such as *Flack*, *Perkins* and *Russell* v. *Wilson* have most to offer English courts. It is important that a problem raised by Holmes a century ago,[170] and of critical relevance to the civilised treatment of discovered antiquities, should now be fully ventilated. The decision in *Flack* may well provide a valuable stimulus to that.[171]

[169] It was approved (subject to explanation) in both *Parker* v. *British Airways Board* [1982] 1 Q.B. 1004 at 1011–1014 *per* Donaldson L.J., 1020 per Eveleigh L.J., 1021 *per* Sir David Cairns, and *Waverley Borough Council* v. *Fletcher* [1995] 4 All E.R. 756 at 759, 762, *per* Auld L.J., for the Court.

[170] Above, p. 23.

[171] On 14th May 1999 the High Court of Australia dismissed an application for the grant of special leave to appeal against the decision of the Federal Court. Gleeson C.J. observed that the case "turned upon the application of well settled and indeed, ancient principles of law to the facts and circumstances of what might well have been regarded as a borderline case."

2

Property and Public Protest

DAVID FELDMAN*

WHEN I FIRST studied land law as an undergraduate in 1973, Brian Harvey's book on strict settlements,[1] among the first to be published in Sweet & Maxwell's *Modern Legal Studies* series, was an invaluable guide. I first met Brian in 1977, when he was an external examiner at the University of Bristol. His careful assessments of students' work and his consideration for a very inexperienced young academic inspired respect and gratitude. Since becoming one of his colleagues at the University of Birmingham, I have learned what an invaluable source he is of sound, thoughtful advice drawing on his vast experience, understanding of people and sense of balance in relation to difficult matters of any sort, whether legal, administrative, managerial, musical, or academic. This essay, for a friend and colleague who will (I hope) forgive the temerity of a public lawyer daring to reflect on some aspects of the law of property, is offered with affectionate thanks.

PRIVATE PROPERTY AND THE INTERESTS OF THE GENERAL PUBLIC

The essay examines the effect on land law of recognising freedom of peaceful assembly and protest as a fundamental right in English law. It will be argued that two separate regimes of real property law have developed, relating to land owned by private people or bodies and public authorities respectively. Generally public-property law has started from the basic principles of private-property law, but has restricted the powers of public-authority landowners by reference to principles of administrative law, so that private-property rules have been at the root of public-property law. The public interest in allowing the local population a degree of access to other people's land for limited purposes has been given effect mainly by presuming a grant of such rights by the landowner in accordance with private law. Although this has long been recognised often to be

* Some of the ideas in this essay were tried out in seminars at the Faculty of Law at the University of Birmingham and the Centre for Criminology at the University of Cambridge. I am grateful to all the participants for their assistance, and particularly to Jack Beatson, Andrew von Hirsch, Frank Meisel and Nicola Padfield for their encouragement and thought-provoking comments. Remaining errors and eccentricities are my own.

[1] Brian W. Harvey, *Settlements of Land* (London: Sweet & Maxwell, 1973).

fictitious, it has served to preserve the forms of private law while permitting public objectives to be achieved. The growing significance of fundamental freedoms and human rights in English law has affected this relationship. For the first time, there are signs that the common law is starting to define the scope of the rights of non-owners over other people's land, and to delimit the powers of landowners accordingly, partly by reference to general statements of public interests and public rights. The advent of the Human Rights Act 1998 is likely to encourage this process in ways which will be explored in subsequent sections of the essay. However, the theme of it is that the process of interaction between public-law and private-law principles and values needs to be managed with care. There are some situations in which an unreflective adoption of principles from public law threatens unexpected and perhaps damaging consequences to private law, and vice versa.

People's rights in property can aid or hinder their own and other people's abilities to express their views to the public. In English law, it has traditionally been the case that anyone is free to use his or her own property[2] as a means or vehicle to express views. Subject to the general law regulating public order and land-use planning, anyone can use a notice on a car, an advertising hoarding, a newspaper advertisement, or a hand-distributed sheet to publicise views, advertise goods and services, and so forth. One can hold meetings on one's own premises, admitting or excluding whomsoever one wishes (subject to the powers of the police to investigate crime and deal with breaches of the peace).[3] On the other hand, owners of property can prevent others from using the property if they want to do so, and normally nobody may lawfully use the property of another for those purposes without that other's consent. Those who have appropriate property or are assisted by accommodating property-owners have an advantage over less fortunate people when it comes to participating in markets, political debate, or other forms of expressive activity.

Legal rules have been developed, through legislation such as the Competition Act 1998, Articles 85 and 86 of the E.U. treaty, and American anti-trust law, to control the creation and abuse of monopolistic and oligopolistic power, and land-use planning controls in the public interest are common, but in economically liberal societies these interferences with an owner's freedom to use property require special justification and legislation. This is true of all property: incursion into it without the owner's consent must be justified by reference to positive law. If public authorities interfere with people's property for public purposes, the assumption is that this incursion is limited as to both its extent and

[2] In order to simplify the terminology, I use the phrase "one's own property", and associated terms such as "ownership", to include not only full ownership of land (which lies in the Crown) but also estates and interests in land which permit one to act in the ways described below without interference from owners of other estates or interests in the land. In respect of personal property, the terms are used as meaning rights over the property allowing one to use it in the ways described below without interference from holders of other rights in that property.

[3] *Thomas* v. *Sawkins* [1935] 2 K.B. 249; *McLeod* v. *Commissioner of Police of the Metropolis* [1994] 4 All E.R. 553, C.A.

its purpose, so that it does not negate ownership. As Professor Tony Honoré wrote in a classic analysis of ownership:

> "We happily speak of the ownership of land, yet a largish number of public officials have the right of entering on private land without the owner's consent, for some limited period and purpose. On the other hand, a general licence so to enter on the 'property' of others would put an end to the institution of property as we now know it."[4]

Real property is, in this respect, little different from other kinds of property. In English law, all land is owned by someone. The notion of *terra nullius*, familiar to international lawyers, has no place in a common-law system of property, and there is little systematic differentiation of types of property and the incidents of ownership by reference to the social function which the property or its owner fulfils (although property owned by the Church of England is subject to a rather different regime from other property). By contrast, Roman law had a classification of property which was more sensitive to the practical and social importance of different kinds of property. It recognised that various kinds of people or bodies might have different rights over property which they owned. Updating the language somewhat, public property (including such things as city walls) was owned by state corporations; common property (such as air, running water, sea and sea-shore, although there had been some disagreement about the legal status of the sea-shore) belonged to everyone; and everything else was capable of being held by individuals as private property to the exclusion of others.[5] Sacred things could be owned by nobody, and wild animals were nobody's property until reduced into possession by capture.

Although Justinian relied on natural law to justify this division of things, there were good economic and social reasons for attaching different incidents to each form of property, as Professor Epstein has shown.[6] For example, maintaining defensive city walls could not safely be left to private owners, even if the necessary co-ordination could easily be established between them. The walls were therefore public property, in the ownership of the state. English law contains no typology of property which can compare with the sophistication and contextual sensitivity of Roman property law. Furthermore, land lawyers have tended to assume that ownership of real property is essentially the same whatever the nature of the real property and whatever the social function of the owner. Where this is not to be the case, a special statutory framework has to be set up.

For those who are excluded from ownership, this means that there have been few, if any, places to which they have had a right of access for expressive

[4] A. M. Honoré, "Ownership", in A. G. Guest (ed.), *Oxford Essays in Jurisprudence (First Series)* (Oxford: Clarendon Press, 1960, 1968) 107–147 at 114.

[5] Justinian, *Institutes*, III.1, 11–48. For the position in the second century A.D., see F. de Zulueta, *The Institutes of Gaius, Part II: Commentary* (Oxford: Clarendon Press, 1953), pp. 55–56, on Gaius, *Institutes*, II.1–11.

[6] Richard A. Epstein, "On the optimal mix of private and common property", *Social Philosophy & Policy* vol. 11(2) (1994), 17–41 at 24–34.

purposes. Private places can be closed to them, and public places, in the sense of places to which people other than the owners can have access as of right, are less and less common. The areas which are usually thought of as being public include the seashore, land over which there are rights of common and public highways such as Trafalgar Square in London (including for this purpose public footpaths, bridleways and roads). Such places are "quasi-public". They are not truly public, because all such ground is, in law, owned and controlled by somebody. Ownership is subject to specified rights of, for example, the travelling public over the property, but any use of the property other than for an authorised purpose by anyone other than the property owner is unlawful. It is a trespass.[7] Such trespasses have often been tolerated, by courts[8] as well as landowners, but toleration does not generally create rights unless the rights are acquired by prescription or statutory provisions relating to long user.[9]

The shortage of public space in which there is a right to gather is emphasised by the battery of legal controls which exist over public assembly, expression and protest. Attempts at expression on quasi-public ground are open to three types of control. First, the owner of the property can use the law of trespass to restrict any use of the ground which goes beyond the purpose for which authority to use it was given. Usually the discretion of the owner is unregulated by law, although where the owner is a public authority certain public-law principles will be applied by way of judicial review, as we shall see in the next section. Secondly, the police and local authorities[10] have extensive powers and duties to regulate expressive behaviour in public places, and sometimes in private, to protect historic monuments and other sites of special interest and to protect the local community from disruption.[11] The police also have a duty to preserve the peace, but they enjoy a very wide discretion as to how they do it.[12] A similarly wide discretion operates in relation to the way in which the police and local authorities exercise their statutory powers to impose conditions on meetings and processions, or to ban classes of processions. Thirdly, the law makes certain kinds of behaviour in public or private places into criminal offences.[13] On occasions, the

[7] *Ex parte Lewis* (1888) 21 Q.B.D. 191, D.C.; *R.* v. *Graham* (1888) 16 Cox C.C. 420.

[8] For example, a court may decide to refuse a discretionary remedy to the owner or occupier. See *Llandudno Urban District Council* v. *Woods* [1899] 2 Ch. 705, where a local authority tried to stop a clergyman from holding services on the foreshore, described by Lord Hope of Craighead (dissenting) in *Director of Public Prosecutions* v. *Jones (Margaret)* [1999] 2 W.L.R. 625 at 647 as a case "where the trespass was so trivial or technical that no reasonable person would have objected to it", a view which leaves out of account the comfort of any non-religious bathers who happened to be on the foreshore at the time.

[9] See Lord Hope of Craighead, dissenting, in *Director of Public Prosecutions* v *Jones (Margaret)* [1999] 2 W.L.R. 625 at 647: "It is the extent of the right of access, not the question whether the activity in question ought to be tolerated, which is in issue in the present case."

[10] In London, the Home Secretary exercises the powers of local authorities elsewhere for this purpose.

[11] Public Order Act 1986, Part II as amended.

[12] See R. v. *Chief Constable of Sussex, ex parte International Trader's Ferry Ltd.* [1998] 3 W.L.R. 1260, H.L.

[13] See e.g. Public Order Act 1986, Part I as amended.

law combines prior and subsequent restraint by giving power to the police or a local authority to control or prohibit gatherings or processions, and then making it a criminal offence to gather or process in violation of the order of the police or local authority.[14] The cumulative effect of these powers is to create a situation in which neither owners wishing to enjoy their property, nor protesters exercising freedom of assembly or expression, nor other people going about their lawful business, can be said to have rights to do so, because when order is deemed to be threatened one's freedom of action hinges on the discretion of a public authority.[15] The lawfulness of their action depends on the discretion, tolerance and broadmindedness of police officers, local authorities, and (sometimes) property owners.

However, the position changes when the fundamental freedoms and human rights protected by treaties such as the European Convention for the Protection of Human Rights and Fundamental Freedoms or principles of administrative law come into play. There is a pressing problem now that the relevant provisions of the Convention (especially Articles 10 and 11, on freedom of expression and of peaceful assembly) have become a full part of domestic law in the United Kingdom for all purposes from 2 October 2000. Articles 10 and 11 are as follows:

Article 10

Freedom of expression

1. Everyone has the right to freedom of expression. This right shall include freedom to hold opinions and to receive and impart information and ideas without interference by public authority and regardless of frontiers. This Article shall not prevent States from requiring the licensing of broadcasting, television or cinema enterprises.

2. The exercise of these freedoms, since it carries with it duties and responsibilities, may be subject to such formalities, conditions, restrictions or penalties as are prescribed by law and are necessary in a democratic society, in the interests of national security, territorial integrity or public safety, for the prevention of disorder or crime, for the protection of health or morals, for the protection of the reputation or rights of others, for preventing the disclosure of information received in confidence, or for maintaining the authority and impartiality of the judiciary.

Article 11

Freedom of assembly and association

1. Everyone has the right to freedom of peaceful assembly and to freedom of association with others, including the right to form and to join trade unions for the protection of his interests.

2. No restrictions shall be placed on the exercise of these rights other than such as are prescribed by law and are necessary in a democratic society in the interests of national

[14] See e.g. Public Order Act 1986, ss. 14A and 14B as inserted by Criminal Justice and Public Order Act 1994, s. 70.

[15] See e.g. R. v. *Chief Constable of Sussex, ex parte International Trader's Ferry Ltd.* [1998] 3 W.L.R. 1260, H.L.

security or public safety, for the prevention of disorder or crime, for the protection of health or morals or for the protection of the rights and freedoms of others. This Article shall not prevent the imposition of lawful restrictions on the exercise of these rights by members of the armed forces, of the police or of the administration of the State.

The obligations imposed on the state in international law by these provisions, and those imposed on public authorities by virtue of the Human Rights Act 1998, section 6, recognise the importance of expression and public assemblies, and accordingly limit the discretion of the police and local authorities when taking steps to preserve public order. There must be a real threat of violence against person or property before it will be proportionate (and so necessary in a democratic society) for freedom of expression and assembly to be interfered with on public-order grounds,[16] and the public authority must have taken adequate steps to ensure that it is in possession of the relevant facts.[17] This requires a balance between the rights of assemblers and protesters under Articles 10 and 11 and the rights of property owners under ordinary rules of property law, supported by Article 1 of the First Protocol to the Convention. Both[18] must be supported by public authorities, particularly the police. It is the task of lawyers to adapt the rules of property law as painlessly as possible to the demands of Convention rights. This may be difficult where property-law rules tend to absolutism and lack contextual sensitivity.

Two broad approaches to the relationship between public-law rules and private-property law are available. The first and less radical one would be to allow property-law principles to operate unchanged except where they produce a result which is incompatible with a Convention right, in which case the right would take priority. Section 6 of the 1998 Act provides that (only) public authorities act unlawfully if they act in a way which is incompatible with a Convention right. This aspect of the scheme of the Act suggests that the rights are to operate only "vertically", i.e. as between citizens and state agencies. If so, the Convention rights would affect public-property law and public-authority landowners, not private-property law and private landowners. However, it is likely that Convention rights will have some degree of "horizontal effect", i.e. affect relationships between private persons or bodies. The reasons for this are, first, that courts and tribunals are themselves public authorities and bound by Convention rights; secondly, the Convention rights sometimes impose positive obligations on public authorities to help private citizens to protect their rights against other private citizens; and, thirdly, courts and tribunals are required by section 3 of the Act to interpret all legislation so far as possible in a way compatible with Convention rights, even if in a particular case the legislation binds

16 *Steel and others* v. *United Kingdom*, Eur. Ct. H.R., Judgment of 22 Sept. 1998.

17 *McLeod* v. *United Kingdom*, Eur. Ct. HR, Judgment of 23 September 1998.

18 On the need for the police to protect the right to assemble and protest, see *Plattform "Ärzte für das Leben"* v. *Austria*, Eur. Ct. H.R., Series A, No. 139, Judgment of 21 June 1988, finding a violation where the police had failed to take reasonable steps to protect anti-abortion protesters against counter-demonstrators.

a private party. These factors are likely to result in courts and tribunals sometimes having to give effect to Convention rights in their judgments in private-law cases.[19]

The second, more radical approach would be to reconceptualise property rights as having intrinsic limits imposed by public rights and freedoms where necessary in order to make Convention rights effective. This method, reading public-law limitations into all private-law (as well as public-law) powers, would be different in theory and would sometimes produce different results in practice from the first approach. It would allow the limits of private-property rights to be set by reference to public-law considerations. Taken to extremes, this could produce what Professor Honoré, in the passage quoted earlier, described as "a general licence" which "would put an end to the institution of landowning as we now know it."[20] For example, it might mean that private landlords would be as much affected as public-authority landlords by the Convention right to respect for private and family life under Article 8. Such a right could significantly affect property law in a number of ways. For example, it would mean that a covenant against accommodating more than a set number of people in premises, or a covenant against children, might be unenforceable if it interfered with the tenants' right to respect of family life, while a covenant against animals might be held to interfere with the tenants' right to respect for private life. Such interference might be justifiable as a legitimate and proportionate response to a pressing social need for an authorised purpose under Article 8(2), but it would be for the landlord to justify it as such. It is probably inevitable that public-authority landlords will face such challenges, but to subject private landlords to similar attack would fundamentally change the balance of private-property law. Another effect of the right, whether it is asserted against private landowners or only against the courts hearing property-related litigation, will be to restrict the circumstances in which landowners will be able to obtain certain discretionary remedies, such as forfeiture of a lease or orders for possession of land, against tenants or squatters.

It is of course possible that the first approach might leave the law of property as it applies to private landowners largely untouched, with public rights (derived from the Human Rights Act 1998 or elsewhere) affecting only public authorities. As the next section explains, even a private law of property can, with a little manipulation of fictions, accommodate some public rights and interests, and, indeed, has done so. There could be no need to resort to public law to give effect to public rights and interests in relation to private property. However, subsequent sections will show that this is unlikely. A separate system of public-property law has already developed, and there is a growing

[19] See Sir William Wade Q.C., "*Human rights and the judiciary*" [1998] E.H.R.L.R. 520–533 at 524–525; Murray Hunt, "*The 'horizontal effect' of the Human Rights Act*" [1998] P.L. 423–443; Gavin Phillipson, "*The Human Rights Act, 'horizontal effect' and the common law: a bang or a whimper?*" (1999) 62 M.L.R. 824–849.

[20] Honoré, *loc. cit.*, n. 4 above.

cross-fertilisation between public law and private law in the real-property field, which has potential pitfalls.

ADAPTING PRIVATE-PROPERTY RULES TO GIVE EFFECT TO PUBLIC INTERESTS: GRANTS, FICTIONS, AND THE EXISTENCE OF RIGHTS OF WAY AND VILLAGE GREENS

The tradition in English law has been to regard the public-interest aspect of the use of land for such purposes by the general public as governed by private law, and as being subordinate to the landowner's private right to determine who may use the land and how. This can be seen in the law governing proof that a person has a right to pass over, or carry out other activities on, another person's land. There is no significant difference between the methods of establishing a private right, or easement, of way and a public right of way. Both depend on private-law principles, needing either a grant (in the case of an easement) or dedication to public use (in the case of a public right of way), or acquisition of the right by prescription. In each case, the prescription at common law arose from proof of use since time immemorial, originally the accession of King Henry I in 1100 but later brought forward by statute in stages to the accession of King Richard I in 1189 as proof of facts dating back over 100 years became practically impossible.[21] As Lord Hoffmann explained in R. v *Oxfordshire County Council, ex parte Sunningwell Parish Council*,[22] this period did not operate as a bar to a claim by the landowner for a remedy but "to presume that the enjoyment was pursuant to a right having a lawful origin", i.e. a grant by the owner. But as time passed and it became more difficult to establish enjoyment since 1189, various fictions were developed at common law so that use for 20 years could give rise to an easement, by way of the fiction either that it was evidence of user since 1189, or that it was evidence of a lost modern grant of an easement, which would be conclusive in the absence of positive proof that such user or grant was impossible.[23] It was necessary to prove that the user had been *nec vi, nec clam, nec precario* (neither by force, nor by stealth, nor with the owner's permission), a need for any of which would have negatived the existence of a (fictitious) grant. In the case of private easements, statute made it impossible for the landowner to allege that the user had arisen later than 1189 once user for 20 years had been established, giving rise to a straightforward prescription without reference to any fiction that there had been a grant.[24] The statute applied where the user had been by someone "claiming right thereto", or "as of right",[25]

[21] Statute of Westminster I, 1275 (3 Edw. 1, c. 39).

[22] [1999] 3 W.L.R. 160 at 165, in a speech on which this section of the essay draws extensively.

[23] See *Bryant* v. *Foot* (1867) L.R. 2 Q.B. 161, 181 *per* Cockburn C.J.; *R.* v. *Oxfordshire County Council, ex parte Sunningwell Parish Council* [1999] 3 W.L.R. 160, 166 *per* Lord Hoffmann.

[24] Prescription Act 1832, s. 2 as amended.

[25] *Ibid.*, ss. 2, 5.

phrases which were interpreted as meaning the same as *nec vi, nec clam, nec precario.*[26]

Establishing public rights of way or common also depended on an actual or presumed dedication. The latter could be established by proving user by the public since 1189. However, user for any period beginning later than 1189 was merely evidence from which a dedication could be inferred, as long as the user had been *nec vi, nec clam, nec precario.*[27] The fictions which operated in English law in relation to private-law easements, such as lost modern grant, were not extended to public rights of way or rights of common. It was therefore very much more difficult to establish rights for the general public over someone's land than to establish an easement benefiting only owners or occupiers of adjacent land. It was only in 1932 that statute provided that enjoyment of a way by the public "as of right" for a period of at least 20 years was to be deemed to have been dedicated to the public use "unless there is sufficient evidence that there was no intention during that period to dedicate such way. . ."[28] Thus the presumption of dedication based on 20 years' enjoyment in the case of public ways, unlike easements of way, can be rebutted by evidence of the landowner's contrary intention during that time.

Rights of common or rights to a village green are even more difficult to establish. English private law has been very unwilling to tolerate such rights. It was consistently held that no private-law easement could be created simply to wander over or remain on private land for unspecified purposes or periods (*ius spatiandi* or *ius manendi*) except by Act of Parliament or, perhaps, express grant.[29] Under the Commons Registration Act 1965, there are only three ways of establishing a right for the general public to do such things on land designated as a town green or village green:

i. allocation of land by Act of Parliament (such as the Inclosure Acts) for the exercise or recreation of inhabitants of the locality;
ii. evidence of a customary right (i.e. dating back at least to 1189) of inhabitants of the locality to indulge in lawful sports and pastimes; and
iii. use by inhabitants of the locality for lawful sports and pastimes as of right for at least 20 years.[30]

Of these, only class iii. made possible the acquisition of new village greens by prescription. Class i. is an example of a right being specially created in the public interest by statute, independently of any presumed grant. Class ii., like other

[26] *Bright* v. *Walker* (1834) 1 C.M. & R. 211, 219 *per* Parke B.; *Gardner* v. *Hodgson's Kingston Brewery Co. Ltd.* [1903] A.C. 229, 239 *per* Lord Lindley.

[27] See *Mann* v. *Brodie* (1885) 10 App. Cas. 378, 385–386 *per* Lord Blackburn.

[28] Rights of Way Act 1932, s. 1(1).

[29] See *Attorney-General* v. *Antrobus* [1905] 2 Ch. 188 (no public right to have access to tracks round the monument at Stonehenge); *In re Ellenborough Park* [1956] Ch. 131, C.A., at 184 *per* Lord Evershed M.R.; *Director of Public Prosecutions* v. *Jones* [1999] 2 W.L.R. 625, 649 *per* Lord Hope of Craighead (dissenting).

[30] Commons Registration Act 1965, s. 22(1).

customary rights, depends on a presumed grant at some stage before the accession of King Richard I. Class iii. is unusual in allowing for a *ius spatiandi* to be acquired by the inhabitants in an area generally by positive prescription, without any need for a presumption of grant or dedication to public use, on the basis of twenty years of continuous use "as of right", which has been interpreted as meaning *nec vi, nec clam, nec precario* without any necessary intention on the part of members of the public to assert a right.[31]

When one looks at all this for signs of the relationship between public and private law, we find that public rights of passage over and access to land depend heavily on private law rights of landowners being exercised in ways which are tolerant towards the activities of the public. Considerations of public law and the public interest are rarely invoked, except under statute (as in the case of class i. and class iii. town and village greens). Generally public rights are based either on express grant, or on long user which is taken to be evidence of a pre-Richard-I grant or dedication or of a lost modern grant. The requirement that the enjoyment of the facility by the public should have been *nec vi, nec clam, nec precario* means that the landowner or his or her agents will have had ample opportunity to observe the activity in question, and to forbid it or impose conditions on it if so desired. It is thus not at all far-fetched to regard the whole of the law of implied grant or dedication and prescription as based on acquiescence on the part of the landowner, a willing acceptance of the limitation of the right to exclude others which is normally an incident of ownership.[32]

This can be contrasted with the position in Scotland, where the influence of Roman law has produced a rule of positive prescription on the basis of proof of continuous possession or enjoyment for 40 years. This does not depend on any presumed or fictitious grant or dedication on the part of the landowner. Instead it is akin to *usucapio* in Roman law: the use for the period of prescription in itself creates the right.[33] This method of acquiring rights depends to some extent on the landowner's acquiescence, but is far more readily adapted to take account of public-interest considerations, including the value of rights of passage etc., than the general English common-law approach under which a public right could be thwarted on proof that the presumed, fictitious grant or dedication could not have been made within the relevant period.

To sum up this section, prescription is a process whereby the interests of people other than the landowner can be given priority over the landowner's rights incidental to ownership, or indeed in some circumstances even over the right of ownership itself. Where the interests of the general public are set against

[31] *R.* v. *Oxfordshire County Council, ex parte Sunningwell Parish Council* [1999] 3 W.L.R. 160, H.L.

[32] See *Dalton* v. *Angus* (1881) 6 App. Cas. 740, H.L., at 773 *per* Fry J. in his advice to the House of Lords.

[33] *Mann* v. *Brodie* (1885) 10 App. Cas. 378, H.L., at 390–391 *per* Lord Watson; *Director of Public Prosecutions* v. *Jones (Margaret)* [1999] 2 W.L.R. 625, H.L., at 644 *per* Lord Hope of Craighead, dissenting.

those of a landowner, a system which depends in theory and still to some extent in practice on the will of the landowner is less well adapted to giving effect to public interests, or fundamental rights to freedom of assembly and expression, than a system which ignores the will of the landowner would be. Statutory intervention to give effect to particular rights in defined circumstances is the clearest and most satisfactory way of dealing with such matters. However, English law has rarely adopted this approach. Instead, our courts concentrate on the private-law rights of all parties, even when dealing with public-law issues, but introduce fictitious presumptions about past events and the intentions of landowners in order to allow public rights and interests to be taken into account while maintaining this concentration on private law principles.

The other possible approach outlined in the previous section of this essay, allowing public law to act directly on the definition of landowners' rights in private law, would merge property law and public law in a way which could lead to a reclassification of ownership according to the nature and location of the property and the legitimate claims of public authorities or of private individuals exercising fundamental rights. Such a move has been advocated strongly by property lawyers such as Professor Gray,[34] who are concerned to ensure that landownership does not preclude public freedom, particularly of access, expression and assembly. It could produce a classification of property-law regimes which approaches the sophistication and contextual sensitivity displayed by sixth-century Roman law. One significant theoretical side-effect would be to problematise the legitimacy of the institution of property. Expressly or by implication, advocates of this approach require that the judges and Parliament reflect on the extent to which the rules of property law perform socially useful functions which can justify excluding a significant number of people from access to and use of huge tracts of land.

If we embark on this enterprise, property law will become a political issue in two ways. First, the scope of property rights, including tax liabilities associated with them, is properly a matter for political discussion. Property as a legal concept has always been dependent on acts of law-making to define the nature and extent of the rights and their incidents, as the legal protection of property requires institutional action by legal authorities. The second approach will require more conscious thought to be given to these matters. That will be no bad thing, as long as the decision-makers give appropriate weight to the legitimate expectations of security which right-holders have, and which must be respected if the institution of private property is to have the beneficial economic effects of which it is capable.[35] There will have to be an express recognition in property

[34] Kevin Gray, "Property in thin air" (1991) 50 *Cambridge Law Journal* 252–307; Kevin Gray, "Equitable property" (1994) 47 *Current Legal Problems* 157–214; Kevin Gray and Susan Francis Gray, "Civil rights, civil wrongs and quasi-public space" [1999] *European Human Rights Law Review* 46–102.

[35] See Stephen R. Munzer, *A Theory of Property* (Cambridge: Cambridge University Press, 1990), pp. 79–80; David Schmidtz, "The institution of property", *Social Philosophy & Policy*, vol. 11(2) (1994), 42–62 at 46–48.

law that the goods and lands which the law allows a person to control may be used as political instruments. Where the law allows right-holders to exclude others from the use of or access to property, the right-holder's *dominium* may be used negatively in order to impede other people's ability to advance their own political views effectively. A broadcasting monopoly or oligopoly may deny opportunities for communication to people who hold views of which the monopolist or oligopolists disagree. In a democracy, it is arguable that ownership rules should not preclude some citizens from participating in politics in these ways while giving to others privileged access to expressive power and influence. Producing a system of property law which is conducive to political and social inclusion and participation would tend to merge the values of private and public law, diluting the liberal (in the economic sense) model of property.

The application of rules of administrative law to publicly owned property, and the passage of the Human Rights Act 1998, would be consistent with the development of limitations on property rights according to the first approach outlined above, restricting rights of ownership only where necessary to protect fundamental rights and public-law values. The next section shows how this has been happening, producing what is really a special system of public-property law. On the other hand, two recent decisions of the House of Lords suggest that a trend towards the second approach, restricting private-law property rights generally by reference to principles of public utility and public law, may be starting to develop, although another recent decision of the House of Lords suggests the contrary. Subsequent sections will therefore assess the impact of the separation and cross-fertilisation between the public and private laws of property in English law.

PROPERTY HELD BY PUBLIC AUTHORITIES: AN ADMINISTRATIVE LAW OF PROPERTY

In a number of recent cases, there have been signs that public-law principles were being applied to local authorities in ways which limited the way in which they could control use of their property. Three examples will suffice.

In *Wandsworth London Borough Council* v. *Winder*,[36] a council brought an action for possession of a council house because the tenant refused to pay an increased rent. The House of Lords held that the tenant could defend the action by arguing that the decision to increase the rent had been unreasonable on administrative law principles, despite that fact that the council's action was in form a private-law action brought in the County Court, and notwithstanding the earlier decision of the House of Lords in *Cocks* v. *Thanet District Council*[37] that a council tenant could not maintain a claim against the council in private-

[36] [1985] A.C. 461, H.L.
[37] [1983] 2 A.C. 286, H.L.

law proceedings where the success of the claim depended in part on establishing that a decision of the council (relating to the tenant's right to be housed as a homeless person) was flawed as a matter of administrative law. In *Winder*, the House of Lords decided that a council tenant should not be deprived of the opportunity to assert the unlawfulness of a claim made against him even if that would involve a court in addressing a public-law issue (the reasonableness of the decision to increase the rent) in a private-law forum. The right not to be evicted on the basis of an unlawful decision was founded on the Rule-of-Law principle of legality, and impliedly accepted that councils, as public authorities, were subject to more controls over the rents which they charged their tenants than were private landlords.

In *Wheeler* v. *Leicester City Council*,[38] the local authority had threatened to refuse permission for Leicester Rugby Football Club to use facilities owned by the council for training. The council were concerned by the club's failure to prevent its players from touring South Africa as part of an international team during the era of apartheid. The club challenged the council's right to refuse to allow it to have access to the training facilities. The land was owned by the council, so on normal principles of property law the council should have been free to decide who, if anyone, could use it and on what terms. However, the House of Lords decided that the council, as a statutory public authority, had to comply with normal public-law principles. Their Lordships accepted that the council's stance was not unreasonable, because it had a legitimate interest in upholding good race relations in its multi-ethnic area. Nevertheless, it was held that the council had acted improperly by, in effect, imposing a penalty on the club for failing to do something which it had no power to achieve, namely to stop its players from travelling to and playing in South Africa.

By imposing a public-law limitation on the freedom of a public authority to deal with its land in the same way as a private landowner, the House of Lords brought land-owning public authorities under a range of restrictions on their powers over the land. These were derived from the general common-law principles of administrative law, not from statutory provisions establishing or conferring powers and duties on the public authorities. The House of Lords did not say that the ownership of the land was outside the local authority's statutory powers; clearly it was not. Instead, their Lordships rewrote the law of property so that a local authority could not claim all the powers and freedoms which are normally incidental to ownership in the same way and on the same conditions as a private landowner could. They were creating a public law of land ownership. In the Court of Appeal, Browne-Wilkinson L.J., dissenting, had wanted to decide the case by reference to the rights of the rugby players to freedom of expression.[39] Had this approach been accepted, it would have made human rights part of the matrix of factors limiting the power of public authorities to

[38] [1985] A.C. 1054, H.L.
[39] [1985] A.C. 1054 at 1061, 1064–1066, C.A.

control access to their land. The House of Lords did not adopt the approach which Browne-Wilkinson L.J. had advocated. Nevertheless, by imposing principles of administrative law on decisions of public authorities relating to the control of land, the decision in *Wheeler* introduced a new type of property, namely public authorities' property, which was subject to some different rules from other types of property by reason of the juridical nature of its owners.

This is not particularly novel in itself. The juridical nature and responsibilities of particular classes of owners have long affected the legal regime governing real property. Land held by trustees is subject to a special set of rights and obligations, and the powers of trustees and beneficiaries to deal with the land are regulated by special rules, which also establish the circumstances in which third parties can enter into transactions which bind the beneficiaries in relation to the land. Local authorities have long been under a reasonably detailed set of statutory rules controlling the circumstances in which, and purposes for which, they might acquire, use, and alienate land. What was new in the *Wheeler* case was the clarity with which a new set of public-law principles, developed at common law, was applied to the local authority as landowner, giving rise to a new class of property (although it was not conceptualised as such): publicly owned property.

The implications of this can be seen in cases relating to the control of stag hunting. Where land is privately owned, the owner can bar the hunt from the land at will, and this applies equally where the owner is a private individual and where land is owned by a campaigning organisation. There is no doubt that a private landowner is entitled to do this. In *League against Cruel Sports Ltd.* v. *Scott*,[40] Park J. held that the master of a pack of hounds was liable for trespass if he intentionally or negligently allowed his hounds to go onto land owned by the League which had prohibited hunting with dogs there. It would also constitute a trespass if the master took the hunt close to the land knowing that it was virtually impossible to adopt precautions which would stop the dogs entering the land but indifferent to the risk. The master was held to be vicariously liable for the actions of hunt servants, agents or mounted followers.

However, different principles apply where land is owned by a local authority. In *R.* v. *Somerset County Council, ex parte Fewings* the county council, under pressure from opponents of stag hunting, had resolved to prohibit the pastime on its own land. When representatives of the Quantock Staghounds challenged the resolution, Laws J. quashed it, characterising it as an illegitimate attempt to impose a particular version of morality on the inhabitants of the council's area: members' views on the ethics of deer hunting were irrelevant considerations when exercising the public power of a local authority.[41] The Court of Appeal upheld the decision.[42] Sir Thomas Bingham M.R. approved the view of Laws

[40] [1986] 1 Q.B. 240.
[41] [1995] 1 All E.R. 513.
[42] [1995] 3 All E.R. 20, C.A.

J.[43] that, unlike a private landowner, a land-owning local authority has to justify every action it takes, including that in relation to its own land, by reference to positive law. On that basis, the question was whether the council's resolution was "for the purposes of . . . the benefit, improvement or development of their area", which are the purposes for which local authorities may acquire land under section 120(1)(b) of the Local Government Act 1972.[44] The Master of the Rolls, unlike Laws J., accepted that the council was entitled to have regard to ethical and animal welfare considerations. However, these matters were relevant only as aspects of the statutory question: did a ban "benefit" the area? Because he decided that the council had been unduly swayed by members' personal views of the ethics of hunting without proper reference to the question whether banning hunting benefited the area, the Master of the Rolls concluded that the resolution had been unlawful, although it was possible that it could have been made lawfully by another route.[45] Swinton Thomas L.J. delivered a judgment quashing the decision on the rather more fundamental ground that the council had never had its attention drawn to the provisions of section 120(1)(b) and so could not say that those supporting the resolution had ever considered whether it would confer a benefit on the area, as required by the section. Furthermore, in his view (unlike that of the other judges) the council could never lawfully have acquired land in order to prevent hunting on it, as this would allow councils to ban many lawful activities of which they happen to disapprove.[46] Only Simon Brown L.J., dissenting, would have upheld the lawfulness of the resolution, on the ground that no sufficient evidence had been produced to show that the council had acted for improper purposes or had taken account of irrelevant considerations. He held that the social and ethical aspects of hunting were necessarily relevant and might legitimately have been decisive, so the council had been legally bound to consider them.[47]

Despite the difficulty in extracting a *ratio decidendi* from it, the decision in *ex parte Fewings* demonstrates that landownership has a meaning when a statutory authority is the owner which is different from its meaning when a private person or body is the owner.[48] For better or worse, the courts have recognised that the principles of the Rule of Law, including the principle of legality (the requirement that public bodies should be able to justify their actions by reference to positive law, and unlike other people are not free to do anything which is not made unlawful by positive law), impose general restrictions on the rights

[43] See [1995] 1 All E.R. 513 at 524 *per* Laws J.

[44] [1995] 3 W.L.R. 20 at 25 *per* Sir Thomas Bingham M.R.

[45] [1995] 3 All E.R. 20 at 28–29 *per* Sir Thomas Bingham M.R.

[46] [1995] 3 All E.R. 20 at 35–36 *per* Swinton Thomas L.J.

[47] [1995] 3 All E.R. 20 at 31–33 *per* Simon Brown L.J. Although the Court of Appeal granted leave to appeal to the House of Lords, no appeal was brought.

[48] It would be interesting, but for present purposes is unnecessary, to consider whether a non-statutory public body such as the Crown is in the same position as a statutory public body or has the same powers of landownership as a private person or body. The scale of the land owned by (for example) the Ministry of Defence makes this a geographically, as well as legally, important question.

of bodies which hold land by virtue of or subject to statute for public purposes. Such bodies may include some charities. In *Scott* v. *National Trust for Places of Historic Interest or Natural Beauty*,[49] Robert Walker J. took the view that the National Trust is a public body, both by virtue of its charitable status and because of its importance to the nation, and could in principle have been amenable to judicial review in respect of its decision to ban stag-hunting on its land on the Quantocks, although, as the aggrieved hunters had a convenient alternative remedy by way of charity proceedings in Chancery Division, leave to apply for judicial review was refused. Now the Human Rights Act 1998 is in force, these general restrictions include those derived from the Convention rights, including the rights to freedom of peaceful assembly under Article 11 and of expression under Article 10. From 2 October 2000, public authorities wishing to prohibit public assemblies and protests on their land have to demonstrate that the interference with freedom of assembly and expression which the prohibition represents is justified by reference to the criteria set out in the Articles, as well as complying with general requirements of English administrative law. These rights will be a central element when establishing the scope of a public authority's power over its land, as advocated by Browne-Wilkinson L.J. in his dissenting judgment in the Court of Appeal in *Wheeler* v. *Leicester City Council*,[50] a suggestion largely ignored by the House of Lords who upheld the appeal on other grounds.

SUBJECTING PROPERTY RIGHTS TO HUMAN RIGHTS: THE HUMAN RIGHTS ACT 1998

The scheme of the Human Rights Act 1998 is to bring the language of most of the rights which bind the United Kingdom under the European Convention on Human Rights into domestic law in the United Kingdom, using the caselaw of the Convention organs as a non-binding guide to the interpretation of the rights for domestic purposes. Section 6(1) of the Act makes it unlawful for any public authority to act incompatibly with a Convention right, unless (a) the incompatible act, rule or decision is mandated by primary legislation (specially defined by section 22) which could not be interpreted in such a way as to allow action which would have been compatible with the right, or (b) the incompatibility consists of a failure to legislate. The House of Lords sitting judicially is a public authority, but otherwise the two Houses of Parliament are not public authorities and so do not act unlawfully if they contravene Convention rights when legislating or conducting their other business. Courts and tribunals, on the other hand, are public authorities, and act unlawfully if their decisions or acts are incompatible with a Convention right.

49 [1998] 2 All E.R. 705 at 716–717.

50 [1985] A.C. at 1061, 1064–1066, C.A.

The Act does not require rules of law to be altered in general. Where rules are contained in primary legislation, courts have a duty to interpret or re-interpret the rules so as to be compatible with Convention rights so far as possible. We can expect courts to adopt fairly robust techniques of interpretation in some cases to achieve compatibility. These methods may include reading words into a statute, ignoring words which are there, or giving words a far wider or more restricted meaning than they would ordinarily be regarded as being capable of bearing. Such techniques may have a restricted application in relation to property law, as courts may feel that parties' rights and legitimate expectations of security of title should not be upset without very clear authority. Where compatibility cannot be achieved by interpretation, superior courts may grant a "declaration of incompatibility" which does not affect the rights of the parties but which triggers methods by which the relevant minister or Parliament may (if they see fit) change the law to make it compatible with the right. On the other hand, where the incompatible rule derives from subordinate legislation, the legislation is invalid to the extent of the incompatibility.

Nothing in the Act deals explicitly with the situation in which a common-law rule or principle is incompatible with a Convention right. The obligations of courts and tribunals in such cases have to be worked out from the general scheme of the Act. Two principles are potentially in conflict here: the idea that the Convention rights mainly bind public authorities rather than private individuals and bodies; and the principle that courts and tribunals are themselves public authorities which are generally under an obligation to ensure that their acts and decisions are compatible with Convention rights. So far as courts and tribunals treat themselves as under an obligation to give effect to Convention rights even when hearing and deciding cases between private parties, the Convention rights will operate not only between private litigants and public authorities but also between private parties *inter se*, giving rise to a degree of what can be described as "horizontal effect". Although the circumstances in which the rights will have horizontal effect and its results are as yet uncertain, there is general agreement that the Convention rights will indirectly operate to some extent as between private persons and bodies.

The areas in which the horizontal effect is likely to be most extensive are those where Convention rights give rise not only to a duty on the State to avoid interfering with citizens' exercise of the rights but also to a positive obligation on the State to help citizens to exercise their rights, protecting them against interference by others. The Strasbourg caselaw demonstrates a number of situations in which this can happen. The relevant state body may violate a person's right to respect for private and family life and the home by failing to take action against polluters who harm the quality of domestic life in the area.[51] The State may violate a person's right to respect for private life and right not to be subjected to inhuman or degrading treatment if it fails to put in place arrangements

[51] *López Ostra* v. *Spain*, Eur. Ct. H.R., Series A, No. 303-C, Judgment of 9 December 1994.

under which a prosecution may be launched against a carer who is alleged to have sexually assaulted a mentally incompetent person,[52] or whereby a conviction may be obtained against and effective penalties imposed on a step-parent who admits having repeatedly beaten his step-son with a garden cane.[53] The police may violate the rights of demonstrators to freedom of expression and of assembly if they fail to take action to protect the protesters against counter-demonstrators.[54]

The last of these examples is particularly relevant to the relationship between public protest and property rights. If property law makes no provision for space in which people can gather without the need for an owner's consent, it imposes a significant constraint on peaceful assembly and protest. It would be possible to justify this infringement of people's rights under Articles 10(1) and 11(1) of the E.C.H.R. in so far as the restriction is calculated to protect a pressing social interest in achieving one of the objectives set out in Articles 10(2) and 11(2), and the means adopted are proportionate to the objective. However, if English law were to allow the owner of land an unconstrained right refuse permission to assemble, and were to give discretion to the police and local authorities to place further hurdles in the way of protesters even after the owner had given permission to assemble, the law would undermine the very essence of freedom of peaceful assembly in a way which would not be compatible with the terms of Article 11.

Until recently, this was largely the position in English law. The few areas in which people could gather more or less freely were limited to those in the ownership of tolerant public authorities, or over which rights of common or of passage could be established. Even there, the right to assemble was constrained, both by the actual or presumed terms of the grant or dedication to public use and by the general provisions of public (including criminal) law governing the use of highways.[55] From 2 October 2000, things may have changed in two ways under the Human Rights Act 1998.

First, a private person or body performing public functions may be treated as a public authority for the purpose of those limited functions. It is possible that a landowner over whose land the public have rights of passage and who has responsibilities to the public in respect of maintaining the footpath or other way might be treated as a public authority in respect of that public function under section 6 of the Act. If so, the landowner would be directly subject to a duty under section 6 to comply with the Convention rights under Articles 10 and 11, and this "vertical effect" of the rights may significantly limit his ability to exclude people from the land. It is well established that the principles of public

[52] *X and Y* v. *The Netherlands*, Eur. Ct. H.R., Series A, No. 91, Judgment of 26 March 1985.

[53] A. v. *United Kingdom*, Eur. Ct. H.R., Judgment of 23 Sept. 1998.

[54] *Plattform "Ärzte für das Leben"* v. *Austria*, Eur. Ct. H.R., Series A, No. 139, Judgment of 21 June 1988.

[55] See e.g. two cases relating to assemblies in Trafalgar Square, *Ex parte Lewis* (1888) 21 Q.B.D. 191, D.C., and *R.* v.*Graham* (1888) 16 Cox C.C. 420.

law apply to some people or bodies which are private, in the sense of being established as a result of private arrangements rather than by the exercise of a statutory or prerogative power, if they are performing functions which courts can categorise as public in the sense that they are of a governmental nature,[56] or they can be regarded as emanations of the state for the purposes of E.U. law.[57] When drafting the Human Rights Act 1998 the Government accepted that the courts would ultimately have to decide what people or bodies were "public authorities" who were to be subject to the duty to comply with Convention rights under section 6(1) of the Act. In the House of Lords, the Lord Chancellor (Lord Irvine) and Lord Lester of Herne Hill Q.C. seemed to think that the courts would have a more or less free rein to build up principles on a case-by-case basis to decide which bodies should be treated as public authorities for this purpose,[58] although in the House of Commons the Home Secretary (Mr. Straw) thought that the courts would need to take account both of the caselaw of the European Court of Human Rights on the kinds of bodies for which the State could be held liable in international law and of the decisions on the bodies which could be subject to judicial review in national law.[59]

Whatever principles emerge from the courts in due course, the Act itself envisages two kinds of public authorities. There are those which are "all-purpose" public authorities, which must always comply with Convention rights in all their dealings. There are then "limited-purpose" public authorities, which for normal purposes are private people or bodies but which become public authorities when and to the extent to which they are performing public functions.[60] In other words, courts will have to apply one test to determine whether a body is an all-purpose public authority, and if it is not they will then have to apply another test to determine whether the private body is exercising a public function so as to make it, for the purposes of the litigation, a limited-purpose public authority which will be directly subject to Convention rights, including the rights to freedom of peaceful assembly and expression.

This may be difficult. For example, consider a private landowner who has a public footpath running across his land. He commits a statutory nuisance if he causes or allows the footpath to become blocked. Does he also commit a wrong in the nature of a breach of statutory duty (the duty under section 6(1) of the Human Rights Act 1998) if he undertakes work on land adjoining the footpath which does not block the path but makes it impossible for a campaigning group to process along the path in groups to protest against (for instance) the growing of genetically modified crops on the farmer's land? If the farmer is for all purposes a private landowner, the answer is "No", because the duty under section

[56] *R.* v. *Panel on Take-overs and Mergers, ex parte Datafin Plc* [1987] Q.B. 815, C.A.

[57] *Foster* v. *British Gas Plc* [1991] 1 Q.B. 405, C.J.E.C., [1991] 2 A.C. 306, H.L.

[58] House of Lords Official Report, 24 November 1997, vol. 583, cols. 784 and 796 (Lord Irvine) and 792–793 (Lord Lester).

[59] House of Commons Official Report, 17 June 1998, vol. 314, cols. 406–409.

[60] Human Rights Act 1998, s. 6(3)(b) and (5).

6(1) applies only to public authorities. On the other hand, if the farmer is treated as performing a public function in maintaining the footpath for use by the general public, he may be a limited-purpose public authority who would have to respect rights of peaceful assembly and expression in his dealings with the footpath. Similar considerations apply to owners of property over which people have rights of common. Such landowners would be subject to the requirements of Article 11 in respect of their use of and control over their land so far as it affects their public role in relation to the footpath or common, although (as section 6(5) of the Act makes clear) not in relation to their purely private activities.

Secondly, even if private landowners do not become limited-purpose public authorities merely by reason of having land over which a public footpath runs, highway authorities are public authorities, and all of them (*a fortiori* those in whom the surface of the highway has been vested) will be required under section 6(1) of the Human Rights Act 1998 to permit use of the highway by members of the public for the purpose of exercising rights to freedom of peaceful assembly and expression, unless the circumstances are such as to justify a restriction on those rights under Articles 10(2) and 11(2). Not only will this have a major impact on rights to assemble on highways, but it will probably have a spill-over effect on the rights of owners of land adjoining public roads.[61] What is more, the courts, as public authorities, will be under a duty under section 6 to ensure that they comply with Convention rights unless compelled not to do so by primary legislation which cannot be interpreted in a manner compatible with a right. This will have an effect on the way they interpret legislation, by virtue of section 3, and the remedies which they are prepared to grant to landowners against those occupying or using land against the landowner's will, and thus will enable the Convention rights to have some "horizontal effect" on the rights of landowners.

Quite apart from the effect of the Human Rights Act 1998, there are signs that the courts are beginning to adapt the law of property and the criminal law relating to highways to the demands of Convention rights, particularly the right to freedom of peaceful assembly. How this is being done, and its implications, are explored in the next section.

HIGHWAYS, PUBLIC-LAW RIGHTS, AND THE PRIVATE-LAW RIGHTS OF LANDOWNERS

The English approach described in the previous sections tends to produce a hybrid system of property law which is part public, part private. While the Human Rights Act 1998 may subject some private land to some Convention rights of the general public, including rights of peaceable assembly under Article

[61] For a less sanguine but very measured view of the likely effect of the Act, see David Mead, "The Human Rights Act—a panacea for peaceful public protest?" (1999) 4 *Journal of Civil Liberties* 7–27.

11, other aspects of the English approach to establishing rights for the public over private property put the principles of private law and the will of the landowner in the forefront of the analysis, even if only fictitiously in order to maintain the appearance of an orderly and monolithic system of property law. As a result, privately owned land may come to be quasi-public for some purposes either through the operation of certain public-law rights and duties or because the bounds of a landowner's rights in private law have come to be defined partly by reference to public-interest and public-law considerations.

As a recent decision demonstrates, this can cause difficulties. In *Director of Public Prosecutions* v. *Jones (Margaret)*,[62] the House of Lords was concerned with a gathering of people protesting against the enclosure of Stonehenge, on the roadside verge beside the main A344 highway adjoining the monument. Salisbury County Council had made an order under section 14A of the Public Order Act 1986, as inserted by the Criminal Justice and Public Order Act 1994, section 70. This prohibited "trespassory assemblies" (i.e. assemblies of 20 or more people on land to which the public has no right of access or only a limited right of access, without or in excess of the limits of the occupier's permission) within a radius of 4 miles of Stonehenge, for four days. Under section 14B(2) of the 1986 Act, it is an offence to take part in a trespassory assembly knowing that it is prohibited by an order made under section 14A. At 6.45 p.m. on the last day, the senior officer at the scene claimed to have counted 21 people on the grass verge of the main A344 highway by the fence surrounding Stonehenge. He asked people to leave, but three people (including Dr. Jones and Mr. Lloyd) refused. They were arrested and convicted by a magistrates' court of the offence under section 14B, although they had been on a public highway and it was accepted that their behaviour was peaceful and did not threaten a breach of the peace or obstruct the highway. Their appeal to the Crown Court was allowed. The Director of Public Prosecutions appealed successfully to the Divisional Court,[63] and Dr. Jones and Mr. Lloyd appealed to the House of Lords.

Because an order made under section 14A prohibits only assemblies which exceed the limits of a person's permission to be on or right of access to land, the scope of that right or permission is crucial when deciding whether an offence has been committed. Where the property in question is a highway, it would be possible to treat the limits of that permission or right as a public-law matter, governed by public-property law rather than private-property law. Public-law principles governing control over publicly owned land could produce more extensive rights for protesters on highways than elsewhere, because extra limitations would be imposed on the public authority landowner's power to exclude people from the land, as in cases like *Wheeler* v. *Leicester City Council*[64] and *R.* v. *Somerset County Council, ex parte Fewings*,[65] discussed earlier.

[62] [1999] 2 W.L.R. 625, H.L.
[63] [1998] Q.B. 563, D.C.
[64] [1985] A.C. 1054, H.L.
[65] [1995] 3 All E.R. 20, C.A.

Indeed, counsel for the appellants advanced just such an argument. However, the courts have always tended to apply private-law rules when considering the extent of people's express or implied permission to enter or use premises owned by others, even when the issue relates to criminal rather than civil liability. As Lord Hope noted,[66] the form of section 14A "brings into the arena of the criminal law the rights, if any, which the public have as against the occupier of the land in private law." Accordingly all five of their Lordships (Lord Irvine of Lairg L.C., Lord Clyde and Lord Hutton in the majority; Lord Slynn of Hadley and Lord Hope of Craighead dissenting) started from the presumption that the question whether the assembly had exceeded the implied permission given to users of the highway had to be decided by reference principally to the private law of trespass, although some were prepared to analyze those rules in the light of a right to freedom of assembly. Furthermore, all five Law Lords agreed that the decision would apply equally to all kinds of highways, including public footpaths or bridleways across private land, although (as Lords Irvine and Hutton held[67]) the tribunal of fact might form a different view as to the reasonableness of an assembly taking place on wholly private land from that of an assembly on a road. Lord Slynn and Lord Hope, dissenting, distinguished toleration of demonstrations and other activities commonly undertaken on highways from a legal right to engage in them,[68] despite Lord Irvine's observation that, "The law should not make unlawful what is commonplace and well accepted."[69] They considered that constructing a right of peaceful assembly on the highway interfered with the rights of occupiers in a way which was undesirable and unsupported by authority. This was an approach closely in line with traditional, English private-property law, concentrating on the landowner rather than the public.

The majority, also purporting to approach the case on a private-law footing, decided that the assembly had not been shown to be trespassory, because the permission actually or impliedly given by occupiers of the soil to users of the highway either already went beyond passing, repassing, and activities necessarily incidental thereto, or (*per* Lord Hutton) should henceforth be treated as extending beyond them. Yet each of the four grounds for limiting the scope of the right of a landowner to prevent people from making use of his or her land on which their Lordships relied is derived from public law rather than private law. It was argued that:

(1) the proper scope of the criminal law does not extend to outlawing what is commonplace and well accepted;[70]
(2) the policy of the criminal law is not well served by treating as a trespass on a highway behaviour which, because reasonable, would not be regarded as a criminal

[66] [1999] 2 W.L.R. at 642.
[67] [1999] 2 W.L.R. at 633, 666.
[68] [1999] 2 W.L.R. at 639 *per* Lord Slynn; see to the same effect Lord Hope at 647.
[69] [1999] 2 W.L.R. at 631; see also 632.
[70] [1999] 2 W.L.R. at 631 *per* Lord Irvine.

obstruction of the highway contrary to section 137 of the Highways Act 1980 as interpreted in *Hirst* v. *Chief Constable of West Yorkshire*,[71] and the test of reasonableness would allow the tribunal of fact to take account of the size, duration and obstructiveness of the assembly;[72]

(3) the common-law right of freedom of assembly, which the majority accepted as a matter of public law, would have been unduly restricted if it could never be exercised on public highways;[73] and

(4) had it been necessary to refer to the European Convention on Human Rights Lord Irvine and perhaps Lord Clyde[74] would have held that undue restrictions on rights of the public on highways would have threatened the right to freedom of peaceful assembly under Article 11 of the European Convention on Human Rights.

Having considered three classic English cases on trespass on the highway,[75] Lord Irvine of Lairg L.C. argued[76] that activities on the highway are not trespassory, even if not strictly incidental or ancillary to the right of passage, so long as they are what Lord Esher M.R. in *Harrison* v. *Duke of Rutland*[77] had called "a reasonable and usual mode of using the highway as such". Assemblies on the highway are not trespassory if they "are reasonable, do not involve the commission of a public or private nuisance, and do not amount to an obstruction of the highway unreasonably impeding the primary right of the general public to pass and repass . . . Subject to these qualifications . . . there would be a public right of peaceful assembly on the public highway."[78] In principle, Lord Clyde agreed that "there is a public right of assembly", subject to certain limitations.[79] His Lordship started from the proposition that passing and repassing on the highway included "a variety of activities, whether or not involving movement, which are consistent with what people reasonably and customarily do on a highway", and "not for some ulterior purpose for which the road was not intended

[71] (1986) 85 Cr. App. R. 143, D.C. See [1999] 2 W.L.R. at 634 *per* Lord Irvine, 664 *per* Lord Hutton. The decision on this point had been anticipated by Hooper J. in *North Yorkshire County Council* v. *Lee and others*, unreported, High Court at Leeds, 22 June 1998, in relation to a peace camp on a lay-by on the A59 near the U.S. Air Force base at R.A.F. Menwith Hill in Yorkshire. I am grateful to Hooper J. for a copy of the judgment.

[72] [1999] 2 W.L.R. at 631, 632 *per* Lord Irvine; 654 *per* Lord Clyde; 666 *per* Lord Hutton. In *North Yorkshire County Council* v. *Lee and others*, unreported, High Court in Leeds, 14 June 1999, Hooper J. applied this, holding that parking a caravan permanently in a lay-by by the A59 went beyond a reasonable user of the highway, but was sympathetic to the view that a trailer or small caravan parked in a safe place, and which could be removed at night, would meet the "reasonable user" test. I am grateful to Hooper J. for a copy of the judgment.

[73] [1999] 2 W.L.R. at 654–5 *per* Lord Clyde and 660–662 *per* Lord Hutton, relying on Lord Denning M.R., dissenting, in *Hubbard* v. *Pitt* [1976] Q.B. 142 at 178, *Hirst* v. *Chief Constable of West Yorkshire* (1986) 85 Cr. App. R. at 151 *per* Otton J., and *Committee for the Commonwealth of Canada* v. *Canada* (1991) 77 D.L.R. (4th) 385 at 391 per Lamer C.J.C.

[74] [1999] 2 W.L.R. at 634–5 *per* Lord Irvine, 654 *per* Lord Clyde.

[75] *Ex parte Lewis* (1888) 21 Q.B.D. 191, D.C.; *Harrison* v. *Duke of Rutland* [1893] 1 Q.B. 142, C.A.; and *Hickman* v. *Maisey* [1900] 1 Q.B. 752, C.A.

[76] See [1999] 2 W.L.R. at 630, 631.

[77] [1893] 1 Q.B. at 146–7.

[78] [1999] 2 W.L.R. at 630; see also 632–3.

[79] [1999] 2 W.L.R. at 654.

to be used".[80] Apart from a requirement of reasonableness, Lord Clyde's restrictions on the right to pass and repass included the following: it does not extend beyond the highway; there is no *ius spatiandi* or *manendi*; it must not interfere unreasonably with the lawful use of the highway by others; and the right may be restricted in accordance with the conditions set out in Article 11(2) of the European Convention on Human Rights.[81] What is significant about this reasoning for present purposes is that, despite purporting to be discussing the private-law limits of permission impliedly given by a landowner to enter land, Lord Irvine and Lord Clyde both eschew any examination of the actual intention of the landowner in the case, of which there was in any event no evidence. The method of reasoning by these judges is thus much more akin to a public-law approach than to an English private-law approach. It is worth noting, however, that (as observed earlier) Scottish private law is much less concerned than English private law with the intention of the occupier. In Scotland, all that is significant is the actual exercise of a right over the land during the period of prescription, and the general law (rather than the owner's will) defines what rights can be acquired in this manner. It is perhaps significant that both Lord Irvine and Lord Clyde hail from north of the border. Lord Hutton, a former Lord Chief Justice of Northern Ireland, considered that it would be necessary to extend the law to create such a right, but was prepared to take that step.[82] His reasons for doing so had nothing to do with the presumed or implied intention of the landowner, and everything to do with the public-law considerations listed above.

The majority interpreted the public's private-law rights against occupiers of property more extensively than did the dissenters for public-law rather than private-law reasons. This is implicit in all three majority speeches, but is made explicit by Lord Hutton, who, while recognising that cases decided under the Canadian Charter of Rights and Freedoms involved principles different from those operating in England and Wales, relied on the following passage from the judgment of Lamer C.J.C. in *Committee for the Commonwealth of Canada* v. *Canada*:[83]

> "the freedom of expression cannot be exercised in a vacuum . . . it necessarily implies the use of physical space in order to meet its underlying objectives. No one could agree that the exercise of the freedom of expression can be limited solely to places owned by the person wishing to communicate: such an approach would certainly deny the very foundation of the freedom of expression."

Once one moves to a position in which people may have a right of freedom of expression, or of assembly, even if they personally control no property on or with which they could exercise those freedoms, the right necessarily imposes

[80] [1999] 2 W.L.R. at 653.
[81] [1999] 2 W.L.R. at 654.
[82] [1999] 2 W.L.R. at 660.
[83] (1991) 77 D.L.R. (4th) 385 at 394.

limits on the private-law property rights of those who do control such property. It is this capacity of fundamental rights and freedoms, whether derived from statute or from common law, to restrict traditional private rights that has been welcomed by some property theorists as recognising the quasi-public nature of some privately owned land such as shopping centres.[84] It is capable of giving rise to what Professor Kevin Gray has called "equitable property" over the land of owners.[85] Despite this nomenclature, these rights are derived less from traditional equitable principles than from public-law notions, particularly fundamental rights. The decision in *Director of Public Prosecutions* v. *Jones (Margaret)* for the first time recognises such rights in English law.

The effect on property law is potentially far-reaching, yet in *Director of Public Prosecutions* v. *Jones (Margaret)* itself only Lord Hope and Lord Slynn (dissenting) and Lord Hutton seem to have recognised that, as Lord Hope put it, the decision represented "a fundamental rearrangement of the respective rights of the public and of those of public and private landowners."[86] Lord Irvine L.C. rejected the suggestion that the decision represented such a realignment, stressing that the test of reasonableness and the usual remedies for trespass would protect the interests of occupiers of land.[87] However, Lord Hutton's acceptance that the decision involved a judicial extension of the rights of the public in relation to highways indicates that the new, or newly extended, right to assemble on highways (including footpaths and bridleways) potentially affects the rights of occupiers to obtain remedies for trespass. This has the capacity to create a category of public-law equitable rights over property of the kind discussed in the work of Professor Gray.

The decision foreshadows one way in which the Convention rights contained in Schedule 1 to the Human Rights Act 1998 may affect not only public authorities in their dealings with private individuals but also, indirectly, the rights and obligations of private individuals *inter se*. Lord Hope, dissenting, was well aware of this. Referring to "the horizontal effect of the defendants' arguments as to the Convention in regard to the private rights of landowners", his Lordship said that he was "not persuaded that the balance which is struck in private law between the rights of the public and those of landowners is in need of adjustment in order to enable members of the public to exercise their freedom of assembly."[88] Now the 1998 Act has come into force, the courts as public authorities are likely to have to give effect to Convention rights in ways which to a greater or lesser extent will impact on private rights. It is therefore important that judges should get used to considering carefully the effect of their decisions on the rights of third parties.

84 See for example Kevin Gray and Susan Francis Gray, "Civil rights, civil wrongs and quasi-public space" [1999] E.H.R.L.R. 46–102.

85 Kevin Gray, "Property in thin air" (1991) 50 *Cambridge Law Journal* 252–307; Kevin Gray, "Equitable property" (1994) 47 *Current Legal Problems* 157–214.

86 [1999] 2 W.L.R. at 650 *per* Lord Hope. See also Lord Slynn at 639.

87 [1999] 2 W.L.R. at 631, 633.

88 [1999] 2 W.L.R. at 652.

Under the Act, there are several different ways in which the Convention rights may affect private landowners. As noted earlier, if the private landowner is a limited-purpose public authority in relation to his or her use of the land, the rights will have direct vertical effect against the landowner *qua* public authority. If the landowner is involved in litigation relating to rights over the property and the other party asserts Convention rights as against the court or tribunal, or compels the court or tribunal to interpret legislation in a novel way to make it compatible with a Convention right in accordance with the requirement in section 3 of the 1998 Act, giving effect to those rights may affect the outcome of the litigation in ways which indirectly limit the previous private-law rights of the landowner (indirect horizontal effect). If the landowner's land adjoins, or is affected by activities on, a highway or other land owned or controlled by a public authority, the rights which can be asserted against that authority (by way of vertical effect) may indirectly affect the private landowner's freedom to use his or her property (incidental horizontal effect).

All of these are legitimate effects of the 1998 Act, in that they are clearly justifiable by reference to the terms of the Act itself. Such limits on private-law rights operate only to the extent that they are necessary to avoid a violation of a Convention right. In all other contexts, it would be legitimate for the previous private-law rules to operate unchanged. This is analogous to the position in relation to direct effect of E.U. directives: previous national law is not changed, but becomes inapplicable to the extent of the incompatibility in cases to which E.U. law applies. However, there is a risk that the effect of the Human Rights Act 1998 will not be limited in this way, and that the Convention rights will seep into private law, changing it for all purposes as it goes. This might produce some desirable outcomes. For instance, it could bolster privacy-related rights in tort against the press and the investigative arms of the State. On the other hand, it could cast a shadow of uncertainty over central elements in property law, including the extent of a landowner's rights to exclude those who would normally be regarded as trespassers. It is likely to occur where private-law powers of landowners and visitors to land fall to be decided by reference to principles and concepts which have their origin in public law, without taking account of the need to be clear about their meaning and scope in their new legal context. This is what happened in *Director of Public Prosecutions* v. *Jones (Margaret)*.

Despite the possible advantages this may have for the protection of public rights and interests, it has dangers in terms of both the coherence of legal doctrine and the ability to ensure that the job of implementing public interests lies in the hands of public authorities which are properly accountable, politically as well as legally, both for their policies and for their chosen means of giving effect to them. Imposing on private individuals the restrictions which the law imposes on public authorities for public-interest or human-rights reasons tends to undermine one of the basic distinctions between human rights and ordinary rights, namely that it is the job of public authorities to uphold people's human rights, and to be accountable for the way in which this is done. While it is permissible, and sometimes necessary, for a public authority to restrict the ordinary rights of private individuals and bodies in order to protect human rights, this should be done and justified openly. The private-law framework for justification, which relies on unfounded presumptions or fictions relating to the actions and intentions of a landowner or landowners over a long period, is ill suited to the task of providing a rational public justification for limiting private rights. As the majority of the House of Lords in *Jones (Margaret)* found, arguments of a public-law kind are needed. They should not be smuggled into private law by the back door.

In the context of *Director of Public Prosecutions* v. *Jones (Margaret)*, their Lordships' approach is understandable. It was forced on them by the drafters of the Criminal Justice and Public Order Act 1994, who ill-advisedly made criminal liability under section 14B of the Public Order Act 1986 depend on private-law concepts. It was never obvious why liability to criminal sanctions should have been made to depend on implied or express permission granted by landowners as a matter of private law, but once a right to assemble peaceably for political or other purposes becomes part of the law (through the Human Rights Act 1998 or by judicial action) it is inevitable that criminal courts will have to decide questions of criminal law by reference to private law while trying to give due weight to human-rights principles. However, this approach is unsatisfactory for two reasons.

First, the consequences of allowing this kind of hybrid decision-making, bringing together public law and private law, is in general as likely to threaten human rights as to advance their cause. Examples of doctrinal cross-over with less than happy consequences for human rights include the recourse to the doctrine of breach of confidence in relation to governmental information in *A-G* v. *Jonathan Cape Ltd.*[89] and the *Spycatcher* litigation,[90] which did little to extend freedom of expression in relation to governmental matters; the extension of contractual and restitutionary doctrines as remedies for public-law wrongs in *A-G* v. *Blake (Jonathan Cape Ltd., third party)*,[91] with potentially damaging consequences for the rights of an author who was not represented before the court; and the use of civil law remedies for public-law purposes, such as injunctions to restrain breaches of the criminal law in ways which pose obvious risks to any right to assemble in public, and injunctions to restrain suspected criminals from disposing of proceeds of crime (later subsumed into statute).

Secondly, the law of private property is based on principles which have developed over a long period to take account of conditions and objectives which had nothing to do with human rights. Nothing in its form or development makes it suitable for balancing public against private interests (since it nearly always assumed the primacy of the latter), or for advancing the objectives of criminal

89 [1976] Q.B. 752.

90 See particularly *Attorney General* v. *Guardian Newspapers Ltd.* [1987] 1 W.L.R. 1248, H.L., and *Attorney General* v. *Guardian Newspapers (No. 2)* [1990] A.C. 109, H.L.

91 [1998] 1 All E.R. 833, C.A., and cp. [2000] 3 W.L.R. 625, H.L.

law in the public-order field in a rational way. The purposes served by rules in property law are very different from those served by criminal law, so attempting to use them for criminal-law purposes may defeat the objectives of the criminal provisions. On the other hand, if courts adapt private-law concepts to suit the purposes of criminal law, and those adaptations are then re-imported into private law, it may significantly alter private rights by a side-wind. Contract law provides a good example of this: the rules on offer and acceptance were derailed by decisions on criminal statutes concerned with offers for sale, which reached results which were sensible in terms of criminal law but disrupted a straightforward area of contract law.[92]

Thirdly, limiting the rights of landowners in criminal proceedings is procedurally questionable, since the landowners are not likely to be represented in the criminal proceedings in which the limits of their private rights are established. Not only are the landowners' private rights restricted, but it is arguable that the method of doing this violates their right to a fair hearing before an impartial tribunal in the determination of their civil rights and obligations, under Article 6 of the E.C.H.R., which has now become a right enforceable in national law under the Human Rights Act 1998.

For all these reasons, even those who applaud the result which was reached in *Jones (Margaret)* are entitled to feel concerned at the implications of the method of reasoning employed, while recognising that a court which wanted to give proper weight to the rights of peaceful protesters might well have felt that, in the light of the legislative and litigation history in relation to that prosecution, it had little choice. Poorly drafted legislation forced a criminal tribunal to decide a question of human-rights law in a context which made it inevitable that it would have an impact on private-property rights. This is regrettable, because it creates a hybrid system of property law which makes it less rather than more likely that English law will be able to develop an approach to property law which will be as sensitive to context and public policy as sixth-century Roman law was. It would be better if legislators and judges kept clearly in mind the different objectives of private and public rights and private and public (including criminal) law, and did their best to ensure that the considerations relevant to each were clearly separated. Only in this way can the real issues be identified and resolved when conflicts between competing interests and rights emerge.

CONCLUSION

The essay has argued that English law has not in the past established clear water between the rules governing ownership of property used for different purposes, public, private, or communal (although a limited special class of sacred property

[92] See *Pharmaceutical Society of Great Britain* v. *Boots Cash Chemists (Southern) Ltd.* [1952] 2 Q.B. 795; *Fisher* v. *Bell* [1961] 1 Q.B. 394; J. Beatson and A. P. Simester, "Stealing one's own property" (1999) 115 L.Q.R. 372–376 at 375, discussing *R.* v. *Hinks* [1998] Crim. L.R. 904, C.A.

has been created). Lawyers have attempted to deal with private, public and communal property on the basis of concepts which were essentially developed for private ownership. Situations in which the public interest has had to be asserted over property-owners have been dealt with by asserting public-law principles against public authorities which own property. When public-law principles are employed in cases which affect (directly or indirectly) private landowners, and this is done in the process of delimiting private-law rights over land, a hybrid system of land law is created which is liable to confuse principles of ordinary private landownership, even if it clarifies principles of public access to land. In *Director of Public Prosecutions* v. *Jones (Margaret)*, the majority of the House of Lords reached the right decision, but by dressing it in reasoning which revolved round private landowning rights Lord Irvine and Lord Clyde in particular failed to appreciate the essential distinction between the principles and concepts which are properly applicable to public authorities and those which are properly applicable to private bodies. The only time when it is appropriate to treat a single landowner as subject to different sets of rules is when the landowner is a private person or body who performs some public functions in respect of land. The public-law restrictions on private landowners should not extend beyond the circumstances in which they are performing public functions.

This is an issue which is likely to arise more often as a human-rights culture develops in English law. If the law is moving gradually towards limiting rights of private property to give greater scope for people to exercise their rights of peaceful assembly and expression, it is a small but welcome indication that the values of political participation and social inclusion are having an effect on the law. However, while saluting the way in which public-law values are being injected into the strictness of the law of private property, one is entitled to express reservations about the effect of the manner in which part of the revolution is being achieved. Restricting private-property rights in circumstances where there is a clash between them and fundamental public-law values or rights is acceptable. Recognizing that public authorities are in a special position, and hold land for purposes which must necessarily take account of public interests, leads to a form of public-land law which is distinctively different from that of private-land law. It begins to establish the distinctions between different kinds of ownership and the incidents of each of them which was familiar to sixth-century Roman lawyers, albeit without a consciousness of the historical, social and economic reasons from which they originated. But an approach which ignores those differences, and seeks to translate public-law values into private law by pretending that their demands are somehow already implicit in the law of private property, puts at risk the coherence and the rationales of both public and private law of property. The challenge for property lawyers and public lawyers in the dawning human-rights era will be to take account of each other's concerns without allowing their distinct areas of law, which advance legitimately different kinds of interests, to collapse into each other to the detriment of each.

3

"Education, Education, Education": Commodity for Sale or Property Right?

TIM KAYE*

> "Ask me my three main priorities for Government and I will tell you education, education, education."
>
> Rt. Hon. Tony Blair MP, 3rd October 1996.

INTRODUCTION

IT IS CLEAR that it has always been possible to purchase a right to education or instruction. For centuries royalty and landed gentry employed the services of tutors for their offspring as household servants. Even with the institutionalisation of education, instruction was available only to those whose families were sufficiently wealthy to pay for it, whether in the "public" schools or colleges or universities. Education has thus always been a commodity for sale available to be purchased by those able to offer some consideration in the form of "some forbearance, detriment, loss or responsibility".[1] But the purchase of commodities creates in law only rights which are personal to the purchaser and governed by the law of contract. Because of the doctrine of privity of contract, according to which only the parties to a contract can obtain rights under it, one important practical effect of this aspect of the law is that any rights regarding the provision of education are likely to belong exclusively to the parent or guardian as the party privy to the contract rather than to the person receiving instruction,[2] and this will invariably be the case where those being educated are below the age of majority.

Of course, whilst a small minority were able to benefit from an education for which their families could afford to pay, the vast majority had no right to any form of education, although the Anglican and Roman Catholic churches did attempt to alleviate this deficiency to some extent by setting up their own

* I am grateful to the editors for their comments on an earlier draft.

[1] *Currie* v. *Misa* (1875) LR 10 Ex 153 *per* Lush J at p. 162.

[2] Unless it can be shown that the parties to the contract intended it to be enforceable by the person receiving instruction under section 1(2) of the Contracts (Rights of Third Parties) Act 1999.

schools in many areas. It was not until the Education Act (EA) 1870, which established school boards to provide elementary schools in areas where the churches had not already done so, that every child could (at least in theory) benefit from some rudimentary education. However, it was only with the passage of EA 1944, which effectively nationalised the church schools and brought them under a degree of state control, that the modern system of state education available to all regardless of means or other personal circumstances was established.[3]

In fact, EA 1944 did not merely make education available to all. It actually compelled a pupil's attendance. Thus section 36 of EA 1944 stipulated: "It shall be the duty of the parent of every child of compulsory school age to cause him to receive efficient full time education suitable to his age, ability and aptitude". It has been argued by Patsy Marson that this parental obligation effectively created "the corollary . . . that each child ha[d] the right to receive an education".[4] But Marson somewhat overstated the rights of the child under EA 1944. The fact that a child's parents were compelled to ensure that he or she attended school on a regular basis did not mean that the child had a right to be educated whilst there; and it certainly could not be taken as implying that any instruction given should have been of a particular type or quality.

Indeed, nowhere in EA 1944 was there any mention of child or parent having any "rights". EA 1944 did not even create a realistic complaints procedure. If parents were unhappy at the decision of a Local Education Authority (LEA) as to the allocation of school for their child, they could supposedly complain under section 68 of EA 1944 to the Secretary of State for Education, who could give "such directions . . . as appear to him to be expedient" if satisfied that the LEA was acting or proposing to act unreasonably.[5] But successive Ministers proved extremely reluctant to intervene and so this parental "right" was rendered virtually useless. David Hunt—then a backbench Opposition MP, but later to become an influential Conservative Cabinet Minister—argued in the mid-1970s that this meant that LEAs were therefore effectively allowed to act as "witness, judge and jury".[6]

It is well known that one of the centrepieces of education reform under successive Conservative administrations in the 1980s and 1990s was the move to give parents a greater say in the decision as to the school into which their children should be admitted. Section 6 of EA 1980, for example, specifically introduced for the first time the "right" of every parent to express a preference for a particular school regardless of whether or not it was situated within the area of the LEA in which the child lived.[7] Of even more practical significance, however,

[3] For a fuller account of the history of education law leading up to the 1944 Act, see M. Barber, *The Making of the Education Act 1944* (London: Cassell, 1994).

[4] P. Marson, "Parental Choice in Education" (1980) *Journal of Social Work and the Law* 193 at p. 196.

[5] This power has now been re-enacted as section 496 of EA 1996 but plays no meaningful part in the admissions process.

[6] HC Deb. Vol. 914, col. 480, 30th June 1976.

[7] EA 1980, s. 6(5).

was the creation under section 7 of a proper appeals system, according to which parents became entitled to challenge an LEA's decision to allocate their child to a particular school before a specially constituted appeals committee—now called an appeals "panel"[8]—whose decisions were binding on both the LEA and school governors. Yet the Children's Legal Centre has pointed out that:

> "The Education Acts of the 1980s . . . tended to give increased rights to parents, but this does not necessarily benefit school students, particularly those whose parents take a less active interest in their children's education or are less sympathetic to their children's needs and opinions. This 'power to the consumer' movement in education has failed to provide more involvement for the pupils, who are in fact the primary 'consumers' of schooling. Indeed the Education (No. 2) Act 1986 made matters worse by abolishing pupil governors, allowing a power of veto over pupils' rights to sex education and imposing restrictions on political activity and discussion in schools (although it did also implement the long overdue reform of outlawing corporal punishment)."[9]

In fact, the new statutory regime founded by EA 1980 can, ironically, be seen as analogous in one sense to the days of education before the Education Act 1870. For whilst the Thatcherite framework was not actually based on legally-enforceable contracts according to which only a child's parents or guardians enjoyed a right to have education provided at a specific institution, it did operate very much on the basis of contractual symbolism. Although never brought into force before being repealed by the Blair administration's School Standards and Framework Act 1998, the "home–school partnership", according to which a school could make it "a condition of the admission of every child to the school that his parent gives the admission authority a signed parental declaration . . . by which he acknowledges and accepts the parental responsibilities specified in the partnership document",[10] is perhaps the prime example of the use of contract as a rhetorical device.[11] In the same way as is the case with contract-based education rights, it was the parent rather than the individual child being educated who, in return for something sufficient to amount to consideration for the purposes of contract law were it not for section 413B(6) of the Education Act 1996, obtained the rights to the provision of education.

Marson may therefore have been guilty of wishful thinking nearly twenty years ago in claiming that section 36 of EA 1944 had the effect of creating for every child in England and Wales a "right to receive an education". But claims of "educational negligence" by former pupils against their Local Education Authority (LEA)[12] suggests that her statement may have turned into an accurate prophesy of the effect of subsequent enactments; the passage of two highly

[8] SSFA 1998, sch. 18.

[9] Children's Legal Centre, *Education Rights Handbook* (London: Children's Legal Centre, 1987) p. iii.

[10] EA 1997, s. 13, creating a new section 413A(1)(b), (2) in EA 1996.

[11] EA 1997, s. 13 also created a new section 413B(6) in EA 1996, which declared: "A partnership document shall not be capable of creating any obligation in respect of whose breach any liability arises in contract or in tort."

[12] *X* v. *Bedfordshire County Council* [1995] AC 633; [1995] ELR 404; [1995] 3 All ER 353 (HL).

significant statutes within the last year[13] may confirm this. In particular, the Human Rights Act 1998 will, when it is brought into force on 2nd October 2000,[14] incorporate into English law Article 2 of the First Protocol to the European Convention on Human Rights, which stipulates that: "No person shall be denied the right to education". Henceforth the question will be not *whether* a person has the right to education, but *what sort* of right it is. Clearly it will not be a contractual right, since neither anyone enjoying the benefits of state education nor their parents or guardians will have a contract with the state school at which they are educated. It could, of course, be a purely statutory right which will exist only in the manner and to the extent specifically laid down in primary or delegated legislation. Alternatively, it could be a property right. This would mean that, far from its ambit being dictated exclusively by explicit legislation, the right would exist "at large" and, in default of specific statutory provisions, it would necessarily be governed by the general law of personal property (including the tort of conversion) and potentially protected from criminal activity by the law of theft. It is therefore important to consider the salient elements of a personal property right so as to determine whether these ingredients also characterise the right to education.

THREE MYTHS OF PERSONAL PROPERTY LAW

The first myth: the classification of personal property

Unfortunately, the elements which are traditionally seen as characterising a personal property right are often somewhat exaggerated. One of the pillars of the orthodox view of property law has been, for example, that personal property rights must be one of two types, *choses* (or things) in possession on the one hand and *choses* in action on the other, so that these categories are mutually exclusive.[15] Items which may become choses in possession are said to be, as their name implies, tangible objects capable of being physically possessed in the everyday sense of this word, for which category a putative right to education could obviously not qualify. Choses in action, by contrast, encompass intangible items of property such as shares, goodwill and debts, all of which have also been held by the European Court of Human Rights to come within the concept of "possessions" to be found in the right to property enshrined in Article 1 of the First Protocol to the European Convention.[16] It has been argued before our domestic courts that there is a distinction to be drawn between debts and other choses in action, but this view has been explicitly rejected in the High Court, where it has been held that: "A debt is but one instance of a chose in action,

[13] The School Standards and Framework Act 1998 and the Human Rights Act 1998.
[14] *Press Release* 18th May 1999.
[15] *Colonial Bank* v. *Whinney* (1885) 30 Ch D 261.
[16] See eg *Tre Traktörer AB* v. *Sweden* (1989) 13 EHRR 309.

though it may be a common one."[17] Thus, according to conventional classification, the category of choses in action "includes all property other than real property, leaseholds and things in possession . . . that is, 'all personal rights of property which can only be claimed or enforced by action and not by taking physical possession'."[18] *Halsbury* thus concludes:

> "The expression [chose in action] is found in the history of English law with so many meanings attached to it, and has been and still is employed to denote so many and such various classes of things, that it is impossible to give an accurate and complete definition of what it means and may include at the present day. The various kinds of property included under the term have little in common beyond the characteristic fact of their not being subject to actual physical possession."[19]

A right to education could therefore potentially qualify as a chose in action.

The orthodox, binary division of personal property is now, however, threatened by the possibility that a third category of property exists, for which a putative right to education may also qualify. As the late Professor Griew recognised,[20] section 4(1) of the Theft Act 1968 provides, for example, that " 'property' includes money and all other property, real or personal, including things in action and *other intangible property*" (my emphasis). This definition clearly allows for the possibility that some forms of intangible property will not be choses in action. Professor John Smith pointed out some years ago that intangible property of this type would certainly include patents and applications for patents because section 30(1) of the Patents Act 1977 expressly declares them not to be things in action.[21] He has also pointed out that, "An invention for which no patent has been granted or applied for is clearly another form of intangible property,[22] whether or not it is a thing in action."[23] There never has been any reason to suppose, however, that the category of "other intangible property" is exhausted by the law of patents and, in the case of *Attorney-General of Hong Kong* v. *Nai-keung*, the Privy Council held that export quotas also qualified as "other intangible property" even though they were not things in action.[24]

It is likely that other quotas fall into the same category since, whilst they appear to be neither choses in possession nor choses in action, they are certainly treated as forms of property by the relevant statutory instruments. EU fishing

[17] *Helstan Securities Ltd* v. *Hertfordshire County Council* [1978] 3 All ER 262 *per* Croom-Johnson J at p. 264.

[18] E. Griew, *The Theft Acts 1968 and 1978* 5th ed. (London: Sweet & Maxwell, 1986) at para. 2–11, quoting Channell J in *Torkington* v. *Magee* [1902] 2 KB 427 at p. 430.

[19] *Halsbury's Laws of England* 4th ed, Vol 6 (London: Butterworths, 1991) para. 1, n 2.

[20] E. Griew, *The Theft Acts 1968 and 1978* 5th ed. (London: Sweet & Maxwell, 1986) at para. 2–11.

[21] Sections (1) and 213(1) of the Copyright, Designs and Patents Act 1988 declare both copyright and design right to be property rights, but there is no indication as to whether or not they are choses in action.

[22] Patents Act 1977, s. 7(2)(b).

[23] These observations are now to be found in J.C. Smith, *The Law of Theft* 8th ed. (London: Butterworths, 1997) at paras. 2-104, 2-105.

[24] (1987) 86 Cr App R 174 (PC).

quotas,[25] for example, are specifically described as "assets" on which capital gains tax is payable;[26] whilst the Dairy Produce Quotas Regulations 1997 make it a criminal offence to dispose of dairy quota which the transferor knows or might reasonably be expected to know is incorrectly registered in his name.[27]

Presumably there may be still more intangible rights, yet to be the subject of litigation in the appellate courts, which may also qualify as "other intangible property". At any rate, it is certainly clear that there is a third category of personal property right, distinct from choses in possession and choses in action which, it is assumed, consists of a variety of amorphous and heterogeneous rights of more recent origin which reflect the growth of trade, consumerism and the culture of rights at the end of the twentieth century rather than the more patrician law of the Victorian era.[28] It may therefore be that a putative right to education would fall within this category of intangible property rather than that of choses in action.

The second myth: property rights are defensible against "all the world"

The essence of a property right is supposed, according to the orthodox view, to be that it is enforceable "against all the world" in contradistinction to a merely personal right, which may be enforced only against a specific person or class of persons. Again, however, such orthodoxy proves on further examination to be an exaggeration of the truth, for property rights can be legitimately undermined in several circumstances. Under section 2 of the Proceeds of Crime Act 1995, for example, a criminal who holds property as a result of, or in connection with the commission of, certain criminal offences may have that property confiscated under a court order. Similarly, a person convicted of drug trafficking who appears to have benefited therefrom is liable to have property confiscated to the value of such benefit.[29] And persons guilty of a terrorist offence may be required to forfeit money or other property in their control or possession at the time of the offence where there is reasonable cause to believe it might be used to assist future acts of terrorism.[30]

Moreover, it is not only through legislation that apparently good title to property can be legitimately supplanted. Someone who has parted with possession of goods because of a misrepresentation will find that his right to have the goods restored to him has been lost if they have since been passed on for value

[25] I am grateful to my colleague, Frank Meisel, for pointing this out to me.

[26] The Finance Act 1993, Section 86(2), (Fish Quota) Order 1999, SI 1999, No. 564.

[27] SI 1997, No. 733, reg. 31(1)(c).

[28] The growth of consumerism in relation to the education system has been well documented by N. Harris, *Law and Education: Regulation, Consumerism and the Education System* (London: Sweet and Maxwell, 1993).

[29] Drug Trafficking Act 1994, ss. 2, 5.

[30] Prevention of Terrorism (Temporary Provisions) Act 1989, s. 13.

to an innocent third party.[31] Indeed, any buyer purchasing goods from a seller who has acquired only a voidable title will nevertheless himself acquire "a good title to the goods, provided he buys them in good faith and without notice of the seller's defect of title".[32]

It is therefore clear that property rights, whilst often maintainable against all the world, do not necessarily enjoy such a characteristic. Professor Michael Bridge has attempted to overcome this difficulty by arguing:

> "The touchstone of a property right is its universality: it can be asserted against the world at large and not, for example, only against another individual such as a contracting partner. If, under a contract of sale, I acquire the ownership of a chattel, my property right to that chattel may be asserted not just against the seller but against the whole world. This is not to say, however, that universal rights are invincible: common law property rights may in certain circumstances be overridden, and equitable rights, for example the interest of a trust beneficiary in the trust assets, are always vulnerable to the *bona fide* purchaser for value without notice of the legal estate."[33]

But it is doubtful if this attempt to distinguish "universality" and "invincibility" amounts to much more than mere verbal quibbling. For example, the property right to a debt cannot be "asserted" *against* anyone in the world other than the debtor or his assignee; it can also not be "asserted" *by* anyone other than the creditor and his assignee. This situation simply mirrors the position with contractual rights: they can be asserted only by one of the parties (or his assignees) against another (or her assignees).There is thus no difference in the breadth of assertion of a (property) right to a debt than there is in respect of a (personal/contractual) right preventing the disclosure of confidential information. Yet, as Lord Upjohn said in *Phipps* v. *Boardman*:

> "In general, information is not property at all . . . confidential information is often . . . described as the property of the donor . . . But in the end the real truth is that it is not property in any normal sense but equity will restrain its transmission to another if in breach of some confidential relationship."[34]

Indeed, a student who "borrowed" an examination paper so as to find out the questions in advance was held to have been rightly acquitted of a charge of theft precisely because the confidential information which those questions comprised could not be classified as property.[35]

The fact that a particular right may (or may not) be "asserted" against all the world will not therefore be a defining characteristic which indicates whether such a right is of a proprietary or personal nature. The most that can be said in this context is that it might produce a sort of "indicative" category of right, but other factors will have to be considered before a full judgment can be made. As

[31] *White* v. *Garden* (1851) 10 CB 919.
[32] Sale of Goods Act 1979, s. 23.
[33] M. Bridge, *Personal Property Law* 2nd ed. (London: Blackstone Press, 1996) at p. 8.
[34] [1967] 2 AC 46 at pp. 127–8.
[35] *Oxford* v. *Moss* (1978) 68 Cr App R 183.

a result, the classification of a putative right to education cannot be founded on this ground alone. Certainly, the courts rarely decide whether a given right is of a proprietary nature or not on the basis of whether it may be asserted against all the world. Indeed, the matter is hardly ever canvassed in judgments at all: it seems to be assumed that the notion of universal assertion flows *as a consequence of* a right's enjoying proprietary status, rather than its being a constituent element which helps to define the right *ex ante*.

The third myth: property rights are capable of assignment

Lord Wilberforce held thirty years ago that, for a right or an interest to be "admitted into the category of property . . . it must be definable, identifiable by third parties, *capable in its nature of assumption by third parties*, and have some degree of permanence or stability" (my emphasis).[36] It is certainly true that, in practice, the courts have tended to find the existence of a property right where the specific item in question can be traded. Thus, as has already been pointed out, the Privy Council was prepared to find that export quotas qualified as property on the basis that they were regularly traded, at least for fixed periods of time.[37] Debts and other intangible forms of property such as patents and copyrights can similarly be bought and sold. Moreover, although the House of Lords affirmed in *Trendtex Trading Corporation* v. *Credit Suisse* the old rule that the bare (personal) right to litigate cannot be assigned[38] on the grounds that it would otherwise permit the "savouring of champerty" or a "trafficking in litigation"[39] and would thus be contrary to public policy, their Lordships opined *obiter* that when the subject-matter involves a right or property or interest in which the assignee has a genuine commercial interest in taking and enforcing for his own benefit, this can be legitimately assigned.

Applying these principles to three cases which had been listed together because they raised similar issues, the Court of Appeal held unanimously that the assignment to a company's creditor of a cause of action by a liquidator or administrative receiver acting under section 214 of the Insolvency Act 1986 was valid and not contrary to public policy even though the assignment had been motivated by the fact that the assignee was a bankrupt entitled to legal aid whereas the assignor was not so entitled.[40] Indeed, Sir Thomas Bingham MR pointed out that such an assignment was actually a sensible course of action by the liquidator, since it relieved the company of any liability for the costs of the action whilst the contract of assignment provided that the proceeds of any success would be applied in the first instance to meeting the claims of the creditors

[36] *National Provincial Bank Ltd* v. *Ainsworth* [1965] 2 All ER 472 at p. 494.
[37] *Attorney-General of Hong Kong* v. *Nai-keung* (1987) 86 Cr App R 174.
[38] [1982] AC 679 (HL).
[39] [1982] AC 679 at p. 694 *per* Lord Wilberforce.
[40] *Norglen Ltd* v. *Reeds Rains Prudential Ltd* [1996] 1 All ER 945 (CA).

and the costs of liquidation. Sir Thomas referred to the observations of Lord Hoffmann in *Stein* v. *Blake*,[41] with which all the other members of the House of Lords had agreed, to the effect that, in Sir Thomas's words, it was acceptable "to enable a bankrupt assignee to sue with the benefit of legal aid which would not be available to the trustee-assignor, to the prejudice of the party sued." He concluded, "There is no obvious reason why it should make any difference if the obtaining of such legal aid was the object of the assignment as well as its effect."[42] Yet the Court of Appeal has also made it clear that the power under section 214 of the Insolvency Act 1986 "does not give the liquidator *carte blanche* to do an illegal act such as entering a champertous agreement."[43]

Nevertheless, this does not mean that the ability to be bought and sold is a characteristic exclusive to forms of property. Confidential information, which has already been shown not to be property, can also be legitimately traded in the market-place in circumstances when, for example, a newspaper purchases information whose publication is in the public interest, or when the information relates to an individual's personal life. As Professor Tony Smith has pointed out:

> "The mere fact that a thing can be bought and sold, or even that there is a developed market in the commodity, is only evidence that it is property. Services can be bought and sold, as can electricity, but they are not property for the purposes of the law of theft, or many other purposes."[44]

The ability to assign is not, therefore, a characteristic distinctive of property rights. Even more seriously, it should be noted that it is not even necessary that something classified as property should be capable of assignment. In *Zim Properties Ltd* v. *Procter (Inspector of Taxes)*,[45] for instance, Warner J held that an employer's rights under a contract of employment could be considered a taxable asset—and thus a form of property—for the purposes of the Capital Taxes Act 1965 even though they were not assignable, because the employee might have paid to be released from his contractual obligations.

In *United Dominions Trust (Commercial) Ltd* v. *Parkway Motors Ltd*[46] the plaintiffs let a motor-van under a hire-purchase agreement which prohibited assignment of the goods or "the benefit of this agreement". Nevertheless, the hirer sold the van to a third party, who sold it to the defendants. Since the hirer was in arrears, the plaintiffs served notice on him terminating the agreement. On the same day the defendants tendered the unpaid balance of the hire and purchase-money. The plaintiffs refused to accept this sum and claimed in detinue for the return of the van or alternatively its value. McNair J held that, since the original hire-purchase agreement expressly prohibited assignment, the hirer had

[41] [1995] 2 All ER 961 (HL) at p. 972.
[42] [1996] 1 All ER 945 (CA) at p. 957.
[43] *Ward* v. *Aitken*, decided on 14th October 1996 (LEXIS transcript) *per* Peter Gibson LJ.
[44] A. Smith, *Property Offences: The Protection of Property Through the Criminal Law* (London: Sweet & Maxwell, 1994) para. 3.15.
[45] [1985] STC 90.
[46] [1955] 1 WLR 719.

been unable to pass any rights in the van or under the agreement to the third party, who could therefore pass no such rights to defendants. Accordingly, the defendants had no interest in the van and no contractual rights against the plaintiffs so that, in default of the return of the van, the defendants were liable to pay the full value of the van to the plaintiffs. The defendants were thus effectively forced to fall back on a contractual remedy against the third party who had failed to pass on the rights specified in the contract between them (although it is, of course, likely that this third party was either untraceable or insolvent). The fact that neither the goods involved nor the benefit of the agreement could be assigned did not, of course, mean that those goods were no longer a form of property. Nevertheless they remained inalienable by the hirer for so long as the contract was in force.

Intangible property, such a chose in action, may also prove to be inalienable. In *Helstan Securities Ltd* v. *Hertfordshire County Council*[47] there had been an assignment to the plaintiff of a debt allegedly owed by the defendant council. The council refused to pay on two grounds. First, it claimed that it had been swindled by the assignor, "Renholds". Secondly, and more relevant in the present context, it pointed to a clause in the contract with Renholds which expressly prohibited the assignment of the contract "or any part thereof or any benefit or interest therein or thereunder" without the written consent of the council. Since the council had not consented, though notified of the assignment by the plaintiff, it argued that it could not be liable. Croom-Johnson J concluded:

> "There are certain kinds of choses in action which, for one reason or another, are not assignable and there is no reason why the parties to an agreement may not contract to give its subject-matter the quality of unassignability."[48]

The assignment was rendered invalid by the terms of the contract, so that judgment was entered for the defendant council, whilst the plaintiff was left to pursue a (presumably worthless) contractual remedy against Renholds.

Lord Browne-Wilkinson has since taken this view much further. In *Linden Gardens Trust Ltd* v. *Lenesta Sludge Disposals Ltd* the House of Lords tackled head-on the question of whether the prohibition of an assignment of property might be contrary to public policy. His Lordship's speech was clear:

> "Certainly in the context of rights over land the law does not favour restrictions on alienability. But even in relation to land law a prohibition against the assignment of a lease is valid. We were not referred to any English case in which the courts have had to consider restrictions on the alienation of tangible personal property, probably because there are few cases in which there would be any desire to restrict such alienation. In the case of real property there is a defined and limited supply of the commodity and it has been held contrary to public policy to restrict the free market. But

[47] [1978] 3 All ER 262.
[48] [1978] 3 All ER 262 at pp. 265–6.

no such reason can apply to contractual rights: *there is no public need for a market in choses in action.*"[49] (My emphasis).

Legislation too, frequently specifies that particular forms of property are incapable of assignment. Social security benefits and child benefit are two such examples; superannuation benefits payable to teachers are another.[50] It therefore appears that the ability to trade a right is not, after all, determinative of whether such a right is proprietary or purely personal. Again, the most that can be said is that the alienability or otherwise of a particular right, such as the right to education, may provide an indication of the legal status of that right.

PROPERTY RIGHTS AND PRAGMATISM

It has thus proved astonishingly difficult either to define a property right *simpliciter* or to do so by means of distinguishing it from other forms of rights and interests known to the law. No doubt these problems do not arise in the vast majority of cases, whether brought before the courts or not. But the relatively undeveloped nature of the subject—to which many writers have adverted—has meant that the fundamental issue of what it means to talk of a property right has hardly been discussed by the courts. As a consequence, it is difficult to know *ex ante* whether newly-created rights may be proprietary or not. Consideration of the cases suggests, indeed, that there is no "common thread" to be found if it is sought in terms of defining characteristics; there are no defining characteristics of a property right which distinguish it from other forms of right or interest. Alienability and, more controversially, universality may be typical features but they are neither necessary nor sufficient conditions on which to predicate the existence of a property right.

It is submitted that, in fact, the only necessary condition for the existence of a property right is that the right in question can be valued in monetary terms (whether or not it can be bought and sold). It was because an employee might pay to be released from his contractual obligations, for example, that an employer's rights under a contract of employment have been considered to be a form of property even though they were not assignable.[51] Non-assignable debts can also be valued in monetary terms—even if they cannot be traded—and are, for this reason, also forms of property.[52] However, the fact that a monetary value can be put on a given right or interest does not mean that it will automatically qualify as a property right. A right to, or interest in, confidential information can be bought and sold and can therefore possess a monetary value, but it

49 [1994] 1 AC 85 at p. 107 *per* Lord Browne-Wilkinson.

50 For a very full list of such inalienable property, see *Halsbury's Laws of England* 4th ed, Vol 6 (London: Butterworths, 1991) paras. 83–86.

51 *Zim Properties Ltd* v. *Procter (Inspector of Taxes)* [1985] STC 90.

52 *Helstan Securities Ltd* v. *Hertfordshire County Council* [1978] 3 All ER 262.

is still not of a proprietary nature.[53] The fact that it has a value capable of being expressed in monetary terminology is therefore a necessary, but not a sufficient, condition of a property right. To put this another way, a right must have some monetary value if it is to be classed as a property right, but not all rights having monetary value are property rights. Once again, this test can provide indicative status only.

In practice, the courts have taken a rather more pragmatic approach. Thus the assignment of a bare right to litigate has been struck down not on the grounds that such a right is purely personal, but on the footing that the arrangement would be champertous.[54] Similarly, it may be argued that the real reason that export quotas have been held to be a form of property was not (as the Privy Council found) that such quotas were often traded, for this would mean that confidential information too should be considered as a form of property. Rather, export quotas had to be held to be a form of property because otherwise it would not have been possible to hold that a company director who sold his company's quotas at an undervalue for his own profit was guilty of theft.[55]

In other words, the courts adopt a flexible approach tailored to the appropriate *function* or *purpose* which may be served, which enables the court to use subtle reasoning to suit the context of the matter in issue and which, in an international context, would be referred to as a "teleological" approach.[56] Coval *et al*. have similarly advocated what they call a "functional theory of property", where what is property is determined by "its function as a means in the satisfaction of the reason for action" in contrast to "descriptive theories of property in which it is claimed that property rights are extendible only to objects which have certain features".[57] Indeed, they have gone further and argued that:

> "with a functional theory of property, the role of physical objects drops out of the centre of the explanatory picture and is replaced by sets of actions . . . The law thus extends . . . by protecting greater possibilities for action through the capacity to give legal recognition to specific kinds of uses as property".[58]

Thus the origin of a putative right is apparently unimportant: property rights may be created by common law (eg debts), equity (eg interests of beneficiaries of trusts) or statute (eg patents or export quotas). The status of the right to education cannot therefore be judged simply according to its inherent characteristics, but can be settled only after consideration of the purpose to be served by classifying such a right in a particular manner.

[53] *Oxford* v. *Moss* (1978) 68 Cr App R 183.
[54] *Trendtex Trading Corporation* v. *Credit Suisse* [1982] AC 679 (HL).
[55] *Attorney-General of Hong Kong* v. *Nai-keung* (1987) 86 Cr App R 174 (PC).
[56] Vienna Convention on the Law of Treaties 1969, Article 31.
[57] S. Coval *et al.*, "The Foundations of Property and Property Law" (1986) 45 *Camb LJ* 457 at p. 460.
[58] *Ibid.* at p. 462.

THE RIGHT TO EDUCATION IN INTERNATIONAL LAW

The United Kingdom is a signatory to three international conventions which contain important provisions relating to the right to education. Ironically, the most recent has the least to offer. Article 28(1) of the United Nations Convention on the Rights of the Child, ratified by the United Kingdom in 1991, thus declares only that "States parties recognise the right of the child to education . . ." Article 26 of the Universal Declaration of Human Rights, adopted in 1948, goes much further:

> "1. Everyone has the right to education. Education shall be free, at least in the elementary and fundamental stages. Elementary education shall be compulsory. . . .
> 2. Education shall be directed to the full development of the human personality and to the strengthening of respect for human rights and fundamental freedoms. . . .
> 3. Parents shall have a prior right to choose the kind of education that shall be given to their children."

Similarly, Article 2 of the First Protocol to the European Convention of Human Rights proclaims:

> "No person shall be denied the right to education. In the exercise of any functions which it assumes in relation to education and to teaching, the State shall respect the right of parents to ensure such education and teaching in conformity with their own religious and philosophical convictions."

But whilst the UN Convention on the Rights of the Child and the Universal Declaration of Human Rights both remain purely international agreements unenforceable at the suit of domestic litigants, the right to education embodied in Article 2 of the First Protocol to the European Convention of Human Rights is due to be incorporated into domestic English law by section 1(1)(b) of the Human Rights Act 1998 (HRA 1998) on 2nd October 2000. Furthermore, in what is commonly known as the *Belgian Linguistic Case (No. 2)*,[59] the European Court of Human Rights held that the meaning of "education" in Article 2 was to be determined according to "economic and social circumstances" and that, since Belgium was a "highly developed country", the right to education included "entry to nursery, primary, secondary and higher education". There is no reason to think that The United Kingdom is any less developed than Belgium, nor that Article 2 would be applied any differently in a British context. It is therefore clear that the right to education extends to persons of all ages, although the precise age from which nursery education must be made available has not been indicated. It is submitted, however, that the fulfilment of the government's pledge to provide a nursery school place to every four-year-old whose parents want one—to be given legal form via Part V of the School Standards and Framework Act 1998—will be sufficient to comply with this aspect of Article 2.

[59] (1968) 1 EHRR 252.

However, on 20th March 1952, the UK entered a reservation to Article 2 of the First Protocol which has never been withdrawn, and which states that:

> "the principle affirmed in the second sentence of Article 2 is accepted by the United Kingdom only so far as it is compatible with the provision of efficient instruction and training, and the avoidance of unreasonable public expenditure".

Sections 1(2) and 15(1)(a) of HRA 1998 will ensure that this reservation becomes the law of the land just as much as the first sentence of Article 2.

It can be seen that Article 2 in fact creates *two* rights which are quite distinct.[60] The second sentence grants a right to parents which has been mirrored by domestic law since the Education Act 1944 was passed and which is now to be found in section 86 of the School Standards and Framework Act 1998 as the parental right to express a preference for a specific school. As was pointed out in the introduction to this essay, this cannot be construed as granting to an individual the right to education. That right is actually created by the first sentence of Article 2, although it may be noted that it is expressed as the right not to be denied education. Nevertheless, the European Court of Human Rights held in the *Belgian Linguistic Case (No. 2)* that, despite this negative formulation, the first sentence of Article 2 can be read as a positive right to education.[61] Since section 2(1)(a) of HRA 1998 requires that a domestic court, when "determining a question which has arisen in connection with a Convention right must take into account any . . . judgment, declaration or advisory opinion of the European Court of Human Rights", it is almost certain that Article 2 will be considered to form the basis of a right to education for all citizens of the UK residing in England and Wales.

The *Belgian Linguistic* case also demonstrates clearly, however, that there is an inherent ambiguity in the concept of the right to education. It may, on the one hand, be taken to mean a right to *some sort* of education, however and whenever delivered. This may be thought of as a *general* right to be educated. On the other hand, it may be seen as a *specific* right to a particular type or form of education more closely associated with the notion of a form of positive freedom. In *Simpson* v. *UK* the Commission observed that Article 2 of Protocol No. 1:

> "is not an absolute right which requires Contracting Parties to subsidise private education of a particular type or level. In principle, it guarantees access to public educational facilities which have been created at a given time and the possibility of drawing benefit from the education received."[62]

The few specific rights associated with positive freedom endowed by Article 2 are those which are necessary to give Article 2 some degree of efficacy. Following the *Belgian Linguistic Case (No 2)*,[63] they include:

[60] See J.R. McManus, *Education and the Courts* (London: Sweet & Maxwell, 1998) at para 10–11 and n. 14.

[61] (1968) 1 EHRR 252.

[62] Application No. 14688/89, (1989) 64 DR 188, at para. 3.

[63] (1968) 1 EHRR 252.

"A right of access to educational institutions existing at a given time; the right to be educated in the national language, or one of the national languages; and the right to obtain official recognition of the studies completed."[64]

However, the incorporation of Article 2 of the First Protocol into domestic law is not necessarily sufficient in itself to transform the right to education into a property right. This is because the European Commission on Human Rights which, until November 1998, decided upon the admissibility of complaints of breaches of the European Convention, held in *Simpson* v. *UK*[65] that such a right to education is not a "civil right" for the purposes of paragraph 1 of Article 6 of the Convention. Article 6(1) provides that:

"In the determination of his civil rights and obligations . . . everyone is entitled to a fair and public hearing within a reasonable time by an independent and impartial tribunal established by law . . ."

The Commission declared in *Simpson* that:

"Although the notion of a civil right under this provision is autonomous of any domestic law definitions, the Commission considers that for the purposes of the domestic law in question and the Convention, the right not to be denied elementary education falls, *in the circumstances of the present case*, squarely within the domain of public law, having no private law analogy and no repercussions on private rights or obligations."[66] (My emphasis).

From this it would appear that the Commission could not accept that the right to education could be a property right, since an interest in property is clearly a matter of private rather than public law. This view will continue to carry weight in domestic English law when HRA 1998 is brought into force, for under section 2(1)(c) of HRA 1998, a domestic court must take account of such a decision by the Commission, although it is not bound by it, in the same way as it must take account of any decision of the European Court. In any event, this decision is highly analogous to the approach taken by Lord Browne-Wilkinson in *X* v. *Bedfordshire County Council*,[67] where he held that there was no tort of breach of statutory duty *simpliciter* in the obligation to provide education suitable to the requirements of an individual child:

"The fact that . . . claims have been successfully brought to enforce public law rights provides no indication that there is a corresponding private law right to damages for breach of statutory duty."[68]

Yet it is important to notice the riders applied to both these decisions. Whilst the Commission could find no "civil right" arising from a public law right "in

[64] J.R. McManus, *Education and the Courts* (London: Sweet & Maxwell, 1998) at para. 10–21.
[65] Application No. 14688/89, (1989) 64 DR 188.
[66] Application No. 14688/89, (1989) 64 DR 188 at para. 1.
[67] [1995] 2 AC 633.
[68] [1995] 2 AC 633 at p. 768.

the circumstances of the present case", Lord Browne-Wilkinson made it clear that although:

> "it is impossible to impose a common law duty of care which is inconsistent with, or fetters, a statutory duty, I can see no legal or common sense principle which requires one to deny a common law duty of care which would exist just because there is a statutory scheme which addresses the same problem."[69]

In other words, if the facts of the particular cases before the courts had been different, a "civil right" to education (in the language of the Convention) or a civil wrong (tort) for failure to comply with such a right might well have been found to exist. Indeed, Lord Browne-Wilkinson's speech has since taken on added significance following the decision of the ECHR itself in *Osman* v. *United Kingdom*, where it held that a blanket refusal by the English courts to countenance a claim of negligence by a public body in its performance of a statutory duty was a disproportionate restriction on an individual's right of access to a court and therefore a breach of Article 6.[70]

These riders suggest that *Simpson* should not be applied too readily in our domestic law. Indeed, it has often been said that the interpretation of the Convention and the Protocols attaching thereto is a dynamic process, whilst the very concept of a "civil right" under the Convention has been considerably widened in a number of cases since the decision of the Commission in *Simpson*. As Wadham and Mountfield have written, the Strasbourg institutions have been "increasingly willing to find a 'civil right' within, or alongside a public law right".[71] Indeed, the European Court of Human Rights held over ten years ago that the fact a signatory state's domestic law classified a particular right as a public law right did not conclusively deny to an applicant the benefit of Article 6(1).[72] Thus, in the instant case, a woman's right to a widow's pension was to be treated as a "civil right" notwithstanding German law's categorisation of it as merely a public law right.

Three other judgments of the European Court of Human Rights are probably even more apposite in the present context. The first is *Pinder* v. *UK*,[73] where it was held that, although the concept of a "civil right" for the purposes of Article 6(1) was autonomous of national law, such a "civil right" could exist only if the same right existed in an individual nation's legal system. The second is *Sporrong and Lönnroth* v. *Sweden*,[74] where the Court held that a property right is "without doubt" a "civil right". The third is *Mats Jacobsson* v. *Sweden*[75] where, in a decision based on an approach very similar to that later adopted by Lord

[69] [1995] 2 AC 633 at p. 765.

[70] [1999] 1 FLR 193.

[71] J. Wadham and H. Mountfield, *Blackstone's Guide to the Human Rights Act 1998* (London: Blackstone Press, 1999) at p. 78.

[72] *Deumeland* v. *Germany* (1986) 8 EHRR 448.

[73] (1984) EHRR 46, at para.5

[74] (1982) 5 EHRR 35, at para. 79.

[75] (1991) 13 EHRR 79.

Browne-Wilkinson in *X* v. *Bedfordshire County Council*,[76] the Court held that rights acknowledged by a nation's domestic legal system will be recognised as constituting "civil rights" for the purposes of Article 6(1) even if the exercise of such rights is subject to conditions laid down in domestic legislation—which the Court itself had recognised in the *Belgian Linguistic* case was almost inevitable in the case of the right to education[77]—which might be varied by successive administrations. In other words, the European Convention represents only the lowest common denominator between the signatory states, so that the right to education in Article 2 of Protocol 1 cannot become a proprietary or "civil" right within signatory states merely through the interpretation of the Convention. However, if a nation's domestic law gives the right to education a proprietary status, then that will be recognised by the Strasbourg institutions and given appropriate effect through the application of Article 6(1).[78] If English law has elevated the right to education to the status of property right, then it will also be capable of being a "civil right" for the purposes of Article 6(1). It is not, therefore, possible to determine whether the right to education is a property right in English law by looking to the decisions of the Strasbourg institutions. On the contrary, the view to be taken when applying the Convention is largely reflective of the nature of the right which is recognised domestically.

THE RIGHT TO EDUCATION IN ENGLISH LAW

The obligation on parents to ensure that their child attends school, which was suggested by Marson to be the basis for a pupil's right to education—and was, at that time, to be found in section 36 of EA 1944—is still in operation, albeit in slightly amended form. It is now to be found in section 7 of EA 1996 and reads:

> "The parent of every child of compulsory school age shall cause him to receive efficient full-time education suitable (a) to his age, ability and aptitude, and (b) to any special educational needs he may have, either by regular attendance at school or otherwise."

LEAs have corresponding obligations. Section 14(1) and (2) of EA 1996, for example, requires that each LEA shall ensure that sufficient schools for providing primary and secondary education are available in its area, and that they will be sufficient only if they are "sufficient in number, character and equipment to provide for all pupils the opportunity of appropriate education". This means that there must be education available offering:

> "such variety of instruction and training as may be desirable in view of (a) the pupils' different ages, abilities and aptitudes, and (b) the different periods for which they may

76 [1995] 2 AC 633.

77 (1968) 1 EHRR 252.

78 See further P. van den Broek, "The Protection of Property Rights under the European Convention on Human Rights" (1986) 1 Legal Issues of European Integration 52.

be expected to remain at school, including practical instruction and training appropriate to their different needs".[79]

In addition, LEAs must ensure that primary, secondary and further education are all available and efficient to meet the needs of the local population.[80] In particular, they need to ensure that special educational provision is made for pupils with special educational needs.[81] All these obligations must be "exercised by the authority with a view to promoting high standards".[82]

Carolyn Hamilton, Director of the Children's Legal Centre, has argued that these rules mean that the right to education currently amounts to little more than the narrow right to a school place, rather than being "directed to the full development of the human personality" in accordance with Article 26(2) of the Universal Declaration of Human Rights, or even including the right to help to get the maximum benefit from education.[83] Such an unsatisfactory position may be a consequence of the fact that, as McManus has argued persuasively:

> "a 'right to education' straddles the distinction between a more traditional civil and political right, in the sense of a negative freedom from interference by public authority, and a more modern economic, social or cultural right, requiring the state to take positive steps to provide what is guaranteed. The tension between the negative and positive nature of the right to education is a constant them in the case law determining the content of the right."[84]

A more positive right is, indeed, to be found in section 402 of EA 1996, which compels the governing body of a maintained school to ensure that:

> "each registered pupil at the school is entered, at such time as they *(sic)* consider appropriate, for each prescribed public examination for which he is being prepared at the school at the time in question in each syllabus for that examination for which he is being so prepared".

However, the governing body is under no such obligation if either it considers that there are educational reasons in the case of that particular pupil for not entering him in that examination or if the pupil's parent requests in writing that the pupil should not be entered for that examination.[85]

Even so, it appears that Hamilton is being unduly downbeat in much the same way that Marson was somewhat over-optimistic back in 1980. During the last few years, the courts have begun to take an approach to the right to education which puts flesh on the skeletal right to a school place. The starting-point may, in retrospect, be seen to have been the case of *X* v. *Bedfordshire County Council*, where Lord Browne-Wilkinson declared:

[79] EA 1996, s. 14(3).

[80] EA 1996, s. 13(1).

[81] EA 1996, s. 14(6)(b).

[82] EA 1996, s. 13A, as inserted by the School Standards and Framework Act (SSFA) 1998, s. 5.

[83] See C. Hamilton, "Current Issues of Children's Rights" in J. de Groof and H. Penneman (eds.), *The Legal Status of Pupils in Europe* (The Hague: Kluwer Law International, 1998) esp. p. 10

[84] J.R. McManus, *Education and the Courts* (London: Sweet & Maxwell, 1998) at para. 10–10.

[85] EA 1996, s. 402 (2).

> "In my judgment a school which accepts a pupil assumes responsibility not only for his physical well being but also for his educational needs. The education of the pupil is the very purpose for which the child goes to the school."[86]

A few years later, Dyson J was called upon to deal with a case involving the interpretation of section 348 of EA 1996, which says that where:

> "(1)(b) the local education authority are satisfied (i) that [a child's] interests require the necessary special educational provision to be made for him at a school which is not a maintained school, and (ii) that it is appropriate for the child to be provided with education at the particular school,
> (2) . . . the local education authority shall pay the whole of the fees payable in respect of the education provided for the child at the school, and if (a) board and lodging are provided for him at the school, and (b) the authority are satisfied that the necessary special educational provision cannot be provided for him at the school unless the board and lodging are also provided, the authority shall pay the whole of the fees payable in respect of the board and lodging."

Dyson J held in *Solihull Metropolitan Borough Council* v. *Finn*[87] that this meant that, since the LEA in this case was satisfied that the child involved had special educational needs—in this case, autism—which required provision to be made for him at a non-maintained (i.e. private or foreign) school, then the LEA was under a duty to pay for that education. That was so even though, in the instant case, it meant an annual bill for the child's education of over £50,000, since he was being educated at Higashi School in Boston, USA.

Similarly, in a case where a boy aged seven was permanently excluded from school, he received no education at all for some fourteen months and only resumed full-time education four terms after his exclusion from primary school. His mother considered that the effect on him was particularly severe because he had special educational needs. She made a number of approaches to the LEA asking for an interim school placement or some form of interim provision while the LEA carried out the statutory assessment. However, there were several sections in the council's education department which had responsibilities relevant to the boy's situation and, whilst co-ordination between them was poor, none took the lead in ensuring the provision of education. Eventually, the council accepted that the delay in making arrangements for the boy's education was unacceptable and the Local Government Ombudsman recommended that the LEA pay £2,000 as compensation for the value of education which the boy had lost. The figure was based on the fact that it cost the council £1,920 per year to educate a pupil in a primary school in its area.[88]

That the right to education in English law certainly does amount to more than a right to a school place is, perhaps, even more clearly seen from a consideration

[86] [1995] 2 AC 633 at p. 766.

[87] [1998] ELR 203.

[88] Local settlement 96/A/3741 in Local Government Commissioner, *Digest of Cases 1997* (London: Commission for Local Administration in England, 1998) pp. 13–14.

of cases concerning the application of section 19(1) of the Education Act 1996 (as amended by section 47 of the Education Act 1997), since this concerns the right to education by means other than at school. It says:

> "Each local education authority shall make arrangements for the provision of suitable education at school or otherwise than at school for children of compulsory school age who, by reason of illness, exclusion from school or otherwise, may not for any period receive suitable education unless suitable arrangements are made for them."

"Suitable education" in this context means "efficient education suitable to his age, ability and aptitude and to any special educational needs he may have".[89]

In *R* v. *East Sussex County Council ex parte T*[90] the applicant was mildly dyslexic and suffered from myalgic encephalomyelitis (ME) which meant that, from the age of seven, she had found it difficult or impossible to attend school. Accordingly, her LEA had provided home tuition for her under section 19 (then section 298 of EA 1993). But in September 1996, the LEA had sought to reduce the home tuition from five hours to three hours per week on the grounds that it had adopted a policy, in order to adapt to a shortage of resources, that three hours' tuition would be the norm. Lord Browne-Wilkinson, giving the leading speech in the House of Lords, found that the LEA was wrong to take the availability of resources into account. There was nothing in what is now section 19 to indicate that the concept of "suitable education" involved consideration of the implications for the LEA's resources. His Lordship also pointed out that the duty in what is now section 19(6) of EA 1996—then EA 1993, s. 298(7)—echoed a parent's duty to ensure that his child received suitable education, and this latter duty could not vary according to the parent's resources.[91] The only way in which the efficient use of resources could become a relevant factor was when there is more than one way of providing "suitable education", so that the LEA would be free to choose the option which involved less expenditure. After all, the LEA had the resources available to it to meet its statutory obligation and it could:

> "divert money from other educational, or other, applications which [were] merely discretionary . . . To permit a local authority to avoid performing a statutory duty on the grounds that it prefers to spend the money in other ways is to downgrade a statutory duty to a discretionary power."[92]

The LEA could therefore choose the most efficient manner in which to provide a suitable education, but could not choose to deny a suitable education on the grounds that it would be inefficient or too expensive to do so.

Lord Browne-Wilkinson also made the significant point that:

> "The majority view [in the Court of Appeal] was largely based on the premise that the duty . . . was owed by the LEA not to each child individually, but to a class of children,

[89] EA 1998, s. 19(6).
[90] [1998] ELR 251 (HL).
[91] [1998] ELR 251 at p. 256.
[92] [1998] ELR 251 at p. 259.

viz all children of school age in their area who, for statutory reasons, might not receive suitable education unless arrangements were made for them . . . On appeal to your Lordships' house, Mr Pleming QC, for the LEA, did not seek to maintain that view. He accepted, in my view correctly, that *the council owed an individual duty to each child in its area who answered the description in s 298(1) to provide an education which was suitable to that individual child*".[93] (My emphasis).

This meant that there was no distinction of substance between the statutory duty to "make arrangements for the provision of education" and the actual provision of that education, for the statutory duty "will not be fulfilled unless the arrangements do in fact provide suitable education for each child".[94] Thus the right to an education cannot be said to amount to no more than a right to a school place. On the contrary, it goes so far as to embrace the right to a "suitable" education. In similar fashion, the Court of Appeal held in *R* v. *Secretary of State for Education and Science ex parte E*[95] held that once an LEA has determined that a child has a special educational need, it must then both set out all such needs of the child and ensure that the special educational provision indicated in the child's statement satisfies all those needs.

EDUCATIONAL NEGLIGENCE

The fact that the right to education in English law is now clearly seen to include more positive rights to specific entitlements other than the right merely to attend school is a significant development not only from the point of view of pupils themselves, but also in terms of whether the right to education can be said to have been elevated to the status of property right. For once it is accepted that there is some substantive content in the right to education, it follows that the failure to deliver such content without good reason can amount to negligence, as Lord Browne-Wilkinson pointed out in *X* v. *Bedfordshire County Council*.[96]

Indeed, although the case itself concerned only an application to strike out a claim on the grounds of disclosing no known cause of action, his Lordship went on to explain just how such educational negligence might occur, especially in relation to the education of children with special educational needs. He said:

"Although . . . it is impossible to impose a common law duty of care which is inconsistent with, or fetters, a statutory duty, I can see no legal or common sense principle which requires one to deny a common law duty of care which would exist just because there is a statutory scheme which addresses the same problem. There is no inconsistency or incompatibility between the statutory scheme for children with special educational needs and any duty owed by headmasters and teaching advisers to give careful advice as to the educational needs of their pupils. If a child were being educated at a

[93] [1998] ELR 251 at p. 255.
[94] [1998] ELR 251 at pp. 256–257.
[95] [1992] 1 FLR 377 (HL).
[96] [1995] 2 AC 633 at p. 766: see footnote 86 above.

> private fee paying school or consulted a private teaching adviser, the existence of the statutory scheme . . . would be irrelevant. Why should it be relevant simply because the school and teaching advice is provided by a local education authority?"[97]

Moreover, it should be noted that any claim for educational negligence would not just be capable of being maintained against teachers and teaching advisers. LEAs should also be aware that they could be vicariously liable for any such breaches of the common law duty of care.[98]

The House of Lords did not consider in X v. *Bedfordshire County Council* the nature of any damage that the plaintiff may have suffered. It is nevertheless important to note that, under domestic English law, a claim for negligence can be sustained only if it can be shown both that the plaintiff has suffered an injury to a legally-protected interest and that such injury can be categorised as a form of personal injury, property damage, economic loss or psychiatric illness. Clearly, the fact that the tort of negligence has apparently been expanded to include educational negligence means that the right to education is a form of legally-protected interest. The question then arises of what form of damage educational negligence might inflict. It is surely clear that there will usually be no question of negligent educational provision causing psychiatric illness: the suffering of "distress" is also is not a type of injury recognised by the law of negligence.

Similarly, although compensation for any damage suffered is always to be measured in financial terms, the negligent provision of education cannot be thought to involve economic loss. It is true that economic loss was alleged by the plaintiff in *Phelps* v. *Hillingdon London Borough Council.*[99] But that was because of the way the case was pleaded. The plaintiff complained that an educational psychologist instructed by the LEA had failed to diagnose the plaintiff's dyslexia and claimed damages for the consequent failure to mitigate this congenital defect. But, as the Court of Appeal held, the failure to mitigate a congenital condition can hardly be said to amount to the causing of an injury: the defect existed as an accident of birth.[100] It was not alleged that the plaintiff's right to suitable education had been violated. Yet a breach of the right to education could not, it is submitted, be classified as causing economic loss. This would be so even though educational negligence might cause someone to be less employable and thus lose future income. For education is about far more than simply providing its recipients with a passage into a job. It is concerned with what Article 26(2) of the Universal Declaration of Human Rights, has called "the full development of the human personality". Any loss of future income would therefore be consequential upon a loss of education in much the same

[97] [1995] 2 AC 633 at p. 765. See now also the decision of the ECHR in *Osman* v. *United Kingdom* [1999] 1 FLR 193.

[98] [1995] 2 AC 633 at p. 771.

[99] [1999] 1 All ER 421 (CA).

[100] The Court of Appeal has since confirmed this view in *Jarvis* v. *Hampshire County Council* (1999) *The Times* 23rd November.

way that loss of future income is treated as consequential in any serious personal injury claim. This means that the damage inflicted by negligence must involve either some form of personal injury or a type of property damage.

But a breach of the right to education cannot be a cause of personal injury.[101] Section 34 of the Limitation Act 1980, for example, provides that:

> " 'Personal injuries' includes any disease and any impairment of a person's physical or mental condition, and 'injury' and cognate expressions shall be construed accordingly."

However, the negligent provision of education does not cause disease and will very rarely lead to the impairment of a person's physical or mental condition. The point about educational negligence is that, rather than causing the plaintiff to be worse off than he was before, it means that he will not have been given the opportunity to make the progress that he should have. His (or her) education has been damaged. He has suffered the loss of something to which he was legally entitled. It is thus submitted that this implies both that education is a form of property and that the right to education is a property right.

Moreover, the apparent availability in future of damages for breach of the right to education also demonstrates the necessary (albeit insufficient) requirement for a property right, namely that it can be valued in monetary terms. Indeed, this new right may be said to be somewhat analogous in form to that of a claim against a company director for misfeasance, which English law has held to be a chose in action and therefore a type of property right for over a hundred years.[102]

Of course, X v. *Bedfordshire County Council* was a case concerned only with a striking-out application. It may thus be thought somewhat premature to argue that English law has elevated the right to education to the status of property right. There is clearly some force in this objection, but probably not as much as might at first appear to be the case. First, the detail of Lord Browne-Wilkinson's judgment in X v. *Bedfordshire County Council*, although strictly *obiter*, is so marked that it is difficult to see how it can be ignored in subsequent cases, especially since the other Law Lords expressed their agreement with it (although it may be difficult to prove on the facts of any given case that a breach of this right has actually occurred). Even if it might be said that English law does not yet recognise the right to education as a property right, it seems clear that it is on the verge of doing so. Secondly, it should be noted that the European Court of Human Rights has already expressly held in *Pressos Compana Naviera SA* v. *Belgium* that a claim for compensation in tort amounts to a type of property right for the purposes of the European Convention.[103] As has already been noted, section 2(1)(a) of the Human Rights Act 1998 will, when it comes into force, require that a domestic court take into account any "judgment, declaration or advisory

[101] See now *Anderton* v. *Clwyd CC* [1999] ELR 1.
[102] *Re Park Gate Waggon Works Co* (1881) 17 Ch D 234 (CA).
[103] (1995) 21 EHRR 301.

opinion of the European Court of Human Rights" when "determining a question which has arisen in connection with a Convention right". Although section 2 will not make *Pressos Compana Naviera SA* v. *Belgium* binding on domestic English courts, it is submitted that they will be slow to depart from it since it seems entirely in line with, for example, the long-standing case of *Re Park Gate Waggon Works Co.*[104]

Thirdly, it will be recalled that it was argued earlier in this essay that the courts have adopted a flexible approach to the classification of property rights whereby what is property is determined by "its function as a means in the satisfaction of the reason for action".[105] The origin of a putative right is apparently unimportant: its status can be settled only after consideration of the purpose to be served by classifying such a right in a particular manner. If there are significant benefits to be gained by classifying the right to education as a property right, then it is submitted that the courts should be prepared to take this option. It is therefore important to consider what purpose would be achieved by admitting the right to education into one of the two possible categories of intangible property right.

THE RIGHTS OF THE CHILD

It will be recalled that, once a domestic legal system recognises a property right, then that right will qualify as a "civil right" for the purposes of Article 6(1) of the European Convention on Human Rights.[106] As a result, and because the Human Rights Act 1998 will soon incorporate the Convention into English law, the holder of a proprietary right to education will become entitled, whenever there is a dispute concerning that right, to "a fair and public hearing within a reasonable time by an independent and impartial tribunal established by law". This could have a potentially significant impact on three particular areas of education law, namely admissions, exclusions and special educational needs (SENs).

This is because education law has—at least until the recent case law outlined above—not been noted for granting rights to those pupils and students actually being educated. Instead, it has focused on promoting the rights of their parents. As Bainham complained a few years ago:

> "We have, for example, the *parent's* charter . . . *parental* choice of school . . . *parent* governors . . . the *parental* right of withdrawal from religious education and collective worship . . . the *parent's* . . . right to withdraw his or her child from sex education . . . [T]he effect of domestic educational policy of recent years has been to eclipse children's rights".[107]

[104] (1881) 17 Ch D 234 (CA).

[105] S. Coval *et al.*, "The Foundations of Property and Property Law" (1986) 45 *Camb LJ* 457 at p. 460.

[106] *Sporrong and Lönnroth* v. *Sweden* (1982) 5 EHRR 35, at para. 79.

[107] A. Bainham, "Sex Education: A Family Lawyer's Perspective" in N. Harris (ed.), *Children, Sex Education and the Law* (London: National Children's Bureau, 1996) at p. 30.

This is in stark contrast to the promotion of children's rights at the expense of their parent's former rights in other areas of law through, for example, the Children Act 1989. The law on school admissions thus provides, for example, that if a pupil is not allocated to the school indicated as preferred by his or her parents, it is only those parents who have a right to appeal to an independent appeal panel.[108] The child is given no right to appeal, or even to be present at such an appeal hearing. This may be acceptable in practice in the vast majority of cases, especially where primary school places are concerned. However, the exclusion of pupils from participation in the appeals process in relation to secondary school places may well be detrimental to a significant minority of disappointed pupils who may have good grounds for appeal but whose parents are unwilling to get involved. Alternatively, the parents may indeed appeal, but fail to present the case as well as a well-motivated pupil might have done. A similar story can at present be told in relation to those pupils having SENs,[109] which affect roughly one in five school children, although there is at least a possibility here that the views of the child may be taken into account as recommended by the relevant Code of Practice.[110] Yet it is still only parents who, when dissatisfied with an LEA's decision either not to make a statutory statement of SENs or with the contents of such a statement, can appeal to the Special Educational Needs Tribunal (SENT).[111]

If, however, pupils are found to possess a proprietary right to education, then it is indisputable that they too will have the right both to appeal, and to be heard at such an appeal hearing, in both admissions and SENs cases. Failure to permit such pupil participation (which may, of course, require the assistance of such bodies as the Children's Legal Centre) would be a clear breach of Article 6(1) of the European Convention and thus a breach of section 6(1) of the Human Rights Act 1998 which, when brought into force, will make it "unlawful for a public authority to act in a way which is incompatible with a Convention right". Perhaps of even more importance is that recognition that a child's proprietary right to education would overcome the problems at present experienced by children in local authority care who, as Harris has pointed out, "have no parents to act as advocates".[112]

It would, moreover, mean that the appeals panels which currently deal with admissions appeals would have to receive much better training and adopt much clearer rules of procedure—in the way that the SENT has done—in order to ensure that the hearing was both truly fair and impartial.[113] The procedure for

108 SSFA 1998, s. 94.

109 A fuller account of the law relating to special educational needs appeals can be found in N. Harris, *Special Educational Needs and Access to Justice* (Bristol: Jordans, 1997).

110 DFE, *Code of Practice on the Identification and Assessment of Special Educational Needs* (London, DFE, 1994) at para. 1.120.

111 EA 1996, ss. 325, 326; *S* v. *Special Educational Needs Tribunal and the City of Westminster* [1996] ELR 228 (CA).

112 N. Harris, *Special Educational Needs and Access to Justice* (Bristol: Jordans, 1997) at p. 5.

113 The reports of the Local Government Ombudsmen abound with investigations into significantly flawed admissions appeals hearings. See further the Annual Reports of the Commission for Local Administration in England.

the hearing of appeals against exclusions from schools by panels constituted in similar fashion to admissions appeals panels[114] would also have to be significantly tightened up. In this way, the granting of proprietary status to the right to education would achieve the significant policy objective of having children's rights to a suitable education put on a footing equivalent to other rights which they are now supposed to enjoy under the Children Act 1989. We would thus be one step closer to realising Article 26 of the 1948 Universal Declaration of Human Rights, in that this modification to the law would be directed, as paragraph (2) of Article 26 requires, "to the full development of the human personality and to the strengthening of respect for human rights".

[114] See SSFA 1998, sch. 18.

4

Compensation, Restitution and Human Rights in Post-Communist Europe

JEREMY McBRIDE

INTRODUCTION

THE ADVENT OF communist rule in Central and Eastern Europe was accompanied by widespread taking of private property into public ownership or control[1]. Following the collapse or political rebirth of the regimes concerned[2], expectations rose for this property to be returned, either to those who had been dispossessed or to their descendants. The strength of feeling on this matter was hardly surprising given that the taking had often been part and parcel of the political persecution of those affected, in many instances leading to the death or exile of the latter. Even without the sense of injustice which this established, such taking did not always have a legal basis and certainly did not involve the payment of compensation. Furthermore a wish for restitution, or at least proper compensation, was an inevitable concomitant of the strong attraction which human rights values held for many of those opposed to communism; concern for the protection of property interests had, after all, been a key feature in the elaboration of such values from the very outset[3]. However, although restitution measures have been adopted in many countries in Central and Eastern Europe, they have not met with universal acclaim. Challenges to them have been mounted in both national and international fora but these have only had limited success.

Concern for restitution in the region has not, however, been restricted to undoing "wrongs" committed several decades beforehand. It has also arisen as a consequence of the more recent dispossession that has been occurring in the

[1] In some countries this had also occurred in the period immediately preceding this development. As to the failure to address this in restitution measures, see I. Pogany, *Righting wrongs in Eastern Europe* (Manchester, Manchester University Press, 1998). See also D. B. Southern, "Restitution or Compensation: The Land Question in East Germany", (1993) 42 *ICLQ* 690 and n 72.

[2] In some countries political leadership continued to lie with high-ranking members of the Communist party, even though they had ceased to operate under that identity.

[3] See M. Cranston, *What are Human Rights?* (London, The Bodley Head, 1973), ch.6.

course of the various conflicts within and between the different republics that once constituted Yugoslavia. Such dispossession, whether as part of a deliberate policy of "ethnic cleansing" or the inevitable by-product of an ever-changing front line and an immediate need to house the homeless, has not only generated much human suffering but also understandable demands for the property concerned to be restored as part of the peace settlements. Although the latter was acceded to in principle, its realisation in practice has not always been achieved and dispossession has indeed continued to take place after such settlements[4]. International human rights norms have thus been invoked as a possible source of help.

This essay looks at the contribution which international standards are able to make to the resolution of these property disputes. It first considers the actual applicability of a guarantee of property rights to these disputes and the extent to which this might give rise to an obligation of restitution[5] or compensation. Secondly it examines the human rights constraints on effecting any restitution where there is no obligation for this to be done but a political choice requiring it has been made. These include the need to respect the interests of persons currently in possession of the property subject to a restitution claim, as well as the requirements of the right to a fair hearing and the prohibition on discrimination. All of these can have a potentially significant impact on both the content of restitution measures and the procedure for their implementation. Overall international human rights norms have so far only required limited changes in the approach adopted towards restitution. Nevertheless the elaboration of their requirements has led to a somewhat clearer framework for handling these matters in the future.

THE EXTENT OF THE PROTECTION FOR PROPERTY INTERESTS

Although some guarantees established under international law directly seek to protect interests in property (and others may do so indirectly), these do not necessarily entail a specific obligation to make restitution where there is a taking in breach of their requirements. In many instances the payment of compensation is all that will be required but this can be substantial. However, before addressing the issue of which remedy might be required with respect to the particular property in dispute, a prior issue has to be resolved. This is the fundamental question of the extent to which these international guarantees are even applicable to the property affected by events in Central and Eastern Europe. In part this is simply a matter of examining the various interferences with property interests in the light of the various guarantees and the case law in which they have been applied.

[4] Ethnic hostility remains a major obstacle to the implementation of commitments.

[5] This term is used in a broad sense and here covers both restoration of possession and ownership, not least because loss of the former in this region often effectively amounts to loss of the latter.

In many instances the position is fairly straightforward, if not entirely helpful. However, it is less certain in relation to some aspects of the dispossession that has occurred during, and after, the conflicts in various parts of former Yugoslavia. Furthermore there is an additional problem of timing which is of considerable significance; did the events occur before the guarantees became legally binding and thus could be invoked?

Applicable guarantees

There has been some reluctance on the part of States to agree to provide explicit protection for property interests in human rights treaties despite their apparent willingness to recognise property as a right in the Universal Declaration of Human Rights[6], the instrument from which those treaties have all been derived. Thus it was not initially included in the catalogue of rights and freedoms found in the European Convention on Human Rights and was only added to this through its First Protocol. Moreover neither of the two instruments which sought to fulfil the Universal Declaration by turning the human rights which it proclaimed into legally binding commitments—the International Covenants on Civil and Political and Economic, Social and Cultural Rights—make any reference to protecting property[7]. The original omission from the European instrument reflected an anxiety—later proved to be unwarranted—that the protection of property interests would obstruct economic and social programmes whereas the character of the philosophical divide between East and West in the era of the Cold War meant that there could never be agreement on having such a guarantee when the global instruments were being adopted and the inclusion of one has not yet become a priority for amending protocols. The property guarantee in Article 1 of Protocol 1 to the European Convention[8] is far from absolute, permitting expropriation or other deprivation of property, as well as various controls over its use, where this is shown to be in the public interest and the law authorising it is accessible, precise and without scope for arbitrariness in the manner of its application[9]. In case of deprivation of property there is generally also an obligation to pay appropriate compensation. "Deprivation" would cover any formal transfer of assets such as the nationalisation of a business

[6] Article 17.

[7] There are, however, property guarantees in the two other existing regional guarantees of human rights, the African Charter on Human and Peoples' Rights and the American Convention on Human Rights.

[8] Hereafter "Protocol 1". On this generally, see D. J. Harris, M. O'Boyle and C. Warbrick, *Law of the European Convention on Human Rights* (London, Butterworths, 1995), ch.18.

[9] Article 1 provides: "Every natural or legal person is entitled to the peaceful enjoyment of his possessions. No one shall be deprived of his possessions except in the public interest and subject to the conditions provided for by law and by the general principles of international law. The preceding provisions shall not, however, in any way impair the right of a State to enforce such laws as it deems necessary to control the use of property in accordance with the general interest or to secure the payment of taxes or other contributions or penalties".

enterprise and the compulsory purchase of property but also anything achieving the same effect, whether done lawfully[10] or without any legal basis at all[11]. The need for a public interest is likely to be something that can be relatively easily established and a State is unlikely to have to demonstrate more than potential for this purpose; the fact that other States choose other means will not be fatal. Moreover ideas about the public interest change; nationalisation of industry was once seen as highly desirable whereas privatisation is now more fashionable so that much of the property deprivation in Central and Eastern Europe might not, if amenable to scrutiny, be regarded as inherently objectionable[12]. A similarly sympathetic view might also be taken of the extensive taking of residential premises and their division into smaller units to meet housing needs[13]. However, such measures might have more difficulty satisfying the requirement elaborated in the Strasbourg case law that a taking should not be arbitrary[14] and that compensation should generally be paid.

The imposition of controls on the use of property and the rather less specific interference with the peaceful enjoyment of possessions[15]—the two other matters which Protocol 1 seeks to regulate—tend to be even more readily accepted. Certainly the disruption caused during, as well as in the aftermath of, conflicts such as in former Yugoslavia has the potential to justify interferences as being in the general interest. This is particularly likely to be so where the situation has

[10] As in *The Holy Monasteries* v. *Greece* (1995) 20 EHRR 1 where a law was adopted which created a presumption that certain land was owned by the State; although purporting to be merely a procedural device, it effectively prevented the monasteries from establishing their title since they could no longer rely on their longstanding adverse possession.

[11] Thus a violation of Protocol 1 was found in *Papamichalopoulos* v. *Greece* (1993) 16 EHRR 440 after the military, during a period of dictatorship, simply occupied the applicants' land, supposedly as a military base but in reality as a resort for officers, and continually frustrated all efforts to recover it through legal proceedings in the national courts. In practice ownership rights could not be exercised and this de facto deprivation was sufficient to found a complaint.

[12] See *Lithgow* v. *United Kingdom* (1986) 8 EHRR 329 which concerned the nationalisation of the aircraft and shipbuilding industries. A good instance of the wide discretion allowed to States can be seen in *Pressos Compania Naviera S A* v. *Belgium* (1996) 21 EHRR 301 where it was not questioned that it was in the public interest to seek to protect the public purse by retrospectively abolishing the State's civil liability for the carelessness of its pilots.

[13] See the acceptance that the social reform involved in requiring a landowner to sell his or her property to the tenants would not entail the latter having to pay its full market value; *James* v. *United Kingdom* (1986) 8 EHRR 123.

[14] A classic instance of this can be found in the *Hentrich* v. *France* (1994) 18 EHRR 440 where the authorities, in an understandable effort to tackle non-payment of tax on land sales, adopted a power permitting the compulsory purchase of land which had recently been transferred. The concern was that vendors and purchasers of land were agreeing a public price below the market value and then sharing the consequential saving on the tax that should have been paid if the transaction had been recorded as showing its true worth. However, the power could be exercised regardless of whether the purchaser whose land was compulsorily bought had engaged in such a fraud but simply to deter others and in the circumstances had to be condemned as arbitrary in character. A similar view would undoubtedly be taken of deprivation of property that was primarily motivated by the owner's supposed political beliefs and was on top of any penalty imposed by the criminal courts.

[15] It can cover the effect of planning blight (*Sporrong and Lönnroth* v. *Sweden* (1983) 5 EHRR 35) as much as difficulties in actually gaining access to the property (*Loizidou* v. *Turkey* (1995) 20 EHRR 99).

led to major difficulties in housing the population, as well as to problems in finding offices for public services. As in the case of the deprivation of property, the principal concern must be to ensure that there is a fair balance between the collective and individual interest, although this does not always require the payment of compensation. However, there will undoubtedly be concern about supposedly temporary measures continuing once it is patently obvious that the circumstances giving rise to them no longer exist or where an entirely different use is being made of the property from that for which it was made subject to controls or occupied without amounting to effective expropriation.

In addition to this specific property guarantee, related interests can also be protected through provisions in both the European Convention and the International Covenant on Civil and Political Rights concerning the right to a fair hearing[16] and against interference with one's home[17]. Also relevant will be the protection provided in these instruments against discrimination; in the case of the International Covenant this is a general guarantee[18] but that provided under the European Convention is dependent upon some other substantive right protected by it being involved[19].

As well as these relatively recent treaty commitments, there is also a much more long-standing obligation to respect property rights under customary law[20]. However, while this only extends to foreign-owned property, the treaty provisions are in principle applicable to citizens and aliens. They are, therefore, potentially of much greater significance to the events under consideration as most of the claims for restitution are by citizens of the States in which the deprivation of property occurred.

Binding effect of the guarantees

Although these various guarantees can justly be regarded as affording, at least in principle, a fairly comprehensive level of protection for property interests, this is not matched by the extent of their applicability to the events under review. The latter commenced in 1918 as regards Belarus, Russia and Ukraine and soon after the end of the Second World War for most other Central and East European States, with those in former Yugoslavia occurring throughout much of the 1990s. Only the requirements of customary international law regarding foreign-owned property were unquestionably in force at all times. However, the

[16] In Articles 6 and 14 respectively.

[17] In Articles 8 and 17 respectively.

[18] Article 26

[19] Article 14. See further D. J. Harris *et al* (n 8), at pp 464–69.

[20] See R. Jennings and A. Watts (eds), *Oppenheim's International Law*, (9th ed) (London, Longman, 1992), pp.911–27. The requirements of customary law, are incorporated into Protocol 1 by its reference to "the general principles of international law", thus reaffirming the special protection for foreign-owned property. Customary international law also permits the requisitioning of foreign-owned property in time of emergency but requires the payment of compensation.

relevance of this body of law at the present time is likely to be very limited. Certainly, insofar as claims were raised following the confiscation of property by communist States, these have generally been settled with the payment of compensation[21]. In the case of former Yugoslavia, the interference with property interests would not have the necessary international dimension since much of the taking was committed or condoned by the States of which the persons affected were citizens. The protection provided is exclusively for foreign-owned property. This would, however, still have some relevance where ownership of this character is established; this might be the case both where the persons involved were not at any of the material time citizens of former Yugoslavia and where those who were such citizens did not acquire the citizenship of the State born out of it and in which their property is located. Nevertheless most persons affected are citizens of the particular State in which their loss has been suffered.

The treaty obligations are not limited to foreign nationals but their applicability is significantly constrained by the fact that they were undertaken, if at all, after most of the events in issue had occurred. Thus the International Covenant only came into force for most of the States concerned in 1976 and those that have ratified the European Convention only began to do so after 1992[22]. The taking of property under communist regimes had generally been completed by the first of these dates and certainly had long ceased by the second. This is of most significance for the ability to invoke the property guarantee in Protocol 1 with respect to any property that has been taken. Any such action which was lawful in the particular State at the time concerned will be regarded as a completed act occurring prior to the acceptance of the obligation in the Protocol, notwithstanding that the loss of property is an enduring one and may be felt as keenly today as at the time of deprivation. As the commitment being made is only prospective in effect, it cannot thus be invoked even if it could be demonstrated that the requirements for finding a violation are otherwise satisfied[23]. This approach has already led to a number of applications under the European Convention being dismissed as inadmissible *ratione temporis*[24]. On the other

[21] A claim can only be made by the State of which the property-owner is a national and such a State may not always have an interest in making one. See the settlement concluded between Albania and the United States; 34 *ILM* 595 (1995).

[22] Armenia, Azerbaijan, Belarus, Bosnia-Herzegovina and the Federal Republic of Yugoslavia (Serbia and Montenegro) are the only former communist States in Europe yet to ratify the European Convention. All of them are parties to the International Covenant. International human rights standards (including the European Convention) have been made applicable to Bosnia-Herzegovina through the Dayton Peace Agreement; Annex 6 to the *General Framework Agreement for Peace in Bosnia-Herzegovina*, 35 *ILM* 75 (1996). On the process dealing with property issues in Bosnia-Herzegovina, see M. Cox, "The Right to Return Home: International Intervention and Ethnic Cleansing in Bosnia and Herzegovina", (1998) 47 *ICLQ* 599 and H. van Houte, "Mass Property Claim Resolution in a Post-war Society—The Commission for Real Property Claims in Bosnia and Herzegovina", (1999) 48 *ICLQ* 625.

[23] The absence of compensation would be a fatal defect, even if a generous view is likely to be taken of the public purpose being served.

[24] See *Brezny* v. *Slovak Republic*, 85 DR 65 (1996), *Geidel* v. *Germany*, 88 DR 12 (1997), *Lupulet* v. *Romania*, 85 DR 126 (1996) and *Mayer et al* v. *Germany*, 85 DR 5 (1996).

hand any taking which was illegal at its inception and never had this defect cured prior to the entry into force of the Convention will be seen as a continuing violation of its requirements. It could thus be the object of a successful application to Strasbourg. The only instance so far of this being established was in *Vasilescu* v. *Romania*[25] where jewellery had been illegally seized by the police and all efforts to bring proceedings to secure its recovery had been frustrated. The European Court of Human Rights considered that the applicant's complete loss of any ability to dispose of her property was, when taken with the failure of all attempts to remedy this situation, enough to amount to a *de facto* confiscation incompatible with the right to peaceful enjoyment of possessions assured by Protocol 1. Such a ruling would be equally applicable to land or premises being occupied by State authorities without any legal basis[26].

The ability to invoke other rights in aid of property interests is less likely to be frustrated by the timing of the ratification. This is not because the bar on the treaties having retrospective effect can somehow be circumvented but because the material events will generally have taken place after their provisions were accepted. This is especially true in the case of the restitution measures since these were adopted after the International Covenant and, in some instances, the European Convention were ratified[27]. However, it would also be so in the case of proceedings to recover property which had been taken without any legal basis. Thus in the *Vasilescu* case there was also a violation of Article 6 because there was no tribunal satisfying that provision's requirements regarding independence before which the applicant could bring her claim to have the jewellery restored to her[28].

The provisions of the International Covenant have been applicable throughout the events occurring in former Yugoslavia but, as has been seen, these do not include any specific protection for property. However, the European Convention has been accepted by all the States born out of Yugoslavia except the Federal Republic of Yugoslavia (Serbia and Montenegro)[29], and the

[25] 22 May 1998.

[26] As occurred in *Papamichalopoulos* v. *Greece*; n 11. This was also effectively the basis of the decision in *Brumarescu* v. *Romania*, 28 October 1999 where title to an estate had been re-established following its nationalisation after a court had ruled that the relevant measure was null and void but a subsequent quashing of that court's final judgment had then made it impossible for the applicant to assert his property right. A similar case pending before the European Court is *Curutiu* v. *Romania*, 29769/99.

[27] A further time constraint exists in respect of the European Convention; applications must be lodged within six months of the final decision on the matter giving rise to the alleged violation. There is no such time limit for the comparable applications by individuals under the International Covenant's First Optional Protocol.

[28] Interference with a property-owner's ability to bring proceedings would also give rise to a successful claim under Article 6; see *The Holy Monasteries* v. *Greece* (n 10, control over proceedings vested in a State body) and *Canea Catholic Church* v. *Greece* (1999) 27 EHRR 521 (legal personality extinguished).

[29] In the case of Bosnia-Herzegovina pursuant to the *General Framework Agreement*; n 22. The European Convention is, however, part of the international human rights standards applicable during the interim administration established in Kosovo under Security Council Resolution 1244 of 10 June 1999.

property guarantee is applicable to all the takings, controls and interferences occurring in them, whether or not they have a legal basis. This is because those which do not have such a basis would satisfy the requirement that the violation had continued after ratification and those which are lawful are not intended to be permanent so that the continued justification for the interference can be subjected to scrutiny.

The nature of the property interest

The conception of property falling within the protection of Protocol 1 is quite wide but is unlikely to extend to all interests affected by the dispossession that has occurred, at least as far as concerns former Yugoslavia. There is certainly no doubt that the land, premises and goods which were taken during the communist era all fall within the understanding given to possessions in Protocol 1 by the European Court of Human Rights. Indeed, apart from also treating it as applying to intangible property interests such as judgment debts, patents and shares, there has even been a willingness by the Court to accept it as extending to some claims over goods that do not amount to ownership[30] and civil claims which have not been determined[31]. However, the important element in all cases has been the legal entitlement to something specific rather than its characterisation by domestic property law. It is this which might be regarded as lacking in many instances in former Yugoslavia where the "property" affected was often a publicly-owned apartment building and the person dispossessed had some kind of interest in it which could not be sold and had no specific rights in these particular apartment which he or she occupied[32]. Although interests such as this can still be sufficient to attract the protection of the right to respect for one's home, there was a reluctance by the European Commission of Human Rights to treat them as amounting to property[33]. However, some qualification on even

30 See *Gasus Dosier- und Fördertechnik GmbH* v. *The Netherlands* (1995) 20 EHRR 403.

31 See *Pressos Compania Naviera* (n 12) which concerned claims against pilots responsible for collision between vessels in a harbour where the State was the organiser of the pilot service and it had sought to evade its potential liability by retrospectively abolishing it through a legislative measure. It may be significant that in this case the factual basis for liability was not in dispute and the collisions could, therefore, be regarded as having given rise to an immediate and incontrovertible right to compensation, a property interest deserving of protection. *Cf* the reluctance of the Court in *National & Provincial Building Society* v. *United Kingdom* (1998) 25 EHRR 127 to reach any firm conclusion as to whether a claim where the law was in dispute amounted to a possession

32 Ownership in the classic sense could still exist in respect of some property; see *Bejdic* v. *Republika Srpska* (1999) 6 IHRR 834 and *Blentic* v. *Republika Srpska* (1999) 6 IHRR 583.

33 See *S* v. *United Kingdom*, 47 DR 274 (1986) where a lesbian was not able to succeed to her lover's tenancy and *Durini* v. *Italy*, 76 DR 76 (1994) where, in accordance with a settlement made by a testator, property passed automatically on death from one male descendant to another, leaving the first male's family without a home. However, in *M J* v. *Republika Srpska* (1999) 6 IHRR 590 the Bosnia Human Rights Chamber was prepared to regard an occupancy right as a possession for the purpose of Protocol 1. This case concerned the failure to enforce a court order for possession after M J had been illegally evicted by an armed group. In reaching its conclusion that there was a violation of Protocol 1, the Chamber laid emphasis on the ability of the holder of this occupancy right to

this requirement can perhaps be seen in *Gaygusuz* v. *Austria*[34] where the European Court was prepared to regard the right to emergency assistance—normally only available where a person has made appropriate contributions to the unemployment insurance fund—as a pecuniary right without there being a need to rely solely on the link between an entitlement and the obligation to pay contributions. There was, therefore, a violation of Article 1 of the Protocol, taken with Article 14 of the Convention, when it was refused to the applicant because the scheme did not apply to non-nationals and there was considered to be no rational and objective justification for this; in this instance it was significant that the non-citizen was paying the same as citizens but still being treated differently. This might be seen as an example of the potential for the prohibition on discrimination to expand the scope of a right where differential treatment in its general area is not justifiable[35]. Where a prohibited ground of discrimination, such as ethnic origin or religion, is the basis on which recovery of a publicly-owned apartment is being denied, this could thus prove to be a sufficient additional dimension to support a claim under Protocol 1. In the absence of such evidence, it is much less likely that claims to be allowed to return to one's former apartment involve a property right[36]. Furthermore, the importance attached to having an entitlement means that the making of a political commitment to restitution

occupy the property concerned indefinitely and, in certain circumstances, to transfer it. It is perhaps significant that the finding arose out of the failure to protect M J's right vis-à-vis another private individual rather than the State but the apparent assignability of the particular occupancy right clearly reinforced its character as a property interest. In any event the position might be seen differently by the European Court—at least for the purpose of a compensation claim—if the interest concerned was used in privatisation programmes as the basis for allowing an occupant preference in purchasing the apartment concerned; see the text at n.71. Furthermore there would be no question about a possession being in existence once an actual contract for purchase had been concluded even though the occupant had not yet become the actual owner; see the finding by the Bosnian Human Rights Chamber of violations of Protocol 1 where such contracts were retrospectively annulled without compensation in *Bulatovic* v. *Bosnia and Herzegovina* (1999) 6 IHRR 573, *Kalincevic* v. *Bosnia and Herzegovina* (1999) 6 IHRR 868 and *Medan, Bastjanovic and Markovic* v. *Bosnia and Herzegovina* (1999) 6 IHRR 562. In *Bulatovic* and *Kalincevic* there were further violations of Protocol 1 arising out of threats to evict the occupants as the application to them of powers relating to "abandoned property" had failed to recognise their property interests. See also the view of the Court in its admissibility decision in *J L S* v. *Spain* (No. 41917/98, 27 April 1999) that a right to live in a given property without being the owner did not constitute "property" within the meaning of Article 1. The case concerned an attempt by a soldier to stay on in accommodation of which he had been given the use because of difficulties in finding accommodation given frequent transfers in postings.

[34] (1997) 23 EHRR 365.

[35] See also *Inze* v. *Austria* (1988) 10 EHRR 394 where the European Court found unacceptable a rule which gave precedence to legitimate children over illegitimate children in the succession to farms where the owner died without having made a will.

[36] The position might be seen differently where the interest concerned is used in a privatisation programme as the basis for allowing an occupant preference in "purchasing" the apartment concerned; see the text at n 71. The issue of being able to occupy a particular apartment should, however, be distinguished from claims that may be made in respect of possessions in them. Generally persons subject to ethnic cleansing had to leave these behind and obstruction in recovering them could sustain a claim under Protocol 1.

subjected to expropriation will be seen as insufficient to establish a possession for the purposes of Protocol 1[37].

Violations and remedies

The fact that international standards are not applicable to many instances of a deprivation of property necessarily precludes a finding of a violation, let alone any requirement that this be remedied by restitution or a particular amount of compensation. However, where the standards can be applied because of the timing of the measure or the continuing effect produced by its unlawful character, the European Court will be able to find a violation of Protocol I. In such cases restitution will undoubtedly be the preferred solution but the Court has no specific authority to order this[38] and it appears not to be inherent in the obligation to comply with its judgment[39]. This is evident from both the *Papamichalopoulos* and *Vasilescu* cases. In the former the Court indicated that the return of the land would be the most effective remedy[40] but made an award of damages to be paid if restitution did not occur within six months. It was the latter part of the ruling that was implemented as Greece maintained that restitution was impossible because of the integration of the property into the country's wartime military structure. In the *Vasilescu* case Romania claimed that it was unable to return the jewellery because it had not been found in the custody of any authority. Thus, although restitution will be the preferred solution where a taking has no legal basis, a State is allowed to provide compensation as an alternative remedy[41]. Where the taking is lawful but does not satisfy international standards in some other respect, compensation can also be awarded and it is unlikely that restitution would even be suggested[42]. Generally the amount of compensation awarded for deprivation of property should reflect the fact that some economic or social objective is involved and less than the full market value may be required[43]. However, in many instances, notably where one individual has had to make a sacrifice for more general economic development, payment of the full

[37] *Brezny* v. *Slovak Republic*, *Lupulet* v. *Romania* and *Mayer et al* v. *Germany*; n 24.

[38] Under Article 41 (formerly 50) of the Convention (as revised by Protocol 11), the Court can only award "just satisfaction", i.e., damages.

[39] Article 46.

[40] *Papamichalopoulos* v. *Greece (Article 50)* (1996) 21 EHRR 439.

[41] The European Court has also recognised the legitimacy of a State choosing to provide compensation instead of restitution for an illegal expropriation when determining the adequacy of the amount paid in *Zubani* v. *Italy*, 7 August 1996.

[42] This might not be so where the public interest supposedly being served was clearly fraudulent; this might be seen as akin to an illegal taking.

[43] For example, the social reform involved in requiring a landowner to sell his or her property to the tenants (*James* v. *United Kingdom*, n 13) or in bringing an industry into public control (*Lithgow* v. *United Kingdom*, n 12). This does not mean that a derisory amount will be acceptable; the monks in the *Holy Monasteries* case (n 10) only had access to a discretionary fund for their future support and that was evidently arbitrary.

market value has been expected[44]. This has also been the basis of assessment where there was no legal basis for the taking, even if it might have served a public purpose, as in the *Papamichalopoulos* and *Vasilescu* cases[45], and will be applicable to any such expropriation in Central and Eastern Europe during or after the Communist era.

Controls over use and interference with peaceful enjoyment of possessions do not generally entail the payment of compensation but, in particular cases, this could be an important factor in concluding that a fair balance had been achieved between the general and the individual interest. Compensation might thus not be required where, to meet the sort of immediate need that arises in a conflict or disaster, persons are temporarily housed in someone else's property, particularly if this is vacant and the owner is not personally dispossessed. Even a requirement to share accommodation in such a situation would probably not be regarded as necessitating compensation. In both situations the inconvenience to the property-owner is unlikely to be seen as particularly great given the general difficulties being experienced. However, the situation is likely to change where this becomes a somewhat more long term measure and the owner is thus prevented from realising the value of the property in question, such as by letting it at a market rent. This would seem to be the implication of the emphasis placed on rent still being paid when the European Court did not object to a bar on landlords being able to recover possession of properties as part of a strategy to meet a housing need[46]. It may be that, given the wider social context, the compensation would not have to correspond to the full market rental value but a failure to make a reasonable contribution to the property-owner's loss would probably be seen as placing an excessive burden on him or her, at least if it is clear that such use would have been made of the property but for its occupation. However, there can be no doubt that compensation would have to be based on the full market rental once the occupation or interference ceased to be justified but was being continued. A similar approach would be appropriate if the genuineness of the measure leading to dispossession was disproved; for example, where the objective was ethnic cleansing. Furthermore, in all cases it might be expected that the State should ensure that any damage sustained during the occupation is made good (whether out of its funds or otherwise). It should also not be overlooked that general international law actually requires compensation to be paid for the loss of the use of, and damage to, foreign-owned property which is requisitioned in an emergency and awards would not necessarily be

[44] See *Howard* v. *United Kingdom* 52 DR 215 (1987), *Schlumpf* v. *France*, 53 DR 76 (1987) and *Thor* v. *Iceland*, 84 DR 89 (1996). Compensation for the loss during the period of deprivation up to judgment will also be expected; see *Guillemin* v. *France*, (1998) 25 EHRR 435.

[45] Full market value is also required under customary international law where a taking has no legal basis; for a review of compensation for expropriation generally, see C F Amerasinghe, "Issues of Compensation for the Taking of Alien Property in the Light of Recent Cases and Practice", (1992) 41 *ICLQ* 22. Restitution may be sought but is rarely the basis on which disputes are settled; see I. Brownlie, *State Responsibility (Part 1)* (Oxford, Clarendon Press, 1983), p.211.

[46] See the cases discussed under "Competing collective and other individual interests", below.

subject to the same balancing considerations. The assumption underlying any temporary dispossession is, of course, that there will ultimately be restitution. Where this is unduly prolonged, the situation will eventually become one in which there has been an effective expropriation and the principles previously considered will become applicable.

Insofar as the right to occupy public housing is not seen as a possession for the purpose of Protocol 1, the dispossessed occupant could still invoke the right to respect for one's home under both the European Convention and the International Covenant. A violation of this right would certainly require compensation for the pecuniary and non-pecuniary losses ensuing[47] but, although the most effective remedy would be the recovery of possession, the provision of comparable alternative accommodation would undoubtedly be seen as acceptable. Violation of the right to a fair hearing and of the prohibition on discrimination in the course of taking property, whether on a permanent or temporary basis, would be factors vitiating the measure concerned from the perspective of international standards and thus be remedied in the manner already discussed. However, these violations might in themselves be seen as meriting a compensatory award[48].

CONSTRAINTS ON RESTITUTION

Although there may be no obligation to afford restitution, there will be considerations which may both encourage and discourage a State to adopt such a measure. Some of these may be a matter of simply weighing different policy options. However, undoing wrongs also has the potential of interfering with other rights, whether ones accrued by virtue of the act of dispossession or ones which human rights standards independently guarantee. These are unlikely to be an absolute barrier to restitution in most cases but they will certainly circumscribe the manner in which it is carried out.

Competing collective and other individual interests

There are undoubtedly important individual, as well as collective interests, in full restitution being made after expropriation[49] or temporary interferences and

[47] See *López Ostra* v. *Spain* (1995) 20 EHRR 277.

[48] However, the finding of a violation is often considered sufficient satisfaction for the non-pecuniary loss involved.

[49] See *Českomoravská Myslivecká Jednota* v. *Czech Republic* (No. 33091/96, 23 March 1999) where the law required the applicant association to make restitution of property which it had bought the year after it had been nationalised without compensation. The Court found the application inadmissible as the deprivation which the applicant suffered took place not only in the interest of individuals (i.e., the original owner or its successors) but also in the general interest since it was promoting the values of a democratic society by providing redress for the previous taking without

measures of control. For the individuals there will either be an undoing of an injustice or, at least, restoration of control over their property. It could also serve the wider interest to try and end abnormal conditions by re-establishing as much as possible the *status quo ante*, as well as to have the economy stimulated through the initiatives of those who recover their property. However, restitution will also have an impact on those persons in occupation, notably where they are the ones whose situation gave rise to the measure being undone or concluded. Furthermore, in some circumstances at least, it could be in the collective interest for the present occupier to remain in possession, particularly if a successful enterprise on which others depend for their livelihood has been established there. These are issues which must be, or have been, faced when considering the approach towards restitution. In the case of expropriated property there is, as has been, scope for choice as to whether this should take place at all. Where, however, the taking or interference was supposed to be a temporary measure, restitution ought to be the eventual policy goal even though it seems that international human rights law will accept compensation as a substitute. Nevertheless individual and collective interests do not just operate as policy considerations; they can also give rise to rights, or justifications for their restriction, which can be asserted to control the demand for restitution.

In the case of expropriation, a significant difficulty may be posed by the fact that title to the property for which restitution is sought or proposed has in the meantime been obtained by a third party. An attempt simply to transfer the property back to the original owner could well entail a breach of Protocol 1, provided this occurs after the obligations in it have been accepted. This would certainly be so if no compensation was paid but, even if it were, the question to be addressed in each case will still be one of finding a fair balance between the interests involved. It may be that where the property simply represents economic potential (such as a factory or land suitable for development), there could not be said to be a pressing need for restitution to the original owner. On the other hand the strength of the association with the original owner (or his or her descendants) of something such as a family home or particular heirlooms could tip the balance in favour of restitution. Full market value would undoubtedly be the appropriate standard for compensation where a fair price had been paid for the property by the third party as he or she would otherwise be bearing the burden of paying for a collectively inflicted injustice. However, there might be no need for compensation, beyond that for any improvements, if the third party's acquisition had actually been achieved through a corrupt practice of the former regime.

It might be thought that the position would be less problematic where the property remains in public ownership but it may still have become someone's home. In such circumstances an unqualified right to restitution could create a

compensation. It was significant that the applicant received the original purchase price and could also claim compensation for revaluation from those benefiting from the restitution. But for a debate on the merits of restitution, see "A Forum on Restitution", 2,3 *EECR* 30 (1993).

housing problem for that person and his or her family. This would not, of course, preclude transfer of title but the collective interest might justify some restriction on the actual recovery of possession as has occurred in analogous cases already considered by the European Court concerning eviction at the end of a tenancy and discussed further below[50]. Indeed, not only might the State be entitled to use this as a justification for deferring restitution but the current occupant could him or herself also bring an international complaint based on the right to respect for the home if national institutions allowed peremptory expulsion[51]. Whether such a complaint could also rely on Protocol 1 would undoubtedly depend on the basis on which the property was occupied; as has already been noted, occupation of much public sector housing is often not founded on any legal entitlement regarding specific premises. However, in neither case is it likely that the assertion of such rights would provide sufficient justification for denying to the original owner the eventual restoration of his or her property concerned. Nevertheless they could probably require alternative accommodation and even compensation to be provided for the occupier before proceeding with restitution[52]

Restrictions on using property which one owns where no one is in occupation of it have been accepted where there was a concern to ensure that there was sufficient accommodation for persons working in a particular locality[53]. A similar approach has also been accepted where there were problems of over-population[54] and such a rationale might also be employed to justify delaying restitution even when a conflict with its immediate problems is over but there is still a shortage of accommodation. However, such a shortage should not be too readily assumed[55]. Nevertheless further support for deferring restitution is likely to be derived from the generally sympathetic response shown by the European Court to decrees suspending the enforcement of evictions, with the only exceptions being where the tenant had not paid the rent or the apartment was needed by the owner for his own family to live in. The general interest recognised as being served here is undoubtedly the need to ensure that people are housed—an obligation under the International Covenant on Economic, Social and Cultural

[50] See *Scollo* v. *Italy* (1996) 22 EHRR 514, *Spadea and Scalabrino* v. *Italy* (1996) 21 EHRR 482 and *Velosa Barreto* v. *Portugal*, 21 November 1995. See also *Stiftelsen Akademiska Foreningens Bostader i Lund* v. *Sweden*, 53 DR 163 (1987) and *Gurel* v. *Turkey*, 67 DR 285 (1990).

[51] The importance attached to a person's right to respect for his or her home is being increasingly recognised; see *Buckley* v. *United Kingdom* (1997) 23 EHRR 101 in which it was accepted that it could even arise from the unlawful occupation of land. See also the complaint before the Court in *Červeňákova and others* v. *Czech Republic* (No. 40226/98) concerning persons of Roma origin who, after the split between the Czech Republic and Slovakia, were forced to leave local authority housing because they were Slovak, not Czech, nationals.

[52] Neither would be necessary if there is an adequate period in which to make other arrangements.

[53] *X and Y* v. *The Netherlands*, 1 DR 86 (1975).

[54] *Wiggins* v. *United Kingdom*, 13 DR 40 (1978) and *Gillow* v. *United Kingdom* (1989) 11 EHRR 335.

[55] Compelling evidence of the supposed problem did not exist in the *Gillow* case.

Rights[56]—and its appropriateness will undoubtedly depend upon the particular circumstances in an individual country. A mere assertion that the property is now needed by the owner would not be regarded as sufficient to justify eviction; his or her actual circumstances must be examined and a wish to have a more comfortable home where he or she already has adequate accommodation, albeit with other members of the family, is unlikely to be compelling[57]. This can certainly be seen as part of the quest for a fair balance; the landowner is still getting an income and has somewhere to live while a housing crisis is not being precipitated[58]. However acceptable this appears to be on the surface, the European Court often seems in these cases to have overlooked the fact that the measures were being regularly adopted over a period lasting nearly forty years and there seemed to be little evidence of alternative measures being taken to tackle the supposed housing crisis; public sector construction might have relieved the problem but the easier course of putting the burden on landowners appears to have been preferred. This has resulted in the latter bearing an excessive burden for what is really a community problem. More recently, in *Immobiliare Saffi* v. *Italy*[59], the Court has recognised that the sort of approach being taken in Italy, under which it can be almost impossible for a landlord to recover possession of residential property except where this is needed for his or her own use, can be too inflexible. Furthermore it called into question the acceptability of the situation created by suspending the eviction process when it endures for a considerable period of time[60].

This last ruling, in particular, points to some delay being accepted before property used to house the homeless after a conflict needs to be restored to its original owner or occupant but also suggests that the longer this lasts the more intense should be the scrutiny of the justification provided[61]. In addition considerable importance should always be paid to the current housing needs of the person "temporarily" dispossessed. In doing so, it is probably unwise to place too much emphasis on the needs of those who were actually in residence at the time of dispossession where this is at the expense of those who were not. Certainly it should be noted that something might be regarded as a person's home even if he or she is not living in it at the time when the interference with its use occurs. Thus in *Gillow* v. *United Kingdom*[62], a couple barred from living in their house because of their prolonged absence abroad had actually been absent from it for almost nineteen years. They had been working outside the

[56] Article 11.

[57] As in the *Velosa Barreto* case; n 50.

[58] Some emphasis has also been placed on the particular needs of the tenants involved.

[59] 28 July 1999.

[60] Over eleven years in the *Immobiliare* case.

[61] See *Loizidou* v. *Turkey* (n 15) in which it was not shown how the need to rehouse displaced Turkish Cypriot refugees and the discussion of property rights in intercommunal talks could justify the continued denial of access to the property owned by Greek Cypriots in the part of Cyprus occupied by Turkish forces. The exceptional nature of the situation in northern Cyprus meant, however, that this denial did not attain the level of a deprivation of property.

[62] n 54.

country but had always intended to return, kept furniture there and saw it as their permanent base. In the European Court's view they had maintained sufficient links for it to be considered as their home and insufficient justification was established for the bar on their returning to live in it, notwithstanding a problem of over-population on the island where it was situated. Although it is still perfectly proper to interfere with established rights on a temporary basis to meet an immediate crisis[63] and the interests of those temporarily in possession should not be regarded as being of no consequence, the principal responsibility to them lies with the State and not the person seeking to recover their home. Moreover it is improbable that loss of possession should be accompanied by loss of the income to be derived from the property for anything but the shortest of periods; a continuous denial of income and other use would eventually become an effective deprivation and the rules already considered would become applicable[64].

Fair hearing

Any legislation adopted recognising that either some sort of restitution might be made or that compensation would be paid for expropriated property, even though there is no obligation for this to be done, needs to pay special attention to the procedure for determining claims. This is because the financial or proprietary interest at stake is sufficient to amount to a "civil right" under Article 6 of the European Convention or a "suit at law" under Article 14 of the International Covenant and thereby obtains the protection of the fair hearing guarantee which both establish. Of particular importance in this respect will be the making of suitable arrangements to ensure that the matter is dealt with by an independent and impartial tribunal with proper regard to the evidence and, in particular, an opportunity for the claimant to produce anything material to his or her claim. The tribunal need not be a court but its members must enjoy full independence from the executive or its decisions must be amenable to review by such a body with full jurisdiction over all the issues addressed[65]. Furthermore the procedure actually followed needs to be fair. There needs to be some recognition of the difficulty in gathering the evidence required to support a claim. This may require some flexibility not only in what is seen as having evidential value but also in setting a time limit for it to be adduced. The latter, in particu-

[63] See *Bejdic* v. *Republika Srpska*, n 32, in which the object of a law providing temporary accommodation for refugees where there was a surplus was held to be legitimate but the particular allocation entailed a breach of Protocol 1 because of the failure to take into account the fact that the apartment concerned had been occupied by the owner's son and family before having been unlawfully evicted. See also the discussion of the *Bulatovic* and *Kalincevic* cases in n 33, as well as *X* v. *Federal Republic of Germany*, 20 DR 163 (1980) and *X and Y* v. *Federal Republic of Germany*, 7 DR 51 (1976).

[64] See *Guillemin* v. *France*, n 44.

[65] *Cf* the finding in *Bryan* v. *United Kingdom* (1996) 21 EHRR 342 that a planning inspector hearing an appeal was not independent because his or her appointment could always be revoked by the minister ultimately responsible for planning matters. However, this defect was cured in the particular case by the possibility of an appeal to a court.

lar, might require some allowance for persons outside the jurisdiction who may not either enjoy the same advantages as someone resident there in assembling a case or even be aware as soon as a resident that an opportunity to make a claim has arisen. This was recognised by the United Nations Human Rights Committee in *Adam* v. *Czech Republic*;[66] in its view the strict observance of a time limit of six months for making a claim for restitution would be unreasonable in the circumstances of a case where the claimants had lived outside the country and were acting through lawyers based in the Czech Republic. It was particularly significant in this case that the deprivation of the property was a factor in leading the claimant to live abroad but there are likely to be other circumstances where due concern ought to be shown for the interests of someone who has good justification for being based outside the jurisdiction[67].

Discrimination

Whereas housing needs may delay or preclude restitution, the approach underpinning the latter must still observe the requirements of prohibitions on discrimination. So far the most significant one has been the one found in the International Covenant, notwithstanding its lack of a property guarantee. Thus in *Simunek, Tuzilova and Prochazka* v. *Czech Republic*[68] the United Nations Human Rights Committee took exception to a restitution law which barred non-citizens and non-residents from recovering property taken during the communist period. In one sense the rule was understandable since it arose out of a general policy of restricting the ownership of land to citizens which is not, in principle, objectionable[69]. However, the restriction applied to the payment of compensation as much as to restitution and the existence of this alternative means of redress meant that a wider interest would not be imperilled by a non-discriminatory approach since title would not have to be transferred when recognising the legitimacy of a claim. Perhaps even more significant was the fact that the measure failed to recognise the circumstances in which many people lost their property; the persecution had been such that they had been forced to flee and it had been confiscated either as part of this process or as a consequence of their departure. In these circumstances it was entirely unreasonable to restrict such persons from recovering the property or receiving compensation; indeed the length of time since their enforced departure made it inevitable that they seek citizenship elsewhere, particularly as in some cases it had been taken from

[66] Communication No 586/1994, 23 July 1996.

[67] A loss of opportunity attributable to flight abroad to evade criminal proceedings could not, however, be expected to elicit much sympathy.

[68] Communication No 516/1992, 19 July 1995.

[69] Such a restriction could be justified by reference to adverse economic effects of allowing foreign ownership, particularly where property would be relatively cheap for overseas buyers. The actual impact on resident non-citizens would, however, need to be monitored.

them once they had left. This decision was endorsed by the Committee in its subsequent decision in *Adam* v. *Czech Republic*[70].

The significant feature in these cases was the differential treatment without any rational justification supporting it. The absence of the latter might also have implications for the acceptability of any compensation criteria that are adopted but a challenge regarding these can only be mounted if there is actually a measure seeking to undo or remedy the deprivation of property; the International Covenant cannot in itself support any claim that there should be restitution or the provision of compensation. The Committee looked at the compensation arrangements in Hungary in the case of *Somers*[71] under which individuals received vouchers that could be exchanged against any property, shares or businesses sold during the privatisation of State-owned property. Former owners were not, however, given any priority in the recovery of the property that they had previously owned but a preference was given to the tenants of residential State-owned property to buy the apartment in which they were living. A tenant thus had an advantage over the former owner of the property but the Committee did not consider this to be unreasonable; it recognised that the interests of persons who may have been occupying the property for years were also deserving of protection. It might, of course, have been different if some former owners were being treated differently than others[72]. It remains to be seen whether the prohibition on discrimination in the European Convention will have a similar effect. Although it has already been established that the protection afforded by Protocol 1 does not extend to the acquisition of property[73], the prohibition on discrimination in Article 14 could have a similar widening effect to that seen in the *Gaygusuz* case previously discussed[74].

CONCLUSION

Restitution and compensation are only part of the approach required to undo serious wrongs[75]. In many instances the former is not obligatory and is also

[70] n 66.

[71] Communication No 566/1993, 23 July 1996.

[72] The prohibition on discrimination could also be relevant to the basis for privatising State assets, such as through the allocation of shares in public companies. Such measures are closely related to but still quite distinct from those concerned with restitution. However, the Human Rights Committee has not seen a decision to require restitution or to provide compensation for only some past injustices as being discriminatory in itself; see *Drobek* v. *Slovakia*, Communication No. 643/1995, 14 July 1997. There would undoubtedly be a violation of Article 26 of the Covenant if such treatment reflected an evident racial motive; see the individual opinion of Medina Quiroga and Klein in this case.

[73] *Linde* v. *Sweden*, 47 DR 270 (1986).

[74] Text at n 34. Furthermore the obligation imposed by the International Covenant on Civil and Political Rights with respect to discrimination cannot simply be ignored, not least because Article 53 of the European Convention (as amended by Protocol 11) provides that the latter instrument is not to be construed as limiting or derogating from other human rights obligations by which a State is bound.

[75] Prosecution may also be needed; see N. Roht-Arriaza (ed), *Impunity and Human Rights in International Law and Practice* (New York, Oxford University Press, 1995).

impractical, as well as posing a new threat to other human rights. Compensation is less disruptive for the individuals now in possession but invariably poses a substantial economic challenge to the State concerned, particularly when its economy is in transition to a market-led system. Nevertheless one or other of these measures has to be undertaken in order to meet the human rights commitments applicable and, even where they are not, they may still be necessary to meet deeply-held expectations. The evolving international case law is far from having solved all the difficulties which dispossession and deprivation of property causes; even restitution, potentially the most effective remedy, is unlikely to repair the anguish suffered with the initial taking and in years that followed it. Nevertheless the approach needed to deal with the problems thrown up by such taking is now much clearer. The most significant deficiency lies not in restitution and compensation measures themselves but in the continuing failure of national legal systems to ensure that the rights they proclaim are observed.

5

The "Prerogative Property" Basis of the English Game Law System: Fact or Fiction?

PETER COOK

(1) INTRODUCTION

IN 1816 THE first major Select Committee on the English Game Laws concluded that

> "by the common law, every possessor of land has an exclusive right ratione soli to all animals ferae naturae, found upon his land; and that he may pursue and kill them himself, or authorize any other person to pursue or kill them; and that he may now by the common law, which in so far continues unrestrained by any subsequent statute, support an action against any person who shall take, kill or chase them".

Yet the Committee felt compelled to admit that certain statutes had in fact limited this common law right. These statutes had

> "subjected to penalties persons, who, not having certain qualifications, shall exercise their common law right; but they have not divested the possessor of his right, nor have they given power to any other person to exercise that right, without the consent of the possessor".[1]

Prior to the reforming legislation of 1831 (1 & 2 Wm.IV c.32), the English Game Laws, which had been given an uncertain and hesitant start by the Game Act of 1390[2], reflected such a continuing conflict between common law (or customary) rights and the claims to precedence of statute law. Nevertheless, most 18th century commentators considered the term "English Game Laws" to be merely synonymous with the statutory "property qualification" upon the taking and killing of game and similar legislation prohibiting the buying and selling of game and preventing unlawful trespasses; but these laws were inseparably connected with aspects of the law of personal property and the theoretical nature of a largely

[1] S.C. (House of Commons) Report on the Game Laws (June 1816), (504), p.2.

[2] 13 Ric.2 st.1 c.13.

mythological (at least by the 18th century) royal prerogative in matters of "game ownership"[3].

In the interests of game preservation and exclusive sporting, the Norman kings had carved out large tracks of land, designated as forests, specially selected for the harbouring and hunting of wild animals of the chase. These animals, later coming under the denomination "game", were the objects of sport and the sources of meat and venison. Under the forest system, such animals were often designated as "royal game" and the right of hunting them in any territory set aside for the purpose was considered to be subject to the royal prerogative. It is only by a considered treatment of the exercise of this prerogative, and of the practice of granting sporting franchises out of a plenitude of royal power in this field, that the true nature of the English Game Law System of the 17th and long 18th century can in large part be comprehended. The royal game prerogative, in its limited application in mediaeval forest and game organisation, fostered questions of "prerogative property law" which were to be fervently debated even into the early nineteenth century[4].

Essentially, however, the arguments for a royal game prerogative, on the one hand, and occupancy rights in game, on the other, were presented long before the game law reform movement began in earnest in the second decade of the 19th century; both considerations of property right and prerogative claim in relation to game were theoretical parts of the foundation of the English game law "system" in operation from the 1671 Game Act[5] until 1831. Such arguments remain essential to both a theoretical and jurisprudential appreciation of the game law system and will consequently form the substance of this piece, which does not pretend to represent a comprehensive survey of these laws.[6]

The conflict between common law right and statutory imposition is an inevitable by-product of a common law system. In the game law context such conflict was ably demonstrated by Richard Burn (1709–1785) in his "Justice of the Peace", the first edition of which appeared in 1755.[7] It appeared to Burn that by the common law "every man" had an equal right to such creatures as were not naturally under the "power of man"; and that the mere capture or seizure of them created a property, albeit qualified and not absolute, in the animal or bird so taken. This common law right was however subject to two "higher" legal

[3] On the concepts of ownership and possession in English law, see A. M. Honore "Ownership" and D.R. Harris "The Concept of Possession in English Law" in A.G. Guest (ed.) "Oxford Essays in Jurisprudence (First Series)" (O.U.P. 1961) chpts. v and iv respectively.

[4] A debate seemingly settled by Edward Christian in "A Treatise on the Game Laws: in which it is fully proved that, except in particular cases, Game is now, and has always been, by the Law of England, the Property of the Occupier of the Land upon which it is found and taken." (London, 1817).

[5] 22 & 23 Car. II c.25.

[6] For a thorough treatment of the English Game Laws in operation between 1671 and 1831, see P.B. Munsche "Gentlemen and Poachers" (Cambridge Univ. Press, 1981).

[7] Richard Burn, "The Justice of the Peace and Parish Officer" vol.ii. (employing the more comprehensive 13th edition, London, 1776) p.218 et seq. (The final and 30th edition of this work appeared as late as 1869).

forms: the royal prerogative and the statutory enactment; it was subject to the greater right of prerogative and the superior law of parliament. Thus, for example, Burn eventually opined (i.e. by the 1770s) that "all those animals ferae naturae, which come under the dominion of game, are styled in our laws 'his Majesty's game': and that which he has, he may grant to another; and consequently another may prescribe to have the game, within such a precinct or lordship . . . and from hence comes the right of lords of manors, or others, unto the game within their respective liberties".[8] Although conceptually mistaken in his analysis of the prerogative–property equation, Burn at least appreciated the three essential themes underlying the English game law system: the application of aspects of the royal prerogative in relation to certain (albeit limited) matters of hunting and sport, the question of property rights in animals (and birds) ferae naturae, and the emergent influence and steadily increasing use of statute-law in this field. As for the purpose of the game laws, Burn considered that they provided "for the recreation and amusement of persons of fortune, unto whom the king with the advice and assent of parliament hath granted the same"; and that they existed to "prevent persons of inferior rank, from squandering their time, which their station of life requireth to be more profitably employed" for "these restrictions do not take from the common people those privileges which before rested solely in the king".[9] At this juncture, there appears to be some logical inconsistency in Burn's recognition of a common law principle, amended and superseded by statute and yet subject to a royal game prerogative, which in itself was capable of denying any such privilege in the common people. Burn's thinking in this matter was however not untypical of his age; as will be discussed later, Blackstone, in his "Commentaries", observed the whole game system resting upon this nebulous prerogative, having an uncertain parentage in the mediaeval forest laws[10]. More recently, and in one of the most influential set of periodical treatments of the English Game Laws, Chester Kirby (an American historian writing mainly in the 1930s) consistently maintained that the game system rested upon a moribund royal game prerogative, from which it nevertheless gained further impetus as late as 1671.[11]

[8] ibid. p.221. It should be noted that this statement does not appear in the earlier editions of the work (e.g. cannot be found in 1755–1756 editions).

[9] ibid. p.221; relying upon Matthew Bacon's "New Abridgement" (1st edition, London, 1736), vol.ii, pp.612–613.

[10] Blackstone's "Commentaries on the Laws of England", (Oxford, 1765–1769), ii. 415–416; iv. 174 (unless otherwise stated in these notes, it is the first edition which is being employed throughout). It is also worth noting that W. Nelson in his "Laws of England concerning the Game of Hunting, Hawking, Fishing and Fowling etc." (London, 1727) devoted 32 pages to "Forests" and only 3 to the question of 'Property' (i.e. in wild animals and birds).

[11] Chester & Ethyn Kirby "The Stuart Game Prerogative" in E.H.R. XLVI (1931) pp. 239–254. The other articles in this "set" are: "The English Game Law System" in American Historical Review, XXXVIII (1933), pp.240–262; "English Game Law Reform" in "Essays in Modern English History in Honor of Wilbur Cortez Abbott", Cambridge, Mass., 1941; and "The Attack on the English Game Laws in the Forties" in Journal of Modern History IV (1932), pp.18–37.

(2) THE PROPERTY QUALIFICATION TO TAKE THE GAME

Whether emanating from within or from beyond the royal prerogative, there had been a "property qualification" to take game animals and birds from the reign of Richard II. The first property qualification act of 1390, sometimes referred to as the first game act, displayed concern that the agricultural labourer was prone to poach by day and on holy days, when good Christian people were in church, hearing the divine service. On these days, he would take his dogs and "other engines" to hunt in the parks and warrens of his social superiors. On occasions, the preamble to the Act recited, these poaching forays were turned into conferences and conspiracies (perhaps not unlike those—whether ideological or not—which preceded the Peasants' Revolt of 1381[12]), and through such "complots" the lower orders would be encouraged to "rise and disobey their allegiance". Accordingly, the Act provided that

> "no manner of artificer, labourer, nor any other layman, which hath not lands or tenements to the value of forty shillings . . . shall use ferrets, heys, nets, harepipes, nor cords, nor other engines for to take or destroy deer, hares, nor conies, nor other gentlemen's game, upon pain of one year's imprisonment"[13].

The term "other gentlemen's game", as literally translated from the French langugage of the Act, has uncertain meaning but at least it can safely be stated that the phrase "the king's game" does not appear in any provisions of the 1390 Act—nor is there evident any express or other reference to any prerogative in game.

The Act's full extent was never tested in an age before the game-bird became popular as an alternative object of sport to the deer, coney or hare. It is likely that all beasts coming within the definitions of "beasts of the forest" and "beasts of the chase" were included in the statutory phrase "other gentleman's game", which would therefore have comprised wild boar, all manner of deer (hart, hind, buck, doe and roe), and the fox, in addition to those animals expressly mentioned in the Act.[14] With the introduction of the game-bird in the fifteenth century, and the new category of "beasts and birds of warren" to include game-fowl,[15] the traditional divisions of animals into those of forest and chase began

[12] Consider R.H. Hilton and H. Fagan, "The English Rising of 1381" (Lawrence and Wishart, London, 1950), pp. 32–36 and 82–89; and R.H. Hilton "Bond Men Made Free. Medieval Peasant Movements and the English Rising of 1381" (Temple Smith, London, 1973), pp.71–74, 221–232; and see comments of Sir William Holdsworth in his "History of English Law", (4th edition, Methuen, London, 1934 as reprinted) vol. iii, p.205

[13] 13 Ric. II st.I.c.13 s.3.

[14] See Edward Coke "Institutes of the Laws of England" (henceforth abbreviated to "Inst.") vol. 4 (London, 1648, 2nd edition), 316. The "Institutes" are in four books: the first Institute was published in 1628; but the second, third and fourth Institutes, although completed earlier, were not published until 1641. Coke died in 1634.

[15] See John Manwood, "A Treatise of the Lawes of the Forest" (3rd edition, London, 1665) pp. 94–96 (the first edition appeared in 1598).

to lose popularity and the concept of game was widened to include all animals and birds expressly protected by the game legislation passed before and during the reign of James I (1603–1625). Pheasants and partridges were mentioned in an Act of 1496,[16] which was both directed towards the better preservation of these birds and clearly intended to promote their position in the game calendar.

The concept of a general class of animals collectively known as game had developed sufficiently by 1603 to be catalogued by two property qualification statutes passed in the first decade of James' reign.[17] Both Acts were promulaged essentially "for the preservation of the game of pheasants and partridges", but they extended statutory protection to "house-dove, pigeon, hearn, mallard, duck, teal, widgeon, grouse, heathcock, moregame, or any such fowl, or any hare". In between the two main qualification Acts of the reign, a statute had been passed in 1605 "against unlawful hunting, stealing of deer and conies", thus completing the category of animals protected by the game legislation.[18] Section 6 of the Act of 1603 gave authority to persons having free warren, to lords of manors, to all freeholders (and their servants) having £10 per annum in lands of inheritance (in fee), to persons having life estates to the yearly value of thirty pounds or to those merely having personal property to the value of £200, to take pheasants and partridges upon their own or their master's free warren, freehold or life estate. (s. 6) These figures or "qualifications" were altered by section 7 of the 1609 Act (7 Ja.1 c.11), which provided that for the values £10, £30 and £200 should be read respectively £40, £80 and £400. Within six years the property qualifications had been far more materially changed than in the preceding two centuries since the Act of 1390. Blackstone overlooked the first qualification Act in his "Commentaries", although he recognised the significance of the Acts of 1603 and 1609. He did however admit that the purpose of the legislation of James I was for the encouragement of hawking, popular with the King and termed by Edward Christian as "the most honourable mode of killing game at that time"[19]. The subsidiary legislative object seems to have been the restriction upon the killing of game with guns, bows, setting dogs and nets. Only certain privileged persons could use nets in the daytime to take pheasants and partridges, while an Act of 1580[20] had enacted that no person should destroy pheasants or partridges "with any manner of engines or devices" in the night, upon pain of forfeiture of 20 shillings for every bird so taken.

As the gentry grew in local and national significance during the seventeenth and eighteenth centuries, the game laws became ever more detailed and covered almost all aspects of game preservation; from regulations pertaining to hunting with greyhounds and limiting the use of firearms in sport, to the generally more

[16] II Hen.7 c.17.

[17] I Ja. I c.27 ss. 1, 2: 7 Ja. I. c.11 ss.8, 9.

[18] 3 Ja. I.c.13.

[19] Bl. Comm. ii (12th edition, 1794) p.418 n.8. Edward Christian was Blackstone's editor (from the 12th edition, 1793–1795) and the author of a "Treatise on the Game Laws" (London, 1817). See earlier footnote 4.

[20] 23 Eliz.c.10.

seriously regarded crime of night poaching, which was eventually (between 1816 and 1828) to become punishable by seven years' transportation. By 1671, the result of a series of property qualification statutes was seen in the amending provisions of an Act seminal to the game system. All persons were prohibited from killing game and keeping guns for that purpose unless they possessed a right of free warren, were lords of the manors or sons and heirs apparent of esquires, or other persons of higher degree; or unless they had lands and tenements of inheritance to a clear yearly value of £100, a life interest or term of ninety nine years to the value of £150, or were "the owners and keepers of forests, parks, chases or warrens, being stocked with deer or conies for their necessary use".[21] Blackstone later pointed out that the freehold property qualification of £100 per annum from lands and tenements of inheritance was fifty times the amount which enabled a man to vote for a knight of the shire.[22] In a similarly critical vein he contended that the 1671 Act raised a little Nimrod[23] in every manor and shire, the activities of which were described by Henry Fielding in some of his finest novels—such as "The History of the Adventures of Joseph Andrews" (1742) and "The History of Tom Jones" (1749). However, it would not be 'all knights of the shire' who were qualified to take or kill game, even upon their own land[24]. The words in the statute, "other persons of higher degree" did not relate "per se" to the squire, or, it was held, to a doctor of physic, with 'degree' from an English or Scottish University.[25]

It was an Act replete with curious anomaly.[26] An esquire of under £100 per annum could not take or kill "his own" game, though it would certainly seem that his eldest son was duly qualified by the Act. Any younger sons of a qualified or unqualified squire or knight could not kill game unless "deputised" as gamekeepers.[27] A further anomaly resulted in a qualified person being permitted to kill game anywhere, and not simply on his own land, subject only to the law of trespass. In the case of a qualified landlord shooting over the land of an unqualified tenant, it was unlikely that the tenant would risk the former's displeasure by bringing an action in trespass, although technically such an action in these circumstances could be coupled with a charge of "poaching" (ie. unlaw-

[21] 22 & 23 Car.II c.25 ss.1, 2

[22] B1.Com.iv. 175.

[23] Nimrod was "the mighty hunter before the Lord": Genesis x.9. In the late eighteenth century et seq. the term was one of mixed affection, commonly bestowed upon sporting gentlemen of no great means. It was however used particularly as an affectionate pseudonym by and for the writing Shropshire Squire, Charles James Apperley (1779–1843). See Bl.Comm. iv, 409.

[24] For a valuable statutory and judicial survey of the persons qualified to take and kill game since the 1671 Act, see J. Chitty, "A Treatise on the Game Laws", (London, 1812), vol.i. chpt.III.

[25] *Jones* v. *Smart* (1785) 1 TR 45 (see Willes J. at p.49)

[26] See E.W. Bovill "English Country Life 1780–1830" (Oxford, 1962) pp. 174–175.

[27] This procedure was known as the "gamekeeper exception" and was frequently used to avoid the provisions of the 1671 Act. It involved a deputation (ostensibly to an previously "unqualified person") by warrant in the form prescribed by the Act, granting the privilege of shooting game. Nominally it was given by a lord of the manor to his gamekeeper, but was frequently used for other purposes. See also 5 Ann c.14, 9 Ann c.25 and 3 Geo.I c.11; and P.B. Munsche, "Gentlemen and Poachers; the English Game Laws 1671–1831", (C.U.P. 1981) pp. 29–32.

ful trespass in pursuit of game). In many cases, the unqualified person was only too pleased to have someone suitably qualified to shoot the voracious game, ravaging crops and damaging fields. It seems that farmers were permitted to shoot rabbits on their own land, but not hares, and that the provision relating to keeping greyhounds or lurchers was avoided by "docking a lurcher's tail and calling it a sheepdog".[28] The right to kill game was as a consequence "the privilege of a class at once artifical and ill-defined".[29]

Chester Kirby has remarked that "the tangle of game legislation, spread over centuries, culminated in 1671 in a law which remained as the principal foundation of the game system for one hundred and sixty years"; and that "this sporting charter disqualified almost all except the landed classes from indulgence in the amusement of pursuing game."[30] In short, the Act of 1671 meant that the permitted class of sportsmen had been more narrowly defined than at any time previous to the passing of that Act. In comparison to previous legislation dating back to 1390, no provision in the 1671 Act included or encompassed the possessors of personal property to a prescribed value. Henceforth the qualification, for at least one hundred and sixty years, would be based upon real property and landed wealth.[31]

The Stuart game laws were essentially examples of legislation for the benefit of an emergent governing class.[32] This class had deep roots in country justice and local government and, by the death of James I in 1625, it had effectively wrested from the Crown most of the benefits of any royal game prerogative and its incidents of forest, chase and warren. In a similar manner, the century was to witness the transfer of effective government from kings and council to parliament and "cabinet". The modern game laws began in the reign of Charles II and the Act of 1671 was a manifestation of a relatively recent social phenomenon, the rise of the gentry, which resulted in a relatively small social class asserting an influence through parliament and local government in order to secure and maintain the legal provision of sporting rights. Questions as to the nature and extent of these rights, usually known as franchises (i.e. royal privileges existing in the hands of a subject), were inextricably interwoven into the fabric of seventeenth century constitutional conflicts. Central to this conflict between Crown and Parliament was the (attempted) application of a seemingly moribund royal prerogative of game control and forest extension. Yet was there in fact or theory a royal prerogative in game still in operation in the seventeenth

[28] C. Chevenix Trench "The Poacher and the Squire: a History of Poaching and Game Preservation in England" (London, 1967) pp.122–123.

[29] J.F. Stephen "A History of the Criminal Law of England" (London, 1883), iii. 281; on the rights of lords of manors see Edinb. Review (1831) vol. 54 p.285.

[30] "English Game Law Reform", in "Essays in Modern English History in Honour of Wilbur Cortez Abbott" (Cambridge, Mass., 1941), p.346.

[31] Cf. the personal property qualification in 7 Ja.I.c.11 s.5; Chester Kirby "The English Game Law System", American Hist.Rev.vol.38, p.241.

[32] Sir George Clark "The Later Stuarts" (2nd edition, Oxford, 1956) p.15, and see p.407 for the reasons for the Game Act of 1671.

century and, if so, how did its exercise affect property rights in beasts and birds of forest, park, chase and warren? The solution to this question, and to others like it, seems central of an appreciation of the English game laws system between 1603 and 1831, by which latter date they had ceased, in all but one aspect, to poison the rural scene.[33]

(3) A ROYAL GAME PREROGATIVE?—AN AMERICAN VIEW IN CONTEXT

Blackstone understood the royal prerogative to be "that special pre-eminence which the kings hath, over and above all other subjects, and out of the ordinary course of the common law, in right of his regal dignity". More particularly, it consists of

> "rights and capcities which the king enjoys alone . . . and not to those which he enjoys in common with any of his subjects: for if once any one prerogative of the crown could be held in common with subject, it would cease to be prerogative any longer."[34].

This recognition of extraordinary "rights and capacities", in their nature "single and eccentrical", outside the common law implies a recognition of their nature and extent by the common law itself. This was certainly not the case at the accession of James I in 1603. The American Historian, Chester Kirby, in a seminal article entitled "The Stuart Game Prerogative", maintained that the royal prerogative, as handed down by the Tudors to James I, was wide-reaching and largely undefined.[35] The lack of precise definition was exemplified by the arguments of Sir John Banks, then Attorney-General, in *R.* v. *Hampden* (The Case of Ship-Money (1637)), in which he attempted to support a prerogative then under siege from all sides.[36] In expounding the extent of the prerogative power in the Crown, he declared that

> "all lands, and all jurisdiction, and all dominion, is derived from the Crown; that whatsoever was not granted from the Crown, remaineth in the person of the King."

Of this Supreme Dominium, he said: ". . . it is so inherent in the King's person, that if he grants away his lands, yet the same must still remain to the King."[37] As a consequence of this not untypical reasoning, Charles I had been seduced (predominantly by the temptation of greater revenue) to use his prerogative power on the advice of the historically-minded Attorney-General Noy, who was

[33] See Chester Kirby "The Attack on the English Game Laws in the Forties" [1840s] in Journal of Modern History, IV (March 1932), 18–37. The "one respect" is the permitted continuation of the practice of reserving all game (including hares and rabbits) to the landlord in what were effectively agricultural leases.

[34] 1 Bl.Comm. 239.

[35] Chester and Ethyn Kirby "The Stuart Game Prerogative" in English Historical Review XLVI (1931) pp. 239–254, at p.239.

[36] Howell's State Trials. Vol.3.825 at pp.1023, 1083. See also Wilfred Prest, "Ship Money and Mr. Justice Hutton" in History Today, vol.41 (January 1991), pp.42–47

[37] Ibid. p.1023.

"able to guide Charles into an aggressive fiscally-inspired legalism in the 1630s"[38] and to revive the forest laws in 1634[39]. This revival was, in effect, an attempt to reclaim all forest land which had once belonged to the king on the pretence that this land had not been "granted from the Crown". It was in fact through such exercise of royal power that the relationship between prerogative and law was clearly established in the Stuart period and that the present theory of the Prerogative is by and large a legacy from the constitutional conflicts of the seventeenth century. However, accepting that the prerogative was to be later more closely defined, its nature and extent in 1603 remains uncertain. Was there, for example, a prerogative in game? And how extensive might such a prerogative have been?

It is widely accepted that when James VI of Scotland also became James I of England in 1603, he succeeded to a prerogative which was stronger than it had ever been before[40]. The Commons complained in the "Apology" of 1604 that "the prerogatives of princes may easily and do more daily grow" while "the privileges of the subject are for the most part at an everlasting stand".[41] James himself had claimed an independent legislative power for the Crown in his "True Law of Free Monarchies" (1598). Later, in 1616, in an address to the judges, he stated that ". . . it is presumption and high contempt in a subject to dispute what a King can do, or say that a King cannot do this or that, but rest with that which is the King's revealed will in his law".[42] The royal claim to extensive extra-legal power had been given bold support by Dr. John Cowell, a Cambridge Civil Law Professor, in his "Interpreter", published in the form of a law dictionary in 1607. Dr. Cowell wrote under the article "King";

> "He is above the law by his absolute power . . . and though at his coronation he take an oath not to alter the laws of the land, yet this oath notwithstanding, he may later on suspend any particular law that seemeth hurtful to the public estate"[43].

This amounted to an admission of a power outside the law to override the law, not simply in an emergency situation and in accord with the nature of "sovereignty",[44] but in order to protect the interest of kingship and the "public estate". James may have had a concept of prerogative power for the public good (or estate) in mind when, in the interests of the national game preservation, he issued an early royal proclamation in May 1603 against unlawful sporting,

[38] Derek Hirst, "Authority and Conflict. England 1603–1658" (Arnold, London, 1986) p.89

[39] See J.R. Tanner, "English Constitutional Conflicts of the Seventeenth Century, 1603–1689" (C.U.P. 1928), pp.74–75

[40] See J.A. Lovat-Fraser, "The Constitutional Position of the Scottish Monarch Prior to the Union" in (1901) 17 L.Q.R. pp. 252–262, especially at 255: "There never was in Scotland anything like the wide royal prerogative which existed in England".

[41] G.W.Prothero "Selected Statutes and Other Constitutional Documents 1558–1625", 3rd. edition (Oxford,1906) p.289.

[42] Cited in J.R. Tanner, supra., p.20.

[43] Cited in J.R. Tanner, supra, idid, footnote 3.

[44] See J.R. Tanner supra. p.19 on prerogative "to deal with emergencies and exceptional situations" and the question of "sovereignty".

phrased in such a way that Chester Kirby deduced that "it seemed he claimed exclusively all the game in England". Significant depreciations in the number of game in particular areas would frequently cause his direct interference. In 1616, for example, Kirby notes that he commanded the gentlemen and qualified persons of Bedfordshire that they should at all events remedy the scarcity of game in the county, under pain of royal displeasure.[45]

However a wide and undefined royal prerogative, an emergency power of legislation for the public good, and a fondness for hunting in the person of King James I do not, of themselves, constitute a royal game prerogative. Further evidence is necessary to satisfy the (legal) historian. Parliament was certainly not in accord with the view of Dr. Cowell. His doctrines were repudiated by the House of Commons and his book ordered, with the reluctant and tacit approval of the King, to be ceremoniously burned by the common hangman in 1610. James himself admitted the extent of his power, or rather its limitations, when he felt compelled to acknowledge that "he had no power to make laws of himself, or to exact any subsidies de jure without the consent of the three Estates."[46] It is highly unlikely that either James I or his son, Charles I, wholeheartedly and genuinely had full concurrence with the sentiments expressed in this message to Parliament; and King Charles' main supporters, including Dr. Sibthorp in 1626, Dr. Manwaring in 1627 and Archbishop Laud after 1633 continued to state and reinterpret the principle of "non-resistance" to the "King's judgements" until the eve of Civil War.[47]

Chester Kirby's evidence for the existence of a Stuart Game Prerogative is based upon the Kings' use of royal proclamation, warrants made out to royal gamekeepers, the granting of free warren and park franchises by the Crown and proceedings in Star Chamber, the most feared of the prerogative courts; but neither case nor statute law are not cited in the main stream of support for the theory. The leading legal treatises are similarly avoided, with the exception of John Manwood, who, in his "Treatise of the Laws of the Forrest", which first appeared in 1598, admittedly recognised an extensive royal hunting right and power to grant franchises out of an equally extensive royal privilege in relation to game[48].

Kirby argued that William the Conqueror had created the New Forest out of a plenitude of power; while in Magna Carta (1215) King John claimed a right not only of establishing forests at will but of making game preserves wherever he wished.[49] He also cited Bracton as authority for his "royal game prerogative"

[45] C. & E. Kirby "The Stuart Game Prerogative", op.cit.p.241.

[46] J.R. Tanner, supra. p.21. The three estates were the Lords Spiritual, the Lords Temporal, and the Commons.

[47] See for eg. Dr. Roger Manwaring "First Sermon on Religion and Allegiance" pp.10–11 (1627), which can be found in J.P. Kenyon, "The Stuart Constitution 1603–1688. Documents and Commentary" (C.U.P. 1969), pp.14–16.

[48] Employing the 3rd edition (London, 1665), chpts. ii, iii and xxiv.

[49] C. & E. Kirby, "The Stuart Game Prerogative", op.cit.p.239; Magna Carta ss.44, 47, 48 in "Stubbs' Select Charters" (9th edition by H.W.C. Davis, Oxford 1913) p.298.

theory. In Bracton's "De legibus et Consuetudinibus Angliae", the author seems to suggest that natural law and Roman law gave wild animals to the first taker although, in English law, they were strictly speaking the prerogative property of the King.[50] Although recognising that any game prerogative was a "moribund prerogative" in 1603, allowed to decline because "the Tudor despots had considered the support of their subjects more important than the literal maintenance of their rights",[51] Kirby displayed a seeming disinterest in the general tendency of the aristocracy, parliament and the common law judges to challenge and limit the prerogatives of the Crown from all sides during the period 1603–1642. He suggested that James I attempted to restore to a state of health and vigour the royal claim "to the right of hunting wherever the king pleased" coupled with a right of control of game preserves throughout England. However, in an age of diminishing royal power outside the common law, it is difficult to accept that James I not only succeeded in resurrecting the game prerogative but also entrenching it so firmly in the popular mind that the legislators, through the last section of the 1671 Game Act, effectively deemed it necessary to still speak of such a prerogative. Yet Chester Kirby felt that Charles II recovered a "somewhat dilapidated game institution", asserting that he was endowed theoretically with "as full a game prerogative as his predecessors had possessed".[52]

Admittedly, Charles II created new parks and free warrens in "gentlemen" and continued to appoint gamekeepers by royal warrant. Warrants giving authority to seize setting-dogs and unlawful sporting equipment were issued. In such warrants and appointments the same reference to "his Majesty's game" is found and, additionally, similar reference to punishment outside the ordinary courts is implied. After 1671, the appointment of royal gamekeepers over large tracts of land continued along with the Privy Council supervision and control of prosecutions for illegal sporting, chiefly around the vicinity of Windsor and Hampden Court[53]. The royal issue of rights to impark and rights of free warren continued at least until the last decade of the seventeenth century. Chester Kirby concluded by stating that the operation of the 1671 Act and subsequent legislation rendered the exercise of the game prerogative less necessary. The advantages of the royal licence to a park as against other rights of park had begun to diminish by statute[54], and from this time the royal game prerogative ceased to have any practical importance and, in the light of an aristocracy coming to

[50] Henry de Bracton "De Legibus et Consuetudinibus Angliae" (edited by G.D.Woodbine, trans. by Samuel E. Thorne, 1922; Harvard Univ. Press. Cambridge, Mass. 1968), ii. 42: "quae nunc sunt ipsius regis de iure civili et non communia ut olim".

[51] C. & E. Kirby, "The Stuart Game Prerogative", op.cit.p. 240.

[52] C. & E. Kirby, "The Stuart Game Prerogative", op.cit.p.247.

[53] Interestingly, as late as 1703, a warrant was issued for preserving game within ten miles of Winchester with instructions that "all poachers and other disorderly persons", using illegal means to destroy game, should be reported to the Privy Council. See Calendar of State Papers, Domestic, 1703–1704, pp. 454–455.

[54] See, for e.g. 3 Wm. & Mary c.10 (Game Act of 1692).

understand that statute-law could more effectively guarantee their sport, it became a merely useless appendage of the constitution.[55]

(4) BLACKSTONIAN GAME PREROGATIVE THEORY AND THE QUESTION OF PROPERTY IN WILD ANIMALS

Sir William Holdsworth in his "History of English Law" classified the royal prerogative into a series of rights and privileges in the Crown, including, inter alia, fiscal or proprietary rights (or those merely quasi-fiscal or quasi-proprietary). He considered Blackstone to have mis-stated Bracton in the matter of "prerogative property" in the Crown as bona vacantia.[56] Edward Christian, Blackstone's editor between 1793 and 1809, had similarly and earlier indicated that Blackstone had contradicted himself in stating that apparently ownerless property belonged to the first occupant (ie. the Crown) by the law of nature. Previously, Blackstone had laid down the "better view", as Christian would have seen it, that ownerless property, or property abandoned by its owner "belongs, as in a state of nature, to the first finder."[57] Historically, only a limited list of ownerless things belonging to the Crown as bona vacantia has been drawn up, including, inter alia, treasure trove, waifs, estrays, royal mines, royal fowl and royal fish. Britton, writing in the early fourteenth century, had maintained that property by prerogative right was a limited concept, merely alluding to a royal property in waifs, estrays and "things lost".[58]. He made no reference to animals ferae naturae or royal fowl, albeit in an age before the 'watershed decision' in the Case of Swans (1592)[59], which is discussed later, and widespread game (including game-bird) preservation.

Christian's reference to the inconsistency in Blackstone and his own subsequent refutation of the view that "the sole right of taking and destroying game belongs exclusively to the King"[60], demonstrates the diversity of views capable of being held on the question of property in those animals ferae naturae, a term which included most game animals and birds. Whereas animals "domitae natu-

[55] C. & E. Kirby, "The Stuart Game Prerogative", op.cit. pp.252–255.

[56] H.E.L. (Methuen, London 1938, 3rd impression 1975) vol.x.p.350; B1.Com.i.299 and see Edward Christian's note (12) at pp. 298–299 of vol.i. of the 12th edition (London 1793).

[57] B1.Com.i.295–296 (12th edition). For earlier criticisms of Blackstone's "prerogative property thesis" see Charles Edward Long, "Considerations on the Game Laws together with Some Strictures on Dr. Blackstone's Commentaries. . ." (London, 1777). See Duncan Kennedy, "The Structure of Blackstone's Commentaries" in 28 (1979) Buffalo L.R. 205 at 288–303 for discussion of Blackstone's use of hierarchies of persons, his inconsistent fusion of public and private law and the resultant confusion of property and jurisdiction in the Commentaries.

[58] "Britton", English translation and notes by F.M. Nichols (Washington, 1901) pp.56–57.

[59] 7 Co.Rep. 15b (Trin 34 Eliz).

[60] Bl.Comm.ii 417: "However novel this doctrine may seem, it is a regular consequence from what has been before delivered; that the sole right of taking and destroying game belongs exclusively to the king. This appears, as well from the historical deduction here made, as because he may grant to his subjects an exclusive right of taking them; which he could not do, unless such a right was first inherent in himself."

rae", or "tame by nature" (ie. domestic animals), can be the subject of an absolute property, there can be no such property in animals "ferae naturae" while living—a proposition well established by the end of the 17th century[61]. Animals "domitae naturae" have been described as those animals which "once thoroughly domesticate, continue habitually with man, will not willingly leave him, and, if they do so accidentally, will probably return."[62] This class includes, inter alia, cattle, dogs and cats. If such an animal, generally regarded as tame and rarely seen wandering at large, should stray from its "owner" and become lost, it was established, again largely in the 17th century, that the "owner" does not lose the property in it[63].

Animals "ferae naturae" (or wild by nature) are not the object of property until killed or caught. There appears to be no authority for the existence of an absolute property or ownership in such beasts or birds as, from time to time, have wandered in and out of this category. At one time dogs were labelled "ferae naturae" and consequently were not distrainable for rent[64]; while Blackstone, in considering animals "of a wild and untameable disposition", wrote that

> "so long as they remain in possession, every man has a right to enjoy without disturbance, but, if once they escape from his custody or he voluntarily abandon the use of them, they return to the common stock, and any man else has an equal right to seize and enjoy them afterwards."[65]

This statement in the Commentaries points toward the presence of a form of property or qualified-ownership in wild animals.[66] Nevertheless, such beasts or birds can have an economic or social value. They may be a source of food, clothing or fuel; they may constitute a social adornment or status symbol, such as deer in a park; or they may be suitable subject-matter for sporting rights. Property law has therefore arrived at a compromise situation between the inapplicability of an absolute property on the one hand, and an economic or social value on the other. This concession takes the form of a "special property", otherwise known as a "qualified property". At its simplest, this notion can be demonstrated by the property of a person in deer in a park, hares or rabbits in a warren or even fish in a pond, subject to a "qualification" that the property will cease if at any time the animals regain their "natural liberty" and cannot be said to possess an "animus revertendi".[67]

[61] See another seminal case in this field, *Sutton* v. *Moody* (1697–1698), 1 Ld. Raym. 250 at 250–251.

[62] John Thrupp "On the Domestication of Certain Animals in England between the Seventh and Eleventh Centuries", translated Ethn. Soc.N.S. iv.164 cited in Glanville Williams "Liability for Animals" (C.U.P., 1939) p.26; and see Williams, ibid., pp.27–30 on the wide meaning of the term 'avers', including cattle, poultry, peacocks, ducks, turkeys etc.

[63] See *Ireland* v. *Higgins* (1588) Cro.E1.125, Owen 93; *Chambers* v. *Warkhouse* (1692) 3 Lev. 336; *Vincent* v. *Lesney* (1625) Cro.Car. 18; *Mason* v. *Keeling* (1700) 12 Mod. 332.

[64] Co.Litt. 47a.

[65] 2 B1.Com.14; and see also 390–394 and 4 B1.Com. 235. See also Henry de Bracton, supra note 50, ii. pp. 41–43.

[66] Co.Litt. 145b.

[67] 2 B1.Com.392.

The interrelation of property and prerogative, and the eventual confusion which flowed from the compounding of these concepts, was demonstrated in the Case of Swans (1592).[68] Swans were subject to a relatively early "game law" which prevented their possession by any who failed to come within a property qualification. A statute of 1483 (22 Edw.IV c.6) enacted that a person not having freehold lands to the value of five marks a year [in pre-decimal terms about sixty six shillings and eight pence] was prohibited from keeping "any mark or game of swans", on pain of forfeiture, half to the Crown and half to the qualified litigant. However, the Case of Swans added something more lasting to the history and development of the English game laws in that it witnessed one of the earliest judicial discussions on the nature of property and prerogative in wild animals. The ratio of the case would appear to be that no person can have absolute ownership of animals ferae naturae, although the Crown was entitled by virtue of its prerogative to swans (presumably white only) swimming in a "common river", having regained their liberty. The Court of Common Pleas found that all white swans, not being marked according to law (i.e. through grant or prescriptive right), and having gained their "natural liberty" swimming in an open and common river, may be seised to the use of the Crown by its prerogative. The basis of this decision was that "a swan is a royal fowl" which, in certain circumstances, may be considered an estray. This exercise of prerogative power by the Crown or its agents in seising swans not in private waters was nevertheless subject to the absence of a personal property in a subject. Thus the Crown's claim to property via prerogative could be defeated by the subject demonstrating "ownership" by a swan-mark or by establishing that possession had not been lost. The Crown was in fact relying on a situation analogous to "bona vacantia", or property in ownerless chattels, and an interpretation of "natural liberty" was made with this in mind. It also seems, from a reading of the case, that tame swans would not be adjudged to have regained their "natural liberty", whether marked or unmarked.[69] The property acquired in tame swans "per industriam" would consequently render the stealing of them felonious (ie. larcenable).[70]

The decision in the Case of Swans has seemingly presented few problems in the history of succeeding "prerogative property" cases in constitutional law. Its major significance lies in its constitutional implications in the wider field of property in wild animals and, with a more general context in mind, the court seemingly gave its opinions "obiter dicta" accordingly. The case is often cited as being a leading authority for the proposition of law that "wild animals are not the subject of ownership." However, the case appears to be authority for no such rule of law. Once the court, in the case of swans, had determined that

[68] 7 Co.Rep. 15b in the Court of Common Pleas; 77 E.R.435; and see the comments of Lord Chancellor Westbury on this case in *Blades* v. *Higgs* (1865) 1 HLC 631 at 638.

[69] 7 Co.Rep.17b.

[70] Ibid.18a.; and see Richard Burn, "The Justice of the Peace and Parish Officer" (2nd edition, London, 1756), i, 490.

> "all white swans not marked . . . having gained their natural liberty . . . in an open and common river, might be seised to the King's use by his prerogative . . . as a swan is royal fowl",[71]

any consideration of property rights in "anything which is ferae naturae" and not royal fowl or "game" would not have contributed to the ratio decidendi of the case. The fact that the court, at some length, discussed various rights of property, absolute, qualified and possessory, in wild animals implies that they may have been leaning away from a conclusion which Sir William Blackstone arrived at a century and a half later. This conclusion was that "the sole right of taking and destroying game belongs exclusively to the King"[72], appropriately appearing in a chapter entitled "Of Title by Prerogative and Foreiture".

On the wider question of property in animals, it was resolved (seemingly obiter) in the Case of Swans that "in some of them which are ferae naturae, a man hath jus proprietatis, a right of property; and in some of them a man hath jus privilegii, a right of privilege"; also, that "there are three manner of rights in property, scil. property absolute, property qualified, and property possessory." It was further resolved that an absolute property could only exist in animals domiae naturae. In relation to ferae naturae, a qualified or possessory property could be acquired in two ways: by industry (i.e. by taming and retaining); and "ratione impotentiae et loci". The example given for the latter mechanism was "as if a man hath young shovelers or goshawks, or the like, which are ferae naturae, and they build in my land, I have possessory property in them, for if one takes them when they cannot fly, the owner of the soil shall an action of trespass". Importantly, the court also identified another means of acquiring a qualified property in wild animals—this was ratione privilegii, as when

> "a man hath savage beasts ratione privilegii, as by reason of a park, warren, etc. he hath not any property in the deer, or conies, or pheasants, or partridges . . . but they do belong to him ratione privilegii, for his game and pleasure, so long as they remain in the privileged place."[73]

It therefore appears, from the Case of Swans, that property qualified or propter privilegium can be acquired in animals ferae naturae through the industry (ie. by the art of reclaiming and taming animals, or confining them to a particular area such as a warren or close); by reason of the impotence of the young or, presumably, injured animals on the land; or through "ratione privilegii". In all of these instances, it would follow that the qualified property or privilege would cease on the animals regaining their liberty, or "natural liberty" as Coke terms the state, unless they could be said to have the "animus revertendi". It is conceivable that these means of acquisition are not indepenent of each other. Property per industriam could be coupled with a privilege ratione soil (by reason of the soil). As applied to "game", while the animals and birds continued to

[71] 7 Co.Rep.16a.
[72] Bl. Comm. ii, 417.
[73] 7 Rep.17b.

exist "in a wild state", both forms of property right would involve the exclusive right to catch, kill and appropriate such creatures. Similarly, when young birds or rabbits become capable of flight or escape from the burrow or warren, a property ratione impotentiae would cease and, depending upon particular facts (eg. location and habit), a right to kill ratione soli or ratione privilegii might arise in the same or a neighbouring "landowner".

Bracton, in his "De Legibus et Consuetinibus Angliae", written around the middle of the 13th century, distinguished the acquisition of 'dominion' of wild beasts "by taking possession of things that are owned by no one" from the acts of fishing, hunting and capture, which are seen as elements in 'the taking of possession'. Bracton wrote (as translated by Samuel E. Thorne) that the

> "taking of possession also includes fishing, hunting and capture. It is not pursuit alone that makes a thing mine, for though I have wounded a wild beast so severely that it may be captured, it nevertheless is not mine unless I capture it; rather it will belong to the one who next takes it, for much may happen to prevent my capture of it; and so if a wild boar falls into a net you have set, and though he is caught fast in it I have extricated him and carried him off; he will be mine if comes into my power, unless custom rules to the contrary or privilege."[74]

The use of the term "privilege" by Bracton at this juncture would presumably have referred to the royal claim to the great and royal fish, wrecks, estrays and the like,[75] and additionally to liberties granted to a subject by the Crown involving rights or privileges over wild creatures. However, as Bracton later submits, he

> "who claims such liberty must show that it belongs to him, for if he has no special warrant he cannot maintain himself therein, even though he puts forward the prescription of long use, for here great length of time does not . . . run against the king . . . nor need he prove that (such things) belong to him since it must be clear to everyone that they belong to the Crown by the jus gentium."

Bracton's analysis of acquisition by jus naturale, jus gentium or "according to civil law" need not concern us in the present discussion, for, by the time of writing (circa. 1250–1268) the three Roman law conceptions had merged sufficiently in this field of early property law to form the radex of its common law development.

The distinction between the acquisition of an absolute or qualified property and rights or privileges of taking or appropriating and killing wild animals may prove central to a legal understanding of the game laws during the seventeenth and subsequent centuries. The law on these matters had been relatively settled (apart from the rights of takers of game on the land of another) before the passing of the 1671 Game Act.[76] In the same way that the decision and arguments in

[74] Henry de Bracton, supra note 50, ii. pp. 42.

[75] Ibid.p.58.

[76] Y.B.2 Ric.3 15b and 16a (Strange and Charlton's Case); Y.B. 3 Hen.6 55b; and *Fines* v. *Spencer* (1572) 3 Dyer. 306b.

the Case of Swans, albeit often difficult to separate, developed from a discussion of prerogative in certain chattels or creatures into the question of property, absolute or qualified; subsequent progress in the development of this area of "personal property" law, through both case-law and statutory enactment, turned from the question of "prerogative property" to the rights correlative or even subordinate to it. There was, in other words, a continuous breaking down of concepts in more realistic notions, based in many cases upon empirical or factual observation. Bracton had hinted at such a distinction in his treatise, perhaps suggesting that dominion (or ownership) was itself the most extensive right allowed to a subject in dealing with property to the exclusion of others. It was to be recognised as a right in rem, itself to be broken down, from its absolute form, into rights of possession, use, enjoyment, alienation, destruction or encumbrance. Ownership is an indefinite right composed of definite or more specific subrights. For the civilians, such subrights were the "jus utendi, fruendi, et abutendi."[77]

Ownership is not unimportant in the development of the English game laws, but the difficulties of demonstrating the concept in terms other than possession, use and other rights requires the discussion to devolve readily upon the nature of rights of taking, killing or disposal by sale in animals ferae naturae and in 'more domestic" game. Bracton again recognised that this was the crucial enquiry in determining dominion and property. By virtue of the jus gentium, he maintained that property in wild beasts and undomesticate birds ought, in accordance with natural law "to be acquired by apprehension and capture or fowling, or by occupation and apprehension", subject to any rights of the Crown or their grantees.[78] The importance of the right of taking is here displayed together with the acceptance of limitations imposed upon it. Clearly, Bracton would have admitted that there could be no right to appropriate or kill the King's game in the royal forests, or in lands designated by grant or prescription as free warren, chase or free fishery and held as such by the subject, "free" of royal claim.

(5) BLACKSTONE'S THESIS REVISITED

In Blackstone's introductory chapter on the "Rights of Things", the idea of a royal game property merely in the nature of prerogative is seemingly overturned.

> "There are things", he stated, "in which a permanent property may subsist, not only as to temporary use, but also in the solid substance; and which yet should be

[77] John Cowell, "Institutiones Juris Anglicani" (Oxon, 1676 edition), see Glossary under "Ownership"; on the civilians see Sir William Holdsworth "History of English Law", vol.v. (2nd edition, Methuen, London 1937 (revised), second impression 1973) pp.4–25.

[78] Bracton, *supra* note 50, ii.pp.166–167; p.339 (on prerogatives relating to wreck, sturgeon and whale).

frequently found without a proprietor, had not the wisdom of the law provided a remedy to obviate this inconvenience. Such are forests and other waste grounds, which were omitted to be appropriated in the general distribution of lands; such also are wrecks, estrays, and that species of wild animals which the arbitrary constitutions of positive law have distinguished from the rest by the wellknown appellation of game. With regard to these and some others, as disturbances and quarrels would frequently arise among individuals, contending about the acquisition of this species of property by first occupancy, the law has therefore wisely cut up the root of dissension by vesting the things themselves in the Sovereign of the State: or else in his representatives appointed and authorised by him, being usually the lords of manor. And thus the legislature of England has universally promoted the grand ends of civil society, the peace and security of individuals, by steadily pursuing that wise and orderly maxim, of assigning to everything capable of ownership a legal and determinate owner."[79]

Blackstone further expounded his theory in a chapter entitled "Title to Things Personal by Occupancy", in which he considered methods of original acquisition of things found without owner. Of property "bona vacantia", he asserted that

"they for the most part belong to the king by virtue of his prerogative; except in some few instances, wherein the original and natural right of occupancy is still permitted to subsist"[80].

By some apparent contradiction with views expressed elsewhere, he included animals ferae naturae among the list of exceptions.

"With regard likewise to animals ferae naturae, all mankind had by the original grant of the Creator a right to pursue and take any fowl or insect of the air, any fish or inhabitant of the waters, and any beast or reptile of the field: and this natural right still continues in every individual, unless where it is restrained by the civil laws of the country."[81]

Blackstone considered that the basic propositions of natural law (or right) and of civil law[82] in relation to the general category of animals ferae naturae to be in uniformity:

"for when a man has once seised them they become while living his qualified property, or if dead, are absolutely his own: so that to steal them or otherwise invade this property, is, according to their respective values, sometimes a criminal offence, sometimes only a civil injury"[83].

Yet this natural right was subject to restrictions, in the same way that the Crown's prerogative of original acquisition might be subject to instances of

[79] Bl.Comm.ii, pp.14–15.

[80] Bl.Comm. ii, 401.

[81] Bl.Comm.ii, 403. Cf. Burn op.cit., 13th edition (1776) vol.ii 220–221.

[82] It is probable that Blackstone is employing the phrase "civil law" at this juncture in the Commentaries to refer to the "corpus juris civilis" (meaning in effect the law of a given State) and not as a term to be employed in contradistinction to "the criminal law".

[83] Bl.Comm. ii, 403; and see the "definitive" (if at times uncertain) decision in *Sutton* v. *Moody* (1698) 1 Ld. Raym. 250.

original occupancy by a subject. Thus, by a typically tortuous mode of reasoning, Blackstone came to regard the English game laws as a notable example of a set of limitations placed by the civil law upon the general property (i.e. in wild animals in their natural state). His views on first occupancy similarly indicate a theoretical tension. It seems, however, that the incorporation of such an evident tension was necessary for the rational extension of his 'royal game theory' into eighteenth century legal theory. For Blackstone, there were two forms of occupancy entitling the occupant to acquisition of property; firstly, and with particular reference to game, the occupier of land would have title to animals on his land by virtue of the land (ratione soli) or by virtue of some privileged position or grant from a superior granting body (ratione privilegii); secondly, there was the occupancy of a first finder. In both instances, it would have been at least theoretcially possible (even in the eighteenth century) to consider the Crown as "occupant". The Crown was thought to be the first occupant of land under the feudal system, and similarly the first occupant of property bona vacantia. The Crown was, additionally the fountain head of "positive municipal law", and capable of designating certain animals ferae naturae as eminently suitable for royal protection and supervision[84]. Blackstone utilised both forms of original occupancy to account for the first game laws of the state. The rights of the individual in relation to the taking of game were superseded by the royal prerogative, "whereby a right may accrue either to the Crown itself, or to such as claim under the title of the Crown, as by grant or by prescription"[85]. This prerogative extended to dominion over things apparently ownerless (bona vacantia), particularly in relation to an earlier period when real property, and therefore rights ratione soli, was subject to the "feudal system", whereby all persons (ultimately) held of the Crown. Consequently, Blackstone considered that the taking of game was made the "exclusive right of the prince, and such of his subjects to whom he has granted the same royal privilege"[86]. Animals not designated as game,

> "are still liable to be taken and appropriated by any of the king's subjects, upon their own territories; in the same manner as they might have taken even game itself, till these civil prohibitions were issued: there being in nature no distinction between one species of wild animals and another, between the right of acquiring property in a hare or a squirrel, in a partridge or a butterfly; but the difference, at present made, arises merely from positive municipal law."[87]

[84] See, for example, Henry Finch, "A Description of the Common Laws of England . . . Compared with the Prerogatives of the King" (London, 1759), pp. 55–56, 123, 145–147. (Based on Finch's "Law", the first edition of which appeared in 1613 and which was arguably the most highly regared elementary work to be placed in the hands of law students until the appearance of Blackstone's "Commentaries".) In a similar vein, see Giles Jacob, "The Student's Companion: or the Reason of the Laws of England" (London, 1725), under "King's Prerogative" (pp.109–111).

[85] Bl. Comm. ii, 408.

[86] Bl. Comm. ii 403.

[87] Bl. Comm. ii. ibid.

The theory reached its zenith in chapter 27, "Of Title by Prerogative and Forfeiture" in which Blackstone declared his judgment on the theoretical "property and prerogative in game" relationship:

> "There still remains another species of prerogative property, founded upon a very different principle from any that have been mentioned before; the property of such animals ferae naturae, as are known by the denomination of game, with the right of pursuing, taking, and destroying them: which is vested in the king alone, and from him derived to such of his subjects as have received the grants of a chase, a park, a free warren, or free fishery."[88]

The natural right to all animals ferae naturae as "first occupant" was thus clearly restricted by "positive laws", enacted, he felt, for the supposed benefit of the community. These restrictions could be threefold in nature: they might pertain to the place in which the right could be exercised; they might regulate the species of types of animals subject (from time to time) to this right, or made exceptions to it; they might determine the persons allowed or forbidden to exercise any such right. Thus far, it is clear that Blackstone considered the royal game prerogative as a form of positive law, overriding any natural or customary right.

In England, Blackstone remarked, "hunting has ever been esteemed a most princely diversion and exercise", and before the Norman Conquest every freeholder had full liberty of sporting on his own territories, provided he abstained from the king's forest (Laws of Cnut, c.77). But, upon the Norman Conquest,

> "a new doctrine took place; and the right of pursuing and taking all beasts of chase or venary, and such other animals as were accounted game, was then held to belong to the king, and to such only as were authorised under him."

His right is both ratione soli and ratione privilegii. As lord paramount in feodal law, "he has a right of the universal soil, to enter thereon, and to chase and take such creatures at his pleasure." His right to game ratione privilegii rests upon "another maxim of common law", that of bona vacantia, whereby things having no owner, "belong to the king by his prerogative." While

> "the former reason was held to vest in the king a right to pursue and take them anywhere; the latter was supposed to give the king, and such as he should authorise, a sole and exclusive right."[89]

Through the forest laws of the Norman Kings, the "right, newly vested in the Crown, was exerted with the utmost rigour."[90] However, as the King had created particular hunting reserves for his own exclusive diversion, he would favour his subjects with the grant of parks or chases, or, alternatively, licences to create the same in their own lands. Similarly, with regard to "all inferior species of game, called beasts and fowls of warren, the liberty of taking or killing

[88] Bl. Comm. ii, 410–411; and see Edinburgh Review Vol.54 (1831) pp.286–289.
[89] Bl. Comm. ii, 415.
[90] Bl. Comm. ii. ibid.

them is another franchise or royalty, derived likewise from the Crown, and called free warren." For Blackstone argued, with some conviction, that the Crown would be unable to grant to its subjects the exclusive right of taking and pursuing game unless that right was inherent in the Crown itself ab initio, although at once compelled to admit that, at the time of writing (c.1770), "this exclusive prerogative of the King is little known or considered." This was particularly evident in the attitude of the qualified eighteenth century sportsman, allowed to sport on his own land, and, sometimes, over the lands of other persons; but, asserted Blackstone,

> "however well qualified he may vulgarly be esteemed, [no man] has a right to encroach on the royal prerogative by the killing of game, unless he can show a particular grant of free warren; or a prescription which presumes a grant; or some authority under an act of parliament."[91]

He observed that the Acts of 1603, 1609 and 1671 merely exempted certain persons from penalties for taking the royal game. They were not property qualifications to sport widely, because even those supposedly qualified

> "are not only liable to actions of trespass by the owners of the land; but also, if they kill game within the limits of any royal franchise, they are liable to the actions of such who may have the right of chase or free warren therein."[92]

In 1817, Edward Christian published a book on the game laws which contained a consistently argued refutation of Blackstone's theory that property in game was vested in the Crown. However, soon after Blackstone's death in 1780, Christian had introduced his argument into the editorial notes of the Commentaries.[93] The substance of this disputation remained constant throughout the twenty four years before publication of Christian's "Treatise on the Game Laws" (1817). Given few admitted exceptions, he argued convincingly that game had always been by the law of England the property of the occupier of the land upon which it was found or taken. Although he recognised the right of parliament to limit or even curtail this right for the national good, he fervently rejected the royal game prerogative thesis. However, Sir William Holdsworth has asserted that it is doubtful that the property in the occupier was applicable in all cases at the time of writing (c.1790):

> "There is authority that occupiers for limited interests were not in all cases entitled. . . but the thesis for which Christian lent support became law as a result of the 1831 Game Act, subject to any contract to the contrary between the landlord and the tenant."[94]

[91] Bl.Comm. ii, 417–418. Reference is here made to the Game Acts of 1603, 1609 and 1671, but no mention is made of the Act of 1389/90.

[92] Bl. Comm. ii, 418.

[93] Christian became editor of the Commentaries in 1793 (12th edition) and remained so until the 15th edition appeared in 1809. See Bl.Comm. Book II p.419 note 10 (12th edition) for Christian's first editorial comments on the Blackstonian thesis.

[94] H.E.L. vol. xiii. (Methuen, London, 1952, second impression 1976) pp. 489–490; 1 & 2 Wm. IV. c. 32.

In the sense that Christian's book is by and large an extension of his notes to the relevant passages in the Commentaries (particularly between pages 417 and 419 of Book II of the 12th edition, 1794), an examination of his theory in context will prove as equally valuable for present purposes as recourse to his later work. Christian challenges the general principles behind the doctrine of royal game. While admitting that game may be said to be "nullius in boniso", he maintained that the principle of bona vacantia related to the first finder or first occupant in fact and not in theory, arguing that "if all wild animals had belonged to the Crown, it would have been superfluous to have specified whales, sturgeons and swans [as royal fish and game]", noting that "these are the only animals which our law has conferred this honour upon."[95] The granting of franchises and liberties by the Crown for the purposes of exclusive sporting to grantees might have provided the learned editor with more problems than are evident in his critique. It is clearly a temptation to conclude that the Crown could only alienate property and rights already in existence and in some person or body. Consequently, the granting of an exclusive privilege might presume that the grantor had possessed that privilege prior to the grant. Irrespective of the fortitude of this part of the Blackstonian thesis, Christian laid seige from all sides. He admitted that it is true historically that our kings prior to the Carta de Foresta (1217)[96] claimed and exercised the prerogative of making forests wherever they pleased over the grounds of their subjects (and within the limits of these forests certain wild animals were preserved, by severe laws, for the recreation of the sovereign). It is equally true that "a district" thus bounded at the king's pleasure might have been granted by the king to any of his subjects who thereafter enjoyed the exclusive privilege either of a forest, chase, park or free warren, according to the extent of the jurisdiction and powers conferred by the royal grant[97]. However, beyond the boundaries of these privileged places, neither the king nor any of his grantees claimed a (prerogative) property in the game: for according to the Law of King Canute, "quilibet homo dignus venatione sua, in sylva, et in agris sibi propriis, et in dominio suo"—which law even Manwood declared was confirmed by many succeeding kings[98].

Blackstone had contended that "upon the Norman Conquest a new doctrine took place"[99] yet, Christian maintained, by the Carta de Foresta, all the new-made forests were disafforested and thrown open again; equally the Norman encroachments (which became known as purlieus) on the ancient Saxon forests were disafforested and landowners were henceforth allowed to enjoy their lands in as full a manner as before any encroachment. Furthermore, the forest law jurisdiction could still apply to others than the landowners. Hence the owner of

[95] See Christian's note 10 at p. 419 around here.

[96] See H.W.C. Davis "Stubbs' Select Charters" (Oxford, 1962 reprint of 9th edition, 1913) pp. 344–348.

[97] See also his Christian's note 17 (12th edition) at Bl. Comm. ii, 38.

[98] Christian, Bl. Comm. ii (12th edition) , 419, note (10) referring to John Manwood's "Forest Laws" supra.

[99] Bl.Comm. vol.ii, p.415.

a purlieu might hunt and kill game within the limits of the purlieu, observed Christian and, with the concurrence of the authorities of Lord Coke and Manwood, he confirmed it has been held that if deer come out of the forest into the purlieu, the purlieu-man may hunt and kill them provided he does it fairly and without forestalling[100]. Christian cited the Year Book 12 Henry VIII, fo.10, as authority for the proposition that

> "if a man drive a stag out of a forest and kill him, he shall gain no property in him, because he shall derive no advantage from his own wrongful act: yet if the stag comes of himself beyond the limits of the forest, then any one (if qualified) may kill and take him for they are animals ferae naturae, et nullius in bonis; and the maxim, as the judges declared, was capiat qui capere potest, ie. catch that catch can."[101]

Christian's decisive authority for his contention that "the king has no property in deer or other game, when they are out of forest" is a case[102] involving an action of trespass for entering the plaintiff's close. The defendant pleaded that the place in which the trespass was supposed to be committed was adjoining the king's forest, and that the plaintiff was bound to impale the said forest, and that for want of paling four deer escaped out of the forest into the plaintiff's land, and that he (the defendant) had entered by the command of the forester to drive the the deer back into the forest. The court held that this plea was not good; for though the plaintiff was in fault for not paling, yet it was not law for the forester or any person to drive the deer out of the ground, or to take them. The reason for this was that the king had no prerogative property in wild animals out of the bounds of the forest: which was a different situation to the case of tame cattle, where the property still remains in the owner though they are out of his ground, for which reason he may retake them wherever he finds them; but it is not so when the beasts are wild. Christian's main authority is certainly illustrative of a property in animals ferae naturae based upon occupancy rather than prerogative, but it should be admitted that there are a few of the "coney cases" which might be capable of a different interpretation.[103]

Not content with this singularly reasoned onslaught upon the Blackstonian "prerogative property" theory, Christian proceeded to debate the justification for the view that the so-called qualification statutes exempted from original penalties rather than permitted certain persons of rank to pursue and take game: ". . . no authority whatever can be found that any penalties were ever inflicted for killing game out of privileged grounds, except those which have been introduced by the modern game-laws, or the qualification acts."[104] Christian felt that

[100] 4 Inst. 303; see John Manwood, op.cit. (3rd edition) chp.xx, especially at 373–376.

[101] Bl. Comm. vol. ii, 419, note (10) by Christian (12th edition, 1794).

[102] Keilwey 30 (Action de Trespas, Mich. Term 12 Hen.7). The reports by Keilwey (of mainly K.B. and Common Pleas cases) cover the period 1496–1531.

[103] See in particular *Boulston* v. *Hardy* (1597) Cro. Eliz. 447; and consider the preamble to 11 Hen. 7 c.17.

[104] See E. Christian in support of this conclusion generally in his "A Treatise on the Game Laws" (London, 1817), pp.22–56.

the proper view had been expressed by Lord Coke in the Case of Monopolies (1602)[105] when he gave judgment that

> "it is true that none can make a park, chase, or warren, without the king's licence, for that is quodam modo to appropriate those creatures, which are ferae naturae et nullius in bonis, to himself, and to restrain them of their natural liberty, which he cannot do without the king's licence; but for hawking, hunting etc. which are matters of pastime, pleasure and recreation, there needs no licence, but every one may in his own land use them at his pleasure without any restraint to be made unless by parliament, as appears by the statutes of II Hen.VII.c.17; 23 Eliz.c.10;3 Jac.I.c.13."

As the final cannonade, Christian launched the Scottish case of *Livingstone* v. *Lord Breadalbane* (1791), maintaining that the decision in the case indicated that Scottish law on the matter

> "is precisely the same as the law of England; for neither a lord of a manor [i.e. a grantee from the Crown], or his gamekeeper can go into any part of the manor, which is not the lord's estate or waste, without being a trespasser like any other person."[106]

In this case the House of Lords decided that the lord of the manor had no right to monopolise the game over his waste or those common grounds not specifically protected by any statutes. The authority of "Balfour's Practice" was chiefly relied upon: viz. "It is leisum and permittit to all men to chais hairis, foxis and all uther wild beistis, beand without forrestis, warrenis, parkis, or wardis".[107]

(6) CONCLUSION

In the light of Christian's criticisms of Blackstone's theory and the previous refutation of Chester Kirby's "royal game prerogative" thesis, (albeit less extensive than the learned Commentator's view and largely unsubstantiated by "legal authority"), the student of the English game laws is directed towards the conclusion that the substance of the "Game Law System", as operating between 1671 and 1831, was constructed upon the existing substructures of franchises and liberties, along with common law (or customary) rights ratione soli, rather than upon the extensive Blackstonian royal game prerogative. Admittedly, the Crown was recognised as the grantor of such liberties and special privileges relating to game; it could grant liberties etc. of chase, park and warren out of a plenitude of power. This aspect of the prerogative continued to be demonstrated into the eighteenth century in the traditional role of the Crown as supreme licence and privilege granting authority in an age before extensive social regulation by the nineteenth century creation, the local authority, which

[105] 11 Co. Rep. 87b; 77 E.R. 1264.

[106] 2 Bl. Comm. (12th edition, 1794) 419, Christian's note (10).

[107] (1791) 3 Pat. 221 (H.L.); Sir James Balfour, "Practicks: or a System of the more ancient Law of Scotland" (Edinburgh, 1754), 542. This work was first published in 1754, although it was probably written c. 1574–1583.

assumed a licensing authority in matters of land use and game certification in the industrial revolution.

However, the game laws were not a "bastard slip"[108] of the forest laws. They can best be appreciated not in the context of a royal game prerogative but as a complementary and comparative system of game preservation which, by the late seventeenth century had usurped the role of forest organisation and the royal interest. The equation between forest and game laws can only be accurately represented in terms of game preservation and the provision of exclusive sport. Both systems produced different sets of regulations, but both systems had a similar (if not the same) object: to preserve the game for the exclusive sport of a social elite. Fears of total extirpation of game through the declining forest organisation resulted in the true game laws of the first decade of the seventeenth century and, following the Civil War period, the legislation of 1671, which further imposed property qualifications upon existing rights of sporting.

Indubitably, the Crown had created both the royal forests and the special sporting privileges granted to subjects under the names of chases, parks and free warren. Almost all the landed gentlemen of any consequence had, at one time, possessed such an exclusive privilege in his own lands, and, sometimes, over the lands of his neighbours. It is likely that the granting of small franchises were either caused or suggested by the King's general control over the forests; but, as the forest law decayed, the sporting rights of landowners ceased to be protected by these smaller franchises; and the landowners began to regard their rights as being "ratione soli" rather than rights ratione privilegii. Protection for rights incidental to ownership or occupation of the soil were, subject to a property qualification, protected by the game laws. In other cases, the common law right was only notional and applicable in supporting actions of trespass against those who sported upon land without licence of the owner or occupier. Statutes prevented persons of humble means from exercising their common law right to game on their own land, ostensibly in the interests of large scale game preservation and the provision of exclusive sporting for those considered to be social superiors. The 1831 Game Act removed any statutory restrictions upon the right to game "ratione soli", and expressly recognised such a right, subject only to game reservation by a landlord in the form of a covenant in a lease.

Accordingly, it is submitted that Blackstone's view of a "royal game prerogative" is insupportable in relation to any aspects of game outside of the forest organisation and the granting of franchises. There is no evidence to establish even its theoretical operation in the game law system of Blackstone's day—or even during the previous century. The very fact of operation of a complex and formerly-efficient forest organisation points to alternative propositions of law in areas unaffected by the forest law. As G.J. Turner argued in his "Select Pleas of the Forests",

[108] Bl. Com. iv. 409.

"the object of charters of warren would be inexplicable if the public had not the right of hunting on unenclosed lands outside forests, chases and warrens"[109].

Similarly, there is no reason to believe that the owners of land outside the forest, chase or warren, and not subject to free chases or free warrens over their own land, could not hunt the game thereon, unless prohibited by statutory enactment passed in the interests of game preservation or other emergent and incidental policy, such as that of disarming the bulk of the population.[110]

The Stuart kings attempted to counteract the rising influence of the gentry by reviving the royal grant of gamekeeperships, foresters and stewardships to its loyal servants, but by 1609 the important implications of the game statutes (and their local enforcement by the country gentry) had subsumed the exercise of prerogative in this field. So, in the final analysis, what is the possible meaning of the "saving provision" in the 1671 Game Act seemingly relating to aspects of prerogative in game? The Act provided that

"... neither this act nor anything therein contained shall extend to the taking away or abridging of any royalty or prerogative royal of His Majesty, nor to abridge, change or alter any part of the forest laws of this realm, but all and every such laws, rights, powers, royalties and prerogatives royal, shall remain and be in as full and ample force and virtue, as the same ought to have been in, if this act had not been made; anything herein contained to the contrary notwithstanding".

The train of legislative thought which continued from "prerogative royal" to the forest laws and "rights, powers, royalties" indicates that the prerogative in question was both pre-franchise and extra-forrestal. Consequently, the inclusion of prerogative could have referred merely to the power of the Crown to grant sporting franchises (and gain revenue thereby) and similar privileges to subjects. It is unlikely that an extensive royal game prerogative was envisaged at this time, after the delimitation of the royal powers by the Acts of the Long Parliament and the Restoration Settlement in 1660. The King may have had a "political right" to hunt anywhere at will, for who save the most powerful in the realm would refuse a monarch permission to hunt on his land; but a legal (or prerogative) right is unlikely to have been entertained by the drafters of the 1671 Act, keen sportsmen in themselves. The reference to the saving of the prerogative royal in this field did not refer to the game prerogative of Blackstone's conception; nor did it allude to a view that selected beasts of the chase were the prerogative property of the Crown by virtue of the doctrines of bona vacantia or occupancy. The Act of 1671 impliedly recognised rights in ratione soli in certain qualified persons; whereas prerogative claim, on the other hand, had been

[109] Publications of the Selden Society, vol. xiii (for 1899), London, 1901, cxxiii.

[110] P.B. Munsche in "Gentlemen and Poachers" (C.U.P. 1981) questions the evidence for such an underlying policy behind the game laws, whereas in practice "a man's gun was relatively safe" (p.82). Blackstone's suggestion that such a policy (among others) lay behind the game laws was controverted by Christian at Bl. Comm. ii (12th edition, 1794), 411 note (2), where he stated that "the modern practice of killing game with a gun has prevailed" and that "every one is at liberty to keep or carry a gun, if he does not use it for the destruction of game".

concerned primarily with rights in alieno solo or ratione privilegii, particularly in those instances where express or demonstrable royal grant or royal demesne lands were not invoked in support of the right or power alleged. When Blackstone wrote of a "new doctrine" introduced into English law and government by the Conqueror, it appears that he was alluding to a "royal game prerogative". Yet the only new doctrine in this field which took place under the Norman and Plantagenet kings was the concept and development of the forest organisation. Since the "forest-game equation" can only usefully be framed in terms of game preservation and exclusivity of sporting, the existence of a distinct forest system is in itself testimony to the absence of a general game prerogative, extending all over the realm and necessitating the appointment of royal gamekeepers and parkers in every shire.

6

An Irish Perspective on Protecting a Non-owning Spouse in the Home

PROFESSOR J. C. W. WYLIE

ONE OF THE most intractable problems to confront the legal system in recent decades is how far a spouse who has no legal title to the matrimonial home should have protection against dispositions by the legal owner (the other spouse) which may jeopardise the "non-owning" spouse's right of occupation. Although such a non-owning spouse has a well-recognised right to occupy the matrimonial home derived from his or her status as a spouse, that spouse's vulnerability was emphasised by the House of Lords in *National Provisional Bank Ltd* v. *Ainsworth*.[1] While it was recognised that the spouse might have protection against the other spouse personally, provided action was taken in time,[2] the law lords refused to countenance that a non-owning spouse had, merely on the basis of his or her status as spouse, any property interest[3] capable of binding a third party dealing with the owning spouse, such as a mortgagee. Of course it has since come to be recognised by the courts that a spouse who has no *legal* title to the home may, nevertheless, have obtained an *equitable* interest by way of, for example, a resulting or constructive trust.[4] However, such a spouse still has the burden of establishing entitlement to such an interest, which is not made easy by years of judicial fumbling in the formulation of the principles to be applied.[5] Even when that hurdle has been overcome, the spouse may still have

[1] [1965] AC 1175.

[2] E.g., an injunction might be obtained to restrain the owning spouse from disposing of the home without making alternative provision for the non-owning spouse: ibid, p1220 (per Lord Hodson) and p1223 (per Lord Upjohn); the Irish courts have also awarded such an injunction: see *Heavey* v. *Heavey* (1974) 111 ILTR 1.

[3] Not even a "mere equity" such as that attributed to a deserted wife in various Court of Appeal decisions during the 1950s (such as *Bendall* v. *McWhirter* [1952] 2 QB 466 and *Jess B. Woodcock & Sons Ltd* v. *Hobbs* [1955] 1 WLR 152), which were overruled by the *Ainsworth* decision.

[4] Confirmed, of course, by the House of Lords in cases like *Gissing* v. *Gissing* [1971] AC 886 and *Lloyds Bank plc* v. *Rosset* [1991] 1 AC 107. Note also the approach of the Court of Appeal in *Midland Bank plc* v. *Cooke* [1995] 4 All ER 562.

[5] See, e.g., the discussion in K. Gray, *Elements of Land Law* (2nd ed, London, Butterworths, 1993), ch 12; R. J. Smith, *Property Law* (3rd ed, London, Longman, 2000), ch 8. The Irish courts have also been somewhat uncertain in their approach to such issues: see J. Mee, "Trusts of the Family Home: The Irish Experience" [1993] Conv 359 and, more generally; J. Mee , *The Property Rights of Co- habitees* (Oxford, Hart Publishing,1999); also A. Lyall, *Land Law in Ireland* (Dublin, Oak Tree Press, 1994), ch 17; A. Shatter, *Family Law* (4th ed, Dublin, Butterworths 1997), ch 15.

to establish that a third party, like a mortgagee, is bound by the equitable interest.[6] Here too the courts have had difficulties, partly because the registration systems governing both unregistered[7] and registered land[8] were developed before such equitable rights came to be recognised and so the legislation appears to operate in a somewhat haphazard manner.[9]

The immediate legislative response in England and Wales to the *Ainsworth* decision, the Matrimonial Homes Act 1967, has been subject to a stream of crit-

[6] Another interesting recent development has been the English courts' protection of even an owning spouse, who has, e.g., joined in a mortgage of a jointly owned property, where there has been at play a vitiating factor such as misrepresentation or undue influence. The plethora of litigation since the House of Lords invoked the doctrine of constructive notice in *Barclays Bank plc* v. *O'Brien* [1994] 1 AC 180 (*cf. CIBC Mortgages plc* v. *Pitt* [1994] 1 AC 200) against a mortgagee has been disconcerting as the English courts have struggled to settle guidelines as to what steps mortgagees should take to protect themselves against this use of the doctrine. Note the Court of Appeal's attempt at a distillation in *Royal Bank of Scotland plc* v. *Etridge* (No 2) [1998] 4 All ER 705 and the House of Lords recent ruling that the burden of proof rests on the party alleging that the mortgagee had constructive notice, *Barclays Bank plc* v. *Boulter* (1999) 149 NLJ 1645; [1999] EGCS 121. For discussion of the theoretical difficulties with this line of authority, see [1994] Conv 140 (Thompson) and 421 (Harpum and Dixon); [1995] Conv 250 (Sparkes); (1995) 15 LS 35 (Battersby); [1996] Conv 35 (Howell). Note also that the Irish courts have cast doubts upon the "policy considerations" favouring "sympathy" for wives underpinning the *O'Brien* decision (*ibid*, p188, *per* Lord Browne-Wilkinson): see *Bank of Nova Scotia* v. *Hogan* [1997] 1 ILRM 407 at 414 (*per* Murphy J); also *R F* v. *M F* [1995] 2 ILRM 572. The Republic's Constitution would also seem to rule out such favoured treatment for wives: see p 155 *infra*. *Cf* the Scottish courts' rejection of the doctrine of constructive notice in this context: see *Mumford* v. *Bank of Scotland* [1996] 1 FLR 344.

[7] Such an equitable interest is not a registrable land charge under the Land Charges Act 1972 and its vulnerability under the doctrine of notice has been of concern ever since the much criticised decision in *Caunce* v. *Caunce* [1969] 1 WLR 286. Later cases have suggested that the burden of investigation under the doctrine of notice on third parties dealing with the legal owner is a high one: see, e.g., *Midland Bank Ltd* v. *Farmpride Hatcheries Ltd* [1981] 2 EGLR 147; *Kingsnorth Finance Ltd* v. *Tizard* [1986] 1 WLR 783. The Irish courts have tended to take a similar view: see *Northern Bank Ltd* v. *Henry* [1981] IR 1; *cf Ulster Bank Ltd* v. *Shanks* [1982] NI 143. Note that there is no equivalent in either part of Ireland of the Land Charges Registry, but unregistered land is subject to a Registry of Deeds system: see J. C. W. Wylie, *Irish Land Law* (3rd ed, Dublin, Butterworths, 1997), ch 22.

[8] In this case the issue has usually been whether the spouse could claim an overriding interest under s 70(1)(g) of the Land Registration Act 1925 (a "right" of a person in "actual occupation"): see leading House of Lords cases like *Williams & Glyn's Bank Ltd* v. *Boland* [1981] AC 487; *Abbey National Building Society* v. *Cann* [1991] 1 AC 56; *Lloyds Bank plc* v. *Rosset* [1991] 1 AC 107. A similar interest can be claimed in respect of registered land in Ireland: see the Republic's Registration of Title Act 1964, s 72(1)(j) (burden affecting registered land *without* registration); (1980) 15 Ir Jur (ns) 211. The same applies in NI: see Land Registration Act (NI) 1970, Schedule 5, Pt I, para 15; H Wallace, *Land Registry Practice in Northern Ireland* (2nd ed, Belfast, SLS Publications, 1987), pp 16–24.

[9] An obvious example is the overreachable/overriding interest dichotomy created in England and Wales by the Law of Property Act 1925 and Land Registration Act 1925 which was exposed by the House of Lords decision in *City of London Building Society* v. *Flegg* [1988] AC 54. A measure of the unsatisfactory state of the law in England and Wales, and of the difficulties of fashioning a satisfactory solution, can be gleaned from the several reports issued by the Law Commission which bear on the issues and illustrate how its thinking has fluctuated over recent decades: see, e.g., Law Com Nos 86 (1978), 115 (1982), 158 (1987), 175 (1988) and 188 (1989). See also the Law Commission's 1998 Consultation Document, *Land Registration for the Twenty-First Century* (Law Com No 254), especially II and IV–V.

icism over the years, but the essential form of the legislation survives,[10] with little likelihood of major change in the foreseeable future.[11] This makes the Irish approach to the problem all the more interesting, especially since the Republic's Parliament (the Oireachtas) took quite a different approach.[12] In order to appreciate the operation of the Irish legislation it may be useful to note some of the essential features of the English (and Welsh) legislation which have given rise to criticism.

MATRIMONIAL HOMES IN ENGLAND AND WALES

Ever since enactment of the original Matrimonial Homes Act 1967, the legislation has conferred on a "non-owning" spouse statutory rights of occupation, now known as "matrimonial home rights".[13] There has never been any question of conferring such rights on an "owning" spouse, in the sense of one holding legal title to the home, but, while the 1967 Act confined the rights to a "bare" spouse holding no interest whatsoever in the property,[14] the statutory rights were later extended to spouses holding an equitable interest only.[15] This remains the case,[16] so that both a spouse with no property interest in the home and a spouse with an equitable interest only can invoke the protection conferred by the legislation.[17] The essence of the statutory rights is that primarily they are personal rights as between the spouses, whereby the non-owning spouse has the right not to be evicted or excluded from, or the right to enter into and occupy, the home[18]

[10] The 1967 Act, together with modifications made by later legislation like the Matrimonial Proceedings and Property Act 1970 and Domestic Violence and Matrimonial Proceedings Act 1976, was consolidated in the Matrimonial Homes Act 1983, but the provisions are now reproduced with minor modifications in ss 30–41 of the Family Law Act 1996 (see also Schedule 4).

[11] See p 144 *infra*.

[12] The provisions in NI introduced by the Family Law (Miscellaneous Provisions) Order 1984 (see now the Family Homes and Domestic Violence (NI) Order 1998) were modelled on the English legislation: see p 155 *infra*.

[13] Family Law Act 1996, s 30 (2).

[14] See *Gurasz* v. *Gurasz* [1970] P 11 at 17 (*per* Lord Denning MR); also *Williams & Glyn's Bank Ltd* v. *Boland* [1979] Ch 312 at 328.

[15] Matrimonial Proceedings and Property Act 1970, s 38, replaced by s 1 of the Matrimonial Homes Act 1983. This was achieved by the somewhat indirect method of treating a spouse holding an equitable interest as if he or she had no entitlement to occupy the property by virtue of that interest (such entitlement was, of course, established by cases like *Bull* v. *Bull* [1955] 1 QB 234): see now 1996 Act, s 30(9).

[16] 1996 Act, s 30(1) and (9).

[17] This is especially significant in the case of the latter where the home is still unregistered land, since it entitles such a spouse to register a land charge under the Land Charges Act which he or she would not be entitled to do otherwise, because the kind of equitable interest under discussion does not come within the classes of charge registrable. It also facilitates protection by a spouse who is unsure as to whether he or she holds an equitable interest.

[18] The legislation refers to a "dwelling-house" which is widely defined by s 63(1) of the 1996 Act so as to include parts of buildings (like flats and apartments) and caravans, house-boats and structures occupied as a dwelling.

subject to the leave of the court.[19] The rights are confined to spouses and, subject to any court orders to the contrary, continue so long as the marriage does.[20] Notwithstanding the personal nature of the statutory rights, the major objective of the legislation from the beginning was to reverse the *Ainsworth* decision and to protect non-owning spouses against dispositions by owning spouses to third parties such as mortgagees. It is how this was achieved that has given rise to the criticism of the scheme.

It is provided that a non-owning spouse's matrimonial home rights are a charge on the owning spouse's estate or interest[21] and that charge has priority as if it were an equitable interest,[22] but protection against a third party is achieved only by registration.[23] Where the home is unregistered land, the charge may be registered as a Class F land charge under the Land Charges Act 1972.[24] Such a land charge is void as against a "purchaser"[25] unless it is registered before the completion of the purchase.[26] Where the home is registered land, the charge does not constitute as overriding interest[27] despite any actual occupation by the non-owning spouse.[28] Instead, in order to obtain protection, registration should be effected by registering a notice under the Land Registration Act 1925.[29] Any dispositions by the registered owning spouse take effect subject to the non-owning spouse's right protected by the notice.[30] On the other hand, a failure to register a notice will mean that a transferee for valuable consideration,[31] when his estate is registered, will take free of the non-owning spouse's rights.[32]

[19] 1996 Act, s 30(2). See the description of the rights given by Megarry J in *Wroth* v. *Tyler* [1974] Ch 30 at 46. The court has wide discretionary powers to make occupation orders: see ss 33–41 of the 1996 Act.

[20] 1996 Act, s 30(8).

[21] 1996 Act, s 31(2).

[22] 1996 Act, s 31(3).

[23] See *Harman* v. *Glencross* [1986] Fam 81 at 94 (*per* Balcombe LJ); also *Perez-Adamson* v. *Perez-Rivas* [1987] Fam 89. If a spouse is entitled to a statutory charge in respect of more than one dwelling-house only one charge can be registered at any one time: see 1996 Act, Sched 4, para 2.

[24] 1972 Act, s 2(1) and (7).

[25] Which means any person (including a mortgagee or lessee) who, for valuable consideration, takes any interest in or charge on the land: 1972 Act, ss 4(8) and 17(1). Cf the discussion of the meaning of "purchaser" in the context of s 4(6) by the House of Lords in *Midland Bank Trust Co Ltd* v. *Green* [1981] AC 513.

[26] 1972 Act, s 4 (8).

[27] I.e., the non-owning spouse given a statutory charge conferring priority as if it were an equitable interest cannot claim to hold a right of a person in actual occupation under s 70(1)(g) of the Land Registration Act 1927: see fn 8 *supra*. Note that registration may be effected by a spouse not in occupation: see *Watts* v. *Waller* [1973] QB 153.

[28] 1996 Act, s 31(10) (b).

[29] 1996 Act, s 31(10) (a). There is no need to produce the land certificate, as would normally be required for registration of a notice: see Matrimonial Homes and Property Act 1981, s 4(1) (adding a new subs (5) to s 64 of the Land Registration Act 1925). The non-owning spouse cannot lodge a caution: 1996 Act, s 31 (11).

[30] Land Registration Act 1925, s 52.

[31] Note the definitions of "purchaser" and "valuable consideration" in s 3 (xxi) and (xxxi) of the 1925 Act, which are at variance with the concept of a "purchaser" under the Land Charges Act 1972: see fn 25 *supra*.

[32] 1925 Act, ss 20(1), 23(1) and 59(6).

The above outline of the statutory regime may suggest that it was a reasonable response to the *Ainsworth* decision, but it has become clear that there are major problems, some of which have been avoided by the Irish legislation. The criticisms which have been levelled over the years range from attacks on the underlying policy to queries about the technical operation of the statutory provisions. The following is a brief summary of the main points.

Policy compromises

The matrimonial homes legislation in England and Wales has never been satisfactory because at its heart lies a compromise of underlying policies. On the one hand, it was clearly designed to effect a major social policy concerned with protecting a vital component of family life, the home.[33] On the other hand, the framers of the legislation were clearly concerned about the danger of upsetting traditional conveyancing practice. Mindful, no doubt, that the home is the most valuable asset held by most people in our society and that most people will engage in several dealings with such property over a lifetime, there was a worry about creating difficulties for third parties likely to acquire interests in the home, like mortgagees. This tension between what might be called the "family" and "conveyancing" aspects of the problem being addressed led to the fundamental principle enshrined in the legislation of conferring rights, but requiring them to be registered in order to secure protection. The trouble is that this compromise has turned out to involve major objections from both the family and conveyancing aspects.

Limited protection

The underlying social policy of the legislation is weakened because the protection conferred is limited and sometimes illusory. A spouse's protection is dependent upon his or her taking positive steps to register the charge conferred by the legislation. As has often been pointed out this requires that the spouse be aware of his or her rights and of the need for registration, an awareness that is likely to be lacking in most cases. Furthermore, even if there is that awareness, many spouses will be reluctant to take action which might, at best, be misconstrued by the other spouse and, at worst, be regarded as a "hostile act."[34] Encouraging a non-owning spouse in a settled relationship with the owning spouse to take such action hardly seems conducive to a continuing harmonious relationship and has been described as an "unsuitable mechanism for protection of interests of a

[33] Arguably the limitation of protection to spouses portrays an outdated attitude to family needs in modern times.

[34] See further p 149 *infra*.

family character."[35] A further point is, of course, that the question of registration is much more likely to arise only when the marriage is in difficulties and the non-owning spouse seeks legal advice. By that time it will often be too late to obtain protection by registration, because the owning spouse will have already engaged in a disposition to a third party.[36]

Considerations such as these led one of the most vociferous critics of the legislation, Megarry J, as he then was, to draw attention to a curious paradox in the statutory scheme.[37] The usual expectation in respect of charges required to be registered in order to protect rights under them against third parties is that they will, indeed, be registered in most cases. In his view no such expectation existed in respect of matrimonial homes charges, so that the legislation "has been operating on a basis of the mass invalidation of the statutory charges for want of registration, with registration being effected only in cases of actual or impending disputes."[38] Indeed, from the practical point of view, it is doubtful if it could be otherwise because, given the huge number of matrimonial homes in existence, mass registration of such charges might well overwhelm the registries.[39]

It must also be pointed out that even where a non-owning spouse protects himself or herself by registration, this does not guarantee the right to stay in the home. That spouse will be particularly at risk if the owning spouse has become bankrupt, because it is one of the features of English law that priority tends to be given to the interests of creditors over the interests of the bankrupt's family.[40] Under the Insolvency Act 1986 the non-owning spouse's matrimonial home rights can be terminated only on an application to the bankruptcy court, but the court is given a wide discretion to make such order as it thinks "just and equitable."[41] Although the court is required to have regard to, *inter alia*, the needs and financial resources of the spouse and any children,[42] this is subject to the injunction that, in any application by the trustee in bankruptcy made after one year from the vesting of the bankrupt's estate in him, the court must "assume,

[35] See R. E. Megarry and H. R. W. Wade, *The Law of Real Property* (5th ed, London, Stevens, 1984), pp 443 and 812; *cf* (6th ed, 2000), p 1063.

[36] See the comments by the Court of Appeal in *Williams & Glyn's Bank Ltd* v. *Boland* [1979] Ch 312.

[37] See his analysis of the operation of the legislation in *Wroth* v. *Tyler* [1974] Ch 30. See further p 141 *infra*.

[38] *Ibid*, p 46.

[39] *Ibid*, p 64.

[40] See the discussion in *Re Citro (A Bankrupt)* [1991] Ch 142; also Palley, "Wives, Creditors and the Matrimonial Home" (1969) 20 NILQ 132; Hand, "Bankruptcy and the Family Home" [1983] Conv 219. *Cf Abbey National plc* v. *Moss* [1994] 26 HLR 249. Note that the non-owning spouse cannot acquire any matrimonial rights in the period between presentation of the petition for a bankruptcy order and the vesting of the bankrupt owning spouse's estate in the trustee in bankruptcy: 1986 Act, s 336 (1).

[41] 1986 Act, s 336 (4). The reference to "rights of occupation" is to be construed as referring to matrimonial home rights: see Family Law Act 1996, Sched 9 para 11.

[42] S 336 (4) (c) and (d).

unless the circumstances of the case are exceptional, that the interests of the bankrupt's creditors outweigh all other considerations."[43]

Quite apart from the risk that the owning spouse may become bankrupt, there is still no guarantee of protection for a non-owning spouse even where he or she has registered a charge before any disposition by the still solvent owning spouse. The purchaser, including a mortgagee, will obviously take subject to the non-owning spouse's matrimonial home rights protected by registration, but those rights are subject to the court's general discretion to make occupation orders.[44] This jurisdiction extends to "persons deriving title under" the owning spouse,[45] so that a purchaser or other person to whom that spouse has conveyed the home may seek an order varying or terminating the non-owning spouse's rights. As *Kaur* v. *Gill*[46] illustrated, it should not be assumed that the court will reject such an application. In that case, the majority of the Court of Appeal took the view that the blind purchaser's immediate need of accommodation outweighed the needs of the non-owning spouse.

Conveyancing problems

Criticism from the conveyancing standpoint has been particularly fierce, as the following passage from Megarry J's judgment in *Wroth* v. *Tyler*[47] illustrates:

> ". . . the Act[48] has put into the hands of all spouses with statutory rights of occupation a weapon of great power and flexibility. Registration is a relatively simple, speedy and secret process, as compared with the necessarily more complex, protracted and less private process of selling a house and carrying through the contract to completion. As this case illustrates, Parliament has made it possible for the protected spouse to go far towards having his or her way as to not moving from the matrimonial home, at the expense of the other spouse and innocent purchasers. No doubt, too, the protected spouse, may, by registering the statutory charge, and particularly by registering at an inconvenient moment, require the owning spouse to buy off the charge. In some cases this may be very proper; in others it may be less so; but the power to do it is a unilateral power, free from any restraints. Of course, the owning spouse always has the possibility of redress by means of an application to the court. . .; but problems of time and costs will often make it prudent to bow to even the most unreasonable demands. The Act thus offers a financial temptation to the protected spouse which may impair marital relations. In the case of multiple matrimonial homes, there are possibilities of the protected spouse frustrating each attempted sale by a timely change of registration. Nor is easy to see why, for instance, if the husband leaves a friend in occupation of matrimonial home A as licensee, moving with his wife's full assent to matrimonial

[43] S 336 (5).
[44] Family Law Act 1996, ss 33–41.
[45] 1996 Act, s 34.
[46] [1988] 3 WLR 39.
[47] [1974] Ch 30 at 46.
[48] He was, of course, referring to the original Matrimonial Homes Act 1967.

home B, it is reasonable for the protection of the wife that she should have a charge under the Act on A which at any time she can protect by registration, making it impossible for her husband to sell A without incurring expense and delay."[49]

As that case itself illustrated, particular problems are caused to the owning spouse who has, for example, entered into a contract to sell the house, but then finds that, following a subsequent dispute with the non-owning spouse, the latter registers a charge. As happened in that case, if he cannot persuade the non-owning spouse to agree to cancellation of the registration,[50] he may face an award of substantial damages[51] for breach of contract.[52] It is little consolation in such cases that the courts will not uphold registration which is not designed to protect matrimonial home rights.[53] The solicitor acting for the vendor faces a particular dilemma, especially where unregistered land is concerned.[54] Arguably a search should be made prior to furnishing the draft contract for sale in order to determine whether a Class F land charge has been registered.[55] This, however, runs counter to recognised practice with respect to such searches[56] and involves the solicitor looking into the delicate personal relations between his client and his or her spouse.[57] For the same reason the purchaser's solicitor will be naturally reluctant to obtain, prior to the contract, a statutory release of

[49] See also *Watts* v. *Waller* [1973] QB 153. *Cf* the views of the Law Commission in Law Com No 86, paras 2.74–90. For discussion of the conveyancing problems raised by these cases, see D. G. Barnsley, "Conveying the Matrimonial Home—Some problems Facing Solicitors and Their Clients" (1974) 27 CLP 76; D. Hayton, "The Femme Fatale in Conveyancing practice" (1974) 38 Conv (NS) 110.

[50] The purchaser's solicitor must make sure that the proper procedure for cancellation is used, otherwise he runs the risk of a negligence claim: see *Holmes* v. *H Kennard & Son* (1984) 49 P & CR 202. See also the Family Law Act 1996, Sched 4, para 5 (2).

[51] *Wroth* v. *Tyler* was, of course, one of the cases where the judiciary demonstrated a reluctance to apply the notorious rule in *Bain* v. *Fothergill*, abolished later by s 3 of the Law of Property (Miscellaneous Provisions) Act 1989. The irony of the *Wroth* case was that the effect of the award of damages in that case was to bankrupt the family: see Megarry J, *op cit*, p 62.

[52] There is an implied term in a contract for the sale of a dwelling-house with vacant possession that the vendor will procure cancellation of any registered Class F land charge or registered land notice protecting a non-owning spouse: see Family Law Act 1996, Sched 4, para 3. The effect of this in the case of *post*-contract registration is to impose a term in the contract retrospectively: see *Barnsley's Conveyancing Law and Practice* (4th ed by M. Thompson, London, Butterworths, 1996), pp 165–6. *Cf* the position in NI: see p 156 *infra*.

[53] See *Barnett* v. *Hassett* [1981] 1 WLR 1385.

[54] If, as is the wise practice in the case of registered land, he obtains an office copy of the entries in the register of title prior to drawing up the contract, this will reveal any notice already registered.

[55] A fortiori if the purchaser's solicitor raises a pre-contract inquiry on the matter: see fn 59 *infra*.

[56] See Barnsley, *op cit*, pp 208–9. Note also Law of Property Act 1969, s 24 (removing the need for searches by the purchaser) and the comments of Millett J in *Rignall Developments Ltd* v. *Halil* [1988] Ch 190 at 201.

[57] However the query has been raised as to whether a failure at least to raise the matter with the client would open the solicitor to a negligence claim if the client later suffers loss because of registration of a charge: see Barnsley, *op cit*, p 166, fn 1. Arguably there is a different level of culpability where a charge has already been registered prior to the contract and where it is only registered after the contract has been entered into. The former is a fact which could easily be discovered by a search, whereas the latter may never occur and, in the nature of things, will not occur in the vast majority of cases.

rights from the non-owning spouse[58] or to insist that this spouse should join in the contract.[59] The fact is that his problem tends to be ignored in practice, perhaps based upon the view that the risk is small because of what Megarry J referred to as mass-invalidation of charges through non-registration.[60]

Reform proposals

The unsatisfactory nature of the statutory scheme operating in England and Wales has from time to time led to proposals for reform. Indeed, in 1978 the Law Commission recommended a statutory scheme of co-ownership for spouses other than legal co-owners, whereby they would be deemed to be *beneficial* joint tenants of the matrimonial home.[61] Although a Private Member's Bill was introduced aimed at implementing these proposals,[62] it failed for lack of parliamentary time. A major criticism that was made of the proposal was that any spouse not on the legal title still had to protect his or her statutory beneficial interest by registration.[63] Although the Commission revived the scheme in 1982[64] and a version appeared in a Bill introduced in 1985,[65] this was never enacted. Subsequently the Commission abandoned the principle that protection should depend on registration,[66] but conceded that its scheme of imposing a statutory co-ownership in equity still left the spouse not on the legal title vulnerable to overreaching by a disposition by two trustees.[67] In the event no progress has been made on such proposals and eventually the Commission proposed[68] re-enactment of the original 1967 scheme, as later modified, which was done in the Family Law Act 1996.[69] This has led some to suggest that what is needed is the imposition of statutory co-ownership of the *legal* title along the lines of the "homestead" legislation operating in other parts of the common law world.[70] This is the appropriate point to turn to the Irish approach to these matters.

[58] See Family Law Act 1996, Sched 4, para 5.

[59] Yet arguably the vendor's solicitor's position is already rendered difficult by the standard inquiry (now included in the Property Information Form which is part of the Law Society's National Conveyancing Protocol documentation) designed to deal with hidden beneficial interests (the *Boland* problem): see Barnsley, *op cit*, p 191. Note the various suggestions made by Hayton (fn 49 *supra*), few of which have been adopted in practice.

[60] See p 140 *supra*.

[61] Law Com No 86.

[62] By one of the law lords, Lord Simon of Glaisdale.

[63] See Megarry and Wade, *op cit*, p 443.

[64] Law Com No 115.

[65] Land Registration and Law of Property Bill 1985: see HL Deb, vol 460 (1984–5), col 1270 *et seq*.

[66] Law Com No 175 (1988). *Cf* the NI Law Reform Advisory Committee's Discussion Paper No 5, *Matrimonial Property* (1999)

[67] See *City of London Building Society* v. *Flegg* [1988] AC 54. See, however, the scheme for protecting beneficial owners in actual occupation from overreaching unless consent is given contained in Law Com No 188 (1989).

[68] Law Com No 207 (1992).

[69] See p 137 *supra*.

[70] See Gray, *op cit*, pp 164 and 604–7.

FAMILY HOMES IN THE REPUBLIC OF IRELAND

Following the enactment of the Matrimonial Homes Act 1967 in England and Wales, much discussion took place in the Republic of Ireland about the vulnerability, in particular, of married women where, as was very common, the legal title to the home was vested solely in the husband. In 1972 the Report of the Commission on the Status of Women drew attention to the problem and urged the enactment of legislation to protect non-owning wives.[71] The result was the enactment of the Family Home Protection Act 1976,[72] one of the most controversial pieces of legislation to have been introduced in the Republic.[73] It is proposed first to summarise the Act's main features,[74] then to discuss how the courts have interpreted it and, finally, by way of further comparison with the English legislation, to consider some conveyancing aspects.

Consent to alienation

The framers of the 1976 Act were determined to avoid what was perceived to be major weaknesses in the English legislation, in particular the need for the non-owning spouse to be aware of his or her rights and of the need to protect them against third parties by registration. Instead the central provision is to require the owning spouse, the holder of the legal title, to obtain the prior consent of the other spouse (whether or not that spouse holds any equitable interest)[75] to any "alienation" of the "family home."[76] This is encapsulated in section 3(1) of the Act, which reads:

[71] Pp 174–6.

[72] See the discussion in the Irish Parliament on the Bill, Dáil Debates, vol 291, col 54 *et seq*.

[73] See the discussion in Lyall's and Shatter's books fn 5 *supra;* also in W. Duncan and P. Scully, *Marriage Breakdown in Ireland* (Dublin, Butterworths, 1990), ch 12; P. Coughlan, *Property Law* (Dublin, Gill & MacMillan1995), ch 19; J. Farrell, *Irish Law of Specific Performance* (Dublin, Butterworths, 1994), ch 7. For the conveyancing aspects see J. C. W. Wylie, *Irish Conveyancing Law* (2nd ed, Dublin, Butterworths, 1996), para 16.61 *et seq*. See also the detailed annotations to the Act in J. C. W. Wylie, *Irish Conveyancing Statutes* (Dublin, Butterworths, 1994), p 355 *et seq*.

[74] Note that some amendments have since been introduced: see pp 151 and 154 *infra*.

[75] Unlike the English legislation, the 1976 Act does not purport to confer on the non-owning spouse any interest he or she does not otherwise have: see *Guckian* v. *Brennan* [1981] IR 478; *Containercare (Ir) Ltd* v. *Wycherley* [1982] IR 143: *Murray* v. *Diamond* [1982] ILRM 113. Note, however, that a notice of the existence of the marriage can be registered in the Registry of Deeds or Land Registry, depending on whether the title to the home is unregistered or registered, under s 12 of the Act. This simply warns third parties of the need for consent to dispositions, but there is no obligation to register such a notice (but there is the incentive that no stamp duty or registration fees are payable: subs (3)) and no inference of non-existence of a marriage arises from a failure to register a notice (subs (2)). Note also s 14 of the 1976 Act which encourages spouses to put the family home in their joint names by again providing that no stamp duty or registration fees are payable on any transaction creating a joint tenancy. Furthermore, s 114 of the Finance act 1990 exempted from stamp duty any instrument transferring any property as between the spouses; see now Stamp Duties Consolidation Act 1999, s. 96.

[76] Defined as "primarily" (i.e., some commercial use does not necessarily exclude the need for consent to alienation) a dwelling in which a married couple ordinarily reside or the non-owning

> "Where a spouse, without the prior consent in writing of the other spouse, purports to convey any interest in the family home to any person except the other spouse, then, subject to subsections (2), (3)[77] and (8)[78] and section 4,[79] the purported conveyance shall be void."

Perhaps not surprisingly the Act has been subject to a plethora of litigation and it is interesting to note how the Irish courts have interpreted its provisions.

Purposive interpretation

Time and again the courts, in particular the highest court (the Supreme Court), have emphasised that the legislation is designed to protect in particular the wife[80] and dependent children and, in so doing, to further the State's constitutional duty to protect the family.[81] This approach was put most forcibly by Walsh J in *Bank of Ireland* v. *Purcell*[82] in the following terms:

> "The Family Protection Act, 1976, is a remedial social statute enacted to protect the interest of the non-owning spouse in the family home and to deal with and to seek to remedy the social problem which was created or could be created by the fact that the spouse who owned the family home could effectively put the other spouse out on the

spouse resides or used to reside before leaving: s 2 (1); see *Somers* v. *W* [1979] IR 94; *H & L* v. *S* [1979] ILRM 105. However,the Act does not apply where the couple have not yet taken up occupation, even though this is intended and imminent (e.g., where they have just acquired the home but not yet moved in): see *National Irish Bank Ltd* v. *Graham* [1994] 2 ILRM 109 at 113–4 (*per* Finlay C J). For these purposes "dwelling" is defined as any building or part of a building (e.g., a flat or apartment), including any garden or other land "subsidiary and ancillary" to the dwelling and a structure not permanently attached to the ground and a vehicle or vessel, whether mobile or not, occupied as a "separate dwelling": see 1976 Act, s 2(2), as substituted by the Family Law Act 1995, s 54(1)(a). *Cf* a "dwelling-house" for the purposes of the English legislation: see fn 18 *supra*.

[77] Subs (2) excepts conveyances in pursuance of a pre-nuptial agreement and subs (3) contains very controversial provisions purporting to protect a "purchaser for full value": see p 151 *infra*.

[78] Subs (8) was added by s 54(1)(b)(ii) of the Family Law Act 1995: see p 151 *infra*.

[79] This confers a wide discretion on the court to dispense with consent in certain circumstances, e.g., where withholding consent is unreasonable given the needs and resources of the family (spouse *and* dependent children). There is also jurisdiction under ss 5–11 to make orders restraining conduct leading to loss of the family home, adjourning proceedings by mortgagees or lessors to recover possession or for a sale, modifying terms of mortgages or leases and restraining disposal of household chattels. See the discussion in Duncan and Scully, *op cit*, ch 11; Shatter, *op cit*, para 15.67 *et seq*.

[80] It must, however, be emphasised that, like the English legislation, the 1976 Act applies to spouses and so protects a non-owning husband: see *Allied Irish Banks plc* v. *O'Neill* [1995] 2 IR 473. Arguably it could not be otherwise because of the provisions in Article 40 of the Republic's 1937 Constitution: "All citizens shall, as human persons, be held equal before the law." See J. Kelly, *The Irish Constitution* (3rd ed by G. Hogan and G. White, Dublin, Butterworths, 1994), p 712 *et seq*. See also p 155 *infra*.

[81] Under Article 41 of the 1937 Constitution, the State "recognises the Family as the natural primary and fundamental unit group of Society"and "guarantees to protect the Family in its constitution and authority, as the necessary basis of social order and as indispensable to the welfare of the Nation and the State." For discussion of these provisions see Kelly, *op cit*, p 989 *et seq*: Shatter, *op cit*, ch 1.

[82] [1989] IR 327 at 333. See also the views expressed in *Somers* v. *W* [1979] IR 94; *Nestor* v. *Murphy* [1979] IR 326; *Hamilton* v. *Hamilton* [1982] IR 466.

street by selling it or mortgaging it. This was sometimes done out of vindictiveness and the other spouse had no redress. Most frequently the victimised spouse was the wife. She and her children could be left to fend for themselves so far as accommodation was concerned. It was to secure the position of such a spouse the Act of 1976 was passed. It made provision for barring a spouse from the family home even when that spouse is the owner of the home, if such spouse was misbehaving in a manner contemplated by the Act. In particular the Act of 1976 secured the position of the non-owning spouse by s 3 which provided that the owning spouse could not, without the prior consent in writing of the other spouse, purport to convey any interest in the family home to any person except that other spouse.

This statute is not be construed as if it were a conveyancing statute. As has been frequently pointed out remedial statutes are to be construed as widely and liberally as can fairly be done. . ."

This approach by the courts has manifested itself in a number of ways, such as the emphasis put on the wide-ranging scope of the statutory provisions and on the burden placed on third parties dealing with the owning spouse.

Scope of provisions

The courts have frequently drawn attention to the fact that the 1976 Act requires consent to a very wide-ranging category of *inter vivos* transactions.[83] The Act defines "conveyance" as a "mortgage, lease, assent, transfer, disclaimer, release and any other disposition of property", and as including an "enforceable agreement (whether conditional or unconditional) to make any such conveyance,"[84] and "interest" is defined as "any estate, right, title or other interest, legal or equitable."[85] Furthermore a "mortgage" includes "an equitable mortgage, a charge on registered land and a chattel mortgage."[86] Thus it requires the consent of the non-owning spouse to one of the most common property transactions in Ireland,[87] the

[83] It does not, however, apply to dispositions by will or a *donatio mortis causa* (s 1(1), presumably because the surviving spouse and children are already protected by the disinheritance provisions in Pt IX of the Republic's Succession Act 1965: see J Brady, *Succession Law in Ireland* (2nd ed, Dublin, Butterworths, 1995), ch 7. Curiously, its does apply to an assent by a personal representative, but it may be that this is designed to cover the common situation in Ireland where the personal representative is a member of the deceased family and has lived in the property with his spouse before or after the death of the relation and fails to take out representation until many years later, when a sale or other dealing is intended to be carried out: see Wylie, *op cit*, para 16.62 (d).

[84] S 1(1).

[85] *Ibid.*

[86] *Ibid.*

[87] See J. C. W. Wylie, *Irish Land Law* (3rd ed, Dublin, Butterworths,1997), ch 12; Lyall, *op cit*, ch 23; W Johnston, *Banking and Security Law in Ireland* (Dublin, Butterworths, 1998), ch 10. Note that there is no equivalent in Ireland of s 2 to the Law of Property (Miscellaneous Provisions) Act 1989 (contracts for the sale or other disposition of land remain governed by the Statute of Frauds (Ir) 1695: see J. C. W. Wylie, *Irish Conveyancing Law* (2nd ed, Dublin, Butterworths, 1996), ch 6; Farrell, *op cit*, ch 3), but in any event it is doubtful whether the Irish courts would follow Chadwick J's view of the underlying principles governing such mortgages given in *United Bank of Kuwait plc* v. *Sahib* [1995] 2 WLR 94, aff'd by CA [1997] Ch 107.

creation of an equitable mortgage by deposit of the title deeds, or land certificate in the case of registered land.[88] Furthermore, it was held in *Bank of Ireland* v. *Purcell*[89] that where, as again is very common, the deposit is to provide the lender with security for "further advances", each such advance is a conveyance within the Act and the security for it will be unenforceable unless the non-owning spouse gave prior consent to each advance.

On the face of it the Act should have no application to a conveyance of property by a company, which *ex hypothesi* cannot have a spouse and so cannot hold a family home. However, there have been indications that the Irish courts may be prepared to apply the Act in cases where a company has permitted an individual (e.g., a director or employee) to occupy property vested in it as that person's house. This is particularly likely to be the case where the company is a small private company controlled by the spouses, or one of them, so that the title to the property occupied by them is held in trust for them or is subject to some licence or other arrangement in their favour.[90] The courts are also likely to be alert to the danger that the legal title has been put by one of the spouses in the company's name as a device to get around the 1976 Act.[91] The result has been that the Law Society's Conveyancing Committee issued a Practice Note advising purchasers' solicitors to determine in particular cases whether the company's property might have been occupied as a family home.[92]

On the other hand, again taking into account the primary purpose of the Act, the courts have been concerned to confine its operation to protecting the non-owning spouse from conveyances by the owning spouse without consent.[93] Thus it was held not to apply where both spouses join in the transaction in question[94] nor, rather more controversially,[95] where a challenge to a conveyance without written consent was made by someone other than the spouse who should have given that consent.[96] Considerable controversy also arose over the issue whether it was possible to "sever" a conveyance without consent, so as to save some its force. This was an important practical point because in Ireland a

88 See *Bank of Ireland* v. *Hanrahan* Unrep (High Court, 10 February 1987); *Allied Irish Banks plc* v. *O'Neill* [1995] 2 IR 473.

89 [1989] IR 327.

90 See *Walpoles (Ir) Ltd* v. *Jay* Unrep (High Court, 20 November 1980); *LB* v. *HB* Unrep (High Court, 31 July 1980).

91 See *Carrigan* v. *Carrigan* Unrep (High Court, 12 May 1983).

92 "An Unmarried Company?" (1983) Gaz ILSI 217.

93 Note that the Act was held not to be retrospective in operation: see *Hamilton* v. *Hamilton* [1982] IR 466.

94 *Nestor* v. *Murphy* [1979] IR 326.

95 In view of the provision in s 3(1) rendering a conveyance without prior consent "void": see pp 145 *supra* and 150 *infra*.

96 *Barclays Bank Ireland* v. *Carroll* Unrep (High Court, 10 September 1986). The purchaser had subsequently mortgaged the family home sold to him without the written consent of the non-owning spouse and it was held that, following his bankruptcy, neither he nor the Official Assignee in bankruptcy could have the original conveyance to him declared void. The court had been informed that the non-owning spouse had agreed to the sale (albeit not in writing as required by the 1976 Act) and did not wish to challenge its validity.

property commonly mortgaged would be a farm comprising the farmhouse, the immediate ancillary land around it (yard, garden etc) and the remaining farm land. For some time doubts were expressed as to whether the property not comprising the family home[97] could be severed so as to save the lender's right to enforce its security at least against that part (i.e., the remaining farm land). Notwithstanding dicta in the Supreme Court casting doubt on such severance,[98] High Court judges have now taken the view that severance is consistent with the remedial purpose of the Act and the definition of "family home" and that it presents no "insuperable difficulty."[99]

A rather more serious limitation on the protection afforded a non-owning spouse by the 1976 Act is the Irish courts' ruling that, if the owning spouse gets into debt and the creditor obtains a judgment for recovery of the debt, which he then registers against the land as a judgment mortgage,[100] this action by the judgment creditor is not a "conveyance" by the owning spouse to which the non-owning spouse must give consent.[101] It is simply a "process of execution" and "not a disposition by a spouse purporting to convey an interest in the family home."[102] The judgment creditor/mortgagee can then seek a court order for sale of the family home in order to discharge the debt out of the proceeds.[103] It is true that in *First National Building Society* v. *Ring*,[104] where the family home was registered in the spouses' joint names and the judgment mortgagee sought an order for sale under the Partition Acts, Denham J refused to make any order, as the resultant disruption to family life was a "good reason to the contrary" within section 4 of the Partition Act 1868. However, the reasoning in this case is dubious[105] and too much reliance should not be put on it. In any event, the juris-

[97] See p 144 *supra*.

[98] See *Hamilton* v. *Hamilton* [1982] IR 466 at 490 (*per* Costello J, dissenting from the majority decision on the issue before the Supreme Court, viz., whether the Act had retrospective operation: see fn 93 *supra*); his doubts were echoed by Blayney J in giving the judgment of the Court in *Bank of Ireland* v. *Smyth* [1995] 2 IR 459 at 471.

[99] *Allied Irish banks plc* v. *O'Neill* [1995] 2 IR 473, following *Bank of Ireland* v. *Slevin* [1995] 2 IRLM 454. *Cf TSB Bank plc* v. *Camfield* [1995] 1 WLR 430: *Dunbar Bank plc* v. *Nadeem* [1997] 2 All ER 253.

[100] Under the Judgment Mortgage (Ir) Act 1850: see J. C. W. Wylie, *Irish Land Law* (3rd ed, Dublin, Butterworths, 1997), para 13.163 *et seq*; W Johnston, *Banking and Security Law in Ireland* (Dublin, Butterworths, 1998), ch 10.

[101] It is arguable that in certain circumstances the owning spouse's actions in getting into the debt in question could be construed as conduct leading to loss of the family home in respect of which a court order under s 5 of the Act could be made: see *CP* v. *DP* [1983] ILRM 380; *S* v. *S* [1983] ILRM 387; Shatter, *op cit*, para 15.84 *et seq*.

[102] *Containercare (Ir) Ltd* v. *Wycherley* [1982] IR 143 at 149–50 (*per* Carroll J). See also *Murray* v. *Diamond* [1982] ILRM 113.

[103] *Ibid*, p154. See also *CP* v. *DP* [1983] ILRM 380 at 384 (*per* Finlay J); *Bank of Ireland* v. *Purcell* [1989] IR 327 at 334 (*per* Walsh J).

[104] [1992] 1 IR 375.

[105] E.g., the judgment creditor had only a charge and not a mortgage because of the provisions of the Republic's Registration of Title Act 1964, so that it could not invoke the Partition Acts (see also, as regards NI, *Northern Bank Ltd* v. *Beattie* [1982] NIJB at 23 (*per* Murray J) and Wallace "Mortgagees and Possession" (1986) 37 NILQ 336 at 353–6, but this was corrected by Art. 48 of the Property (NI) Order 1997; Art 48 is not without its difficulties: see the Consultation Paper issued in

diction under the Partition Acts cannot be invoked where no co-ownership exists, i.e., where the non-owning spouse does not even have an equitable interest in the family home.[106] On the other hand, if the owning spouse becomes bankrupt, section 61(5) of the Republic's Bankruptcy Act 1988 gives the court jurisdiction "to order postponement of the sale of the family home having regard to the interests of the creditors and of the spouse and dependants of the bankrupt as well as to all the circumstances of the case." It remains to be seen how the Irish courts will interpret this jurisdiction and, in particular, whether they will be less willing to favour the creditors than the English courts.[107] There are strong arguments in favour of the view that the creditors would not be given greater weight. One reason is that the express weighting in favour of the creditor's interests in the English legislation does not appear in the Irish legislation. Another is that the Irish courts have already shown a distinct willingness, wherever statutory discretion exists, to exercise it in the light of the protection of the family enshrined in the Constitution and bolstered by the Family Home Protection Act.[108]

Conveyancing implications

Notwithstanding the Family Home Protection Act's broad social policy and family law purposes, it must be recognised that these are effected by interfering in the most drastic fashion with the conveyancing process, and in the most common of transactions, i.e., those relating to peoples' homes. Despite warnings to the legal profession,[109] it was slow to appreciate fully the implications for conveyancing practice and the changes needed to take account of its provisions.[110] It was not until the Irish courts, in particular the Supreme Court in some very

July 1999 by the N I Office of Law Reform, *Orders Charging Land and the Innocent Spouse)* and it is questionable on the authorities relating to the Partition Acts whether the court has the discretion to refuse any order, i.e., it should order either a partition or a sale. See the discussion in J Mee, "Partition and Sale of the Family Home" (1993) 15 DULJ 78. *Cf* cases where one spouse invokes the Partition Acts directly against the other spouse in order to try to force a sale, where the Irish courts have frequently invoked the Family Home Protection Act and the constitutional protection of the family as a "good reason" to refuse an order for sale: see *O'D* v. *O'D* Unrep (High Court, 18 November 1983); *AL* v. *JL* Unrep (High Court, 27 February 1984).

[106] See Shatter, *op cit*, pp 830–2. The *Report of the Joint Oireachtas Committee on Marriage Breakdown* (March 1985) (p 66) recommended that " legislative action should be taken immediately in order to prevent the spirit of the [1976] Act being defeated whereby judgment mortgages can be used to enforce the sale of the family home without the consent of either or both spouses."

[107] See p 140 *supra*.

[108] See fn 105 *supra*. See also M. Sanfey and B. Holohan, *Bankruptcy Law and Practice in Ireland* (Dublin, Round Hall Press, 1991), ch 9.

[109] See, e.g., the 1st edition of J. C. W. Wylie, *Irish Conveyancing Law* (Oxford, Professional Books, 1978), para 6.31 *et seq*.

[110] This slow reaction was recognised by both the Law Society (see (1981) Gaz ILSI 151) and the Law Reform Commission (see *Report on Land Law and Conveyancing Law: (1) General Proposals* (LRC 30–1989), para 39 et seq). See also p 151 *infra*.

important cases decided in the late 1970s and early 1980s,[111] hammered home the dire consequences of failing to take the 1976 Act into account in conveyancing transactions, that the proper procedures were put in place to deal with it. The following is a summary of the main points.

The first crucial point is that, on the face of it, section 3(1) of the Act imposes a draconian sanction on any disposition of a family home without the prior consent of the non-owning spouse. It is declared to be "void", not "voidable"[112]. The courts have never really resolved clearly whether this should be given its usual meaning, i.e., that the transaction is "of no effect" whatsoever,[113] which, of course, would normally vitiate subsequent transactions dependent on it. Cases holding that a mortgage obtained without the requisite consent deprives the lender of any interest suggest that this is indeed the effect of the Act,[114] yet other decisions cast doubt on this interpretation, for example, where it has been held that a mortgage without consent cannot be challenged by a party other than the non-consenting spouse.[115] As time passed this matter became a pressing one because it raised the issue of the validity of subsequent transactions executed on the assumption that the first one carried out after the 1976 Act came into force, to which prior consent in writing[116] should have been obtained, had, indeed, been valid. If that initial transaction was void, did this render all subsequent transactions void, on the well-recognised principle, *nemo dat quod non habet*? The position was not entirely clear from the wording of the Act dealing with the position of purchasers for value,[117] but it has been argued that subsequent purchasers did get good title provided they could claim to have no notice of the invalidity of the previous transaction.[118] The situation was exacerbated by the fact that, as pointed out earlier, solicitors were slow to react to the passing of the 1976 Act and checks on early sales would often not have been as rig-

[111] *Somers* v. *W* [1979] IR 94; *Nestor* v. *Murphy* [1979] IR 326; *Hamilton* v. *Hamilton* [1982] IR 466.

[112] See p 145 *supra*.

[113] For dicta suggesting support for this view see *Hamilton* v. *Hamilton* [1982] IR 466 at 485–6 (*per* Henchy J); *Bank of Ireland* v. *Purcell* [1989] IR 327 at 334) (*per* Walsh J). It was also the view of the Law Reform Commission, *op cit*, para 41 (see fn 118 *infra*). And see J. Farrell, *Irish Law of Specific Performance* (Dublin, Butterworths, 1994), para 7.18.

[114] *Bank of Ireland* v. *Purcell op cit*; *Bank of Ireland* v. *Smyth* [1995] 2 IR 459; *Allied Irish Banks plc* v. *Finnegan* [1996] 1 ILRM 401.

[115] *Barclays Bank Ireland* v. *Carroll* Unrep (High Court, 10 September 1986): see fn 96 *supra*.

[116] The need for "prior" consent rules out retrospective validation by execution of a subsequent consent. Of course, in due time if a purchaser under a void conveyance, and his successor, remain in possession, unchallenged title may be acquired under the doctrine of adverse possession.

[117] The key is s 3(3)(b) of the 1976 Act (see p 152 *infra*), which was not a model of clear drafting: see Lyall, fn 118 *infra*.

[118] See A. Lyall, "The Family Home Protection Act, 1976 and Conveyances other than by Spouses" (1984) 6 DULJ 158 and *Land Law in Ireland* (Dublin, Oak Tree Press, 1994), pp 470–5. See also *Walpoles (Ir) Ltd* v. *Jay* Unrep (High Court, 20 November 1984). On the other hand, the Law Reform Commission regarded the notion of a void conveyance as "completely foreign to the basic doctrines of the law of property": *op cit*, para 41.

orous as has now become common practice.[119] In the end, following a recommendation of the Law Reform Commission that subsequent unchallenged conveyances should be deemed valid,[120] an amendment to section 3 of the 1976 Act was introduced by the Family Law Act 1995.[121] This adds a new subsection (8) to section 3 of the 1976 Act[122] and introduces important changes from the conveyancing point of view. One is that it declares that a conveyance "shall be deemed not to be void and never to have been void" unless declared void by a court or, if void, the parties to it so state in writing within six years from its date.[123] It is further provided that proceedings to have a conveyance declared void cannot be instituted after six years from the date of the conveyance.[124] These provisions provide considerable relief to Irish conveyancers.

The second vital point about section 3(1) of the 1976 Act was that the sanction of "voidness" was made expressly subject to exceptions, initially those set out in subsections (2) and (3).[125] It is worth quoting the provisions of subsection (3) in full, for they are the key to understanding the conveyancing implications of the 1976 Act:

> "(3) No conveyance shall be void by reason only of subsection (1)—
> (a) if it is made to a purchaser for full value;[126]

119 E.g. often statutory declarations as to the status of the parties would not have been obtained: see p 151 *infra*. The Law Society's Conveyancing Committee issued the pragmatic advice to the profession that solicitors should rely on consents endorsed on deeds without seeking further evidence as to the position of spouses: (1981) Gaz ILSI 115. It was also held in *Guckian* v. *Brennan* [1981] IR 478 that this problem did not arise in subsequent purchases of registered land because the purchaser could rely upon the "conclusiveness" of the vendor's title conferred by s 31 of the Republic's Registration of Title Act 1964. However, it has been pointed out that it is difficult to square this decision, however convenient from the conveyancer's point of view, with other provisions of the 1964 Act, in particular s 59 (1) which states that nothing in the 1964 Act affects any enactment "by which the alienation . . . of any land is prohibited or in any way restricted." See J. Mee, "The Family Home Protection Act and Registered Land: a Reassessment of *Guckian* v. *Brennan*" (1997) 2 (4) CPLJ 58.

120 Fns 113 and 118 *supra*.

121 S 54 (1)(b)(ii).

122 See p 145 *supra*.

123 Subs (8)(b). Any such statement must be registered, as appropriate, in the Land Registry or Registry of Deeds within the six year period: subs (8)(c).

124 Sub (8)(a)(i), but this does not apply where the spouse who should have consented has remained in occupation, i.e., purchasers are protected by the six year rule where the family home is sold and the spouse has vacated the property in the usual way, but not, e.g., lenders taking mortgages or charges on a home still occupied by the borrower's spouse: subs (8)(a)(ii). Note also that the six year rule does not deprive the non-owning spouse of other remedies, e.g., against the owning spouse: subs (8)(a)(iii). Any proceedings to challenge a conveyance must be entered as a *lis pendens* in the Judgments Office: subs (8)(d).

125 And the provisions in s 4 enabling the court to dispense with consent in cases of "unreasonable" withholding or to give it on behalf of a spouse subject to mental incapacity or whose whereabouts are unknown. It was pointed out in the 1st edition of J. C. W. Wylie, *Irish Conveyancing Law* (Oxford, Professional Books, 1978), para 6.45, at a time when the age of majority was still twenty-one, that this did not cover minor spouses; confirmed by *Lloyd* v. *Sullivan* Unrep (High Court, 6 March 1981). As a result s 10 of the Family Law Act 1981 was enacted, declaring that consent under the 1976 Act "shall not be invalid by reason only that the spouse is under age."

126 This rather odd concept is defined in subs (5) as meaning "such value as amounts or approximates to the value of that for which it is given." It clearly rules out nominal consideration or, indeed, any consideration less than the market value in the case of a purchase; presumably a

(b) if it is made by a person other than the spouse making the purported conveyance referred to in subsection (1), to a purchaser for value,[127] or
(c) if its validity depends on the validity of a conveyance in respect of which any of the conditions mentioned in subsection (2)[128] or paragraph (a) or (b) is satisfied."

These provisions are, then, reinforced by subsection (4), which provides that in any proceedings concerning the validity of a conveyance the burden of proving validity rests on the person who alleges it, and by subsection (6), which defines a "purchaser" as a "grantee, lessee, assignee, mortgagee, chargeant or other person who in good faith acquires an estate or interest in property." The courts have from the beginning emphasised that the effect of these provisions is to incorporate the doctrine of constructive notice, as enshrined in section 3 of the Conveyancing Act 1882,[129] so that the issue in each case is whether the purchaser, or his solicitor,[130] has made the appropriate "inquiries and searches" in relation to compliance with the 1976 Act.[131] In response to this, and under the guidance of the Law Society's Conveyancing Committee, a standard procedure[132] has developed which involves initially: (1) the purchaser raising pre-contract[133] inquiries[134] or requisitions on title; (2) the vendor responding by furnishing statutory declarations verifying the responses to the inquiries and requisitions, and exhibiting, as necessary, supporting documentation, such as a copy of the marriage certificate. The form of the various statutory declarations covering different situations has been approved by the Law Society and lending

mortgagee lending less than the market value of the home which is the security for the loan, in accordance with standard lending practice, still gives full value for the security interest being advanced, but also for future advances (which may or may not be made) and for previous advances long since made and which were previously unsecured: see *Bank of Ireland* v. *Smyth* [1993] 2 IR 102 at 108 (*per* Geoghegan J) (the point was not raised on appeal to the Supreme Court [1995] 2 IR 459).

[127] See p 150. Especially fns 117 and 118 *supra*.

[128] I.e., a conveyance executed in pursuance of an ante-nuptial agreement.

[129] The equivalent of s 199 of the Law of Property Act 1925 and still in force in Ireland: see JCW Wylie, *Irish Land Law* (3rd ed, Dublin, Butterworths, 1997), para 3.069 *et seq*.

[130] This duty is heightened by s 3(7) of the 1976 Act, which states that s 3 of the 1882 Act is to apply in relation to s 3 of the 1976 Act as it the words "as such" in s 3(1)(ii) of the 1882 Act were omitted, i.e., notice gained by the purchaser's solicitor in whatever capacity (but it must still be in the same transaction) will be imputed to the purchaser, e.g., in acting also for the purchaser's lending institution: see *H & L* v. *S* [1979] ILRM 105 at 108 (*per* McWilliam J).

[131] *Somers* v. *W* [1979] IR 94; *Hamilton* v. *Hamilton* [1982] IR 466; *Allied Irish Banks plc* v. *Finnegan* [1996] 1 ILRM 401.

[132] For detailed discussion, see J. C. W. Wylie, *Irish Conveyancing Law* (2nd ed, Dublin, Butterworths, 1996), para 16.63 *et seq*.

[133] Since the 1976 Act defines "conveyance" as including an agreement for a conveyance (see p. 146 *supra* and *infra*) this is an occasion when a pre-contract inquiry should be made (using, if necessary, the standard requisitions on title form). Such pre-contract inquires have not been used, until recently, in Ireland as extensively as in England and Wales, see Wylie, *op cit*, ch 5.

[134] Rq 24 of the Irish Law Society Standard Requisitions on Title form requires the vendor's solicitor to confirm whether or not the property is a family home within the 1976 Act. For judicial approval of such procedure see *Somers* v. *W*, *op cit*, p 111 (*per* Henchy J).

institutions and it is unwise to use other forms.[135] If it transpires that consent is required under the 1976 Act, this must be put in writing "prior to the conveyance." The Law Society has again produced recommended forms and the usual practice is for one to be endorsed on the contract for sale and another on the deed of conveyance.[136] This remains the recommended practice despite the Irish courts' ruling that a consent endorsed on the contract is sufficient, since the conveyance simply puts this into effect.[137] This, however, leads to one of the most interesting developments in recent years.

It was pointed out above that section 3(4) of the 1976 Act clearly puts the burden of proof in any proceedings concerning the validity of a conveyance of a family home on the party arguing that the requisite consent has been given. In several cases involving mortgages, the Irish courts have emphasised that this involves the lender establishing that the consent given was an "informed" one.[138] In the leading case, *Bank of Ireland* v. *Smyth,*[139] the Supreme Court took the view that the doctrine of constructive notice, as it applied under the 1976 Act, put a duty on the lender to ensure that it obtained a valid mortgage or charge over the family home. It is not so much a duty of care owing to the non-owning spouse, rather it is a duty to itself as a lender intending to obtain security for its loan.[140] This involves taking steps to ensure that the non-owning spouse gave the consent in the full knowledge of what he or she was doing and was given the opportunity to obtain independent legal advice on the matter.[141] Unfortunately the Court did not spell out in detail what those steps should be and it remains to be seen whether the Irish courts will evolve principles similar to those developed by the English courts in relation to cases where it is alleged that a borrower joining in a mortgage has been subjected to some vitiating factor like undue influence.[142] What authority there is suggests that a lender is

[135] The purchaser's solicitor is entitled to take such declarations at face value and "good faith" does not require him to go behind them unless he has other knowledge to the contrary: *Reynolds* v. *Waters* [1982] ILRM 335; see also *Martin* v. *Irish Permanent Building Society* Unrep (High Court, 30 July 1980). This assumes that the declaration sets out the appropriate facts: see *Hegarty* v. *Morgan* Unrep (High Court, 15 March 1979). It will clearly not be acting in "good faith" if the purchaser's solicitor colludes with the vendor's solicitor in what is obviously a false statement or a "wild and inaccurate leap in the dark": *Somers* v. *W*, *op cit*, p 107 (*per* Henchy J).

[136] See Wylie, *op cit*, para 16.69. The point is again that "conveyance" is defined as including an enforceable agreement: 1976 Act, s 1(1).

[137] *Kyne* v. *Tiernan* Unrep (High Court, 15 July 1980). The danger is, of course, that the contract may not be preserved subsequently with the title deeds and so a consent endorsed on the deed is important for later proof of title. See the Law Society's Conveyancing Committee's views (1981) Gaz ILSI 79.

[138] Thereby raising the issue which has given rise to a flood of litigation in England following the House of Lords decision in *Barclays Bank plc* v. *O'Brien* [1994] 1 AC 180: see fn 6 *supra*.

[139] [1995] 2 IR 459. See the discussion of this decision by J. Mee, "The Family Home Protection Act: The Practical Implications of *Bank of Ireland* v. *Smyth*" (1996) 14 ILT (ns) 188 and 209; M. Sanfey, "Consenting Adults: The Implications of *Bank of Ireland* v. *Smyth*" (1996) 3 CLP 31.

[140] *Per* Blayney J, *op cit*, p 469.

[141] *Op cit*, pp 468–9.

[142] See e.g., *post O'Brien* (fn 138 *supra*), *Royal Bank of Scotland plc* v. *Etridge (No 2)* [1998] 4 All ER 705. But note the ruling of the House of Lords in *Barclays Bank* v. *Boulter* [1999] 4 All ER 513; that the burden of proof rests on the party alleging that the mortgagee had constructive notice.

entitled to assume that, if the spouses are being advised by their solicitor, he will explain the implications of the transaction to them, including the non-owning spouse.[143] If, on the other hand, the lender employs the same solicitor to act for it as well, as is very common in Ireland, its instructions should require the solicitor to give the appropriate advice and to confirm in due course that these instructions have been carried out.[144]

Finally, in the context of consents, it is worth noting that an important provision relating to "general" or "blanket" consents was enacted in the Family Law Act 1995. Prior to this, doubts had been raised as to whether such a consent was valid, e.g., a consent to a mortgage securing not just the current debt but also future advances contemplated under the terms of the loan. That Act added a new subsection (9) to section 3 of the 1976 Act validating, both retrospectively and prospectively, a "general consent in writing to any future conveyance of any interest" in the family home.[145] It must, however, be emphasised that this does not reduce in any way the need to ensure that any such consent is "informed"; indeed, given the consequences for the spouse executing such a consent, the likelihood is that the courts will be even more vigilant about this point.[146]

Conclusion

Notwithstanding the conveyancing complications created, and the legal profession's early difficulties in adjusting to its provisions, it is fair to say that the Family Home Protection Act 1976 has to a large extent achieved its overriding purpose of providing protection to non-owning spouses. There have been difficulties in interpreting some of its language, which has resulted in rather too much litigation for comfort, but the Irish courts have striven to make it work, taking a suitable purposive approach and, on occasion, adopting a pragmatic attitude. The Oireachtas has also, as we have seen, been prepared to enact some useful adjustments. In this sense it is fair to say that the Act has been more successful in achieving its purpose than the English matrimonial homes legislation, particularly in not requiring a non-owning spouse to take action, such as registering a charge, in order to secure protection.

Having said that, it is clear that, despite the legislative adjustments over the years, there remain fundamental weaknesses in the scheme. Far and away the most serious is the fact that no real protection is given to a spouse holding no interest (legal or equitable) in the home against the owning spouse getting into debt and his creditor registering a judgment mortgage against the home and then enforcing that through a court sale.[147] It was considerations such as these

[143] See *Doherty* v. *Doherty* [1991] 2 IR 458; *Bank of Nova Scotia* v. *Hogan* [1997] 1 ILRM 407.
[144] See *Allied Irish Banks plc* v. *Finnegan* [1996] 1 ILRM 401. See Wylie, *op cit*, para 16.69.
[145] S 54 (1)(b).
[146] See Wylie, *op cit*, para 16.69 (h).
[147] See p 148 *supra*.

which led the Government in 1983 to take up again a suggestion made in the report of the Commission on the Status of Women in 1972 which led to enactment of the 1976 Act. This was that a statutory scheme of joint ownership of the home by the spouses should be introduced.[148] However, no immediate steps were taken to implement this, but the Second Commission on the Status of Women revived the proposal.[149] The Matrimonial Home Bill 1993 was introduced to put into effect automatic joint ownership of all matrimonial homes but, on reference to the Supreme Court, it was ruled that it violated the Constitution.[150] The Court accepted that it was permissible for the Oireachtas to encourage joint ownership in furtherance of the State's duty under the Constitution to protect the family,[151] but what was offensive about the 1993 Bill was that it operated retrospectively. By interfering with decisions as to ownership of homes made by families in previous years, as part of the authority of the family which the State was supposed to protect, the Bill did not constitute a "reasonably proportionate intervention" with the rights of the family.[152] It seems clear that legislation which only operates prospectively would be regarded as constitutionally acceptable, but the Government appears to have abandoned the notion of joint ownership. The Family Home Protection Act will, therefore, remain the primary means of protecting the non-owning spouse for the foreseeable future.

MATRIMONIAL HOMES IN NORTHERN IRELAND

There is little to be said about the provisions relating to protection of a non-owning spouse now contained in the Family Homes and Domestic Violence (NI) Order 1998.[153] These are almost an exact replica of the provisions contained in the English Family Law Act 1996 which were discussed earlier.[154] In particular, as under the 1996 Act, the 1998 Order confers on a non-owning spouse (both one with no interest at all in the home and one with an equitable interest only)

[148] Report, p 176. The Government's proposals were announced in a statement by the Minister for Justice, *Irish Women—Agenda for Practical Action*, pp 274–5. The notion of "community of property" was also supported by the *Report of the Joint Oireachtas Committee on Marriage Breakdown* (1985). See Shatter, *op cit*, para 15.209 and P O'Connor, *Key Issues in Irish Family Law* (Dublin, Round Hall press, 1988), Pt 4. *Cf* the English proposals: see p 143 *ante*.

[149] Report (1993), pp 39–41.

[150] *Re Matrimonial Home Bill* [1994] 1 IR 305. See G. Hogan, "The Matrimonial Home Bill Reference" (1994) 16 DULJ 175; Slatter, *op cit*, pp 26–8 and 837–9.

[151] Under Art 41 (see fn 81 *supra*): note that judicial invocation of Art 41 to impose joint beneficial ownership (see Barr J in *L* v. *L* [1989] ILRM 528; but *cf EN* v. *RN* [1990] 1 IR 383) had already been ruled out by the Supreme Court: see the appeal in *L* v. *L* [1992] 2 IR 77 and in *EN* v. *RN* [1992] 2 IR 116. See also Kelly, *op cit*, pp 1010–2.

[152] *Per* Finlay CJ, *op cit*, pp 323–6.

[153] Largely re-enacting provisions in Pt II of the Family Law (Miscellaneous Provisions) (NI) Order 1984.

[154] P 137 *supra*.

matrimonial home rights,[155] which constitute a charge with the same priority as if it were an equitable interest,[156] but which, as under the English legislation, must be protected by registration[157] if it is to secure protection against third parties.[158] The scheme is, therefore, subject to the same limitations as the English system and it should be noted also that the Northern Ireland insolvency legislation has the same provision recognising the priority to be given to the interest of creditors.[159]

There is, however, one important difference from the English position which bears on the conveyancing problems illustrated by cases like *Wroth* v. *Tyler*.[160] Article 6(3) of the 1998 Order[161] provides that a matrimonial charge on a legal estate is void as against the purchaser[162] unless it is registered before the purchaser enters into a "contract to purchase that estate."[163] Thus vendors and purchasers in Northern Ireland are spared the problems which arise in England from a *post*-contract, but *pre*-completion, registration of a matrimonial charge.

CONCLUSION

This brief comparative study of how the jurisdictions on both sides of the Irish Sea have tackled the same basic problem has shown how quite different approaches can be taken. The markedly different approach taken by the Republic of Ireland was, no doubt, to a large extent influenced by social considerations, in particular the position of the family under its written Constitution. Of especial interest has been the attitude of the Republic's courts and their endeavour to make unsatisfactorily drafted legislation work according to the legislators' intentions. The ultimate conclusion must be, however, that, despite the courts' efforts, the scheme still contains many flaws, although probably not as many as the English legislation and, to a rather lesser extent, its Northern Ireland equivalent.

155 Art 4: see p 137 *supra*.

156 Art 5: see p 138 *supra*.

157 In the Land Registry, if the home is registered land and since there is no Land Charges Registry in NI, in the Registry of Deeds where it is unregistered land. See p 138 *supra*.

158 Art 6: see p 138 *supra*.

159 Insolvency (NI) Order 1989, Art 309 (5).

160 [1974] Ch 30: see p 141 *supra*.

161 A similar provision was to be found in Art 6(3) of the original 1984 Order (fn 153 *supra*).

162 Defined in Art 2(1) as "any person (including a lessee or mortgagee) who, for valuable consideration, takes an estate in land".

163 Para (a), or, in the case of the common transaction in Ireland of creating an equitable mortgage by deposit of the title deeds or land certificate (see p 147 *supra*), before the deposit: para (b).

7

Monied Might or Social Justice? Mortgage Repossessions and the Protection of Occupiers

M. P. THOMPSON

THERE CAN BE little doubt that one of the most serious problems affecting home ownership in recent times has been the high rate of possession actions brought by mortgagees to enforce their securities. In 1997, over 67,000 such actions were brought and, including cases where orders for possession were suspended, over 57,000 orders were made. While this does represent a 16% decrease in such actions from the previous year, and is considerably less than the high point of 1991, when over 145,000 actions were entered and over 103,000 orders were made[1], the figures provide eloquent testimony to the scale of the problem. As such actions have become more prevalent, a tension in the legal response to the issue has become apparent. From the point of view of commercial lenders, their principal interest is to be able, in the event of mortgage default, to realise their securities as easily as possible. From the point of view of the borrower, a principal concern will be to be able to retain the property as a home, a concern that will frequently be shared by other occupants of the property.

As the action for possession by a mortgagee has become more common, so the law has increasingly had to develop to deal with the particular issues which have arisen. As will be seen, the development of the law has been marked by desire to achieve a balance between protecting the legitimate commercial interests of the lenders on the one hand and to provide a degree of consumer protection[2] to borrowers and other interested persons on the other. The purpose of this essay is to trace the development of this area of law, to assess how this balance has been struck between the competing interests and to highlight areas where, because

[1] (1997) Judicial Statistics, Cm. 3950, table 4.6

[2] A greater harmonisation of the practice of different lenders and greater publicity to the approach taken in the event of mortgage default would, of itself, improve the lot of borrowers. See Lisa Whitehouse, "The Right to Possession: The Need for Substantive Reform" in P. Jackson and D.C. Wilde, *The Reform of Property Law* (Dartmouth, 1997) and "The Home-Owner: Citizen or Consumer", in S. Bright and J. Dewar, *Land Law: Themes and Perspectives* (Oxford University Press, 1998).

the development of the law has been incremental rather than comprehensive, problems still remain.

THE LEGAL BACKGROUND

In recent years, there has been a plethora of case law relating to possession actions brought by mortgagees and a substantial academic literature has developed. This activity may well have been difficult to foresee, given that, in 1966, the leading textbook, Megarry and Wade, a work noted for its comprehensiveness, managed to devote only a single paragraph to the topic.[3] This comment is not intended as a criticism. Quite simply, there was not a great deal to say. The basic position was stated in the oft-quoted dictum of Harman J. that:

> "the right of the mortgagee to possession in the absence of some contract has nothing to do with default on the part of the mortgagor. The mortgagee may go into possession before the ink is dry on the mortgage unless there is something in the mortgage, express or by implication, whereby he has contracted out of that right."[4]

At one time, it was thought that this absolutist position had been modified so that the court could, under its inherent jurisdiction, adjourn possession proceedings so that, "in proper cases the wind was tempered for the shorn lamb, time being given for payment and so forth."[5] The assertion of this inherent jurisdiction to adjourn possession proceedings failed to command assent, however, and in *Birmingham Citizens Permanent Building Society* v. *Caunt*[6], Russell J. held that the only relief available to a mortgagor, who had got into arrears with his payments and was faced with possession proceedings, was to allow him a short period to enable him to redeem the mortgage by repaying the whole sum borrowed. Clearly an unlikely prospect.

While the law afforded little or no protection to a mortgagor who had fallen behind with the mortgage repayments, the same was also true for other occupiers of the home. In *National Provincial Bank Ltd* v. *Ainsworth*[7], a husband left his wife. After having done so, and without telling her, he mortgaged the property to a bank, who, when the husband defaulted on his repayments, sought possession of the house. She argued that, as a deserted wife, she had an equity in the house which was binding upon the bank. This was rejected by the House of Lords. Overruling previous authority, where Lord Denning had sought to create and develop a new species of equitable right based upon the concept of

[3] Megarry and Wade, *The Law of Real Property (3rd ed)* (Stevens, 1966) p. 908.

[4] *Four-Maids Ltd* v. *Dudley Marshall (Properties) Ltd* [1957] Ch.317 at 320. See M. Haley (1997) 17 L.S. 483.

[5] *Redditch Benefit B.S.* v. *Roberts* [1940] Ch. 415 at 420 *per* Clauson L.J.

[6] [1962] Ch. 883. See R.E.M. (1962) 78 L.Q.R. 171.

[7] [1965] A.C. 1175.

the deserted wife's equity[8], it was held that there was no such right known to English law. Consequently, she had no interest which was capable of binding the bank which was, therefore, entitled to possession.

In reaching this conclusion, the House of Lords was acutely concerned with the conveyancing dimension of the case. Despite some sympathy being expressed for the position of Mrs Ainsworth,[9] their Lordships were most concerned with the consequences for banks and other lending institutions had her argument prevailed. Famously commenting that "it has been the policy of the law for over a hundred years to simplify and facilitate transactions in real property",[10] Lord Upjohn was strongly influenced by the repercussions of finding for the wife. Before it was safe for the bank to lend money by way of mortgage, it would need to address enquiries to her to ascertain what, if any, rights she had in the house. In his view, "[i]t does not seem to me that an enquiry as to the marital status of a woman in occupation of property is one that the law can reasonably require to be made. . . ."[11]

To an extent, one can sympathise with this perspective, in that a central feature of the right claimed by Mrs Ainsworth derived from the fact that she had been deserted by her husband and one can readily see why the law should shy away from requiring mortgagees to enquire as to the stability of a marriage.[12] Questions such as "do you think it likely that your husband is going to leave you?" are not the staple diet of commercial transactions. On the other hand, however, a wife who has been deserted will be in exclusive possession of the property and it might be thought to be reasonable to expect some enquiry to be made of a person who is living in a house which is being mortgaged by someone who, although the legal owner of the house, does not actually live there himself.[13] Be that as it may, the underlying ethos of the decision is clear: it is a reluctance to impose upon mortgagees the burden of having to make enquiries of occupiers of houses before granting the legal owner of it a mortgage. In so doing, the policy of making conveyancing efficiency paramount was furthered, albeit at the cost of refusing protection to occupiers of the property who, without being consulted by anyone, are at risk of losing their home.

This policy was continued in *Caunce* v. *Caunce*[14]. In what was to become a

[8] *Bendall* v. *McWhirter* [1952] 2 Q.B. 466; *Street* v. *Denham* [1954] 1 W.L.R. 624; *Jess B. Woodcock & Sons Ltd* [1955] 1 W.L.R. 152. The deserted wife's equity was later described by Baroness Summerskill as "the Denning Convention": H.L. Deb. Vol 275, Col. 21.

[9] See, e.g., [1965] A.C. 1175 at 1228 *per* Lord Cohen.

[10] *Ibid.* at p.1233.

[11] *Ibid* at p.1234. Contrast the view of Professor F.R. Crane (1964) Conv. (N.S.) 254, 464 at 467, "one cannot help but feel that the inconvenience to the banks must be a small matter when compared to their total loan transactions".

[12] Although contrast *Royal Bank of Scotland* v. *Etridge (No.2)* [1998] 4 All E.R. 705 717 *per* Stuart-Smith L.J.

[13] An obvious possibility is that the occupier is a tenant, in which case the mortgagee would be bound by the tenancy. See also the unfortunate decision in *Lloyds Bank plc* v. *Carrick* [1996] 4 All E.R. 630, criticised by M.P. Thompson [1996] Conv. 295.

[14] [1969] 1 W.L.R. 286.

familiar factual scenario, the legal title to the house was vested in the husband but his wife was an equitable co-owner of it. At all material times she lived in the house with her husband. Without telling her, he then mortgaged the house to a bank, who made no enquiries of her. When he defaulted on the mortgage, the bank sought possession. She defended the action arguing that the bank's failure to make enquiries of her meant that it had constructive notice of her rights and that, therefore she could not be evicted. This argument failed. Stamp J. held that, as she shared occupation of the home with her husband, her presence was not inconsistent with him being the sole legal and beneficial owner of the house. Consequently it was not reasonable to expect the bank to make enquiries of her. The result, which was described as a welcome one for conveyancers[15], was that, without ever having been consulted, she lost her home as a result of her husband's actions.

It should, therefore, occasion little surprise that discussion of the mortgagee's right to possession should, at that time, be brief. As the right was virtually unfettered, there was not a lot to say. Currently, however, this is not the case, the topic being one which is now a matter of keen discussion. Much has changed over the past thirty years. In part this is a result of legislative intervention. Arguably as important, however, is the changed judicial attitude to the subject, where the tendency has been for the courts to react more sympathetically to the position of occupiers of mortgaged property. Because, however, there has not been a systematic reform of the law, there are instances where it may still be the case that the law does not provide adequate protection for occupiers.

PARLIAMENTARY REFORM

The first move to improve the lot of house occupiers when faced with an action for possession by a mortgagee came as a response to the decision in *Ainsworth*. A Private Member's Bill, was introduced by Baroness Summerskill, with Government support, to give spouses, with no beneficial interest in the matrimonial home[16], the statutory right to occupy it.

This statutory right was to be binding upon a purchaser if, but only if, it was protected as either a land charge or on the register of title.

This, seemingly modest reform, which eventually came to be enacted as the Matrimonial Homes Act 1967[17], met with initial opposition. One of the objections was that, if a wife registered her right of occupation, this would prevent her husband from dealing with the property without her consent; something which, to some, was objectionable[18]. Others thought that there should be no

[15] Barnsley, *Conveyancing Law and Practice* (1st ed) (London, Butterworths, 1973) p.333.

[16] The statutory right was extended to equitable co-owners in 1970: Matrimonial Proceedings and Property Act 1970, s.38. See now Family Law Act 1996, s.33.

[17] See now Family Law Act 1996, s.31.

[18] See H.L. Deb. Vol. 275, Col. 645 *per* Lord Derwent.

automatic statutory right but that any such right would have to granted by a court.[19] More extreme still, there was almost outright opposition, thus Lord Hodson, a party to the decision in *Ainsworth*, spoke rather disparagingly of Lord Denning's attempts to secure a degree of protection for wives, saying that he:

> "moves us to tears every time he mentions a deserted wife, the poor woman he has been protecting in the Court of Appeal for years. Then he comes to this House and, in sepulchral terms, says 'When the House of Lords got the case of a bank, what did they do? They protected the bank.' "[20]

Despite the criticisms, a number of which were squarely based upon a desire not to do anything to cause difficulties to banks in realising their securities, the Act was passed. It had, however, what might be perceived as a fatal flaw. For the statutory right of occupation to be enforceable against a mortgagee, it had to be registered. The obvious problem is that, unless the wife is in receipt of legal advice, which normally will occur only when divorce proceedings are in train, she will never have heard of the statutory right of occupation or the need to protect it by registration. This, despite Lord Denning's somewhat tongue in cheek remark, that immediately the wedding is over a wife should register her statutory right of occupation, something he considered "ought to become a custom of the country"[21], the reality is the mortgage will have been created prior to the wife learning of her statutory rights and so find that the mortgagee has taken free from them. While well-meaning, the Act does little to protect a wife when her husband has mortgaged the house without consulting her.

THE ADMINISTRATION OF JUSTICE ACTS

The second area of Parliamentary intervention was designed to deal with the decision in *Birmingham Citizens Permanent Building Society* v. *Caunt* discussed earlier[22]. Acting on the recommendation of the Payne Committee[23], section 36 of the Administration of Justice Act 1970 was passed. This section was designed to give the courts a discretion to suspend, or postpone, possession orders when a mortgagor was in arrears, such discretion to be exercised when there appeared to be a realistic possibility of the mortgagor being able to pay off those arrears within a reasonable time, while also being able to service the mortgage. This reform was prompted in part by the realisation that, under the Rent Acts,

[19] *Ibid* Col, 633 *per* Lord Wilberforce.

[20] *Ibid*. Col. 650.

[21] *Ibid*, Col 45. Some years later, commenting on the need to register, he said of the Act that "it was of precious little use. at any rate when she was still living at home in peace with her husband. She would never have heard of a Class F land charge; and she would not have undertood it if she had": *Williams & Glyn's Bank Ltd* v. *Boland* [1979] Ch. 312 at 318.

[22] See n.6, *ante*.

[23] Enforcement of Judgment Debts (1969) Cmnd. 3909.

tenants enjoyed considerable security of tenure against their landlords, even when rent arrears had accrued and that it was anomalous that mortgagors should be in a worse position *vis a vis* the bank or building society when arrears had accrued than was the case for tenants with regard to their landlords in respect of rent arrears. The aim, therefore, was to afford a mortgagor some breathing space when arrears had occurred to put matters back on an even keel. In the course of a penetrating article on the subject, however, it was said that "however clear the goal of this promised land, the meanderings of the law towards it have made the wanderings of the children of Israel in the wilderness look positively direct."[24]

The first difficulty to be encountered with the section was potentially serious. In focusing on mortgage arrears, the section made reference to money due under the mortgage. The problem was that certain mortgages include default clauses, whereby if there is default in the monthly payments, the whole capital sum becomes instantly payable upon demand. In that situation, the question for the courts was whether the sum due meant the accumulated arrears or the whole sum borrowed. Unfortunately, in *Halifax Building Society* v. *Clark*[25], the judge opted for the latter alternative and concluded that there was no prospect of the whole sum borrowed being repaid within a reasonable time and, therefore, refused to postpone a possession order.

This judgment, which effectively restored the decision in *Caunt,* also stultified the intention of Parliament. After some touching, and unusual, statements of fallibility by leading politicians, such as Sir Michael Havers confessing to being "a complete novice about mortgages"[26], Parliament intervened again to seek to close the gap. This led to the enactment of section 8 of the Administration of Justice Act 1973, which was intended to reverse the decision in *Clark,* so that a court, when assessing whether a person could repay the sums due within a reasonable time, should disregard the effect of a default clause. Unfortunately, the drafting of the section was extremely obscure with the result that, for a time, it was not clear whether the section was applicable to endowment mortgages[27]. Happily, by a purposive interpretation of the section, part of which was effectively dismissed as being meaningless[28], the Court of Appeal extended the protection of the section to all types of mortgage normally used to finance the acquisition of a house. This left open the important questions as to how the court should exercise its discretion and the effect, if any, the Act had on the general law relating to the mortgagee's right to possession.

[24] Stephen Tromans [1984] Conv. 91.

[25] [1973] 2 All E.R. 33. Contrast the more sensible approach taken in *First Middlesbrough & Trading Co.* v. *Cunningham* (1974) 28 P. &. C.R. 29.

[26] H.C. Deb. Vol. 338, col. 1760.

[27] See the valuable discussion of *Habib Bank* v. *Tailor* [1982] 1 W.L.R. 1218 by Stephen Tromans [1984] Conv. 91.

[28] *Bank of Scotland* v. *Grimes* [1985] Q.B. 1179 at 1188 *per* Sir John Arnold P.

The Exercise of Discretion

In considering how to exercise the discretion given by the Act, the courts, initially took a fairly hard line. The postponement of possession had to be for a determinate and not an indefinite period[29]. Any counterclaim that the mortgagor might have against the mortgagee was disregarded in assessing the amount which was actually owing under the mortgage[30] and the courts would insist that a financial plan was put forward, which was both within the mortgagor's means to comply with and would also allow the debt to be repaid within a reasonable period, while also servicing the normal mortgage payments[31]. At the outset, however, little attention was given to the important question of what was considered to be a reasonable period in which to clear the debt.

Although in one, poorly received, decision, the Court of Appeal seemed to regard this as being a matter for the almost unfettered discretion of county court judges[32], it became apparent that a practice had built up of allowing, at most, four years in which to clear the arrears[33]. This practice has now been overturned in the important case of *Cheltenham & Gloucester Building Society* v. *Norgan*[34]. The mortgagor had experienced constant difficulty in meeting the mortgage payments and several actions had been brought for possession and orders postponed. Finally, although the amount of the arrears was disputed, an order for possession was made in the county court and Mrs Norgan appealed. Allowing her appeal, the Court of Appeal set out wholly new guidelines as to how the statutory discretion should be exercised.

The court took the view that, in assessing what is a reasonable time in which to repay the accrued arrears, the starting point should be the agreed length of the mortgage term. To obtain relief, the mortgagor should present a financial plan which, if implemented, would result in the loan itself, including the arrears, being paid off by the term date of the mortgage. Spread over the agreed period of the mortgage, it will be more feasible than was previously the case for the mortgagor to come up with a workable scheme and thus be able to remain in occupation of the house. On the other hand, it was also held that, because the courts were interfering, substantially, with what was previously considered to be the mortgagee's almost sacrosanct right to possess the property, the mortgagor should only have one bite of the cherry. If, having been granted a reprieve when the mortgagee had brought an action for possession, default occurred again, then, it was anticipated, no further postponement should be granted.

29 *Royal Trust Co of Canada* v. *Markham* [1975] 1 W.L.R. 1157.

30 *Citybank Trust Ltd* v. *Ayivor* [1987] 1 W.L.R. 1157; *Ashley Guarantee plc* v. *Zacaria* [1993] 1 All E.R. 254.

31 *First National Bank plc* v. *Syed* [1991] 2 All E.R. 250.

32 *Cheltenham and Gloucester B.S.* v. *Grant* (1993) 24 H.L.R. 48, criticised by M.P. Thompson [1995] Conv. 51.

33 Although see *Citybank Trust* v. *Ayivor* [1987] 1 W.L.R. 1157 at 1164 *per* Mervyn-Davies J., who seemed to consider 18 months to be an appropriate period.

34 [1996] 1 All E.R. 449. See further, M.P. Thompson [1996] Conv. 118.

While the decision is to be welcomed, in that it shows an increased judicial willingness to display a greater concern for the protection of a person's right in the home than had previously been the case, the coda to the judgment, while understandable, may be a little unfortunate in that it smacks a little of a "two strikes and you're out" policy. A person who has got into financial difficulties once, but has been able to resolve them, may in the future, perhaps due to illness or the loss of a job, again find himself with temporary difficulties in paying the mortgage. The stance of confronting the issue of successive applications for a postponement in a way that is unsympathetic to the mortgagor is, however, symptomatic of piecemeal reform of the law. The legislative approach, namely of focusing on one aspect of mortgage possession actions, has consequences when a mortgagor finds it difficult to come within the terms of the Acts.

The Right to Possession

There can be little doubt that the Administration of Justice Acts represent, so far as dwelling-houses are concerned, a substantial inroad into the mortgagee's right to possession. Because of this, it has been argued that it was no longer correct to see it as a right at all but that, in all cases, the court should have a general discretion as to whether possession should be granted[35]. That this is not so was recently confirmed in *Rapaigelach* v. *Barclays Bank plc*[36]. In this case, the bank had re-entered the property and sold it at auction. No possession order had been sought because the house was empty. It was held that where there had been a peaceful re-entry, without recourse to the courts for possession, there was no jurisdiction to interfere under the Acts.[37]

This result appears anomalous. It is, perhaps, not too serious, however, in that, if the house is in residential occupation, a mortgagee would be highly unwise to seek possession without first obtaining a court order[38]. Where the statutory jurisdiction to postpone a sale is less helpful is where it is not envisaged that the arrears will be paid off by periodic payments but by a lump sum when the house is sold at some time in the future. This scenario occurred in *Bristol & West Building Society* v. *Ellis*[39]. Mrs Ellis, who had separated from her husband, continued to live in the matrimonial home which was mortgaged to the building society. Arrears of some £16,000 had accrued and the loan outstanding was £60,000 making a total sum of £76,000. When possession pro-

[35] Alison Clarke [1983] Conv. 293. See also *Western Bank Ltd* v. *Schindler* [1977] 1 W.L.R. 1; *Quennell* v. *Maltby* [1979] 1W.L.R. 318 at 322 *per* Lord Denning M.R. For a highly sensible discretionary approach, see *Albany Home Loans Ltd* v. *Massey* [1997] 2 All E.R. 609 discussed by M.P. Thompson [1998] Conv. 391.

[36] [1999] 4 All E.R. 235.

[37] Contrast *Billson* v. *Residential Apartments Ltd* [1992] A.C. 494 (forfeiture of a lease).

[38] Housing Act 1988, ss.28, 29.

[39] (1996) 73 P. &. C.R 158. See also *National and Provincial Building Society* v. *Lloyd* [1996] 1 All E.R. 630. See M.P. Thompson [1998] Conv. 125.

ceedings were brought, the evidence was that she could pay a lump sum of £5,000, maintain the existing interest repayments and pay off the arrears at £10.00 a month. Reversing the first instance decision, the Court of Appeal ordered possession.

It was clear that, in this type of case, the principle laid down in *Norgan* was inapplicable because, given the rate at which the arrears were to be paid off, it would take 98 years for them to have been cleared: on any view, not a reasonable period. What is more interesting is the alternative solution proposed by Mrs Ellis. She argued that, given her current financial position, the level of debt would be stabilised. She then sought a postponement of sale for five years, to allow her children to complete their university education and, at the end of that period, the house would be sold and the proceeds would be sufficient to pay off all that was owed. On the facts, this was rejected.

The principal difficulty faced by Mrs Ellis was the traditional reluctance of the courts to allow a postponement of possession on the basis that the mortgagor will be able to sell the house at some time in the future. The jurisprudence with regard to this issue is still affected by the approach taken in *Caunt,* where the courts were only prepared to allow a short postponement in order for the mortgagor to sell the house and pay off the debt. Thus in *Royal Trust Co. of Canada* v. *Markham*[40], Simon Brown L.J. was of the view that there should only be a postponement if "there was clear evidence that a sale was going to take place in the near future."[41] This was softened to some extent subsequently to indicate that a period of up to a year may be a reasonable period to postpone a sale[42] and, in *Ellis*, this was recognised as not being a rule of law but a statement of general guidance[43]. Nevertheless, it is evident that lengthy postponements would appear to be unlikely.

This reluctance to allow a postponement of several years on the basis that the house will be sold is understandable but it is to be hoped, that it is not adopted mechanically. In *Ellis*, Auld L.J. stressed that:

> "the critical matters are the adequacy of the security for the debt and the length of the period necessary to achieve a sale. There should be evidence, or at least some informal material . . . before the court of the likelihood of a sale of the proceeds of which will discharge the debt and of the period in which such a sale is likely to be achieved."[44]

In looking at these two criteria, it would seem to be uncontroversial that, in considering whether to postpone a sale, the interest of the mortgagee must be an important factor[45]. In assessing the security of that position, the size of the

[40] [1975] 3 All E.R. 433.

[41] *Ibid.* at 438. See also *Target Home Loans Ltd* v. *Clothier* [1994] 1 All E.R. 439.

[42] *National and Provincial Building Society* v. *Lloyd* [1996] 3 All E.R. 630 at 638 *per* Neill L.J.

[43] (1996) 73 P. &. C. R. 158 *per* Auld L.J.

[44] *Ibid* at 162.

[45] This is also the case when it is the mortgagor who is seeking a sale in cases of negative equity, See Law of Property Act 1925, s.91(2) and *Cheltenham and Gloucester B.S.* v. *Krausz* [1997] 1 W.L.R. 1558. Contrast the unsatisfactory decision in *Polonski* v. *Lloyd's Bank Mortgages Ltd* [1998] 1 F.L.R. 896. See M.P. Thompson [1998] Conv. 125.

mortgagor's equity would seem to be an important factor. In *Ellis,* the redemption figure was £70,000 and the house had been valued at either £80,000 or £85,000, both figures being disputed by the building society. Arguably, therefore, in the light of this dispute, and given the volatility of the housing market, there may have been an insufficient equity to justify a five year postponement of a sale. On the other hand, the situation in *Ellis*, where the mortgagor is in receipt of social security, and the position has been stabilised so that the arrears do not increase, there may be much to be said for the courts allowing rather longer postponements than seems to be the case at the moment, particularly if the mortgagee is given leave to reapply for possession of the property if the market appears to be weakening with the result that the value of the mortgagee's security is endangered. As to the second criterion, the likelihood of a sale, it is, of course, difficult to predict how easy it will be to sell a particular property in five years time. Taken on its own, however, it is suggested that this should not be a crucial factor. Provided that the overall security of the mortgagee's position is maintained, the difficulty of predicting the state of the market should not, it is thought, in itself, be an impediment to a lengthy postponement of possession where it is hoped to sell the house in a few years time in order to repay the loan.

It is certainly the case that the Administration of Justice Acts have done much to improve the lot of mortgagors and have introduced a considerable measure of consumer protection into an area previously dominated by the mortgagee's paramount right to possession of the property. Nevertheless, although the judiciary have, in the main, sought to interpret the legislation sympathetically, the legislation is poorly drafted, giving rise to various problems. A more satisfactory approach would be to reconsider this aspect of mortgage law, so that, while it may not be practical to expect the implementation of a wholesale restructuring of the law of mortgages, to remove some of the historical oddities afflicting the subject[46], there is much to be said for a rationalisation of the law relating to the mortgagee's right to possession: an important practical area, where the judges are left to grapple with piecemeal legislative reform.

CO-OWNERSHIP

While the position of the mortgagor has been considerably improved from the common law position as the result of legislative intervention, as striking has been the additional protection afforded to other occupiers of the mortgaged property: on this occasion as result, largely, of judicial development of the law.

[46] See (1991) Law Com No. 204.

The Background

As will be recalled, occupiers who shared the house with a mortgagor had virtually no prospect of resisting a possession action brought by a mortgagee. In the case of wives, the development of the deserted wife's equity, championed by Lord Denning, was nipped in the bud by the House of Lords in *National Provincial Bank Ltd* v. *Ainsworth*[47]. While it is true that the position of spouses was, to an extent, alleviated by the introduction of the statutory right of occupation introduced by the Matrimonial Homes Act 1967, the enforceability of this right against a mortgagee was dependent on it having been registered prior to the creation of the mortgage; a consideration which meant that the protection was largely illusory. At least as significant, however, was the position of co-owners. Increasingly it is the case that both parties to a relationship, be it marital or neo-marital, go out to work and contribute to the purchase of their home. Where the house is only in person's name, usually the man's, then, despite her contribution to the household budget resulting in her having a beneficial interest in the house[48], the risk is that he will enter into a transaction involving it without consulting her. If things turn out badly, then she could be at risk of losing her home as a result of his transaction: a risk highlighted only too clearly by the decision in *Caunce* v. *Caunce*[49].

The Decision in *Boland*

The decision in *Caunce* had never been universally popular and had been doubted, *obiter,* in *Hodgson* v. *Marks*[50]. This in turn stimulated an academic debate as to whether it remained good law, arguments being put that a co-owner, sharing accommodation with a sole legal owner, should have rights binding upon a mortgagee[51]. This matter was central to the landmark decision in *Williams & Glyn's Bank Ltd* v. *Boland*[52].

The facts are well known. Mr Boland was the sole registered proprietor of the matrimonial home which he shared with his wife who was an equitable co-owner of it. Without consulting her, he mortgaged the house to the bank to secure his business indebtedness. The bank made no enquiries of her, although she lived in it at all material times. On default the bank sought possession and she claimed to have an overriding interest binding upon the bank.

47 [1965] A.C. 1175.

48 This is, of course, a massive oversimplification. The law relating to the acquisition of an interest in the home is beyond the scope of this essay. See Mee, *The Property Rights of Cohabitees,* (Hart Publishing, Oxford, 1999).

49 [1969] 1 W.L.R. 286.

50 [1971] Ch. 982 at 932 *per* Russell L.J.

51 F. R. Crane (1958) 22 Conv. (N.S.) 14 at 24; Farrand *Contract and Conveyance* (2nd ed) (Oyez Publishing, London, 1973) 199. For the opposite view, see D.J. Hayton (1969) 33 Conv. (N.S.) 254.

52 [1981] A.C. 487.

At first instance, Templeman J. aligned himself squarely with the conveyancing lobby. To decide for Mrs Boland would mean that mortgagees would not only have to enquire if the mortgagor's spouse was in the property and, if so, when, but also whether she was claiming to have a beneficial interest in it; consequences he regarded as "almost catastrophic"[53]. Predictably, the Court of Appeal took a less apocalyptic view. Referring to his earlier attempt to establish the deserted wife's equity, Lord Denning M.R. said: "[i]n this court we gave her the protection she rightly deserved. But the House of Lords stripped her of it."[54] Turning his attention to a wife who was a co-owner, as was not the case in *Ainsworth*, his sympathies were clear. He concluded that:

> "We should not give monied might priority over social justice. We should protect the position of a wife who has a share—just as years ago we protected the deserted wife. In the hope that the House of Lords will not reverse us now as it did then."[55]

Perhaps to his surprise, his hopes were fulfilled and the House of Lords decided in Mrs Boland's favour.[56]

The leading speech was given by Lord Wilberforce. Interestingly, he seemed to have been converted by some of the arguments put forward favouring the interests of wives, as he had been a party to the decision in *Ainsworth* and, in the debates leading to the enactment of the Matrimonial Homes Act 1967, had been very concerned with the conveyancing implications of the statutory right of occupation[57]. In *Boland*, however, these concerns seemed to impress him less. While he expressed some sympathy with Templeman J.'s concerns, he, nevertheless concluded that:

> "all that is involved is a departure from the easy-going practice of dispensing with enquiries as to occupation beyond that of the vendor and accepting the risks of doing so. To substitute for this a practice of more careful enquiry as to the fact of occupation, and if necessary, as to the rights of occupiers can not, in my view of the matter, be considered as unacceptable except at the price of overlooking the widespread development of shared interest of ownership."[58]

Similarly, Lord Scarman was unimpressed with supposed conveyancing difficulties should Mrs Boland win, describing them as "exaggerated".[59]

[53] *Williams & Glyn's Bank Ltd* v. *Boland* (1978) 36 P. &C. R. 448 at 454.

[54] *Williams & Glyn's Bank Ltd* v. *Boland* [1979] Ch. 312 at 328.

[55] *Ibid* at 333.

[56] *Williams & Glyn's Bank Ltd* v. *Boland* [1981] A.C. 487. The same result was soon after reached in a case concerning unregistered land, thereby consigning *Caunce* v. *Caunce* to history: *Kingsnorth Finance Co. Ltd* v. *Tizard* [1986] 1 W.L.R. 783.

[57] See n.19, *ante*. Viscount Dilhorne, who had supported Lord Wilberforce's amendment, again agreed with him in *Boland*. Lord Templeman, on the other hand, remained unmoved, commenting, somewhat acidly, that responsibility for further litigation, with the resulting high costs, should be shared by the decision in *Boland*: *Winkworth* v. *Edward Baron Development Co. Ltd* [1986] 1 W.L.R.1512 at 1515.

[58] [1981] A.C. 487 at 508,9.

[59] *Ibid* at 510.

With the benefit of hindsight, the decision might seem to be fairly uncontroversial but, when it was decided, it certainly was not, and it received a distinctly mixed press. Some commentators were overtly hostile to it[60], while others offered a more balanced reaction[61]. The issues involved were, however, considered to be sufficiently serious for the matter to be referred to the Law Commission, whose report recommended the legislative reversal of the decision in *Boland*[62]. In its view, the rights of persons in the position of Mrs Boland should only be enforceable against purchasers if they were protected in the appropriate manner by registration.

The only legislative response was the misguided Land Registration and Law of Property Bill 1985. Under the terms of the Bill, the beneficial interest of a wife, who was in actual occupation of the home, would, unless she had consented to the mortgage, be binding upon the mortgagee, whereas the same interest of any other occupant of the property would not be unless it was protected by registration. The implementation of this Bill would have necessitated an enquiry as to the marital status of any person who shared the house with the legal owner: an absurdity[63]. Thankfully, the Bill was abandoned and it was left to the judiciary to develop the law.

The Aftermath of *Boland*

Undoubtedly the decision in *Boland* generated shock waves in the property market. Building societies were concerned on two counts. First, there was the worry that existing mortgages might not be good security because possession might be unobtainable against people who shared the house with the mortgagor. Secondly, they were concerned that, when granting mortgages in the future, they would be unable to ensure that the rights of any equitable co-owner of the property would be unenforceable against them. With regard to the latter problem, there was one particular nightmare scenario. This involved a situation where a man would apply to a building society for a mortgage to enable him to buy a house. Unbeknown to the society, he was planning to share the house with a partner who was providing part of the initial deposit on the house but, for some reason, was not to be the joint legal owner of it. Because of her financial contribution to the purchase of the house, she would become an equitable co-owner of it and the fear was that this interest would then be binding upon the society. This fear was exacerbated in the case of registered land because of the gap between the transfer of the house and the subsequent application for registration. During this period, the woman could go into actual occupation and so, at the time of registration, be able to establish an overriding interest.

[60] Stephen Freeman (1980) 43 M.L.R. 692.
[61] Jill Martin [1980] Conv. 361.
[62] (1982) Law Com. No. 115.
[63] This point was made in *Ainsworth*, See n.12, *ante*.

These were very real concerns. The latter problem was sought to be met by adopting what became the commonplace practice of asking a single mortgage applicant if he was going to be sharing the house with anyone. If the answer was yes, the practice developed of insisting that the title to the house be put into joint names. The difficulty with this, however, was, that, if the applicant lied, a question addressed to him about the potential rights of another person in the property would not suffice to prevent that other person from later asserting those rights as an overriding interest[64]. As matters developed, it soon emerged that these concerns were overstated.

The first, and most important limitation on *Boland* was directed at mortgagees' greatest fear. In *Bristol and West Building Society* v. *Henning*[65], a house was conveyed into the sole name of Mr Henning for £12,900 of which £11,000 was borrowed by way of mortgage from the society. The balance was raised from the proceeds of sale of an earlier house which had been co-owned by Mr and Mrs Henning[66]. As she was a co-owner of the first house, it followed that she was also a co-owner of the second house. The society had no idea that the house was going to be shared and, therefore, addressed no questions to Mrs Henning. When he defaulted on the mortgage, the society sought possession and she argued that they were bound by her equitable interest in the house. It was held that the society was entitled to possession. According to Browne-Wilkinson L.J., because Mrs Henning knew that the house was being mortgaged—it could not have been bought without a mortgage—and benefited from it, the intention would be imputed to her that the interest of the building society should have priority to her's.

This decision, which has since, somewhat controversially, been extended[67] is a major limitation on *Boland*. There can be very few situations where a potential co-owner of a house does not know that her partner is taking out a mortgage to finance the purchase of it[68]. In such cases, it is now clear that the beneficial co-owner cannot claim that her interest has priority to that of the mortgagee. So, when a mortgage is being used to finance the purchase of a home, an equitable co-owner, be it wife, girlfriend, or relative of the legal owner, will not, by virtue of that beneficial interest, be able to resist possession proceedings brought by a mortgagee in the event of default.

The related problem of the "registration gap" has also been addressed. In *Abbey National Building Society* v. *Cann*[69], the House of Lords held that, for the purposes of section 70(1)(g) of the Land Registration Act 1925, the key time

[64] *Hodgson* v. *Marks* [1971] Ch. 892 at 932 *per* Russell L.J.

[65] [1995] 1 W.L.R. 778, followed in *Paddington B.S.* v. *Mendelsohn* (1985) 50 P. &. C.R. 244. See M.P. Thompson (1986) 49 M.L.R. 245; [1986] Conv.57.

[66] The couple were not married. The marital status of the co-owners is immaterial in this type of situation.

[67] *Equity and Home Loans Ltd* v. *Prestidge* [1992] 1 W.L.R. 137; *Locabail (UK) Ltd* v. *Waldorf Corporation* [1999] *The Times*, March 9. For criticism, see M.P. Thompson [1992] Conv. 206.

[68] For a rare example, see *Lloyds Bank plc* v. *Rosset* [1991] A.C. 107.

[69] [1991] A.C. 56. See Simon Baughen [1991] Conv. 116; P.T. Evans [1991] Conv. 155.

for determining whether a person was in actual occupation was not, as one might have expected, the date of registration, when the transferee acquires the legal title[70], but the date of the transfer, thereby preventing the possibility of an occupier who goes into actual occupation of the property between those dates from acquiring an overriding interest.

Second Mortgages

The approach taken to the above issues seems to be pragmatic and sensible. In balancing the interests of mortgagees and occupiers, there does not appear to be any convincing case as to why occupiers who know perfectly well that a mortgage is necessary for the house to be bought at all, and thereby benefit directly from it, should be able, subsequently, to assert proprietary rights against the mortgagee. The effect of these decisions is that the effect of *Boland* is to provide protection for occupiers when the legal owner mortgages the property for some purpose of his own; overwhelmingly, this will involve a second mortgage of the property. In this situation, the law provides, in most cases, protection to occupiers, with interests in the property, to ensure that the house is not put at risk with their consent[71]. To that proposition, however, there is a significant exception.

In *City of London Building Society* v. *Flegg*[72], a married couple were registered proprietors of a house and they held it on trust for themselves and her parents. Without informing the parents, the legal owners created a number of mortgages over the house until, finally, they created a mortgage in favour of the plaintiffs, the money being used to redeem the existing mortgages. No enquiries were addressed to the parents who, when the mortgagee sought possession, claimed that, because they were in actual occupation of the property at all material times, they had an overriding interest. The Court of Appeal, in a highly controversial decision[73], considered the case to be indistinguishable from *Boland*, and decided in favour of the parents. The House of Lords reversed that decision.

Once more, the House of Lords were much exercised by the conveyancing implications of the case. Lord Oliver commented that:

> "[t]his appeal is . . . of considerable importance not only to conveyancers but to anyone proposing to lend money on the security of property in respect of which there is any possibility of the existence of beneficial owners which have not been disclosed by the apparent absolute owner."[74]

[70] Land Registration Act 1925, s.20. But see the article to the contrary by Peter Sparkes [1986] Conv. 309.

[71] This puts co-owners in a similar position to other occupiers of residential property, almost all of whom have some protection against arbitrary eviction: see (1989) Law Com. No. 188, para. 3.5.

[72] [1988] A.C. 54.

[73] [1986] Ch. 605. For strong criticism, see D.J. Hayton (1986) 130 N.L.J. 208. For a lone defence, see M.P. Thompson (1986) 6 L.S. 140.

[74] [1988] A.C. 54 at 71.

He then opined that to have decided in favour of the parents would have the consequence that "financial institutions [would] face hitherto unsuspected hazards"[75]; a prospect he viewed with some degree of alarm.

There are, of course, sound technical reasons for distinguishing *Boland's* case, in that capital money was paid to two trustees[76] and so the beneficial interests existing behind the trust were overreached. It was also true that the decision accorded with the overwhelming weight of academic opinion[77] and confirmed the sanctity of the overreaching machinery and was consequently welcomed by conveyancers. Nevertheless, it does represent a setback for those who argue that occupiers of property, who own a beneficial interest in it, should not be at risk at losing their homes as a result of the actions of the legal owner or owners mortgaging the property in order to raise money for their own purposes. This argument received a fillip when the Law Commission, in a marked shift in its position, recommended that *Flegg* be reversed by legislation[78].

Such a change would be desirable. While a conveyancer might appreciate why it makes a crucial difference that a mortgage has been granted by two legal owners, as opposed to one, it is doubtful whether lay people such as the Fleggs would. Moreover, the conveyancing implications would not appear to be unduly serious. As has been seen, it is only when the house is being used as security for collateral borrowing that a mortgagee needs to be concerned with the rights of occupiers of property who, in any event, may be tenants rather than co-owners[79], when overreaching would not occur. To impose the burden on mortgagees to ensure that all adult occupiers[80] of a house are consulted before a home is used as security for a loan would not, it is suggested, be unreasonable[81] and it is unfortunate that when the legal structure of co-ownership was reformed by the Trusts of Land and Appointment of Trustees Act 1996 the opportunity to implement this Law Commission proposal was not taken[82].

[75] [1988] A.C. 54 at 72.

[76] The same result occurs even if no capital money arises but the mortgage is created by two legal owners: *State Bank of India* v. *Sood* [1997] Ch. 276. See Charles Harpum [1980] C.L.J. 277; M.P. Thompson [1997] Conv.134.

[77] See, e.g., H. Forrest [1978] Conv. 194 at 199–201; M.D.A. Freeman (1981) Fam Law 37 at 40; Stephen Freeman (1980) 692 at 695; Jill Martin [1980] Conv. 361; W.T. Murphy (1979) 42 M.L.R. 467. For the contrary view, see M.P. Thompson (1986) 6 L.S. 140.

[78] (1989) Law Com No.188. Of course, the the Commission was differently constituted. It is interesting to note that the Commission whose previous report dealing with *Boland,* and which gave priority to the conveyancing interest, contained as one of its members the distinguished Family lawyer, Dr Stephen Cretney, while one of the members responsible for the latter report, which favoured the the rights of occupiers was the leading conveyancing lawyer, Dr Julian Farrand.

[79] *Cf Woolwich B.S.* v. *Dickman* [1996] 3 All E.R. 204.

[80] See *Hypo-Mortgae Services Ltd* v. *Robinson* [1997] 2 F.C.R. 422.

[81] See also *State Bank of India* v. *Sood* [1997] Ch.276 at 290 *per* Peter Gibson L.J.

[82] The argument that the Act has, seemingly unintentionally had this effect, seems unconvincing: Graham Ferris and Graham Battersby [1998] Conv.168 at 179–183. See A.J. Oakley [1997] Conv.401 at 404–5. See, also, Gravells, *Land Law, Text and Materials* (2nd ed) (London, Sweet & Maxwell, 1999) 205, referring, in particular to the Government's response to the Law Commission Report: *Hansard*, HL, March 19, Written Answers 213.

UNDUE INFLUENCE

The reconciliation of the competing interests of institutional lenders and occupiers seemed to have been settled with the decision in *Flegg* and the ensuing Law Commission report. The essential problem was seen to be that of balancing the interests of co-owners, who were not on the legal title with those of the person or persons who were and the mortgagee. What has recently come to prominence is the potential conflict of interest between legal co-owners.

Initially, the position was that, if a mortgagee entrusted one co-owner to get the signature of the other co-owner to a mortgage and the former employed undue influence or misrepresentation to obtain that signature, then the mortgage would not be valid against the latter[83]. Alternatively, if the mortgagee was actually aware that the signature had been obtained as a result of the application of undue influence, then. again, the mortgage would not be enforceable[84]. Apart from these situations, the mortgage would be upheld, notwithstanding that some wrong had been perpetrated by one co-owner upon the other[85]. Matters changed decisively as a result of the decision in *Barclays Bank plc* v. *O'Brien*[86].

Mr O'Brien was closely involved with a company and had agreed to act as guarantor of its overdraft. When that overdraft reached £60,000, the bank sought security for it, the security being the matrimonial home. At this stage, it was envisaged that the loan would be repaid within a month. At the time that the mortgage was signed the level of indebtedness was £135,000. Mrs O'Brien went to the bank and signed the mortgage deed and a side letter confirming that she fully understood the mortgage transaction. In fact she had read neither document. The mortgage was to secure the total indebtedness of the company which, at the time possession proceedings were brought, stood at £154,000. She argued that the mortgage was not binding upon her claiming she had signed the mortgage as a result of undue influence and misrepresentation. She thought she had agreed to a short term mortgage to secure the sum of £60,000; not open-ended liability.

The Court of Appeal unearthed some, hitherto, little known principle of equity[87] that a benevolent attitude is taken towards wives who stand surety for their husbands and held that the mortgage was only enforceable against her to

[83] *Kings North Trust Ltd* v. *Bell* [1986] 1 W.L.R. 119; *Avon Finance Ltd* v. *Bridger* (1979) [1985] 2 All E.R. 281.

[84] *Bank of Credit and Commerce International* v. *Aboody* [1990] 1 Q.B. 923.

[85] See *Coldunell* v. *Gallon* [1986] Q.B. 1184; *Lloyds Bank Ltd* v. *Egremont* [1992] 2 F.L.R. 351.

[86] [1994] 1 A.C. 180. For the fullest discussion of the issues arising in this case, see Fehlberg, *Sexually Transmitted Debt: Surety Experience in English Law* (Oxford, Clarendon Press, 1997).

[87] Based to a large extent on *Yerkey* v. *Jones* (1939) 63 C.L.R. 649. This approach has been continued in Australia: *Garcia* v. *National Australia Bank Ltd* (1998) 72 A.J.LR. 1243. See P.J. Clarke [1998] All E.R.Rev.271.

the extent of her understanding: £60.000[88]. On appeal, the House of Lords took an entirely different approach and held the mortgage to be completely void against her[89].

According to Lord Browne-Wilkinson, certain relationships give rise to presumptions of different types. If the transaction is between parent and child, or solicitor and client, then a presumption of undue influence will automatically arise. In the case of husband and wife[90], there is no such presumption. If, however, the transaction is to the manifest disadvantage to the wife[91], it will, unless the contrary is proved, be assumed that some vitiating factor was present which will, as against him, entitle her to set the transaction aside. This equity will then be binding upon the mortgagee if it has notice[92]. To avoid being fixed with notice, the mortgagee must take certain precautions. It should arrange to see the wife independently from the husband, to ensure that she fully understands the transaction and she should be counselled to take independent legal advice[93].

O'Brien represented a major sea-change in judicial attitudes towards the position of wives and people in similar relationships. It shows a concerted effort to balance the competing interests of facilitating commercial transactions on th e one hand and protecting people form losing their home on the other. The decision did not, however, give total protection to spouses. First, the bank has to be put on notice that some vitiating factor is present. If, on the face of it, the loan appears to benefit both parties, the bank need not take any special precautions when obtaining the wife's signature; a factor which, paradoxically, benefits the banks if they are dealing with a particularly dominant and unprincipled husband[94]. Difficulties will arise in determining whether a loan for the benefit of a company in which both parties have an interest will put a bank on notice, a matter which was the subject of considerable debate at a Chancery Bar Association conference which met to discuss the implications of *O'Brien*[95]. The better view, particularly in the light of research which shows that such companies are often not a combination of equals, even though the couple are married[96] is that this is

[88] [1993] Q.B. 109.

[89] [1994] 1 A,C, 180. See also *TSB* v. *Camfield* [1995] 1 All E.R. 951, discussed by A. Dunn [1995] Conv. 325; P. Ferguson (1995) 111 L.Q.R. 356.

[90] This is also true of non married relationships. See *Midland Bank plc* v. *Massey* [1994] 2 F.L.R. 342; *Credit Lyonnais Bank Nederland NV* v. *Burch* [1997] 1 All E.R. 144.

[91] See *CIBC Mortgages plc* v. *Pitt* [1994] 1 A.C. 208.

[92] For different views as to the proper role of noice, see M.P. Thompson [1994] Conv. 140; C. Harpum and M. Dixon [1994] Conv. 221; P. Sparkes [1995] Conv. 250. The views of Harpum and Dixon would now seem to be vindicated; see *Barclays Bank plc* v. *Boulter* [1997] 2 All E.R. 1002 at 1010; *Royal Bank of Scotland* v. *Etridge (No.2)* [1998] 4 All E.R 705 at 717; M.P. Thompson [1999] Conv. 126 at 128–129.

[93] *Barclays Bank plc* v. *O'Brien* [1994] 1 A.C. 180 at 189–190 *per* Lord Browne-WIlkinson. For some well-justified scepticism as to the utitlity of such advice, see B. Fehlberg (1996) 59 M.L.R. 675 at 683. See also *Royal Bank of Scotland* v. *Etridge (No. 2), supra*, at 711 *per* Stuart-Smith L.J.

[94] See *CIBC Mortgages plc* v. *Pitt* [1994] 1 A.C. 200.

[95] See [1994] Conv. 349. See also *Royal Bank of Scotland* v. *Etridge (No.2)*, supra, at 716, 717 *per* Stuart-Smith L.J.

[96] See B.Fehlberg, n.92, *ante*.

a situation where precautions should be necessary[97]. The other issue is what precautions will suffice.

With regard to this latter issue, the approach of the courts has been somewhat disappointing and there has been some rowing back from the guidance issued by Lord Browne-Wilkinson in *O'Brien*[98]. If a solicitor certifies that he has advised the wife as to the mortgage then, save for exceptional cases[99], or where the mortgagee is aware of relevant circumstances pertaining to the loan which it does not reveal to the solicitor[100], the bank can rely on this despite the fact that the solicitor is acting for the company that will benefit from the loan[101], or even for the mortgagee itself[102]. Although in such circumstances, one might anticipate that the bank should be regarded as having notice of the potential conflict of interest facing the solicitor, and, consequently, unable to proceed on the basis tat she has been fully and independently advised, this is not the approach that the courts have taken.

Neither have they insisted that mortgagee comply with the guidance given by Lord Browne-Wilkinson to see the wife independently from her husband. Interestingly, however, in these cases, the courts have stressed that the cases before them have involved facts which occurred prior to the decision in *O'Brien*[103] and it may well be the case that, in cases where the facts postdate the guidance given by Lord Browne-Wilkinson, a less lenient line will be taken to lenders who do not follow the guidelines given in *O'Brien* and see the wife independently of her husband[104]. This is a matter which awaits determination, although it is submitted that it would be preferable if such a prospective view of *O'Brien* was taken.

While it is true that the way that the courts have developed the law following *O'Brien* has entailed a degree of watering down the guidelines put forward by Lord Browne-Wilkinson, the same cannot be said for the potential liability of solicitors. Although, quite recently, the Privy Council took the view that the role of the solicitor was effectively limited to explaining the legal nature of a mortgage[105], subsequent cases have taken a rather more robust line in considering the obligations of solicitors when there is a potential conflict of interest between

[97] But see *Royal Bank of Scotland* v. *Etridge (No.2)* , *supra*, at 716 *per* Stuart-Smith L.J.

[98] See Fehlberg, *Sexually Transmitted Debt*, p.46; M.P. Thompson [1997] Conv. 216; S. Wong [1998] Conv. 457.

[99] See *Credit Lyonnais Bank Nederland NV* v. *Burch* [1997] 1 All E.R. 144.

[100] See *Northern Rock Building Society* v. *Archer* (1998) 78 P. &. C. R. 65.

[101] *Banco Exterior International* v. *Mann* [1995] 1 All E.R. 936, where Hobhouse L.J. dissented with much force. It is the majority decision in this case which is probably responsible for the somewhat relaxed view taken of the protection available to mortgagees when a solicitor has advised a wife prior to her signing the mortgage.

[102] *Barclays Bank plc* v. *Thomson* [1997] 4 All E.R. 816; *Royal Bank of Scotlamd* v. *Etridge (No. 2)* [1998] 4 All E.R 705. For criticism, see M.P. Thompson [1997] Conv. 216; [1999] Conv. 126.

[103] See *Massey* v. *Midland Bank plc* [1995] 1 All E.R 929 at 936 *per* Steyn L.J.; *Northern Rock Building Society* v. *Harper* , *supra*, at 72 *per* Chadwick L.J.

[104] See M.P. Thompson [1999] Conv. 126 at 135.

[105] *Clark Boyce* v. *Mouat* [1994] 1 A.C 428. For convincing criticism, see Rosemary Tobin [1994] Conv. 404.

clients[106] and, in an extreme case, the view was expressed that if advice not to proceed with a particular transaction is disregarded, the solicitor should decline to act[107]. So, although the mortgagee will in most cases be able to rely on the fact that a wife has been advised by a solicitor prior to her signing the mortgage deed, the solicitor may well incur liability if the advice given is not regarded as having been adequate: a position which is most likely to occur when the solicitor is acting for more than party involved in the mortgage transaction. In the end, if there is mortgage default, although the wife may not be able to resist a possession action, who may have a pecuniary remedy against her legal adviser.

CONCLUSIONS

As has been seen, over the past few years, the law has developed enormously from a position where the attitude was one of caring little for the rights of occupiers of property and regarding the interests of mortgagees and conveyancers as paramount. As with much legal development, the path has not been direct. Thus, with hindsight, the decision in *Flegg* can be seen as representing a reversion to previous attitudes and. although clearly distinguishable, does not sit easily with the ethos underlying *O'Brien*. Nevertheless, by a combination of legislation an d judicial decision, a considerable degree of consumer protection has been introduced into this area of law. While it is true to say, that a comprehensive redrawing of the law has not occurred; the developments having taken place in a somewhat piecemeal manner, a much fairer balance has now been struck between monied might and social justice than was previously the case.

[106] See, e.g., *Mortgage Express Ltd* v. *Bowerman* [1996] 2 All E.R. 836; M.P. Thompson [1996] Conv.204, where the inconsistency between this case and the Privy Council approach is pointed out. See also the quite detailed account of what can be expaected of a solicitor in cases where undue influence or misrepresentation may be in issue in *Royal Bank of Scotland* v. *Etridge (No.2), supra,* at 715–717 *per* Stuart-Smith L.J. and the comments in *Northern Rock Building Society* v. *Harper, supra*, at 79 *per* Chadwick L.J.

[107] *Credit Lyonnais Bank Nederland NV* v. *Burch* [1997] 1 All E.R. 144 at 156 *per* Millett L.J.

8

Is Justice a Priority in Priorities? Law Reform and the Re-Introduction of Morality to Registered Conveyancing

JOHN STEVENS

THOSE RESPONSIBLE FOR framing the property legislation of 1925 anticipated that title to all land in England and Wales would be registered within a thirty year period. It is only now, some seventy five years later, that the accomplishment of total registration is within sight. Registered land will thus form the new paradigm of English Land Law, as has been recognised by the Law Commission[1] and by academic authors.[2] During the intervening period the nature of property ownership has radically changed. Perhaps the most significant development has been the increasing importance of informal rights of co-ownership and occupation, arising either by way of a resulting or constructive trust, or through an application of the doctrine of proprietary estoppel.[3] Since the recognition of such rights by the House of Lords in *Pettitt* v. *Pettitt*[4] and *Gissing* v. *Gissing*[5] the courts have struggled to tackle the difficult problems of priority which they have occasioned. Much of this difficulty reflects a fundamental tension generated by the inherently competing policy objectives of land law, and the system of registration in particular. The 1925 legislation was intended to make conveyancing more efficient and land more easily marketable.[6] In contrast the emergence of informal trusts interests in land reflects a desire to protect the rights of individuals. It will be argued that the solutions adopted in the property legislation of 1925 do not accomplish an appropriate balance for today between the competing objectives of efficient conveyancing

[1] *Land Registration for the Twenty-First Century*, Law Com No 254, 1998.

[2] See for example, Sparks, *A New Land Law*, Hart Publishing, 1999.

[3] *Transfer of Land, Overreaching: Beneficiaries in Occupation*, Law Com No 188, 1989, paras 2.7. & 3.1–3.3.; Ruoff and Roper, *Law and Practice of Registered Conveyancing*, 5th ed., (1986), p. 822.

[4] [1970] AC 777.

[5] [1971] AC 886.

[6] *State Bank of India* v. *Sood* [1997] 1 All ER 169, 172–173, per Peter Gibson L.J.

and the protection of individual rights in land, and that the time has come to recognise that the "new wine" of informal rights cannot be satisfactorily accommodated by the "old wine skins" of the 1925 legislation.

The Law Commission has recently published a significant consultation document suggesting major reform of the system of registration.[7] However it has rejected any suggestion of re-introducing a moral dimension, founded upon the concept of notice, to the resolution of issues of priority. It is clear that the doctrine of notice incarnated moral concepts of fairness, justice and conscience into the resolution of priorities issues in land. A purchaser of land was expected to protect his own interests by inspecting the documents of title and the land itself. He was expected to act as a prudent, careful man. If he failed to do so, *caveat emptor* operated strictly against him. The moral foundation of the doctrine of notice was recognised by the House of Lords in *Midland Bank Trust Co Ltd* v. *Green,* where Lord Wilberforce analysed the essential characteristics of "equity's darling":

> "The character in law known as the bona fide (good faith) purchaser for value without notice was the creation of equity. In order to affect a purchaser for value of a legal estate with some equity or equitable interest, equity fastened upon his conscience and the composite expression was used to epitomise the circumstances in which equity would or rather would not do so. I think that it would generally be true to say that the worlds 'in good faith' related to the existence of notice. Equity in other words, required not only the absence of notice, but genuine and honest absence of notice. As the law developed this doctrine became crystallised in the doctrine of constructive notice. . . ."[8]

Such terms as "conscience", "good faith," "genuine" and "honest" emphasise the moral dimension of the doctrine of notice. Lord Wilberforce further stressed that even once the doctrine of constructive notice had taken statutory form in s3 Conveyancing Act 1882 "Equity still retained its interest in and power over the purchaser's conscience." Thus by means of the doctrine of notice equity operated such that a purchaser took land subject to pre-existent equitable interests, which ought morally to bind them, and from which there was no just escape.

In contrast, one central objective of the comprehensive scheme of land registration introduced in 1925 was the replacement of the doctrine of notice as a means of determining issues of priority between interests in land with a mechanistic system of statutory rules.[9] It is submitted that registered conveyancing requires the re-injection of just such a moral dimension. In order to make the case for a more radical reform three areas will be examined. First the mechanism

[7] *Land Registration for the Twenty-First Century*, Law Com No 254, 1998.

[8] [1981] AC 513 at 528.

[9] See: H.W.R. Wade, [1956] CLJ 216; Stuart Anderson, "The 1925 Property Legislation: Setting Contexts," Chp 4 in Bright & Dewar, *Land Law: Themes and Perspectives* (OUP 1998), p. 108. Professor Gray suggests, in the context of land charges in unregistered land, that the doctrine of notice was replaced by "an amoral rule," *Elements of Land Law*, 2nd ed, (Butterworths, 1993), p. 121.

of overreaching and its impact upon the rights of beneficiaries in actual occupation of land. Second, the relevance of actual notice to issues of priority in registered land. Third, the place of estoppel interests in registered land. In the course of the examination of these areas it will be argued that, at the very least, the current law should be amended so as to protect the rights of a person in actual occupation of land from the averse consequences of overreaching, and that informally created interests should be binding upon purchasers who have not acted in good faith because they were aware of their existence.

OVERREACHING AND THE RIGHTS OF BENEFICIARIES IN ACTUAL OCCUPATION OF LAND

Overreaching provides perhaps the single most important means by which a purchaser may acquire title to, or a mortgage over, land free from the existing trusts interests of third parties, whether such trusts have arisen expressly or informally. The mechanism of overreaching is the lynch pin of the so called "curtain" principle of land registration, whereby the existence of trust interests need not appear on the face of the register of title, and potential purchasers need not concern themselves with their existence if they observe certain statutory procedures.[10] In essence, a person who purchases land where the title is owned by two or more trustees may acquire it free from any pre-existing beneficial interests. The rights of the beneficiaries are not destroyed per se, as would have been the case in the past where land subject to a trust was acquired by a bona fide purchaser for value without notice,[11] but rather their rights are transferred to the purchase moneys paid over to the trustees.[12] Their interest in the land is thus converted on sale, without their consent, into a mere interest in money.

This mechanism clearly seeks to draw a balance between the protection of the legitimate rights of beneficiaries and the facilitation of conveyancing simplicity. At the time at which the legislation was introduced it may have achieved an appropriate balance between these competing objectives. Earlier in the century the majority of trusts of land would have been created expressly, and most would have sought to facilitate the creation of successive interests in land, thereby falling under the regime of the Settled Land Act 1925. Since the legal title to land subjected to a strict settlement was vested in the beneficiary it was impossible for his or her interests to be defeated by a purchaser without his knowledge. The rights of other beneficiaries were protected by the requirement that any capital moneys arising form a sale of the land must be paid to the trustees of the settlement,[13] who exercised an independent supervisory role. The difficulties associated with the operation of overreaching have only become

[10] See s74 Land Registration Act 1925, which imposes the curtain principle.

[11] *Wilkes* v. *Spooner* [1911] 2 KB 473.

[12] Law of Property Act 1925 s2(2).

[13] s 18(1) Settled Land Act 1925.

apparent in more recent years in the context of co-ownership rights in land arising by way of an informal trust, and especially in relation to the interaction between overreaching and the operation of overriding interests under s70(1)(g) of the Land Registration Act 1925.

In *City of London Building Society* v. *Flegg*[14] the question arose whether the mechanism of overreaching would operate so as to defeat the interests of beneficiaries who were in actual occupation of registered land. The case concerned a house, somewhat ironically named "Bleak House," purchased in the names of Mr and Mrs Maxwell-Brown, who were the registered proprietors. Part of the purchase price was provided by Mrs Maxwell-Brown's parents, Mr and Mrs Flegg, who thereby gained an equitable interest in the property by way of a resulting trust. Mr and Mrs Flegg were not absentee beneficiaries. The house was their home. Some time later, following severe financial difficulties, Mr and Mrs Maxwell-Brown mortgaged the property to the tune of £37,500. Following their default the mortgage company sought possession of the property. Whilst the advance of the mortgage moneys to Mr and Mrs Maxwell-Brown clearly satisfied the statutory conditions for the operation of overreaching, this could not alone provide a straightforward determination of priority between the rights of the mortgagee and the undoubted beneficial entitlement of Mr and Mrs Flegg. They appeared to satisfy the statutory requirements for an overriding interest under s70(1)(g) Land Registration Act 1925, which protects the rights of persons in actual occupation of land by granting them statutory priority. The case thus necessitated the resolution of a fundamental tension in the structure of the legislation. Should the overreaching mechanism operate so as to negate the statutory protection of beneficial owners in actual occupation of land, or does the protection of occupiers prevent their interests being destroyed by overreaching? The House of Lords concluded that the overreaching mechanism took precedence, such that at the moment that the mortgage was executed Mr and Mrs Flegg no longer had any interest in the land itself which could form the subject matter of an overriding interest. At the moment that the mortgage was registered they enjoyed only an interest in the mortgage moneys paid over to the Maxwell-Brown's.

This interpretation of the relevant legislation, and in particular of the interaction between the Law of Property Act 1925 and the Land Registration Act 1925, was clearly motivated by policy considerations rather than being the result of mechanistic statutory construction. Lord Templeman stressed that to hold that the mortgage company was subject to the rights of an actual occupiers would frustrate the compromise between "the interests of the public in securing that land held in trust is freely marketable and, on the other hand, the interest of the beneficiaries in preserving their rights under the trusts," which he considered was one of the main objects of the 1925 legislation.[15] However it is precisely

[14] [1988] AC 54. See: [1986] Conv 379; [1987] Conv 451; [1987] CLJ 392; (1987) 103 LQR 520; (1988) 51 MLR 565; [1988] Conv 108.

[15] *ibid*. at p. 73–74.

the terms of the alleged compromise embodied in the legislative scheme which is open to question. In *Williams* v. *Glynn's Bank* v. *Boland*[16] the House of Lords had already accepted the proposition that rights of a beneficiary in occupation of would bind a mortgagee as an overriding interest where land was owned by a sole trustee under a trust for sale. This amounted to a seismic shift in understanding of the rights of beneficiaries under a trust for sale, recognising that they enjoyed real proprietary interests in that land itself, and not purely personal rights in the proceeds of sale arising by application of the doctrine of conversion. This shift reflected the practical reality that individuals felt that they owned "land" and not merely an interest in the notional proceeds of sale of their home. The House of Lords thus introduced a substantial derogation in the efficacy of the curtain principle, which was affirmed in subsequent cases,[17] and ultimately enshrined by legislative reform.[18]

The contrasting outcomes of *Flegg* and *Boland* thus point to the crucial significance of overreaching as currently understood. Where there are two trustees the curtain principle is held to apply in its full rigour. Where there is only one trustee the rights of the beneficiary are protected and a purchaser, or mortgagee, cannot seek the shelter of the curtain but must take action to protect himself from adverse interests, usually by inspecting the land for evidence of undisclosed occupants who might enjoy an interest therein. This arbitrary distinction is clearly driven by the desire to achieve conveyancing simplicity, but leaves an occupier vulnerable. *Flegg* itself demonstrates that the presence of two trustees is no adequate protection for the beneficiaries of a trust of land. In the light of these considerations it would surely have been equally legitimate for the House of Lords to follow the lead of the Court of Appeal[19] and to conclude that the compromise should have been drawn in favour of the occupiers of land, so that a person in actual occupation would be able to assert his or her rights against a third party even if that person had purchased the land from more than one trustee.

This position was subsequently advocated by the Law Commission in *Overreaching: Beneficiaries in Occupation*.[20] The proposed reforms were condemned by Harpum on the ground that they would amount to a negation of the curtain principle enshrined in the 1925 legislation.[21] However this is to miss the point of the proposal, which recommends a redrawing of the compromise between conveyancing efficiency and individual justice in favour of the rights of occupiers. The curtain principle is not inherently sacrosanct, and it is not an intolerable burden to expect the purchasers of land to investigate the entitlements of any persons who might be in actual occupation of land. In *Abbey*

[16] [1981] AC 487.
[17] *City of London Building Society* v *Flegg* [1998] AC 54.
[18] Trusts of Land and Appointment of Trustees Act 1996, ss 3 and 12.
[19] [1986] Ch 605.
[20] Law Com No 188, 1989.
[21] [1990] CLJ 277, at 330. See also J. E. Adams [1998] Conv. 349.

National v. *Cann*[22] the House of Lords considered that it was perfectly reasonable to require a mortgagee to inspect land to identify potential occupiers with rights until a transaction is completed, a position accepted by the Law Commission in its more recent consultative document *Land Registration for the Twenty-First Century*. Whilst *Cann* may be distinguished on the grounds that it concerned land owned by a sole trustee, the argument that a purchaser acquiring an interests from two or more trustees need not be concerned physically to inspect the land because he will enjoy the protection of overreaching is flawed. As not every category of overriding interest is capable of being overreached,[23] every purchaser would be well advised to carry out an inspection of the land if he wishes to be sure that he will acquire it free from such adverse interests. Any alteration of the balance between conveyancing simplicity and the protection of individual rights inevitably imposes greater burdens upon those who wish to acquire an interest in land. However in *Boland* the House of Lords was prepared to accept that such costs would be justified in the interests of the protection of individual rights. Similarly, in *Barclay's Bank* v. *O'Brien*[24] and *CIBC Mortgages* v. *Pitt*[25] the House of Lords preferred to protect mortgagors from exploitation by the exercise of undue influence, even though this would inevitably impose greater costs upon mortgage companies and necessitate changes in business practice.

Harpum also argues against the introduction of reform on the grounds that it would strike an unfair balance between those beneficiaries who are in actual occupation and those who are not. However this reasoning is also unsatisfactory. First, s70(1)(g) inherently draws a distinction between those persons who fall within its ambit and those who do not. This distinction is as fundamental to the 1925 scheme as the principle of overreaching, and derives from the common law rule that the fact of occupation constitutes notice of rights.[26] Secondly, s70(1)(g) also protects the rights of persons who are in receipt of rent and profits derived from the land. Thus the legislation fails to protect only beneficiaries who neither occupy the land nor obtain any economic benefit from it. Third, in any event it is no argument against reform that it would not protect all beneficiaries. The decision to protect only the rights beneficiaries in actual occupation of land is no more arbitrary than the decision to protect only purchasers who acquire land from two trustees.

[22] [1996] 1 AC 56.

[23] For example a legal lease for less than 21 years, which is an overriding interest under s70(1)(k) Land Registration Act 1925. See also, *Land Registration for the Twenty-First Century*, Law Com No 254, 1998, paras 5.87–5.94.

[24] [1994] AC 180. See: [1994] CLJ 21; [1994] Conv 140, 421; (1994) 110 LQR 167; (1994) 57 MLR 467; [1994] RLR 3; (1995) 15 LS 35; (1995) 15 OJLS 119.

[25] [1994] AC 200.

[26] *Holmes* v. *Powell* (1856) 8 De G M & G 572. See also *Land Registration for the Twenty-First Century*, Law Com No 254, 1998, para. 5.57.

It has now become clear that the reforms advocated by the Law Commission will not be implemented.[27] Whilst Ferris and Battersby[28] have argued that one unintended effect of the Trusts of Land and Appointment of Trustees Act 1996 has been to reverse the decision in *Flegg*, on the grounds that under the new legislation the mortgage would have been *ultra vires* the power of the trustees and therefore deprived of overreaching effect, this does not address the central question whether the rights of occupiers should be subordinated to those of purchasers who comply with statutory mechanisms for the payment of purchase moneys. They are surely correct to state that at present it is "assumed that a disposition by two trustees of land allows a purchaser to rely on sections 2 and 27 of the Law of Property Act 1925," and that as a result "any overriding interests arising under a trust for sale of land would be overreached and cease to affect the land.[29]" The weakness of the beneficiary's position is compounded by the fact that overreaching will take place even where the purchaser had actual notice of the existence of the trust[30] and that the beneficiary need not consent to the transaction. The recent case of *State Bank of India* v. *Sood*[31] marks a further derogation in the protection of the trustees as the Court of Appeal concluded that the rights of beneficiaries in occupation of land will be overreached even where there is no payment of any purchase moneys to the trustees, thus undermining the very basis of overreaching, which is the transfer of rights in land to rights in money.[32]

It is submitted that the modern law should provide greater protection for the rights of beneficiaries who are in occupation of land, and that legislative reform is needed to make clear that a beneficial interest which enjoys overriding status cannot not be overreached. This would not undermine the curtain principle as such. There would still be no need for beneficial interests to appear on the face of the register. The additional burden imposed upon potential purchasers and mortgagees would not significantly exceed what is currently expected from them.

ACTUAL NOTICE AND PRIORITY OVER UNPROTECTED MINOR INTERESTS

There is something instinctively unsatisfactory about a system which allows a purchasers to acquire land free from third party interests of which they were aware. As Lord Buckmaster remarked in *Waimiha Sawmill Ltd Co* v. *Waione Timber Co Ltd*[33] "if the designed object of a transfer be to cheat a man of a

[27] [1998] 12 *L.S.G.* 4.
[28] [1998] Conv 168.
[29] *ibid.* at 187.
[30] s27(1) Law of Property Act 1925.
[31] [1997] Ch. 276.
[32] Ferris and Battersby argue that this case was wrongly decided because counsel for the beneficiaries had conceded that the mortgage was *intra vires* when it was not: [1998] Conv 168 at 182.
[33] [1926] AC 101, 106.

known existing right, that is fraudulent." In stark contrast to these sentiments, in *Midland Bank Trust Co* v. *Green*[34] Lord Wilberforce stated, in the context of a unprotected land charge in unregistered land, that it was not fraud for a purchaser to take advantage of rights conferred by statute. Thus a mother, who had purchased a farm from her husband for a paltry sum with the express intention of defeating an option to purchase which had been granted to her son, was held to have acquired the land free from the option, which had not been properly protected as a class C(iv) land charge. This result was considered to be just because the son had failed to take steps necessary to protect his position by registration. Whilst this argument may have some merit in respect of a commercial transaction, albeit conducted in a family context, it is less compelling where the interest concerned arises informally, such that the person entitled may be unaware of its existence, still less of the need to register. If the land at issue in *Midland Bank Trust Co* v. *Green* had been registered then the case would have been decided differently as the unprotected option would have enjoyed automatic priority as an overriding interest under s70(1)(g), thus emphasising the greater protection given to the rights of occupiers in registered land. However even the statutory protection of overriding interests does not fully address the problem. Imagine that a person contributes to the purchase of a shared house in London but is not a registered proprietor thereof. She decides to take a six month working holiday in Australia. During her absence the registered proprietor sells the property to a friend who is fully aware that she had contributed to the purchase. It is highly unlikely that in such circumstances the contributor would be able to maintain an overriding interest against the purchaser or mortgagee, since she would not have been in actual occupation at the date of the completion of the purchase,[35] nor was she in receipt of any rent or profits from the land.[36] This problem highlights the fact that the central difficulty lies with the structure of the land registration system as a whole. The protection accorded to overriding interests does not provide a comprehensive solution to the problem of purchasers of land who are fully aware of the existence of an unprotected right which does not otherwise rank as an overriding interest. The question thus arises whether there should be any place within the land registration system for continued operation of the doctrine of notice.

Historically the reforms of 1925 were intended to rid the system of the complexities of the doctrine of notice. In *Williams & Glynn's Bank Ltd* v. *Boland*[37] Lord Wilberforce stated that the system adopted by the Land Registration Act

[34] [1981] AC 513.

[35] It is unlikely that she would be able to claim continued symbolic actual occupation for such a period of time: *Hoggett* v. *Hoggett* (1980) 39 P & CR 121; *Chhokar* v. *Chhokar* [1984] FLR 313; *Abbey National* v. *Cann* [1996] 1 AC 56.

[36] She would be in an identical position to the father in *Strand* v. *Casewell* [1965] Ch 373, who was an equitable tenant of land but was not entitled to the protection of s70(1)(g) because he was neither in actual occupation of it nor in receipt of rents and profits from his daughter who was occupying the property rent free.

[37] [1981] AC 487, 503; [1985] CLJ 280 (Thompson).

1925 was "designed to free the purchaser from the hazards of notice—real or constructive—which, in the case of unregistered land, involved him in enquiries, often quite elaborate, failing which he might be bound by equities."[38] However it has proved impossible to shake off the perception that this renunciation of the doctrine of notice has replaced a fundamentally moral mechanism for the determination of priorities with one with lacks any moral dimension. The cynical and calculating are thus able to defeat the interests of the inefficient or uncomprehending.

An attempt to reintroduce a moral dimension by means of a re-incorporation of the doctrine of notice was mounted by Graham J in *Peffer* v. *Rigg*.[39] Mrs Peffer had purchased a house from her ex-husband, who was the sole registered proprietor and who held it on trust for himself and Mr Rigg, who had contributed half the purchase price. Mr Rigg was not in occupation of the property, nor was he in receipt of any rent or profits deriving therefrom. His beneficial interests were not protected as overriding interests, nor were they overreached by the transfer. Graham J held that in the circumstances the purchaser took the land subject to the beneficial interest because she had only given nominal consideration, thus rendering her incapable of claiming the protection of s20(1) Land Registration Act. However he further considered what the result would have been if he had upheld the contention of the purchaser that the transfer had occurred as part of a wider divorce settlement, such that she had provided valuable consideration so as to entitle her to enjoy the protection of s20(1). In such circumstances Graham J held that she would have been bound by the beneficial interest because she had acquired the land with actual notice thereof.

This novel conclusion was only made possible by reason of a difference in drafting between relevant provisions of the Land Registration Act 1925. Graham J held that the term "transferee or grantee" in s20(1) should be given the same meaning as the word "purchaser" in s59(6), where the different term was used. Since by s3(xxi) the term purchaser is given the meaning "purchaser in good faith for valuable consideration"[40] he held that s20 should be interpreted so as to be subject to a requirement of good faith, which would not be satisfied where the purchaser had notice of the existence of an interest. Whilst his interpretation is convoluted, and can be challenged on the grounds that it equated the phraseology "transferee or grantee" with "purchaser," and the concept of a lack of good faith with actual notice, he approached the question from the premise that there should be some moral element operative in the determination of priorities issues. He considered that it was "a remarkable proposition"

[38] See also: *Strand Securities* v. *Casewell* [1965] Ch 373 at 390 per Cross J; Parkash v. Irani Finance Ltd [1970] Ch 101, at p. 109, per Plowman J.

[39] [1977] 1 WLR 285. See: [1977] CLJ 227 (Hayton),; (1977) 40 MLR 602 (Anderson); (1977) 93 LQR 341 (Smith); (1977) 41 Conv 207 (Crane).

[40] According to the Law Commission the definition of the term "purchaser" in s3(xxi) Land Registration Act 1925 was a "legislative accident" arising by "some quirk". See *Land Registration for the Twenty-First Century*, Law Com No 254, para 3.41.

that s20(1) had intended to grant statutory priority to any person meeting its criteria, irrespective or whether they were acting in good faith or not.

It seems highly unlikely that the resourceful obiter dicta of Graham J in *Peffer* v. *Rigg* have successfully reintroduced an element of the doctrine of notice into registered conveyancing. His comments equating the absence of good faith with the presence of actual notice are impossible to reconcile with the definition of fraud adopted by the House of Lords in *Midland Bank Trust Company* v. *Green,* and are inconsistent with the sentiments of Lord Wilberforce in *Williams & Glynn's Bank Ltd* v. *Boland* that the whole object of the 1925 reform was to consign the doctrine of notice, in respect of registered conveyancing, to history. However despite the dubious reasoning employed, the fundamental question has refused to go away, namely whether a purchaser should take free of an interest of which he or she has actual notice. Indeed the Law Commission has recently suggested that the point remains "not wholly free from doubt,"[41] such that it recommends legislative clarification by a statement of general principle that the doctrine of notice should have no application in dealings with registered land except where otherwise specified. This recommendation runs counter to the arguments of distinguished academic commentators calling for the explicit re-introduction of the concept of actual notice within registered land,[42] and it is submitted that the reasoning of the law Commission remains unconvincing.

First, the Commission argues that there should be no place for the concepts of knowledge or notice because "it was intended that the system of registration under the Land Registration Act 1925 should displace the doctrine of notice." In reality this is no argument at all. The mere fact that a particular policy was pursued in 1925 does not ensure that it is efficacious for all time. As was argued in relation to overreaching above, the very question at issue is whether an appropriate balance was struck between the interests of conveyancing efficiency and the protection of individual rights in the legislation of 1925. To restate the policy adopted in 1925 does not advance that debate in one direction or the other.

Secondly, the Commission argues that "there is little evidence of which we are aware that the absence of the doctrine of notice in dealings with registered land has been a cause of injustice in the seventy-two years in which the present system has been operative." This amounts to an argument that, since the outcome of few cases would have been different, there is no need for change. However this might equally serve as a strong argument for amendment. If there are very few cases which would be affected, then the introduction of a clear principle that a purchaser with actual notice takes subject to unprotected interests would have very only marginal impact upon the integrity of the system. The reasoning of the Commission seems to be driven by a dogmatic commitment to the replacement of notice by registration. The recent employment of the concept of constructive notice as the touchstone to determine when a mortgagor may set

[41] *Land Registration for the Twenty-First Century,* Law Com No 254, para 3.44.

[42] Battersby (1995) 58 MLR 637; Howell [1996] Conv 34; Smith, "Land Registration: Reform at Last" in Paul Jackson and David C Wilde (ed), *The Reform of Property Law* (1997) p 129.

aside a mortgage entered under the undue influence of a third party other than the mortgagee also suggests that it is not true to say that there have been "no cases" where the absence of notice in dealings with registered land has been a cause of injustice. Since the role of constructive notice was only introduced by the House of Lords in this context in *Barclays Bank* v. *O'Brien*[43] presumably there must have been earlier cases where a mortgagor had acted under the influence of a spouse or third party but had been unable to set the mortgage aside.

Thirdly, the Commission suggests that the ethical argument in favour of the incorporation of actual notice is weaker than it appears because the creation of many interests will be required to be completed by registration, and especially that "when electronic registration is introduced, it seems probable that many rights will be incapable of being created except by registering them." However it is submitted that this is also a non-argument. The problem of unprotected rights arises most acutely in respect of those interests which arise informally, for example under resulting or constructive trusts, or rights arising by way of proprietary estoppel. It is precisely in the context of such rights that the supposedly essential feature of registration of title, namely its attempt to "substitute a system of registration of rights for the doctrine of notice,"[44] cannot operate fairly. The Law Commission's proposal to extend full proprietary status to rights arising by way of estoppel, such that they will be capable of binding third parties, inevitably means an increase in the number of informal rights which have to be integrated within the system of registered land. Perhaps more significantly, there is a presupposition that the mere fact of electronic trading will mean that dealings in land must be made notice free. There is no logical reason why this should be the case. Where shares are traded, electronically or otherwise, the doctrine of notice is still applied so as to protect the interests of beneficiaries if the shares are subject to a trust, and the law has proved sufficiently mature to tailor the requirements of the doctrine in such circumstances so as to ensure that commercial freedom is not unduly circumscribed.[45] It is ironic that as the Law Commission seeks to treat land as a more tradable commodity comparable to shares, the rights of third parties appear to be less well protected than the similar rights of third parties in personal property. Whilst it remains the case that land and shares cannot be treated identically, especially since there are many more third party rights likely to affect a piece of land than a bundle of shares, it is also the case that land no longer enjoys a unique place as the pre-eminently valuable asset in modern society. If the doctrine of notice is considered efficient to determine whether a purchaser should acquire shares free from a pre-existing security interest, or from the rights of beneficiaries, then it cannot be so flawed as to be a priori inappropriate for determining such issues in relation to land.

Fourth, the Commission argues that the introduction of a concept of actual notice would inevitably result in the reintroduction of constructive notice, since

[43] [1994] AC 180.
[44] *Parkash* v. *Irani Finance Ltd* [1970] Ch 101, at p. 109, per Plowman J.
[45] *Macmillan Inc* v. *Bishopsgate Investment Trust Ltd* [1995] 3 All 747.

"it would then be very difficult to prevent the introduction by judicial interpretation of doctrines of constructive notice." This follows from the Commission's view that the boundary between actual knowledge and constructive notice is unclear and incapable of precise definition, and that "if actual knowledge sufficed, the question would inevitably be asked: why not wilful blindness as well?" The very fact that the Commission poses its objection in this manner reveals the underlying moral question at stake. The question posited would only be asked precisely because there would be an instinctive sense of injustice if a person were able to avoid conceding priority by reason of a deliberate and wilful blindness to the obvious. However the mere fact that the concept of notice may be difficult to apply does not, in itself, mean that a mechanical alternative is preferable. As has already been noted, in the context of mortgages executed where undue influence was exercised, the courts have readily seized upon the concept of constructive notice as the touchstone determining whether a mortgagee should be entitled to enforce the mortgage. In relation to trusts of personal property the modern law has demonstrated the ability to develop a more sophisticated approach to the concept of "knowledge" which is less bedevilled by distinctions between shades of actual and constructive notice.[46] The traditional five-fold categorisation of knowledge derived from land law, which was spelt out by Peter Gibson J in *Baden Delvaux*[47], has given way to a requirement of "dishonesty" as the foundation for personal liability.[48] There is no reason why the concept of actual notice cannot be applied with similar maturity in the context of land itself. In fact, the concept of "dishonesty" which has emerged in recent cases begins to look identical to the criteria of "lack of good faith" which was read into s20(1) of the Land Registration Act 1925 by Graham J in *Peffer* v. *Rigg*. Understood in this way, the issue is not primarily one of notice at all, but whether dishonest purchasers should enjoy the right to acquire land free from pre-existing rights.

Finally the Commission argues that the re-introduction of an element of actual notice would inevitably weaken the security of title provided by registered land at the moment. This, they fear, would lead to increased litigation, and "because of the nuisance value of such threats, purchasers would often settle out of court." Whilst there is some merit to this objection, the mere fact that some uncertainty would ensue cannot provide a determining criteria by which to judge whether the concept of actual notice should be re-introduced. The issue is

[46] Although some commentators would prefer the concept of fault based personal liability in Equity to be replaced by a strict restitutionary liability balanced by the availability of the defence of change of position. See, for example, Lord Nicholls, "Knowing Receipt: The Need for a New Landmark," Ch 17 in Cornish, Nolan O'Sullivan and Virgo, *Restitution Past, Present and Future* (1998).

[47] [1983] BCLC 325.

[48] *Royal Brunei Airlines* v. *Tan* [1995] 3 All ER 97. See also: *Re Montagu's Settlement Trusts* [1987] Ch 264; *Re Clasper Group Services* [1989] BCLC 143; *Agip (Africa) Ltd* v. *Jackson* [1990] Ch 265; *Eagle Trust plc* v. *SBC Securities* [1992] 4 All ER 488; *Cowan de Groot Properties Ltd* v. *Eagle Trust plc* [1992] 4 All ER 700.

whether the greater justice achieved thereby would be outweighed by the uncertainty introduced. The perceived danger of uncertainty cannot be used as a trump card, since to do so is already to prejudge the merits of any debate as to the objectives of land registration in favour of the attainment of certainty. The vast explosion of informal rights which have been recognised as enjoying protection as overriding interests under s70(1)(g) is already a far more significant derogation from the security of title envisaged by the framers of the 1925 legislation than would be the introduction of some limited concept of actual notice. In any event, given the Commission's opinion that there are few cases which would be affected by such a change, the adverse consequences are in danger of being overstated.

It is therefore submitted that the Law Commission has wrongly rejected the opportunity to introduce a clear moral element into the determination of priorities in registered land. At a matter of principle, a person who is actually aware of the existence of a right affecting land, or of the circumstances giving rise to the existence of such a right, should not be entitled to acquire title free from it. The emphasis on conveyancing simplicity embodied in the 1925 legislation should not be sacrosanct. It is somewhat ironic that at the same time as rejecting the introduction of such a straightforward principle for protecting rights, the Law Commission is recommending a drastic restriction in the operative scope of the doctrine of adverse possession, such that a squatter will generally only be entitled to claim title by virtue of possession if he or she "had entered into adverse possession under a mistaken belief as to his or her rights and that that mistake was a reasonable one to have made."[49] This proposal is clearly grounded in a moral objection to the acquisition of title from a registered proprietor where a squatter was aware, or should have been aware by inspection of the register, that the land was not his or her own. This is evidenced by the fact that such reasonable mistakes might include cases where "the boundary between the squatter's land and that of the registered proprietor was uncertain; there had been some misrepresentation to the applicant as to the extent of his or her land; or the natural features of the land had led him or her to believe that the disputed land was his or hers."[50] In other words, if the adverse possessor knew, or ought to have known, that he or she enjoyed no entitlement to the land possessed, he or she cannot acquire title by virtue of his or her possession. In effect this proposal amounts to a re-introduction of concepts of actual and constructive notice of title in place of the current straightforward mechanical requirement that the land must be possessed for a specified period, albeit with the requisite intent. If title to land cannot be acquired by an adverse possessor because he or she knew, or should have known, that he or she was not entitled to the land concerned, why should a purchaser or mortgagee acquire title to land free from the rights of third parties of which they had actual notice?

[49] *Land Registration for the Twenty-First Century*, Law Com No 254, 1998, para 10.50.
[50] *ibid.* para 10.54.

ESTOPPEL INTERESTS IN REGISTERED LAND

It has been argued above that in important respects the current resolution of issues of priority in registered land is deficient. The law relating to overreaching is unsatisfactory because the beneficial interests of occupiers may be overreached, such that they do not enjoy protection as overriding interests. The law regarding unprotected minor interests is also inadequate, because a purchaser of land can take title free from rights of which he had prior actual knowledge. It is further submitted that these deficiencies will be exacerbated if the Law Commission's proposal to accord proprietary status to an equity arising by way of estoppel is adopted.[51]

The status of an estoppel equity has long been a matter of controversy. Some commentators have taken the view that such an equity is incapable of binding a third party because it does not fall within the catalogue of rights and interests historically recognised as proprietary,[52] a view supported by older authorities.[53] However other commentators,[54] alongside more recent authorities,[55] have tended to stress that an estoppel equity should enjoy proprietary status, with the inevitable consequence that it might be binding upon a person acquiring title to the land. In *Canadian Imperial Bank of Commerce* v. *Bello*[56] Dillon LJ suggested that an estoppel equity was an insufficient interest in land to attain overriding status within the meaning of s70(1)(g). The Law Commission has proposed that this should be reversed, provisionally recommending that "an equity arising by estoppel or acquiescence in relation to registered land should be regarded as an interest from the time at which it arises."[57] This will "make clear that such an equity is a minor interest and that it may also exist as an overriding interest where the person having the benefit of it is in actual occupation."[58] The conferral of proprietary status upon such estoppel equities will inevitably generate problems of priority which do not appear to have been addressed by the Law Commission, and which, if the proposal is adopted, provide strong support for the reforms advocated in the preceding sections.

First, it seems that such an estoppel equity would, without further statutory amendment, be capable of being overreached. Overreaching operates in respect of "any equitable interest or power affecting" an estate in land,[59] and an

[51] *Land Registration for the Twenty-First Century*, Law Com No 254, 1998, para. 3.36.

[52] [1983] Con 99 (Bailey); [1990] Conv 370 (Hayton).

[53] *Plimmer* v. *Wellington Corporation* (1884) 9 App Cas 699; *Jones (AE)* v. *Jones (FW)* [1977] 1 WLR 438; *Pennine Railway* v. *Kirklees Council* [1983] 1 QB 382; *Fryer* v. *Brook* [1984] LSGazR 2856.

[54] [1991] Conv 36 (Battersby); (1994) 14 LS 147 (Baughen); (1995) 58 MLR 637.

[55] *ER Ives Investments Ltd* v. *High* [1967] 2 QB 379; *Re Sharpe (a bankrupt)* [1980] 1 WLR 219; *Voyce* v. *Voyce* (1991) 62 P & CR 290; *Lloyd's Bank Plc* v. *Carrick* [1996] 4 All ER 630.

[56] [1992] 64 P & CR 48.

[57] *Land Registration for the Twenty-First Century*, Law Com No 254, 1998, para. 3,36.

[58] *ibid.*

[59] Law of Property Act 1925, s2(1). See (2000) 116 LQR 341, where Harpum argues that in some circumstances estoppel rights may be overreached.

inchoate estoppel equity is not exempted from the scope of overreaching by s2(3) Law of Property Act 1925. It is thus extremely hard to see how estoppel equities could be integrated within the registered land system, as it currently stands, without creating inconsistencies. The Law Commission has proposed that the grant of registered dispositions should be completed by registration.[60] However some such rights are also capable of arising informally by way of proprietary estoppel, for example easements[61] or a leases,[62] as the Commission itself explicitly recognises.[63] Thus, if the Commission's proposals are implemented, where land is burdened by a properly created legal or equitable easement overreaching would not effect its existence and it would be binding upon a successor in title as an overriding interest, but if there was an inchoate estoppel equity giving rise to an identical entitlement the right would be overreached. The facts of *ER Ives Investments Ltd* v. *High*[64] will serve as an example, although the case concerned unregistered land. The defendant had acquired an equitable easement over neighbouring land by way of estoppel. His neighbour had transferred the land to the plaintiff, who had expressly agreed to take it subject to the defendant's rights. The plaintiff subsequently brought an action for trespass against the defendant, claiming that his easement did not enjoy priority because it had not been protected by registration as a class D(ii) land charge. The Court of Appeal held that the issue of priority was to be determined by application of the doctrine of notice because it concerned a claimed estoppel equity,[65] or an easement of a type which was not required to be registered as a class D(ii) land charge.[66] Since the plaintiffs had acquired the land with actual notice of the defendant's right they took subject to it. However if the land had been registered, and subject to a trust of land,[67] the outcome would have been very different. The transfer of title would have effected overreaching, such that the inchoate estoppel equity giving rise to the easement would not have bound the purchaser, who would have acquired the land free from it. Such a result would appear to be inconsistent with the intentions of the overreaching mechanism, since such rights as easements and restrictive covenants cannot be converted into money.[68] This example makes clear that the conferral of proprietary status upon inchoate estoppel equities must be accompanied by their removal from the category of overreachable interests if they are to enjoy any real protection where land is not owned by a sole trustee.

[60] *Land Registration for the Twenty-First Century*, Law Com No 254, 1998, para. 22.1.

[61] *ER Ives investments Ltd* v. *High* [1967] 2 QB 379; *Crabb* v. *Arun District Council* [1976] Ch 179.

[62] *Grant* v. *Williams* (1977) 248 EG 947.

[63] *Land Registration for the Twenty-First Century*, Law Com No 254, 1998, para 11.12.

[64] [1967] 2 QB 379.

[65] per Danckwerts and Winn LJJ.

[66] per Lord Denning MR.

[67] Which would be much more likely today since most couples are co-own their house, inevitably giving rise to a trust of land.

[68] Sparks, *A New Land Law*, Hart Publishing, 1999, p. 116.

If such a development were to occur, further problems would be highlighted, since it would be impossible to reconcile the treatment of estoppel rights with those of the beneficiaries of trusts of land. It has been seen that in *City of London Building Society* v. *Flegg* the House of Lords held that overreaching operated so as to deprive the defendants of their beneficial interests, such that they were not able to assert an overriding interest binding the mortgage company by virtue of s70(1)(g) Land Registration Act. However if estoppel equities were to be exempt from the operation of overreaching a further unacceptable inconsistency would ensue. If Mr and Mrs Flegg asserted a right by way of proprietary estoppel to enjoy occupation of the house on the basis of a representation to that effect from Mr and Mrs Maxwell-Browne, rather than beneficial interests by way of a resulting trust, their interests would not have been overreached and the estoppel equity would have satisfied the requirements of s70(1)(g) and would have bound the mortgagee as overriding interests. Thus, if the Law Commission's proposal is adopted, the law will be faced with the invidious choice between permitting all estoppel equities to be overreached, differentiating between different types of inchoate estoppel equities so that only some would be overreachable, or excluding all estoppel equities from the scope of overreaching, with the consequence that a strict distinction would have to be drawn between proprietary estoppel and resulting and constructive trusts, concepts which the courts already recognise to be close relations, if not identical. The simplest solution, if estoppel equities are to be fully integrated into registered land as full-blown proprietary rights, is to amend the legislation so that estoppel equities cannot be overreached, and to reverse the effects of the decision in *Flegg* such that the rights of occupiers are protected as overriding interests irrespective of the overreaching mechanism. To this extent the proposal of the Law Commission that estoppel equities be accorded proprietary status provides unintentional support for the implementation of its earlier proposals in *Overreaching: Beneficiaries in Occupation*.[69]

The call to confer of full proprietary status upon inchoate estoppel equities also provides support for the argument that a purchaser of land should be bound by informally created interests of which he has actual notice. Consider again the case of *ER Ives Investments Ltd* v. *High*.[70] If the land concerned had been registered, it is hard to see how the defendant's right would have been binding on the plaintiff. The defendant was in no sense in actual occupation of the plaintiff's land, such as to entitle him to claim protection of his right as an overriding interest under s70(1)(g). If his right is properly to be categorised as an inchoate estoppel equity,[71] rather than an equitable easement, then it would not constitute an overriding interest under s70(1)(a) even if the generous interpretation of that provision adopted by Scott J in *Celsteel* v. *Alton House Holdings*

[69] Law Com No 188, 1989.
[70] [1967] 2 QB 379.
[71] As Danckwerts and Winn LJJ so held.

Ltd,[72] whereby equitable easements which are openly exercised and enjoyed by the dominant owner at the time of a transfer of the land constitute overriding interests binding on the transferee, were to be accepted. In such circumstances it would therefore appear that the plaintiff would take free from the estoppel right because it had not been properly protected as a minor interest. Thus the Law Commission proposal to accord proprietary status to estoppel equities also demands that some further provision is made to ensure that such rights are properly integrated within the land registration system. If estoppel interests are to be given full proprietary effect, the comment of Cross J in *Stand Securities* v. *Casewell*[73] that "it is vital to the working of the land registration system that notice of something which is not on the register of the title in question shall not affect a transferee unless it is an overriding interest" cannot stand. An inchoate estoppel equity, which may ultimately be satisfied by the grant of an easement, can neither be expected to be protected by registration, nor will it attain overriding status. Whilst the Commission recommends that all expressly granted easements should have to be completed by registration,[74] thus guaranteeing that they are protected, this is obviously not appropriate for estoppel rights. Estoppel provides a means by which rights may be created informally, and it is unacceptable to require persons to take active steps to protect such interests by registration as they are unlikely to be aware of their entitlement, or at the very least of their need to take steps to protect it. For this reason informal rights, such as estoppel based easements, cannot be brought satisfactorily within the conventional regime governing the priority of minor interests, and since they are not accompanied by actual occupation of the servient tenement they affect, they cannot fall within the ambit of s70(1)(g). It would be inappropriate to confer automatic overriding status upon them, since purchasers would then be incapable of protecting themselves against adverse interests which might only become apparent after they had acquired title. The only realistic solution to the problem of estoppel interests is to introduce some priority rule based on the doctrine of notice, such that a purchaser of land will be bound by an estoppel equity of which he was aware at the time that he acquired the land. This was the solution adopted by Lord Denning MR in *ER Ives Investments Ltd* v. *High*. If such a rule is necessitated by the recognition of proprietary character of estoppel equities, then it would be hard to justify the refusal to extend similar protection to other informally created interests, such as those arising under constructive and resulting trusts. Thus the Law Commission's proposal to accord proprietary status to estoppel equities also leads to the need to reintroduction some concept of notice to registered conveyancing. Given the difficulties associated with the concept of constructive notice, this would probably have to be confined to a concept of actual notice, achieving much the same effect as the purposive interpretation of the legislation advocated by Graham J in *Peffer* v. *Rigg*.

72 [1985] 1 WLR 204.
73 [1965] Ch 958, 987.
74 para. 5.9.

CONCLUSIONS

A resurgence of the traditional role of Equity as a means of ensuring justice and fairness is increasingly evident in the modern law. The emergence of constructive trusts and proprietary estoppel, the development of the doctrine of unconscionability and the introduction of concepts of constructive notice to determine whether a mortgage obtained by the use of undue influence should be set aside are all examples of this tendency. The doctrine of notice, as historically applied to determine issues of priority between rights in land, was rooted in a concern for fairness and justice. The land registration system was framed on the assumption that a mechanistic procedure could be designed which would eliminate complexity and uncertainty yet also achieve fairness. As Cross J observed in *Strand Securities* v. *Casewell*[75] "it is vital to the working of the land registration system that notice of something which is not on the register of the title in question shall not affect a transferee unless it is an overriding interest." Whilst this objective may be laudable, it is submitted that it is also unattainable if proper recognition is to be accorded to the role of proprietary interests arising without the need for formality, and pre-eminently to constructive and resulting trusts and inchoate estoppel equities. Unlike the beneficiary of a commercially valuable estate contract, such as the son in *Midland Bank Trust Company* v. *Green*[76], the possessors of such informally arising interests cannot be expected to have to take steps to protect their rights, since by their very nature most remain ignorant of their existence, or importance, until some difficulty arises. The proper protection of such informal interests should not be sacrificed for the sake of achieving conveyancing efficiency, if the consequence is injustice. Such rights cannot be protected satisfactorily as s70(1)(g) overriding interests because they are not universally enjoyed by occupiers, and they remain vulnerable to the effects of overreaching. The only solution to this problem is therefore to accept that they deserve special protection. This can only be done by ensuring that such interests arising informally are not defeated by overreaching where the owner thereof is in actual occupation of the land affected, and that a purchaser is bound by all such interests of which he was actually aware. If such measures are introduced then justice will enjoyed a proper place in determination of priorities between interests in registered land. It is submitted that any consequent degradation of the certainty of title accorded by the current system would be minimal. However, in the light of the decision of the government not to the implement the recommendations of the Law Commission report *Overreaching: Beneficiaries in Occupation*,[77] and the refusal of the Commission to countenance any role for actual notice in its consultative document *Land Registration for the Twenty-First Century*,[78] it seems that there is no prospect of such reform.

[75] [1965] Ch 373, 390.

[76] [1981] AC 513.

[77] Law Com No 188, 1989.

[78] Law Com No 254, 1998.

9

Co-ownership of Property, Valuation, vires *and Entitlement to Means-tested Benefits*

NICK WIKELEY*

IT IS BOTH my pleasure and privilege to contribute this chapter to Brian Harvey's Festschrift. Brian was Dean of the Law Faculty at the University of Birmingham when I applied for my first academic post. During the interview he asked me which I regarded as more complex: national insurance law or supplementary benefits law. When I suggested the former, his response was along the lines of "Well, what about the assessment of capital resources under the supplementary benefits system?" I had no answer to that but still managed to be appointed. It is therefore particularly appropriate that this contribution addresses an important interface between Brian's scholarship in Property Law and his judicial service in the field of Social Security Law. Brian was first appointed a part-time Chairman of the former supplementary benefit appeal tribunals (SBATs) in May 1982 (from April 1984 these became social security appeal tribunals, or SSATs). He was subsequently appointed a medical appeal tribunal (MAT) chairman in November 1985 and a disability appeal tribunal (DAT) chairman in December 1991, retiring in 1999. He was a source of great support and wise counsel to me as I developed my own research in social security law. He was also instrumental in encouraging me to take up a similar judicial appointment. I am indebted to Philip Larkin for his invaluable research assistance.

INTRODUCTION

Income support is, by definition, a last resort for the impoverished citizen. It represents the principal safety net of the modern welfare state with a lineage that can be traced back through supplementary benefit, national assistance and unemployment assistance to the Poor Law. Today income support is payable to those people who meet various prescribed conditions and who have either no

* Professor of Law, University of Southampton.

other sources of income or insufficient income to live on, as judged by the minimum subsistence level laid down by the State.[1] It is therefore a means-tested benefit; people are expected—within certain constraints recognised by the legislation—to rely on their own resources before turning to income support for assistance. There is accordingly no entitlement to income support if the claimant possesses £8,000 or more in capital.[2] For these purposes the claimant's capital is treated as including assets owned by a member of his family, except in prescribed circumstances.[3] The definition of "family" in social security law is such that this deeming rule effectively only brings in the capital of a married or unmarried partner living in the same household.[4] A more generous limit of £16,000 has applied since April 1996 for claimants who live permanently in residential care or nursing homes, or similar accommodation.[5] Parallel provisions apply for the other means-tested benefits.[6] However, certain forms of capital are expressly disregarded in assessing the claimant's resources.[7] A claimant who owns between £3,000 and £8,000 in capital is deemed to receive a "tariff income" from such assets which may, independently of the capital rule, disentitle him from receiving income support when aggregated with other forms of income.[8]

The primary legislation furthermore vests the Secretary of State with sweeping powers to deal with the treatment of capital in regulations. Thus "capital shall be calculated or estimated in such manner as may be prescribed".[9]

[1] Social Security Contributions and Benefits Act (SSCBA) 1992, s.124.

[2] SSCBA 1992, s.134(1) and Income Support (General) Regulations 1987 (S.I. 1987 No. 1967), reg 45(a). The upper limit for income support was originally £6,000 but was raised to £8,000 in 1990.

[3] SSCBA 1992, s.136(1) and S.I. 1987 No. 1967, reg. 23. The principal exceptions relate to children's capital: *ibid.*, regs 44 and 47.

[4] SSCBA 1992, s.137(1) and S.I. 1987 No. 1967, reg. 23.

[5] *Ibid.*, regs. 45(b) and 53(1B), inserted with effect from April 8, 1996 by Income-related Benefits Schemes (Miscellaneous Amendments) Regulations 1996 (S.I. 1996 No. 462) reg. 12(1). Regulation 53(1B) has since been further amended by Income-related Benefits and Jobseeker's Allowance (Miscellaneous Amendments) Regulations 1997 (S.I. 1997 No. 65), reg. 8. Identical provisions apply to income-based jobseeker's allowance: Jobseeker's Allowance Regulations 1996 (S.I. 1996 No. 207), regs. 107 and 116(1B).

[6] The capital limit is £8,000 for family credit and income-based jobseeker's allowance but £16,000 for all claimants of housing benefit, council tax benefit and disability working allowance: Family Credit (General) Regulations 1987 (S.I 1987 No. 1968), reg. 28, Housing Benefit (General) Regulations 1987 (S.I. 1987 No. 1971), reg. 37, Council Tax Benefit (General) Regulations (S.I. 1992 No. 1814), reg. 28, Disability Working Allowance (General) Regulations 1991 (S.I. 1991 No. 2887), reg. 31 and Jobseeker's Allowance Regulations 1996 (S.I. 1996 No. 207), reg. 115 (on the latter, see the argument below at p.000). Family credit and disability working allowance were renamed with effect from October 5, 1999 as working families' tax credit and disabled person's tax credit: Tax Credits Act 1999, s.1.

[7] There is an extensive and detailed list of exemptions, or "disregards", in S.I. 1987 No. 1967, Sched. 10. These include most obviously, for example, "the dwelling occupied as the home": *ibid.*, para. 1.

[8] SSCBA 1992, s.136(2) and S.I. 1987 No. 1967, reg. 53. The tariff income is £1 per week for each £250 or part thereof of assets worth between £3,000 and £8,000. Thus a claimant with savings of £6,100 is treated as receiving £13 investment income per week (assuming a non-taxpayer, this would actually require an interest rate in the order of 11 per cent).

[9] SSCBA 1992, s.136(3).

Moreover, section 136(5) of the Social Security Contributions and Benefits Act 1992 provides, with "chilling simplicity"[10] that:

"Circumstances may be prescribed in which—
(a) a person is treated as possessing capital or income which he does not possess;
(b) capital or income which a person does possess is to be disregarded;
(c) income is to be treated as capital;
(d) capital is to be treated as income."

As Lord Donaldson observed in *Chief Adjudication Officer* v. *Foster*,[11] these enabling powers allow the Secretary of State "to prescribe that black is white and nothing is something and vice versa in the context of income and capital".[12] The breadth of section 136(5) has been confirmed more recently by the Court of Appeal in *Owen*,[13] in which a terminally ill claimant had left his employment with a month's sick pay, paid in arrears. His claim for income support was refused as his sick pay was attributed to a forward period under the relevant regulations.[14] Mummery L.J. concluded that the relevant provision was *intra vires* s.136(5)(a): "By their very nature deeming provisions have the effect of treating a fact or a state of affairs as existing for a stated purpose when that fact or state of affairs does not in truth exist."[15] Moreover, a challenge based on irrationality also failed: "The fact that the regulation produces a hard case or an anomaly does not necessarily make it irrational."[16]

The Income Support (General) Regulations 1987 also take full advantage of this extensive licence in relation to capital. Chapter VI of Part V of the Regulations accordingly provides that all the claimant's capital, actual and notional,[17] along with that of any partner, is taken into account, subject to the disregards specified in Schedule 10.[18] There is also provision for various forms of income to be treated as capital.[19] Regulation 49 specifies that capital held in the United Kingdom is to be calculated:

"at its current market or surrender value, less—
(i) where there would be expenses attributable to the sale, 10 per cent; and
(ii) the amount of any incumbrance secured on it."[20]

[10] The expression is that of Commissioner Howell in *CIS/4312/1997*, starred decision **81/98* (para. 9), upheld on appeal as *Owen* v. *Chief Adjudication Officer*, April 29, 1999, Court of Appeal, unreported.

[11] [1992] Q.B. 31 at 45.

[12] See also *Chief Adjudication Officer* v. *Palfrey*, *The Times*, 17 February 1995, C.A. where Hobhouse L.J. observed that "the maker of the regulations has a considerable latitude": official transcript, p.13.

[13] Above, n.10. See also (1999) 6 J.S.S.L. 108.

[14] Income Support (General) Regulations 1987 (S.I. 1987 No. 1967), reg. 29(2).

[15] Transcript of C.A. decision, above n.10, p.12.

[16] *Loc. cit.*; but "the situation would, however, appear to be unsatisfactory and would justify a review of the operation of the Regulations by the Secretary of State."

[17] On the complex nature of "notional capital", see above n.14, regs. 51 and 51A.

[18] *Ibid.*, reg. 46.

[19] *Ibid.*, reg. 48.

[20] *Ibid.*, reg. 49(a). On the treatment of incumbrances, see *R(IS) 21/93*. There are separate rules

The principal focus of this chapter is the treatment of jointly-owned capital for the purpose of assessing an individual's eligibility for income support.[21] The central provision is regulation 52 of the Income Support (General) Regulations,[22] the heading to which is "Capital jointly held". This regulation in effect governs the position where a claimant is the co-owner of property with one or more persons other than a partner living in the same household.[23] Regulation 52 treats each beneficial co-owner as having an equal share of the equity, irrespective of the true position as regards beneficial title. The text of the regulation has undergone a number of transformations as a result of amending secondary legislation issued in response to the developing case law, most notably the decisions of the Court of Appeal in *Chief Adjudication Officer* v. *Palfrey*[24] and of Commissioner Goodman in *Tucker*.[25] It is therefore important to trace the chronology of these developments before analysing some of the wider lessons to be drawn.

THE POSITION BEFORE *PALFREY*

The supplementary benefits legislation in place between 1966 and 1988 made no specific provision for the assessment of jointly owned property.[26] The official guidance, as published in the departmental 'S' Manual, was quite specific. Staff were directed that:

> "Where a claimant has an interest in property which is jointly owned:—
> (1) do **not** simply apportion the value of the property between the owners; instead
> (2) ascertain the value of the claimant's **interest** in the property from the District Valuer."[27]

The legal authority for this advice was the decision of Commissioner Morcom in *R(SB) 21/83*. The claimant was the beneficiary under a will trust, the assets of

for the valuation of National Savings Certificates (reg. 49(b)) and for capital outside the United Kingdom (reg. 50).

[21] At the outset, of course, it must be established that there is indeed joint ownership, applying orthodox principles of property law. In *R(IS) 4/96* the claimant had transferred his entire interest in the former matrimonial home to his ex-wife in return for a charge equal to 16/57ths of its value, not to be enforced until she died, remarried or cohabited for six months or more. The tribunal treated the claimant as owning a 16/57 share in the property; as the Commissioner held, in fact he had no more than a secured debt payable at some future date which was worth substantially less than 16/57 of the property's current value.

[22] S.I. 1987 No. 1967.

[23] As explained above (see text accompanying notes 3 and 4), if the other joint owner is a partner, whether or not married to the claimant, and lives in the same household, then that person's assets are aggregated with those of the claimant.

[24] *The Times*, 17 February 1995, C.A.

[25] *CIS/15936/1996*.

[26] Supplementary Benefits (Resources) Regulations 1981 (S.I. 1981 No. 1527), reg. 5 was the only relevant statutory provision, and this merely stated the general rule on valuation now to be found in Income Support (General) Regulations 1987 (S.I. 1987 No. 1967), reg. 49.

[27] DHSS, "S" *Manual*, HMSO, 1983, para. 6208 (original emphasis).

which comprised 12 cottages with a total value of £25,000, at a time when the capital limit for supplementary benefit was £2,000. The Commissioner held that:

> "An undivided share in a trust fund has a current market value of less than the amount provided by merely dividing by the number of beneficiaries. As the value of the claimant's undivided share is less than the amount provided by dividing the total value of the trust fund by the number of beneficiaries a reduction in value from a merely proportionate basis of anything between 5 and possibly 30 per cent is a question of evidence and argument. However as a question of valuation the value of the beneficiary's share must be subject to possible litigation, that is if the trustee refused to sell the beneficiary's recourse would be to the court and of course the costs of the sale would in any case diminish the value of the beneficiary's interest."[28]

Commissioner Hallett concluded to similar effect in *CSB/1189/1983*:

> "a one third share in the proceeds of sale of property is not necessarily (and indeed normally will not be) worth one third of the value of the property, because a purchaser will usually (if not always) pay less for a share than its proportion of the whole. . . Accordingly, the *share* must be valued."[29]

These subtleties, predicating an awareness of the distinction between the property itself and rights in the property, and between legal and beneficial title, were often lost on staff working on the ground, who tended to operate in the diametrically opposite fashion to that advocated in the guidance. As Mesher observed, "the simplistic DHSS view has usually been to value the totality of the assets and then divide it up to reach the relevant share."[30] This approach was "entirely wrong" as it was "the value of the share, which may well be lower, which has to be taken".[31]

In April 1988 the supplementary benefits scheme was superseded by income support. The new scheme made express provision for situations in which capital was jointly owned. The original formulation of regulation 52 of the Income Support (General) Regulations 1987[32] was as follows:

> "Except where a claimant possesses capital which is disregarded under regulation 51(4) (notional capital), where a claimant and one or more persons are beneficially

[28] *R(SB) 21/83*, para. 8.

[29] *CSB/1189/1983*, para. 4 (original emphasis).

[30] J Mesher, *Supplementary Benefit and Family Income Supplement: The Legislation* (2nd ed., 1986) London: Sweet & Maxwell, p.213.

[31] *Loc. cit.*

[32] S.I. 1987 No. 1967. Identical provision was made for family credit (Family Credit (General) Regulations 1987 (S.I. 198 No. 1968), reg. 35) and housing benefit (Housing Benefit (General) Regulations 1987 (S.I. 198 No. 1971), reg. 44) and later for disability working allowance (Disability Working Allowance (General) Regulations 1991 (S.I. 1991 No. 2887), reg. 39), council tax benefit (Council Tax Benefit (General) Regulations 1992 (S.I. 1992 No. 1814), reg. 36) and income-related jobseeker's allowance (Jobseeker's Allowance Regulations 1996 (S.I. 1996 No. 207), reg. 115). A parallel provision also appears in the extra-statutory Earnings Top-Up Rules 1996, r.42. These various provisions have all been amended in the light of subsequent amendments to reg. 52.

entitled in possession to any capital asset they shall be treated as if each of them were entitled in possession to the whole beneficial interest therein in an equal share."[33]

As Mesher commented, this was "an extraordinary rule".[34] It stipulated that a claimant who had *any* beneficial interest in an asset was to be treated as having an *equal* share. "Thus if a person has a 10 per cent interest in a house, and another person has a 90 per cent interest, each is treated as having a 50 per cent interest."[35] The inevitable outcome, when combined with the rules on capital disregards in Schedule 10 of the 1987 Regulations, was that "a claimant is fixed with capital assets which he is not legally entitled to at all, let alone unable [*sic*] to realise immediately."[36]

Within six months of the introduction of the income support scheme, regulation 52 had been amended by the inclusion of a further sub-clause.[37] It now read:

> "Except where a claimant possesses capital which is disregarded under regulation 51(4) (notional capital), where a claimant and one or more persons are beneficially entitled in possession to any capital asset they shall be treated as if each of them were entitled in possession to the whole beneficial interest therein in an equal share *and the foregoing provisions of this Chapter shall apply for the purposes of calculating the amount of capital which the claimant is treated as possessing as if it were actual capital which the claimant does possess.*"

This was described by the Explanatory Note to the amending regulations to be one of a number of "miscellaneous amendments".[38]

So far as valuation of the deemed share was concerned, the majority of the early Commissioners' decisions reflected the construction advanced by Mesher

[33] Regulation 51(4) is concerned with deemed ownership of a company's assets in a one person company or similar small enterprise.

[34] J. Mesher, *C.P.A.G's Income Support, The Social Fund and Family Credit: The Legislation* (1988) London: Sweet & Maxwell, p.100. Judicial eyebrows were also raised: in *CIS/408/1990* Commissioner Hoolahan echoed Mesher's comment (at para. 5) and in *CIS/449/1990* Commissioner Johnson observed that "it is not appropriate for me to discuss in this decision that regulation's wider implications or the injustices to which it may give rise" (para. 7). Similarly, the provision was described as "draconian" by Commissioner Rice in *CIS/807/1991*.

[35] Mesher, above n.34, p.100. Such an extreme scenario appears not actually to have arisen, at least in any Commissioners' decisions which I have seen. However, in *CIS/408/1990* (see further below) a claimant who owned a 50 per cent beneficial share was treated as owning only a one-third interest, as the other half was jointly owned by two others. Conversely, in *CIS/240/1992* the claimant had a one-quarter share in a property with his mother owning the remaining three-quarters. Commissioner Mesher (as he had by then become) explicitly held that the effect of regulation 52 was to deem the claimant to own a one-half share (para. 15).

[36] Mesher, above n.34, p.100.

[37] The amendment was with effect from September 12, 1988: Income Support (General) Amendment No. 4 Regulations 1988 (S.I. 1988 No. 1445), reg. 13.

[38] No reference to the Social Security Advisory Committee was required as they were made within 12 months of the commencement of the enabling provisions: Social Security Act 1986, s.61(5) (now 6 months under Social Security Administration Act (SSAA) 1992, s.173(5)). These amending regulations were not debated in Parliament. The purpose of this amendment is by no means clear; probably it is an example of departmental "belt and braces" drafting of regulations. The amendment was prayed in aid before the Social Security Commissioners by the adjudication officer in *Palfrey* (*CIS/391/1992*), para. 26.

and contained in the official guidance (if not the practice) in the context of the supplementary benefits scheme. Thus it was held in *CIS/024/1990* and *CIS 408/1990* that the correct approach was not to take the market value of the property and simply divide it into the appropriate number of shares. Rather, the assumption should be made that the claimant has an interest of the deemed percentage, the market value of which should then be calculated. This approach might "depending on the circumstances, produce a much lower valuation".[39] As the point has been well put, "the difference between the approaches can be summed up as being between 'half the value' and the 'value of half'."[40]

In *CIS/024/1990* the claimant and her daughter were joint owners of a house in which they lived. The claimant then moved into a residential care home, leaving her daughter alone in the house, precisely the scenario which was to recur in *Palfrey* and other cases. The original adjudication officer and appeal tribunal took the simplistic view that the claimant's capital included half of the vacant possession value of the house. On appeal to the Commissioner, the adjudication officer then concerned supported the appeal, relying on *R(SB) 21/83* and agreeing that the value of the claimant's beneficial interest might be quite different to her proportionate share of the overall value, and indeed might arguably be nil. The Commissioner upheld the appeal accordingly with no further discussion of the issues.

The merits of *CIS/408/1990* were undoubtedly less compelling in terms of the underlying policy issues. Here the claimant, a widow, lived in a nursing home and owned a half share in a retail property valued at £100,000 which was let to Boots the chemists. Although she owned a 50 per cent interest as an equitable tenant in common, the owner of the other 50 per cent interest had since died and her share had been inherited by two people. To this extent regulation 52 worked to the claimant's advantage: whilst her actual interest was clearly one half of the whole, there were now three co-owners and so she was deemed by regulation 52 to be entitled to a one-third share. The lay majority of the appeal tribunal concluded, somewhat perversely, that the value of the claimant's share was still less than £6,000, the then capital limit, given the expenses of sale and the unwillingness of the other co-owners to buy out her share. The legal chairman, dissenting, took the view that, notwithstanding the difficulties of valuation, the claimant's capital assets clearly exceeded £6,000.[41] Commissioner Hoolahan set aside the decision of the majority of the tribunal as erroneous in law, concluding on the evidence available that the claimant was not entitled to income support. Although the point is not made explicitly in the Commissioner's judgment, this conclusion appears to be premised on the assumption that it was the deemed

[39] J. Mesher, *C.P.A.G's Income Support, The Social Fund and Family Credit: The Legislation* (1991) London: Sweet & Maxwell, p.146.

[40] L. Findlay, R. Poynter, P. Stagg and M. Ward, *CPAG's Housing Benefit and Council Tax Benefit Legislation* (11th ed., 1998/99) (London: CPAG, 1999), p.236.

[41] The claimant also had savings of nearly £2,500.

share which had to be valued in its own right, rather than on the basis of a straightforward arithmetical division.

This interpretation was also echoed in advice issued by the Chief Adjudication Officer in December 1990, which recognised that "the value of a claimant's beneficial interest shared amongst relatives will be most probably nil", assuming that there was no willing buyer amongst the relatives or indeed outside the family.[42] Subsequent Commissioners' decisions reaffirmed and elaborated upon the approach taken in *CIS/024/1990* and *CIS/408/1990*. In *CIS/357/1990* the claimant was one of three trustees and four beneficiaries under a trust created by will. The settlement comprised three houses, each with a sitting tenant, which could not be sold without the consent of the other trustees. The claimant's interest was valued at nearly £12,000, allowing for the tenants' security.[43] Commissioner Hoolahan concluded that the claimant's undivided share in the property had to be valued taking into account a wider range of considerations than the simple fact of sitting tenants, including the prospect of an application to court to enforce a sale and the probable costs. This was likely to lead to "a heavy discount of the open market valuation".[44]

However, not all Commissioners adopted this approach. Two later decisions applied a simple division of the value of the whole to arrive at a valuation for the individual share. In *CIS/807/1991* a father and son, both bricklayers, had jointly bought a plot of land as equitable tenants in common on which the son had built a house for his own family. The property was subsequently valued at £75,000. On the father's claim for income support, Commissioner Rice dismissed an argument that the son had sole beneficial ownership through the operation of proprietary estoppel and concluded that the value of the father's half share "came to something in the region of £26,250",[45] after allowing for the mortgage and related costs. The Commissioner's decision assumed, without discussion, that a half share under regulation 52 was automatically worth half the value of the property itself. In *CIS/210/1991* the same broad brush approach was taken. Here the claimant was joint beneficial owner with her grandson of a house worth £30,000. After deductions for the costs of sale, she was fixed with a share worth £13,500 so as to disentitle her from income support. Commissioner Morcom's brief decision made no reference to any of the earlier decided authorities on the point, but again assumed that a simple division of the market value of the property as a whole was appropriate. According to Commissioner Morcom:

> "Though the above construction of regulation 52 would appear to operate in some instances somewhat harshly, it is to my mind as a question of construction clear that

[42] "Guidance for Adjudication Officers—Income Support", para. 18, cited in *CIS/391/1992*, para 9(2) and included as the first Appendix to that decision.

[43] This was on the basis that there were only three beneficiaries; in fact, to complicate matters further, one of the original beneficiaries had died, leaving his interest to two infants.

[44] *CIS/357/1990*, para. 14.

[45] *CIS/807/1991*, para. 17.

its effect is as stated above. I would add that I have no overriding or dispensing powers. My task is to construe the legislation as I see it. Amendment to the law is a matter for Parliament and Parliament alone and regulation 52 is of course a fairly recently introduced provision."[46]

Given the obscurity of regulation 52, the divergent views of the Commissioners were perhaps to be expected. Indeed, it seems clear that the question of the proper construction of regulation 52 was one on which views changed over time within the DSS Solicitor's Office itself. In *CIS/357/1990*, decided in 1991 following an oral hearing, the departmental solicitor had argued that the provision required a sophisticated valuation. It was not sufficient to divide the market value between the appropriate number of beneficiaries; rather, the individual deemed beneficial share had to be valued.[47] Two years later, in *Palfrey*, when the same version of regulation 52 was in issue, the same individual adopted the converse position.[48]

THE DECISION IN *CHIEF ADJUDICATION OFFICER V. PALFREY*

The proper construction of the original regulation 52, as amended in 1988, was fully considered by a Tribunal of three Social Security Commissioners[49] and subsequently by the Court of Appeal in *Chief Adjudication Officer* v. *Palfrey*.[50] In *Palfrey* the claimant was an 81 year old widower who lived with his 52 year old daughter. The house in which they had lived since the early 1950s was a local authority property. In 1982 Mr Palfrey, as the secure tenant of the property, wished to exercise his right to buy. He had already been retired for 10 years and was not able to afford the purchase. Accordingly, the house was conveyed to Mr Palfrey and Miss Palfrey as legal and equitable joint tenants. Mr Palfrey contributed nothing to the purchase of the property; part of the purchase price and all of the mortgage repayments were met by Miss Palfrey. In March 1991 Mr Palfrey, in failing health, became a permanent resident in a residential care home. The adjudication officer, on reviewing the award of income support, decided that Mr Palfrey was disentitled to benefit as his capital now exceeded the capital limit of £8,000.[51] The house of which he was a co-owner but in which

[46] *CIS/210/1991*, para. 5.

[47] *CIS/357/1990*, para. 14.

[48] *CIS/391/1992*, paras 25 and 26.

[49] Under SSAA 1992, s.57, the Chief Commissioner had the power so to direct if it appeared to him that the appeal "involves a question of law of special difficulty" (see now Social Security Act 1998, s.16(7)). Many years ago, commenting on a draft of one of my first articles on social security adjudication, Brian Harvey pointed out (quite correctly) that the Latin root for tribunal is not tri-, and so a tribunal by definition can comprise any number of individuals.

[50] Somewhat curiously, this decision has never been properly reported. There is an inadequate summary report in *The Times* (1995) February 17; the full report of the Court of Appeal's decision on 8 February 1995 is available on LEXIS. References in this chapter to *Palfrey* are based on the official transcript of the Court's decision, for which I am indebted to Godfrey Cole.

[51] One might note in passing that had Miss Palfrey herself been aged 60 or over or incapacitated then there would have been an indefinite disregard of this capital: Income Support (General) Regulations 1987 (S.I. 1987 No. 1971), Sched. 10, para. 4.

he no longer lived had been valued at £40,000 by the District Valuer; with deductions for the expenses of sale and outstanding mortgage, the equity was almost £32,000, and so Mr Palfrey's "share" was calculated to be nearly £16,000. It was clear that Miss Palfrey was unwilling to move or to join in any sale of the property.

The Tribunal of Commissioners held that regulation 52 deemed a claimant to have an equal share of any relevant capital asset together with any co-owners and that "it is the current market value of that share which requires to be calculated".[52] In that context the District Valuer's valuation was "worthless", because it referred to the market value of the house, not the market value of a half share of the proceeds of sale of the equity of redemption.[53] The Commissioners went on to give detailed guidance as to the proper factors to be considered in valuing such an interest.[54] Although the Commissioners found against the Chief Adjudication Officer on the point of construction, they ruled that regulation 52 was neither *ultra vires*, given the broad scope of the enabling power in the primary legislation,[55] nor void for irrationality.

The Court of Appeal upheld the ruling of the Tribunal of Commissioners on the issue of valuation, but made no comment on the question as to whether regulation 52 was *ultra vires* or void for irrationality. Each of the three Lords Justices of Appeal delivered his own judgment, reaching their unanimous decision by somewhat different routes and with declining degrees of certainty as to the inevitability of the outcome of the appeal. Nourse L.J. took the view that the key issue of valuation turned on the proper interpretation of the stipulation in regulation 52 that the co-owners "shall be treated as if each of them were entitled in possession to the whole beneficial interest therein in an equal share".[56] His Lordship held that this necessarily required the claimant's deemed (or actual) beneficial interest in an equal share in a tenancy in common to be valued.[57] Under regulation 49, this had to be assessed according to its current market value, "with the probable result that it will be given a nil value".[58] Dealing

[52] *CIS/391/1992*, para 38; see N. Wikeley, "Joint Ownership of Property and Entitlement to Income Support" [1994] Conv. 303. It should be noted that Mr Palfrey was unable to afford representation before the Commissioners; the arguments which prevailed were those advanced by an *amicus curiae*, instructed by the Treasury Solicitor.

[53] *CIS/391/1992*, para. 51.

[54] *Ibid.*, paras. 53–54. See also *CIS/413/1992*, applying the Commissioners' decision in *Palfrey* in the context of Scots real property law (claimant, who lived in England, owned a ¼ *pro indiviso* share in a holiday chalet in Scotland with her siblings).

[55] SSCBA 1992, s.136(5).

[56] *Palfrey*, above n.24, official transcript, p.7.

[57] "So in the case of a freehold or leasehold property the persons beneficially entitled in possession are to be treated as if each of them (including the claimant) were (a) entitled in possession to the whole beneficial interest in the property (b) in an equal share. . . The only entitlement known to the law where (a) and (b) above can coexist is a tenancy in common in equal shares, each tenant, while the property is undivided, being entitled to the whole in common with the other or others and, on its division, to an equal share": *loc cit*.

[58] *ibid.*, p.8. Nourse L.J. had concluded earlier that "It is evident that there would be no market for Mr Palfrey's interest. Miss Palfrey, being no doubt content to rely on her right of survivorship

with the submissions of the Chief Adjudication Officer and the Secretary of State on the proper interpretation of the statutory language, Nourse L.J. observed:

> "The appellants' construction of regulation 52 requires the crucial words to be rewritten as follows:
>
> > 'they shall be treated as if each of them were entitled in possession to an equal share of the value of the whole beneficial interest therein.'
>
> But the crucial words as drawn have no concern for the beneficial interest as a whole, far less for its value. They are concerned only with the beneficial interest of each of the persons entitled. The appellants' construction is quite simply not open to them on the wording."[59]

Hobhouse L.J. noted, by way of introduction, that the extremely wide enabling provisions meant that the regulations could provide for the application of wholly artificial criteria.[60] Given that statutory context, His Lordship concluded somewhat disarmingly that:

> "it is very difficult for a court to approach any question of construction of the Regulations on the basis that there is any intention that the Regulations shall have, in their application, a relationship to reality or any identifiable statutory policy of justice. There is, therefore, in my judgment no escape from adopting a construction of the Regulations which derives little, if any, assistance from anything other than the literal meaning of the actual language used. The detailed policy of the Regulations is in many respects obscure and equivocal."[61]

Notwithstanding the absence of any clear underlying principle, Hobhouse L.J. indicated that he was prepared to assume that:

> "there is an overall intention that income support should be paid, and only paid, to those who have inadequate financial means to support themselves; that ease of administration of the scheme and the avoidance of complication are considerations which may have motivated those responsible for drafting the Regulations; and that the creation of artificial situations by means of deeming provisions has not been adopted as an end in itself."[62]

Turning to the language of regulation 52 itself, Hobhouse L.J. took the view that the use in two places of the term "treated as" demonstrated that it was deeming some situation to exist which in truth did not exist. Moreover, it was

under the joint tenancy, has made it clear that she has no intention of buying it. Equally, no outsider would be willing to buy into a house whose occupation would have to be shared with her. Accordingly, Mr Palfrey's interest would in all probability have to be brought into account at a nil value"; *ibid.*, p.4.

[59] *ibid.*, p.8.

[60] "Situations which do not exist are liable to be treated as if they did; those which do exist are liable to be treated as if they did not. A person may be treated as if he possessed capital which he does not possess and *vice versa*": *ibid.*, p.13.

[61] *loc. cit.*

[62] *ibid.*, pp.13–14.

"a reasonable inference that this is being done for the sake of simplicity of calculation".[63] In contrast to Nourse L.J., Hobhouse L.J. regarded both of the constructions advanced by the two parties as equally viable at face value.[64] However, he preferred the claimant's contended meaning because "the draftsman has chosen language which . . . must have been specifically directed to the creation of a deemed tenancy in common."[65] This approach both reflected the statutory language used and resulted in a conclusion "less extreme in its artificiality"[66] than that advocated by the Department. Furthermore, having analysed the case law on applications under section 30 of the Law of Property Act 1925,[67] Hobhouse L.J. dismissed the pragmatic argument advanced by the Chief Adjudication Officer and the Secretary of State:

> "The Appellants were not right to argue that it was impossible or even disproportionately difficult to calculate the amount of the capital which the claimant is deemed to possess as a tenant in common. Where the capital asset is a jointly owned dwelling house held for the purpose of accommodating the joint owners and that purpose is still subsisting, there is nothing obscure or abstruse in the conclusion that the amount of the capital which the applicant's joint possession of that dwelling house represents may fall, for the time being, to be quantified in a nominal amount."[68]

The third member of the Court of Appeal, Sir Ralph Gibson, agreed with Hobhouse L.J. that either of the meanings being advanced by the parties was consistent with the statutory language.[69] Accordingly, "the issue must be decided by reference to the legislative context in which the regulation appears".[70] However, in contradistinction to Hobhouse L.J., Sir Ralph Gibson found no assistance in the notion that regulation 52 might be particularly directed towards treating joint tenants as tenants in common.[71] Sir Ralph Gibson also concluded that the goal of simplification might have led Parliament to accept the broad-brush approach contended for by the Department.[72] Ultimately, however, he concluded that it was safest to assume that:

> "where Parliament intends that an applicant shall be excluded from benefit because he is to be treated as possessing capital, or capital of a particular value, which he

[63] *ibid.*, p.16.

[64] "I consider that both arguments are plausible and must confess that, on this question, my mind has shifted. I do not accept the argument of the Respondents [the claimants] that the language used is inappropriate to achieve the result contended for by the Appellants [the Chief Adjudication Officer and the Secretary of State]; *ibid.*, p.17.

[65] *loc. cit.*

[66] *ibid.*, p.18.

[67] Now Trusts of Land and Appointment of Trustees Act 1996, ss.14 and 15.

[68] *ibid.*, p.20.

[69] *ibid.*, p.24.

[70] *loc. cit.*

[71] His reasoning appeared to be that regulation 52 was not confined to dealing with freehold property: "There is no limitation upon the meaning of the words 'any capital asset'; they include, but are not limited to, real property such as a dwelling house. The words apply to money, to shares in a company, and to an enforceable claim": *ibid.*, p.24.

[72] *ibid.*, p.25.

does not or may not in fact possess, clear language will be used to express that intention."[73]

If the outcome of the Court of Appeal's decision was "to impose unacceptable burdens upon the administration of the scheme, or to increase unacceptably the burden upon the taxpayer, Parliament may be invited to approve such amendment of the scheme as may be thought to be necessary."[74]

Palfrey was heard by the Court of Appeal along with four other appeals, *Dowell*[75], *McDonnell*,[76] *McNamara*[77] and *Pelter*.[78] The first two had been heard together with *Palfrey* by the Tribunal of Commissioners. In *Dowell* the claimant, an 80 year old widow, owned and lived with her daughter and son-in-law in a property valued at £75,000 and not subject to a mortgage. On this occasion, the beneficial interest was held under a tenancy in common. She then had to move into residential care and claimed income support but was disallowed on the same basis as Mr Palfrey. The Commissioners held that regulation 52, if it applied at all to an asset held in trust for persons in equal shares, had no practical effect. In *Dowell* the claimant had an actual one-third share, the current market value of which had to be valued under regulation 49. If regulation 52 applied, she had a deemed one-third share but the same principles would apply on valuation. Thus in both *Palfrey* and *Dowell* the Commissioners were faced with claimants who, by operation of law, had equal interests. They expressly reserved their position on whether regulation 52 operated so as to deem actual *unequal* shares as equal shares.[79] The Court of Appeal similarly found no need to address that particular issue.[80]

In *McDonnell* the claimant was joint owner of a house with her husband, from whom she was separated. The house, which was valued at £65,000 and subject to a mortgage of £47,000, was let out to tenants. The Commissioners held that the co-owned freehold interest in the property was a "reversionary interest" within the meaning of one of the statutory disregards,[81] and so was exempt from valuation as her capital.[82] The application of regulation 52 therefore did not apply in this case. The Court of Appeal confirmed this conclusion,

[73] *ibid.*, p.26.
[74] *loc. cit.*
[75] *CIS/417/1992.*
[76] *CIS/085/1992.*
[77] *CIS/127/1993.*
[78] This case turned on the "reversionary interest" point which was also raised in the *McDonnell* case and did not concern regulation 52.
[79] *CIS/417/1992*, para. 24. This point was subsequently resolved in the affirmative by Commissioner Mesher in *CIS/240/1992*: see above n.35.
[80] "Although [the regulation] might well work to the detriment of a claimant who was a tenant in common with less than an equal share, none of the claimants here is in that position and no argument has been advanced against the apparent effect of the regulation in that respect" *per* Nourse L.J., *Palfrey*, official transcript p.6. But as Hobhouse L.J. noted, regulation 52 could also apply to the credit balance in a joint bank account or a joint shareholding. "The only puzzle in such a situation is why the share should be deemed to be equal and the true entitlement not used": *ibid.*, p.18.
[81] S.I. 1987 No. 1967, Sched. 10, para. 5.
[82] *CIS/085/1992*, para. 38.

but the wording of the relevant exemption was subsequently amended to reverse the effect of this decision with effect from October 1995.[83]

In *McNamara* the claimant, an elderly widow suffering from senile dementia, was resident in a nursing home. She was the joint owner with her daughter of a house which had been their home for more than 30 years and in which the daughter continued to reside. The adjudication officer calculated her interest to be worth nearly £11,000, applying the strict arithmetical construction of regulation 52 and after making allowances for the costs of sale and for the outstanding mortgage debt. A social security appeal tribunal allowed her appeal on the basis that her deemed share effectively had a nil value. Commissioner Mesher formally allowed the adjudication officer's appeal on the basis of errors of law in the tribunal's judgment.[84] However, applying the decision of the Tribunal of Commissioners in *Palfrey*, the Commissioner found for the appellant on the central issue of the valuation under regulation 52, accepting evidence from a surveyor that the claimant's interest was not a marketable commodity and was accordingly of no value.[85]

THE POST-*PALFREY* AMENDMENT AND THE *ULTRA VIRES* CHALLENGE IN *TUCKER*

The Department of Social Security subsequently sought to reverse the effect of the Court of Appeal's decision in *Palfrey* through amending regulations which came into force on October 2, 1995.[86] Regulation 52 was redrafted so that it read as follows:

> "Except where a claimant possesses capital which is disregarded under regulation 51(4) (notional capital), where a claimant and one or more persons are beneficially entitled in possession to any capital asset they shall be treated as if each of them were

[83] Income-related Benefits Schemes and Social Security (Claims and Payments) (Miscellaneous Amendments) Regulations 1995 (S.I. 1995 No. 2303), reg. 6(10)(a).

[84] Brian Harvey, along with many other tribunal chairmen, will doubtless smile wryly at the Commissioner's comments: "I agree that the appeal tribunal's decision does disclose errors of law. However, I should say that the appeal tribunal displayed an admirable grasp of the difficult legal issue before it and set out its reasoning on that issue fully, and in the main clearly. Unfortunately, as I recognise can happen all too easily happen under the pressure of time which often affects appeal tribunals, the concentration on the central issue seems to have led to a failure to make all the necessary findings of fact and to deal with the consequences of the determination of the central issue": *CIS/127/1993*, para. 11.

[85] According to the surveyor: "In effect the value of this asset cannot be realized in the market place. The property would be occupied as a residence, but non income producing and therefore would not be attractive to an investor. Moreover a speculative purchaser of the share in the hope of obtaining vacant possession in the future would I believe be unlikely in the present circumstances"; *ibid.*, para. 19.

[86] *Ibid.*, reg. 6(6). Guidance to adjudication officers was subsequently issued as AM(AOG)12 (November 20, 1996) that for the period before October 2, 1995 the principles in *Palfrey* should be applied: "In the absence of real evidence of an **actual** willing purchaser, the value of a claimant's deemed share in jointly held property should be accepted as **nil**" (original emphasis).

> entitled in possession *to an equal share of the whole beneficial interest therein; and the value of that equal share shall be calculated by taking the value of the whole beneficial interest calculated in accordance with the foregoing provisions of this Chapter, as though—*
>
> *(a) that interest is solely owned by the claimant; and*
>
> *(b) in the case of a dwelling, none of the other joint owners occupies the dwelling concerned,*
>
> *and dividing the same by the number of persons who have a beneficial interest in the capital in question.*"

The policy intention is entirely clear: the difficulties of valuing an equitable interest in co-owned property were to be sidestepped by a crude arithmetical exercise, as the Chief Adjudication Officer had unsuccessfully argued in *Palfrey* was the effect of the original 1988 version of regulation 52. Thus under the new formulation the value of the property in question was to be taken, as determined under regulation 49,[87] and then simply divided by the number of beneficiaries. The law had come full circle, seeking to prescribe a method of valuation which had been the practice under the former supplementary benefits scheme, albeit in contravention of the then departmental guidance. The belt and braces wording of assumptions (a) and (b) in the amended Regulation 52 was clearly designed to avoid the complications which would be introduced by the types of considerations relevant to an application to force a sale of jointly-owned property. Given the history of the saga over the drafting of this provision, the editor of *Mesher and Wood* predicted that the validity of the new regulation 52 would be subject to further scrutiny, and she was not to be disappointed.[88]

The 1995 variant on regulation 52 was subject to a successful *ultra vires* challenge in *Tucker*,[89] heard by Commissioner Goodman together with *Wilkinson*[90] and *Moharrer*,[91] with a common Appendix, dealing with the general legal principles, being given for all three decisions.[92] In *Tucker* the claimant, a 73 year old widow, owned what was thought to be a one-third share in a property with her daughter and son-in-law; the net value of the total equity was nearly £18,000. As in *Palfrey* she then moved out, presumably into some form of residential care (the decision is short on facts) and was fixed with tariff income on the basis that she had some £5,380 in capital. In *Wilkinson* the appellant, an elderly woman, jointly owned and lived in a bungalow with another elderly woman (not a relative).[93] The claimant was then admitted to a nursing home and her claim for

[87] Thus allowing deductions from the gross value of 10 per cent for the costs of sale and in respect of any incumbrances secured on the property.

[88] Wood, *Income-related Benefits: The Legislation*, 1995 Supplement (1995), p.19.

[89] *CIS/15936/1996.*

[90] *CIS/263/1997.*

[91] *CIS/3283/1997.*

[92] It is interesting to note that the Chief Commissioner expressly decided not to appoint a Tribunal of three Commissioners to hear these appeals (see above n.49). The not unreasonable assumption was perhaps that the case was bound to go to the Court of Appeal in any event.

[93] It is unclear from the brief report whether they were joint tenants or tenants in common in equity, but nothing turns on the point given the breadth of regulation 52.

income support refused on the basis that she had capital assets exceeding the prescribed limit (in this instance £16,000, as she was resident in a nursing home). The bungalow had been valued at £40,000, and her share under regulation 52 was calculated to be £18,000.[94] In *Moharrer* a flat worth £100,000 was owned under a tenancy in common by the claimant (a one-fifth share), her step-mother (a two-fifths share) and her two step-siblings (a one-fifth share each). The claimant applied for income support less than a fortnight after the post-*Palfrey* amendment to regulation 52 in October 1995. Her share was accordingly regarded under regulation 52 as being £18,000,[95] so excluding her also from entitlement to benefit.

It will be recalled that a direct challenge to the *vires* of the pre-*Palfrey* version of regulation 52 failed before the Tribunal of Commissioners in that case. Commissioner Goodman specifically declined to depart from that ruling in the *Tucker* trio of cases.[96] However, Commissioner Goodman was of course directly concerned with the post-*Palfrey* formulation of regulation 52, which he recognised was "clearly introduced to 'reverse' the decision of the Court of Appeal in the *Palfrey* etc. cases."[97] Not only did this deem the co-owners to have equal shares, but it also deemed that share to be freely realisable. The adjudication officer's contention was that this "double deeming" was authorised by the combined effect of sections 136(3)[98] and 136(5)(a)[99] of the Social Security Contributions and Benefits Act 1992. The Commissioner observed that the 1995 amendments "derogate considerably" from the principle enshrined in regulation 49 and concluded, moreover, that section 136(3) of the 1992 Act:

> "does *not* authorise a departure from the normal principle that a valuation of property of whatsoever nature must bear some relationship to its *actual* value. The 1995 Amendments violate that principle fundamentally in that they provide for a method of valuation of shares in capital jointly held which has no relationship to the sum which may actually be realisable for that share."

Furthermore, section 136(5)(a) was concerned solely with the attribution of capital and made no provision for matters of valuation. His conclusion was therefore that the new regulation 52 was not authorised by the statutory powers in the primary legislation. Given his decision on the *vires* point, there was no need for Commissioner Goodman to reach a view on the wider question as to whether the 1995 amendments were void for irrationality. The Commissioner was careful not to express an opinion either on that specific issue or, more generally, on the scope of the Commissioners' jurisdiction to take such a point.[100]

[94] i.e. one half of the valuation less 10 per cent of the costs of sale under reg. 49.

[95] Being one-fifth of the overall value less 10 per cent for the expenses of sale.

[96] Common Appendix to *CIS/15936/1996*, *CIS/263/1997* and *CIS/3283/1997*, para. 8.

[97] *Ibid.*, para. 9.

[98] This provides that ". . . capital shall be calculated or estimated in such manner as may be prescribed".

[99] See p.000 above.

[100] Above n.96, para. 14. See also *CIS/14141/1996* for an example of the difficulty of establishing a challenge to *vires* on the basis of irrationality, especially at para. 21.

The immediate and practical consequence of Commissioner Goodman's decision was that regulation 52 had to be read henceforth as if the amendments made by the 1995 amending regulations were null and void. It followed necessarily that the only valid version of regulation 52 was that in force at the time of the rulings of the Tribunal of Commissioners and the Court of Appeal in *Palfrey*, and so those authorities still applied as to the principles of valuation of co-owned property. In respect to the individual cases under appeal (*Tucker, Wilkinson* and *Moharrer*), it was conceded by the adjudication officer that in each case the value of the claimant's share in the relevant asset was either nil or too low to warrant either a disentitlement for exceeding the capital limit or the attribution of tariff income.[101]

As a coda to his decision, Commissioner Goodman considered the application of regulation 52 to different forms of co-ownership. Although not strictly necessary for the proper disposal of these appeals, the Commissioner expressed the view that regulation 52 *in all its forms* applied to both joint tenants and tenants in common.[102] The basis for this conclusion was the generic language of the regulations, which refer to property being "jointly held" and to "joint owners" and so connote co-ownership generally.[103] It was also noted that *Dowell* had involved a tenancy in common and the Tribunal of Commissioners in that case had proceeded on the assumption that regulation 52 applied. This being so, it remains inevitable, as a matter of principle, for a tenant in common as to a one-tenth share (which might be readily valued, and certainly more readily valued than an interest under a joint tenancy) to be fixed with a one-half share where there is only one other co-owner. Such a conclusion was the "inescapable result of the application of regulation 52, as adjudicated on by the Tribunal of Commissioners in the *Palfrey* and *Dowell* cases."[104] In this context, it is pertinent to note that the Tribunal of Commissioners in *Palfrey*, given the breadth of the enabling powers, expressly rejected the argument that such an outcome necessarily meant that the regulation was void for irrationality.[105]

The decision in *Tucker* was of particular significance to people moving into residential care and leaving a non-partner joint owner in occupation of the property, and to separating and divorcing couples who remained joint owners after six months of separation,[106] as claimants in these situations would be

[101] *Ibid.*, para. 15.

[102] *Ibid.*, para. 17.

[103] The Commissioner accordingly distinguished *CIS/7097/1995* (on which see advice to adjudication officers issued as AM(AOG)50 (4 September 1997)), both on "its very special facts relating to a joint bank account, containing also third party's monies" and also as a matter of general principle (*loc. cit.*). See also *CIS/449/1990.*

[104] Above n.96, para. 18.

[105] "It cannot conceivably be said that such a provision, if indeed that is what the regulation provides, is wholly outside the intention of Parliament and that the Secretary of State has taken leave of his senses": *CIS/391/1992*, para. 46. See also n.100 above and now *O'Connor* v. *Chief Adjudication Officer and Secretary of State for Social Security* [1999] E.L.R. 209.

[106] D. Thomas and S. Robertson, "Recent developments in social security law", *Legal Action*, August 1998, p.11 at p.12.

unable to avail themselves of any of the capital disregards under the income support scheme.[107] Moreover, the principles laid down by Commissioner Goodman in *Tucker* necessarily applied *pari passu* to the other means-tested benefits schemes, given that regulation 52 was replicated (with its various amendments) within the relevant sets of regulations. Thus in *CFC/16105/96* the corresponding regulation in the family credit scheme was held to be *ultra vires*.[108] The facts of that case were similar to those in *McDonnell*, in that the claimant jointly owned a house with her ex-husband which was let to tenants. On the question of valuation, Deputy Commissioner Fellner observed that the difficulties in realising the half-share might include "the lack of a market for a share already subject to contested ancillary matrimonial proceedings and the likelihood that any application for sale of the property might have been successfully resisted".[109]

THE POSITION SINCE *TUCKER*

It was originally anticipated that the Department might seek to challenge the decision of Commissioner Goodman in *Tucker* before the Court of Appeal. However, wiser counsel prevailed and the Department's response was to promulgate yet another amendment to regulation 52 with effect from 12 October 1998.[110] As it currently stands,[111] the regulation now states that:

> "Except where a claimant possesses capital which is disregarded under regulation 51(4) (notional capital), where a claimant and one or more persons are beneficially entitled in possession to any capital asset they shall be treated as if each of them were entitled in possession *to the whole beneficial interest therein in an equal share and the foregoing provisions of this Chapter shall apply for the purposes of calculating the amount of capital which the claimant is treated as possessing as if it were actual capital which the claimant does possess.*"

The wheel had thus come full circle again, with regulation 52 reverting to its revised 1988 formulation. This retains the crude deeming rule which regards all co-owners as having equal shares, but restores the more sophisticated approach to valuation affirmed in *Palfrey*.

How did this reversal of the Department's position affect other claimants? An unknown number of claimants for income support and for other means-tested benefits will have been denied entitlement to benefit as their claims for benefit were determined on the basis of the post-*Palfrey* version of regulation 52 found to be invalid in *Tucker*. The immediate advice to claimants in this position was to apply for a review or (if the decision was within the previous three months)

107 Income Support (General) Regulations 1987 (S.I. 1987 No. 1967), Sched. 10.
108 Family Credit (General) Regulations 1987 (S.I. 1987 No. 1968), reg. 35.
109 *CFC/16105/1996*, para. 12.
110 Social Security Amendment (Capital) Regulations 1998 (S.I. 1998 No. 2250).
111 At least at the time of final revisions, namely October 2000.

to lodge an appeal.[112] However, this only provided limited solace for those concerned. The Department's interpretation of the "anti-test case rule" was such that it sought to pay arrears on review only as far back as 21 May 1998, the date of Commissioner Goodman's decision in *Tucker*.[113]

There were, however, two further complications which appear to have been overlooked in the literature to date. First, as Commissioner Goodman had held in *Tucker* that the 1995 amendments to regulation 52 were *ultra vires*, accordingly that regulation and its companions in respect of disability working allowance and family credit reverted to their pre-1995 formulation, without the offending words. But jobseeker's allowance (JSA) was not introduced until October 1996, i.e. after the 1995 amendments; the parallel provision to regulation 52 for income-based jobseeker's allowance (regulation 115)[114] was thus enacted for the first time using the post-1995 formulation. The effect of *Tucker* was to remove the final part of regulation 115, leaving it to read as follows:

> "Except where a claimant possesses capital which is disregarded under regulation 113(4) (notional capital), where a claimant and one or more persons are beneficially entitled in possession to any capital asset they shall be treated as if each of them were entitled in possession."

This was, even by the standards of social security legislation, nonsense, and could not be rescued by the remainder of the original regulation 52 as that had never been part of the regime for income-based JSA.[115] Logically it followed that, so far as claimants for income-based JSA were concerned, there was simply no meaningful provision governing the valuation of jointly-owned capital at least from the date of the Commissioner's decision in *Tucker* (21 May 1998) until the 1998 amendments were brought into operation (12 October 1998).[116]

The second problem revolved around housing benefit and council tax benefit. The parallel provisions had undergone the same series of legislative amendments as had taken place in the income support scheme.[117] But whereas adjudication officers deciding claims for family credit, disability working allowance and (subject to the above discussion) income-based JSA were bound to apply

[112] *Welfare Rights Bulletin* 145, August 1998, p.14 and *Disability Rights Bulletin*, Winter 1998, Update p.1.

[113] For the counter view, see *Welfare Rights Bulletin* 145, August 1998, p.14.

[114] Jobseeker's Allowance Regulations 1996 (S.I. 1996 No. 207).

[115] The advice to adjudication officers was less than helpful: "The JSA jointly-owned capital regulation has been the same since the start of JSA and was not introduced by amendment. The AO should nonetheless treat the regulation as not containing the words that require deemed shares to be valued in a special way" (Memo AOG Vol 8/17).

[116] If, as is arguable, s.69 of SSAA 1992 did not "bite on" a successful *ultra vires* challenge (see further n.113 above), then this legal vacuum went back to the inception of the JSA scheme in October 1996. I am indebted to Penny Wood for talking this through with me.

[117] Strictly from 1988 in relation to housing benefit and from 1992 in relation to council tax benefit. Thus regulation 44 of the Housing Benefit (General) Regulations 1987 (S.I. 1987 No. 1971) has been described by the authors of *CPAG's Housing Benefit and Council Tax Benefit Legislation*, above n.40, as having "probably the most chequered legislative history of any regulation in this book" (p.235).

Tucker and treat the 1995 amending regulations as *ultra vires*,[118] local authority officials determining claims for housing benefit and council tax benefit had no legal authority to treat a statutory provision as *ultra vires*, as they stand outside the hierarchy of statutory adjudicating authorities.[119] As a matter of strict law, they should have continued to apply the regulations in those schemes, the parallel provision to which in the income support scheme had been ruled to be *ultra vires* in *Tucker*. Theoretically it would therefore have been possible that a co-owner claiming both income support and council tax benefit would have had their interest in the jointly-owned property valued differently for each benefit. This merely re-emphasises the continuing unsatisfactory nature of the arrangements for determining claims for housing benefit and council tax benefit.[120]

VALUATION: A COMPARISON WITH INHERITANCE TAX

We have seen that the Commissioners have generally taken the view that the market value of an interest in jointly-owned property will be at best minimal and often nil, given the right of the other owner(s) to remain in that property. This appears to be a matter of judicial notice; in no cases has any further evidence been sought beyond that which may have been available at first instance. In particular, the Commissioners have not, in any of these cases, used their power to seek specialist advice, either by commissioning an expert's report[121] or indeed by sitting with an assessor.[122] In fairness it should be noted that these provisions are very rarely used.

The social security case law has also been conspicuous for its failure to consider the ways in which jointly-owned capital is valued in other legal contexts. For example, the Commissioners' decisions discussed above, and indeed the Court of Appeal in *Palfrey*, have not sought to make any comparisons with the law governing inheritance tax. The fundamental principle as regards valuation in the latter context is established by section 160 of the Inheritance Act 1984:

> "Except as otherwise provided by this Act, the value at any time of any property shall for the purposes of this Act be the price which the property might reasonably be expected to fetch if sold in the open market at that time; but that price shall not be assumed to be reduced on the ground that the whole property is to be placed on the market at one and the same time."

[118] Following the decision of the House of Lords in *Foster* v. *Chief Adjudication Officer* [1993] A.C. 754 (see D. Feldman and N. Wikeley (1993) 109 L.Q.R. 544), adjudication officers and appeal tribunals are in principle bound to consider a *vires* argument, and certainly to apply a decision of a Commissioner on the point.

[119] This may account for the statement in HB/CTB Circular A30/98 that "a recent Commissioner's decision has thrown doubt on the *vires* of the regulations concerning the valuation of jointly-owned property", advice which was described by CPAG as "disingenuous": above, n.113.

[120] Ogus, Barendt and Wikeley, *The Law of Social Security*, 4th ed., (London: Butterworths, 1995), p. 684. See now Child Support, Pensions and Social Security Act 2000, s. 68 and Sched. 7.

[121] SSAA 1992, s.53. See now Social Security Act 1998, s.16(6).

[122] SSAA 1992, s.56 (see *R(I) 14/51*).

The underlying assumption is thus broadly the same as for regulation 49 of the Income Support (General) Regulations 1987, namely that the current market value prevails, albeit that regulation 49 makes provision for specified reductions to allow for the costs of sale. However, a very different approach has been adopted by the limited case law on the valuation of co-owned property in this context.[123]

In *Wight* v. *Commissioners of Inland Revenue*[124] two unrelated spinsters, Miss Moss and Miss Wight, bought a house in Weston-super-Mare in 1952. They contributed equally to the purchase price and occupied the house together, living as one household. The property was conveyed to them as joint tenants on trust for sale with a further declaration that, in the event of disposal, the net proceeds of sale were to be held on trust for themselves as tenants in common. In 1979 Miss Wight died; Miss Moss continued to occupy the house as her home. The value of the freehold interest was agreed to be £22,500; it was also agreed that a fair rent for the property at that time would have been £800 per annum. The issue for the Lands Tribunal was the appropriate valuation of Miss Wight's interest for the purposes of capital transfer tax (now inheritance tax).

The executors of the deceased's estate argued that the property should be valued as if let at a fair rent (presumably as there was effectively a sitting tenant in Miss Moss). They then contended that the resulting valuation should be halved (given it was a joint interest) and then rounded up to reflect a possible bid by the survivor and the possibility of future appreciation. This produced a value of £4,000. On the other hand, the Commissioners of Inland Revenue adopted the District Valuer's traditional approach, namely to take half the vacant possession value of the freehold and then to deduct 10 per cent to allow for the restricted demand for this type of interest. Using this methodology, the value of the deceased's interest was assessed at £10,000. This approach is clearly more in line with the valuation policy formerly adopted by the DSS in income support claims in relation to co-owned capital assets.

It was agreed by the parties that what had to be valued was an equitable tenancy in common. The Lands Tribunal considered whether a purchaser of that interest would succeed in an application under section 30 of the Law of Property Act 1925, concluding that no order would be made so long as Miss Moss was alive as the purpose of the original trust subsisted. It was accordingly not "highly likely", as the District Valuer had assumed, that an order for sale would be made. However, the argument for a valuation based on a fair rent was also rejected as such an approach would only be appropriate if an order for sale was made but postponed. The Lands Tribunal recognised that the 10 per cent deduction had become customary, but held that in this case a more suitable discount was 15 per cent, leading to a valuation of £9,560. The appeal was allowed to that extent, but clearly the Lands Tribunal's valuation was much closer to that

[123] I am indebted to my colleague Natalie Lee for drawing this provision and the case law to my attention.

[124] (1982) 264 E.G. 935.

advocated by the Inland Revenue. As the Lands Tribunal concluded, "that [the Revenue's] valuation is nearer the mark than [the executors'] is indicated by supposing that the two half shares were each worth £4,000. If Miss Moss purchased Miss Wight's share at that figure she could sell the whole at a very large profit".[125]

What if, rather than having died in 1979, Miss Wight had left Miss Moss in residence in their co-owned house in Weston-super-Mare and had moved into a nursing home and claimed supplementary benefit?[126] If the advice in the then departmental guidance had been followed, the District Valuer would have been asked for his valuation of the interest and she would have been excluded from benefit. If the *Palfrey* approach to valuation were to be followed, her interest would almost certainly have been valued at nil and (assuming she had no other assets) her claim for benefit would have succeeded.

This raises the interesting prospect that the very same interest may be valued in very different ways for different purposes. It is, however, possible to reconcile this. There is a body of social security case law which suggests that the methods of valuation for revenue purposes should not necessarily be applied in the context of supplementary benefit or income support.[127] The point was addressed directly by Commissioner Mesher in *CIS/767/1993*, decided after the Court of Appeal's judgment in *Palfrey*. The claimant, a woman of 81, owned a farmhouse and surrounding farm land with her husband. She then had to move into a residential care home; the farmhouse itself could be disregarded,[128] but the value of the farm land fell to be assessed. The District Valuer's report indicated that the value of the entirety was £36,000 (subject to the farm's trading partnership) or £40,000 (with vacant possession); applying the revenue principles, he then arrived at a valuation of £15,000 for the claimant's interest, allowing for the trading partnership. This assessment was rejected by the Commissioner on two grounds. First, as a result of *Palfrey* "one must ask what could actually be obtained for the asset in question in the current market",[129] rather than applying the revenue approach which starts with a division of the vacant possession value and then applies a discount to reflect the restricted demand for such an interest. Secondly, the District Valuer had assumed that an order for sale of the farm would be likely to be granted. Given that the property was farmed by the claimant's husband and son in partnership, it was by no means certain that an application for sale under section 30 of the Law of Property Act 1925 would succeed.[130] In this context it is interesting to note that the editors of one of the standard works on the taxation of real property argue

125 At p. 937.
126 In other words, the scenario in *Wilkinson*, above n.90.
127 See e.g. *R(SB) 18/83*, para. 16 and *R(IS) 2/90* paras. 5–8.
128 Income Support (General) Regulations 1987 (S.I. 1987 No. 1967), Sched. 10, para. 4.
129 *CIS/767/1993*, para. 27.
130 See n.67.

that the traditional revenue approach may be difficult to sustain in future, which suggests that there may be some convergence in valuation practices.[131]

CONCLUSION

The complexity of regulation 52 in its various guises has been such that the Social Security Commissioners (and indeed social security appeal tribunals) have been "obliged to referee a game of competing statutory construction. The claimant's needs, which the system is, after all, supposed to address, may easily get submerged in a sea of technicality."[132] The saga of the *Palfrey* and *Tucker* litigation thus holds several lessons for the development of social security law.

In the 1970s the courts took the view that supplementary benefit (S.B.) law should be "administered with as little technicality as possible. It should not become the happy hunting ground for lawyers."[133] This non-interventionist approach was strongly criticised in contemporary academic writing.[134] At that time the basic structure of supplementary benefits law was laid down in primary legislation; much of the detail was left to the written and unwritten policy of the then Supplementary Benefits Commission (S.B.C.) and Department of Health and Social Security (D.H.S.S.). By the time Brian Harvey was first appointed as a tribunal chairman, the legal framework of supplementary benefits law had changed beyond recognition. In particular, departmental guidance was transformed into the force of law by its incorporation into densely-drafted statutory instruments.[135]

This pointed to the indispensable nature of legal qualifications and expertise for those involved in chairing appeal tribunals. *Palfrey* and the other Commissioners' decisions discussed in this chapter have been simply the tip of the iceberg; other "lookalike" cases have been heard before social security appeal tribunals, and often held back pending the outcome of lead cases such as

[131] In M. Gammie and J. de Souza, *Land Taxation* (London: Sweet & Maxwell, 1986), it is argued that the days of a fixed 10 per cent discount when valuing an undivided share in non-residential property have passed, and that there is no logical reason to start with the valuation of the whole when the stakeholder has little prospect of being able to force a sale. "It needs to be borne in mind, when valuing, say, a half share in a property, that what falls to be valued is the half share and not half the whole": Vol. 1, para. B6.022C. Note also an early American treatise, which reported typically discounts of 10 to 25 per cent when valuing fractional interests in realty for inheritance tax purposes: "the particular percentage that is used is based, not on concrete studies of the relative market values of divided and entire interests, but on arbitrary rules of thumb": J.C. Bonbright, *The Valuation of Property*, 1st ed. (Charlottesville: Michie, 1937, reprint 1965), Vol. I, pp.707–708.

[132] D. Thomas, "Access Denied" (1993) 90(44) *Law Society Gazette* 19, p.20.

[133] R. v. *Preston Supplementary Benefit Appeal Tribunal, ex p. Moore* [1975] 1 W.L.R. 624, at 631, *per* Lord Denning M.R.

[134] See especially T. Prosser, "Politics and Judicial Review: The Atkinson Case and its Aftermath" [1979] *Public Law* 59 and *Test Cases for the Poor* (London: CPAG, 1983).

[135] See generally I.B. McKenna, "The Legalisation of Supplementary Benefits—More Power to the Claimant?" [1985] *Public Law* 455.

Palfrey and *Tucker*.[136] In this context it is noteworthy that the previous Conservative administration proposed to introduce arrangements for non-legally qualified decision makers sitting alone in appropriate types of benefit appeals.[137] This proposal found its way into draft legislation brought forward by the incoming Labour Government. However, by the time the Social Security Act 1998 was enacted, the central role of the lawyer had been resurrected with the panel of lay members on social security appeal tribunals being abolished.[138]

There are also implications for first tier decision making; cases such as *Palfrey* and *Tucker* emphasise the importance of the availability of specialist advice to staff in local offices charged with making decisions on the ground.[139] More fundamentally, the very existence of regulation 52 points to the constant tensions inherent in operating a mass means-tested benefit scheme. The administrative and bureaucratic imperative is to devise a streamlined, efficient system which can process large numbers of claimants whilst deploying relatively low grade civil service staff and utilising computers, wherever possible, for routine tasks. The drive for such operational efficiency was a key reason behind the overhaul of supplementary benefits in 1980 and the introduction of income support in 1988. It has also lain behind a whole raft of individual changes to specific aspects of the income support scheme, such as the decision to implement a "standard rate of interest" for income support housing costs in 1995, irrespective of the individual claimant's own mortgage interest rate.[140]

Against these pressures, the very rationale of a means-tested benefit scheme is that it is premised on an assessment and comparison of the individual claimant's resources and needs. This presupposes that the adjudication process should resolve disputes about legal rights and the allocation of benefits accordingly. Regulation 52 thus represents one of the pinch points in the modern welfare state: from an operational point of view the need is for a simple rule which can be applied with minimal administrative costs. Logic therefore dictates that, where a claimant is a joint owner of a capital asset, then her individual share should be calculated by dividing the market value by the number of co-owners. As well as being easy for local office staff to understand, such an approach means that an estate agent's simple market valuation of the property is all that

[136] As Brian Harvey can attest from his own judicial experience, this phenomenon is not unique to regulation 52; indeed, *Palfrey* "lookalikes" were relatively infrequent. Along with other experienced tribunal chairmen, Brian presided over whole lists of "lookalike" appeals relating to entitlement to the severe disability premium in income support in the wake of the House of Lords' decisions in *Foster* v. *Chief Adjudication Officer* [1993] A.C. 754 and *Chief Adjudication Officer* v. *Bate* [1996] 1 W.L.R. 814.

[137] These would have been in relation to "straightforward disputes on non-medical facts": DSS, *Improving decision making and appeals in Social Security*, Cm. 3328 (London: HMSO, 1996), p.25.

[138] See N. Wikeley, "Decision making and appeals under the Social Security Act 1998" (1998) 5 *J.S.S.L. 104* and M. Adler, "The Lay Member: A Sorry Goodbye" (1999) 6 *J.S.S.L.* 99.

[139] Formerly designated "adjudication officers", these staff will now all be formally acting on behalf of the Secretary of State following the coming into force of Social Security Act 1998, s.1. See generally the contributions in M. Adler and R. Sainsbury (eds.), *Adjudication Matters: Reforming Decision Making and Appeals in Social Security* (Edinburgh: Department of Social Policy, 1998).

[140] N. Wikeley, "Income support and mortgage interest: the new rules" (1995) 2 *J.S.S.L.* 168.

is required, with no necessity to delve into the technicalities of the underlying beneficial co-ownership. The decision of the Court of Appeal on valuation in *Palfrey* can be viewed as an attempt to reassert the centrality of individualised justice. The 1995 amending regulations can then be seen as an example, in microcosm, of Mashaw's justice model of bureaucratic rationality.[141]

From a policy perspective the most disappointing feature of the saga of regulation 52 is that the battle over the appropriate method of valuing a co-owned share has effectively been fought out within the confines of a series of elegant legal disputes over the construction and *vires* of the regulation in question. Thus the elderly Mr Palfrey was left a winner,[142] and the terminally ill Mr Owen a loser,[143] on the basis of judicial deliberations on the scope of section 136(5) with regard to regulations governing capital and income resources respectively. It is of the very essence of delegated legislation that such provisions do not receive adequate scrutiny at Westminster.[144] This explains in part the vain attempts by the Court of Appeal in *Palfrey* (and especially by Hobhouse L.J.) to discern the purpose of regulation 52. Thus, given the nature of the parliamentary and judicial arenas, there has been no serious attempt to engage publicly with some of the crucial underlying social policy issues involved: to what extent should claimants be expected to realise their interests in co-owned property before claiming income support, especially where that property is occupied by a family member? The Rent Acts and Housing Acts have long accepted, albeit now in an attenuated form, the claim of a member of the tenant's family to security in their joint home.[145] The income support scheme also already recognises that it is inappropriate to take into account the value of the house in which the claimant lives.[146] A further indefinite capital disregard applies where premises are occupied by a partner or relative who is aged 60 or over or is incapacitated.[147] Other property

141 "The administrative goal in the ideal conception of bureaucratic rationality is to develop, at the least possible cost, a system for distinguishing between true and false claims. Adjudication should be both accurate (the legislatively specified goal) and cost-effective. This approach can be stated more broadly by introducing trade-offs between error, administrative, and other 'process' costs such that the goal becomes 'minimise the sum of error and other associated costs' ": J. Mashaw, *Bureaucratic Justice* (New Haven: Yale University Press, 1983), p.25.

142 As David Thomas, formerly legal officer at CPAG has commented, "Mr Palfrey won the valuation argument. It is doubtful whether he has any idea why. So much time and taxpayers' money, not to mention worry for him and his daughter, could have been avoided with clearer drafting": above n.132, p.25.

143 See above p.000.

144 See G. Ganz, "Delegated Legislation: A Necessary Evil or a Constitutional Outrage?", ch. 3 in P. Leyland and T. Woods (eds), *Administrative Law Facing the Future: Old Constraints and New Horizons* (London: Blackstone Press, 1997).

145 See most notably the decision of the House of Lords in *Fitzpatrick* v. *Sterling Housing Association* [1999] 3 W.L.R. 1113; for a critique of the decision of the Court of Appeal, see N. Wikeley, "Same-sex partners and succession to Rent Act tenancies" (19980 10 *Child & Family Law Q*. 191.

146 Income Support (General) Regulations 1987 (S.I. 1987 No. 1971), Sched. 10, para. 1. According to *Social Assistance* (London: D.H.S.S., 1978), "we think it unacceptable that people should actually have to sell their homes, and then live on the proceeds, before they could claim benefit. This could be a savage deterrent to claiming in circumstances of real need" (para. 8.15).

147 Income Support (General) Regulations 1987, Sched. 10, para. 4.

which is not occupied by the claimant (or monies derived from the sale of property) can be disregarded for 26 weeks or, in certain instances, such longer period as is appropriate.[148] However, the restrictive nature of several of these disregards made the controversy over the 1995 amendments to regulation 52 inevitable.

Whilst the present formulation and construction of regulation 52 is broadly favourable to the interests of claimants, the provision remains unsatisfactory in at least two respects. First, the legislation fails to make any distinction between property held on trust for "use", e.g. as a family home, and that held for investment.[149] Property which is held on trust as an investment may well have a genuine realisable value, as with the retail chemists in *CIS/408/1990*. It would be entirely consistent with the principle of means-testing and the current scope of the capital disregards to argue in such a case that a claimant should realise their share in such an asset before turning to the State for support.[150] To apply the same reasoning in the case of a beneficial interest in the family home will, necessarily, either compel the other beneficiaries to provide support or force an application for sale. Yet it is well established that only the claimant's resources and those of any partner and dependants are taken into account in establishing title to means-tested benefits. Since the passage of the National Assistance Act 1948 the ability of other relatives (e.g. an adult son or daughter) to maintain the claimant has been irrelevant.[151] The attribution of an artificially inflated value to a beneficial interest in a family home would therefore subvert that principle. Forcing an application for sale, on the other hand, would generate both legal costs and considerable uncertainty for all the affected parties.[152]

Secondly, regulation 52 continues arbitrarily to deem co-owners as having equal shares. The whole purpose of this deeming provision was presumably to facilitate a straightforward method of assessing the value of a claimant's interest based on the overall market valuation (i.e. the "half the value" as opposed to "value of half" approach where two co-owners are concerned). Yet this methodology has been undermined by the decision in *Palfrey*. If the adjudicating authorities have to go to the trouble of obtaining a valuation of a deemed proportionate share in the property, they may as well obtain a valuation of the claimant's *actual* proportionate interest rather than some notional legislative construct. Furthermore, the fact that the deeming rule applies to all forms of co-owned property, and not just real property, may still result in serious anomalies. As Hobhouse L.J. wondered aloud in *Palfrey*, why should regulation 52 apply

[148] *Ibid.*, paras. 2, 3 and 25–28.

[149] I am grateful to my colleague Nick Hopkins for his insights on this point.

[150] For example, a claimant previously in self-employment has the benefit of a disregard for business assets "for such period as may be reasonable in the circumstances to allow for disposal of any such asset": Income Support (General) Regulations 1987 (S.I. 1987 No. 1967), Sched. 10, para. 6.

[151] R. v. *West London Supplementary Benefits Appeal Tribunal, ex p. Clarke* [1975] 3 All E.R. 513.

[152] On the construction of s.15 of the 1996 Act, see N. Hopkins, "The Trusts of Land and Appointment of Trustees Act 1996" [1996] Conv. 411 at pp.421–423 especially.

to cash assets?[153] The fact that it does provides the scope for some imaginative benefits planning. Thus in principle it would enable an individual with assets over the capital limit to pool them in a joint bank account, along with nominal contributions from several other parties, and hence to fix the real owner of the great majority of the fund with a notional (and much reduced) proportionate share, so as to bring her within the scope of entitlement to income support.[154]

The *Palfrey* and *Tucker* line of cases also indirectly raise wider issues about the justification for capital limits. The standard explanation is that capital disregards exist so as not to penalise the thrifty.[155] Yet this in no way assists us in determining as a matter of policy the level at which such a limit should be set or how it should operate. The treatment of capital assets under the supplementary benefits and later the income support schemes has varied over the years. Originally the capital thresholds were laid down in primary legislation, albeit that the precise mechanisms for taking capital resources into account (or disregarding them) varied over time.[156] With the advent of the 1980 regulation-based scheme, the capital limits became buried in regulations. The maximum capital allowed was initially £2,000,[157] later raised in quick succession to £2,500 in 1982[158] and then to £3,000 in 1983.[159] The upper limit remained fixed at that level until 1988, when it became the lower limit and a tariff income was assumed on capital between £3,000 and £6,000.[160] The £6,000 limit in turn was raised to the current level of £8,000 in 1990,[161] since when it has remained unchanged until recently with the exception of claimants in residential care or nursing homes.[162] There is no statutory mechanism for up-rating the capital (or indeed the income) disregards in line with inflation each year; as the Social Security Advisory Committee has commented, this failure "means an expenditure saving achieved at the expense of a poor section of the community."[163] On the other hand, as the report of the 1978 departmental review of the supplementary benefits scheme observed, "priority has rarely been given to improving the disre-

153 Above n.80.

154 See the worked example provided in *CPAG's Housing Benefit and Council Tax Benefit Legislation* (11th ed., 1998/99) , above n.40, p.236.

155 *Social Assistance*, above n.146, para. 8.10 and D.H.S.S., *Reform of Social Security*, Cmnd. 9517, Vol. 1, para. 9.7.

156 From 1948 until 1966 a basic amount was disregarded and an income assumed on savings between the basic amount and the upper limit. Under the Supplementary Benefit Act 1966 (Sched. 2, para. 22) there was a basic disregard of £300, an assumed income between £300 and £800 with no upper limit but a steeper rate of income assumed on capital above £800. Under the Social Security Benefits Act 1975, Sched. 3, paras. 2 and 3, the lower limit of £300 was replaced by one of £1,200, with a single rate of tariff income above that level and no upper limit.

157 Supplementary Benefits (Resources) Regulations 1981 (S.I. 1981 No. 1527), reg. 7. This operated as a simple cut-off, with no tariff income above this level.

158 Supplementary Benefit Up-rating Regulations 1982 (S.I. 1982 No. 1127), reg. 4.

159 Supplementary Benefit Up-rating Regulations 1983 (S.I. 1983 No. 1245), reg. 3.

160 Income Support (General) Amendment Regulations 1987 (S.I. 1987 No. 1971), regs. 45 and 53.

161 Income-Related Benefits (Miscellaneous Amendments) Regulations 1990 (S.I. 1990 No. 671), reg. 5.

162 For whom the limit was raised to £16,000 in 1996: see n.5 above.

163 S.S.A.C., *First Report* (London: HMSO, 1981), para. 4.23.

gards, mainly on the ground that claimants with disregarded resources were already better off than others and that priority should be given to changes which would benefit all claimants".[164]

In 2000 the Government announced its decision to raise, with effect from April 2001, the lower capital threshold to £6,000 and the upper capital limit to £12,000 for claimants of income support or jobseeker's allowance where either the claimant or his partner is aged 60 or over. (This assumes the claimant does not already have the benefit of the special rule for those in residential care or nursing homes).[165] The tariff income rule in such cases is only to apply to income above £6,000 and below the relevant upper capital limit. The new lower capital threshold of £6,000 also applies to housing benefit and council tax benefit claimants (or partners) aged 60 or over. This development has all the hallmarks of an *ad hoc* response to the Government's political difficulties over the value of the state retirement pension, rather than a considered reappraisal of the role of capital disregards in general.

Moreover, the appropriateness of the level at which the capital limit is set, of the scope of the capital disregards and of the mechanism for valuing co-owned property all have broader ramifications. Many of the cases discussed in this chapter have involved claimants who have moved into residential care or a nursing home, leaving a family member in the co-owned property.[166] The treatment of such property thus raises difficult policy issues in relation to the arrangements for supporting people with long term care needs and the problematic demarcation line between social security and social services.[167]

Finally, the tortuous legislative history of regulation 52 of the Income Support (General) Regulations 1987,[168] and the associated case law, is testament to the all-embracing nature of social security law. All too often, social security law has been seen as a rather technical, self-contained discipline with limited relevance to the more traditional and mainstream branches of legal scholarship. *Palfrey* and *Tucker* illustrate one of the key interfaces between social security law and property law. Indeed, in this context regulation 52 is remarkable for establishing, for benefit purposes at least, a form of statutory severance which has not been acknowledged by the standard texts in property law. Academics are prone to berate law students for their propensity to think in boxes; Brian Harvey's distinguished academic and judicial career is testament to the need to make those connections across sub-disciplines.

[164] *Social Assistance*, above n.146, para. 8.11. The cost of abolishing the capital limits for the income-related benefits has been estimated at between £0.75 billion and £1 billion. An increase in the lower limit from £3,000 to £5,000 and in the standard upper limit from £8,000 to £10,000 would cost about £110 million: *Hansard*, H.L. Debs., Vol. 601 col. 277 (18 May 1999) *per* Baroness Hollis of Heigham.

[165] Social Security Amendment (Capital Limits and Earnings Disregards) Regulations 2000 (S.I. 2000 No. 2545).

[166] This was, of course, the case in *Palfrey* itself, but also in *CIS/024/1990*, *CIS/408/1990*, *CIS/417/1992*, *CIS/127/1993*, *CIS/767/1993*, *CIS/7097/95* and *CIS/263/1997*.

[167] On which see Royal Commission on Long Term Care, *With Respect to Old Age: Long Term Care—Rights and Responsibilities*, Cm. 4192–I and II (London: The Stationery Office, 1999).

[168] S.I. 1987 No. 1967.

10

The Impact of the European Community on the UK Consumer[1]

DEBORAH L. PARRY

APRIL 2000 MARKED the twenty fifth anniversary of the adoption of the *European Economic Community's Preliminary Programme For a Consumer Protection and Information Policy*.[2] It, therefore, seems an appropriate time to review the activities of the European Community (EC) and to consider the consequential impact on laws protecting the consumer in the UK. The word "impact" has been chosen specifically as it can be argued that, in some respects, the position of the UK consumer has been unaffected or has even deteriorated, rather than been improved.

First, the history of EC consumer protection policy will briefly be considered, then its effect on UK law will be examined. Finally an attempt will be made to determine the extent to which European aims and objectives have been achieved and to assess the overall impact on the UK consumer. The debate on the legal basis for European consumer protection policy has been conducted extensively elsewhere and will not be rehearsed.[3] Instead, the focus is on the substantive changes to UK laws and other protective measures that have been prompted or required by membership of the European Community and consideration of their effect on UK consumers.

EUROPEAN CONSUMER PROTECTION POLICY

The 1975 EEC Programme promulgated five basic rights for consumers:

(a) protection of health and safety;
(b) protection of economic interests;

[1] Ideas from which this chapter developed were first presented as a paper at the meeting of the Consumer Law Group of the Society of Public Teachers of Law. Brian Harvey has written on this area see, inter alia, Brian W. Harvey and Deborah L. Parry, *The Law of Consumer Protection and Fair Trading* 5th Edition , (London, Butterworths, 1996), Chapter 2; C. J. Miller, Brian W. Harvey and Deborah L. Parry, *Consumer and Trading Law, Text, Cases and Materials* (Oxford, Oxford University Press, 1998), Chapter 1.

[2] OJ 1975 C 92/1.

[3] See, for example, S. Weatherill, *EC Consumer Law and Policy* (London, Longman, 1997).

(c) redress;
(d) information and education; and
(e) representation (the right to be heard).

Initial progress on achieving these rights proved relatively slow,[4] but a second programme of action for 1981–1986 was eventually approved.[5] Very similar objectives were identified, with greater emphasis on consultation with, and representation of, consumers in the framing of decisions affecting their interests.

1986 saw the Commission critically examining the achievements of a decade of Consumer Programmes in *A New Impetus for Consumer Protection Policy*.[6] This analysed the reasons for delays in achieving the main objectives and indicated the Council action necessary to achieve consumers' wishes namely: that products should conform to acceptable safety and health standards, consumer benefit be obtained from the common market and more account being taken of consumer interests in other Community policies. The Council Resolution of 23 June 1986[7] welcomed this review and endorsed its objectives.

In 1989 a Council Resolution on future priorities for relaunching consumer protection policy was issued,[8] encouraging the integration of consumer protection policies with other policies, improving consumer representation at Community level, promoting the safety of, and information about, goods and services and facilitating access to legal redress. This was accompanied by a three-year plan of action for 1990–1992.[9]

In 1992 the Maastricht Treaty on European Union upgraded the role of consumer protection by adding a new title (XI) on consumer protection to the EC Treaty:

> "The Community shall contribute to the attainment of a high level of consumer protection through:
>
> a) measures adopted pursuant to Article 100A in the context of the completion of the internal market;
>
> b) specific action which supports and supplements the policy pursued by the Member States to protect the health, safety and economic interests of consumers and to provide adequate information to consumers. . . ." (Article 129a).

This, for the first time, made consumer protection a specific objective of the Community.

A now familiar pattern of events followed, with a Council Resolution[10] identifying pre-existing priorities on integration, representation, legal redress and

[4] See Annex to Commission proposal for a draft resolution on the second programme for consumer protection and information, OJ 1979 C 218/3.

[5] Council resolution of 19 May 1981 on a second programme of the European Economic Community for a consumer protection and information policy, OJ 1981 C 133/1.

[6] COM (85) 314 .

[7] OJ 1986 C167/01.

[8] OJ 1989 C 294/1.

[9] COM (90) 98.

[10] Council Resolution of 29 June 1992 on future priorities for the development of consumer protection policy, OJ 1992 C 186/1.

safety and health, and additional priorities for consumer information and education and protection of economic interests. A second three-year action plan for 1993–1995[11] was devised. In March 1995 the Consumer Policy Service of the Commission was upgraded to a Directorate, now DG XXIV Consumer Policy and Consumer Health Protection. The Plan for 1996–1998[12] proposed ten priorities, indicating new areas for action including public utilities, financial services, and the Information Society.

The Treaty of Amsterdam (1997) revises Article 129a[13] to read:

> "1. In order to promote the interests of consumers and to ensure a high level of consumer protection, the Community shall contribute to protecting the health, safety and economic interests of consumers, as well as to promoting their right to information, education and to organise themselves in order to safeguard their interests.
> 2. Consumer protection requirements shall be taken into account in defining and implementing other Community policies and activities.
> 3. The Community shall contribute to the attainment of the objectives referred to in paragraph 1 through:
> (a) measures adopted pursuant to Article 100a in the context of completion of the internal market;
> (b) measures which support, supplement and monitor the policy pursued by the Member States. . .."

1998 saw a further review of progress in *Consumer Policy: Past Achievements*[14] and the Plan for 1999–2001[15] followed, focusing on the tasks identified in the Treaty of Amsterdam namely strengthening the consumer voice, high levels of health and safety and respect for economic interests. Most recently, in 1999, a Decision of the European Parliament and Council establishes a general framework for Community activities in favour of consumers.[16]

To examine the impact of these European initiatives on UK consumers it is necessary to consider developments in Contract, Tort, Criminal Law and administrative regulation.

CONTRACT LAW

The European Community has had a noticeable effect on UK contract law, regarded in some instances as "neutral", in others as largely beneficial to UK consumers. It is submitted that, initially, European measures failed to make a global impact on contract law. Most were fragmented, concerning specific

[11] *Placing the single market at the service of consumers*, COM (93) 378. See also R. Evans, "Time for Action: EU Consumer Policy" (1994) 4 Consumer Policy Review 18.

[12] *Priorities for consumer policy*, COM (95) 519.

[13] To be renumbered as Article 153 when fully adopted.

[14] Commission staff paper, SEC (1998) 564.

[15] COM (98) 696.

[16] 25 January 1999, Decision 283/1999/EC, 1999 L 34/1.

contracts identified by subject matter, such as package travel,[17] or the circumstances under which contracts arise, for example door-step selling.[18] Such measures were designed to provide information to enable consumers to make informed pre-contractual choices or "escape routes" where contracts were entered unwisely.[19] There was no "new order" compared with criminal law, where whole areas of consumer protection have been subject to a "new European approach" and new regimes introduced.[20] More recently, contractual reforms having a wider and more direct impact on the contents of contracts have been introduced or proposed. Of particular note are those concerning unfair terms[21] and the sale of consumer goods and associated guarantees.[22]

Cancellation

Taking formation of a contract as a starting point, the effects of Europe are immediately apparent. Traditionally, in the absence of an operative mistake or fraud, once agreement, consideration and contractual intention are established a binding contract is formed. Termination by the agreement of the parties is permissible; otherwise breach occurs if one party unilaterally decides to end the arrangement. Now, European initiatives mean this is often not the case.

Door-step selling

When a consumer,[23] purchases goods or services following unsolicited door-step selling, the Consumer Protection (Cancellation of Contracts Concluded away from Business Premises) Regulations 1987[24] may apply. If the contract price is £35 or more, the contract, providing it is not an excepted one,[25] will be unenforceable against the consumer if appropriate written notice of cancellation rights has not been delivered (regulation 4(1)). Additionally, the consumer has seven days following the making of the contract to serve, on the supplier, written notice cancelling the contract (regulation 4(5)), at no cost to the consumer. Although the UK had, independently, previously implemented a similar

[17] The Council Directive on package travel, package holidays and package tours, 90/314/EEC, OJ 1990 L 158/59.

[18] Council Directive to protect the consumer in respect of contracts negotiated away from business premises, (85/577/EEC) OJ 1985 L 372/31.

[19] See further S. Weatherill, *EC Consumer Law and Policy* (London, Longman, 1997), Chapter 3.

[20] See below p 232.

[21] Council Directive on unfair terms in consumer contracts (93/13/EEC) OJ 1993 L 95/29.

[22] Council Directive on certain aspects of the sale of consumer goods and associated guarantees (99/44/EC) OJ 1999 L 171/12.

[23] As defined in reg 2(1) of the Consumer Protection (Cancellation of Contracts Concluded away from Business Premises) Regulations 1987, SI 1987/2117.

[24] SI 1987/2117, as amended, implementing Council Directive 85/577/EEC (OJ 1985 L 372/31).

[25] For example insurance, investments agreements, food and drink supplied by regular roundsmen.

right of cancellation where certain regulated credit agreements of £50 or over were signed off trade premises,[26] the Directive further extended these rights to credit agreements over £35.[27]

UK consumers clearly gain from additional cancellation rights but one practical problem that became apparent[28] was the lack of consumer awareness of such statutory rights and the need for individual consumers to enforce them. This led to the introduction of strict liability criminal offences for failure to provide notification of cancellation rights, with an enforcement obligation placed on weights and measures authorities.[29] A private law European measure has thus, eventually, required additional public law measures to ensure that UK consumers receive its full benefit.

Timeshare

UK laws pre-dated European measures regarding timeshare. The Timeshare Act 1992 provided cancellation rights for timeshare agreements governed by UK law or if at least one party was in the UK when the agreement was entered into. The European Directive on Timeshare[30] was adopted two years later and was implemented by amending the 1992 Act.[31] Protection has been extended by, for example, applying to accommodation in the UK and other European Economic Area (EEA) States (where the offeree is ordinarily resident in the UK), additional information requirements and enhanced cooling-off periods in the absence of particular terms in the agreement. It is significant that, in addition to implementing a private law measure by contractual provisions, the UK has made several requirements also enforceable by strict liability criminal offences.

Although UK law has been enhanced, the main impact of the Timeshare Directive will, it is suggested, be felt by UK consumers who purchase timeshares whilst on holiday in other EEA States. Previously, little, if any, protection was provided by UK legislation,[32] and consumers were often without adequate protection under the national laws where the property is situated. The incorporation of the Directive into the domestic laws of all EEA States will achieve a far greater level of protection.

[26] Under s 67 of the Consumer Credit Act 1974.

[27] Reg 9 of SI 1987/2117, amending s 74 (2) of the Consumer Credit Act 1974.

[28] *Doorstep Selling: Improving the protection of consumers*, DTI Consultation Paper, June 1998.

[29] Regs 4A and 4D of the 1987 Regulations as inserted by the Consumer Protection (Cancellation of Contracts Concluded away from Business Premises) (Amendment) Regulations 1988, SI 1988/3050 as of 31 December 1998.

[30] European Parliament and Council Directive 94/47/EC of 26 October 1994 on the protection of purchasers in respect of certain aspects of contracts relating to the purchase of the right to use immovable properties on a timeshare basis (OJ 1994 L 280/83).

[31] See the Timeshare Regulations 1997 (SI 1997/1081).

[32] Unless under the Consumer Credit Act 1974, s 75, see *Jarrett* v. *Barclays Bank plc; Jones* v. *First National Bank plc; Peacock* v. *First National Bank plc* [1997] 2 All ER 484.

Distance selling

The most recent European measure concerning cancellation rights, implemented mainly by the Distance Selling Regulations 2000, is the Directive on the protection of consumers in respect of distance contracts.[33] This applies to organised distance sales or service schemes using "distance communications" such as direct mailings, catalogues, telephone calls, electronic mail, fax, teleshopping etc. There are information requirements, a minimum of seven working days' withdrawal provision, restrictions on the use of automated calling machines and faxes, prohibitions on inertia selling and performance requirements.

An extensive range of contracts are affected and, in conjunction with the door-step provisions, consumers dealing with businesses will usually only be left without cancellation rights if making face to face contracts on trade premises. This makes substantial inroads into UK contractual rules, allowing hasty or pressurised consumers time for reflection in many but, significantly, not yet all, contractual situations. Consumer education is needed regarding the availability of cancellation rights, their differing applications and time limits, and, importantly their non-availability in certain situations.

Terms of contracts

European measures have had a considerable impact on terms in contracts. Although the proposed Directive on Services[34] was abandoned, there have been notable changes both regarding specific contracts, for example package travel agreements and also for non-negotiated contract terms. Most recently a directive has been adopted on sale of consumer goods and associated guarantees.[35]

Package travel

The Council Directive on package travel, package holidays and package tours,[36] implemented in the UK as the Package Travel, Package Holidays and Package Tours Regulations 1992,[37] has improved package holiday contracts for UK travellers. Consumers[38] have a civil action for compensation,[39] including for disappointment, if affected by misleading information concerning the package, its

[33] 97/7/EC, OJ 1997 L 144/19.

[34] Draft Directive on Liability of Suppliers of Services, COM (90) 482.

[35] Directive 1999/44/EC, OJ 1999 L 171/12.

[36] 90/314/EEC, OJ 1990 L 158/59.

[37] SI 1992/3288.

[38] This covers, in addition to the person booking the package, others members of the party included on the booking form, thereby extending full liability, irrespective of privity arguments, cf *Jackson* v. *Horizon Holidays Ltd* [1975] 1 WLR 1468 and in advance of the Contracts (Rights of Third Parties) Act 1999.

[39] Reg 4.

price or the conditions applying to the contract. This is wider than pre-existing provisions for misrepresentation and breach of contract. Particulars in brochures constitute implied warranties in contracts based upon them, subject to certain exceptions,[40] thus obviating the need to distinguish representations and terms. The form, content and presentation of contracts are regulated by creating an implied condition that the specified requirements are complied with (Regulation 9) and contractual measures regulate transfers of bookings, price revisions, significant alterations of essential terms, withdrawal by consumers and cancellations by organisers (Regulations 10–13). There is also codification of the pre-existing UK law whereby liability is placed on organisers and/or retailers to ensure proper performance of the contract by themselves and other suppliers of services (Regulation 15). Also of note, although not relating to contractual terms, are the bonding, insurance and trust provisions to cover insolvency and the several criminal offences created by the Regulations regarding the supply of information.

Many aspects of the Package Travel Regulations were already covered by the ABTA Codes of Practice for Tour Operators and Travel Agents. Such codes do not, however, apply to all travel businesses. Clearly, the consumer has much stronger protection from legal provisions enforceable by civil and/or criminal actions, rather than relying on pressure from trade organisations on their members to comply with codes. There were few, if any, signs of moves to enhance UK protection in the absence of the Directive and consumers certainly have gained considerably from European intervention.[41]

Unfair terms

The most significant contractual development to date is the Council Directive on unfair terms in consumer contracts,[42] incorporated into UK law originally by the Unfair Terms in Consumer Contracts Regulations 1994,[43] now replaced by the Unfair Terms in Consumer Contracts Regulations 1999.[44] Both versions of the Regulations supplement pre-existing measures, and, although it is comparatively early to assess their impact, they appear very beneficial for consumers, in enabling an extensive range of terms to be challenged.[45]

Briefly, the 1999 Regulations apply, with certain exceptions, to terms in contracts, made by consumers with business sellers or suppliers, where those terms have not been individually negotiated—*ie* standard terms. Such terms are subject to a test of "fairness"—an "unfair term" being one which "contrary to the

[40] Reg 6.

[41] The Regulations are described as the "catalyst" for an increased willingness for consumers to pursue their grievances, see Jonathan Ungoed-Thomas in *The Sunday Times* 19 July 1998.

[42] 93/13/EEC, OJ 1993 L 95/29.

[43] SI 1994/3159, applicable to contracts made on or after 1 July 1995.

[44] SI 1999/2083, applicable to contracts made on or after 1 October 1999.

[45] See also the discussion of the powers given to the Director General of Fair Trading and other bodies at p 240.

requirement of good faith, . . . causes a significant imbalance in the parties' rights and obligations arising under the contract, to the detriment of the consumer".[46] A further requirement is that terms must be presented in plain, intelligible language.[47] Factors to be considered in assessing the fairness of a term are specified,[48] and Schedule 2 provides an "indicative list" of terms that might be regarded as unfair. A term judged to be unfair is unenforceable against the consumer, although the contract will continue if capable of subsisting without the offending term.

There is considerable overlap between the Regulations and the pre-existing statutory controls in the Unfair Contract Terms Act 1977, but many new aspects are also introduced. For example the Regulations are not solely concerned with exemption clauses, unlike the 1977 Act. Any non-negotiated term, apart from those defining the subject matter of the contract and the contractual consideration, may be subject to the fairness test. Many other examples could be cited. The Directive has thus led to a considerable extension of the UK courts' powers to question the fairness of non-negotiated terms in consumer contracts.

An example of applying the 1994 Regulations demonstrates their benefit. In *Falco Finance Ltd* v. *Michael Gough*[49] possession proceedings were brought against the defendant for failure to pay instalments on a second mortgage. It was argued, inter alia, that a term, considerably increasing the interest rate following non-payment or late payment of any instalment, was an unfair term under the Regulations. The County Court agreed with this submission. It also considered there was unfairness in calculating interest on a flat-rate, rather than a reducing, basis and in the amount of payment required to redeem the mortgage early. Although the Consumer Credit Act 1974 was also of some assistance to the consumer here, without the 1994 Regulations he would have remained bound by several onerous terms.

In time, an extensive jurisprudence on the meaning of "good faith" will develop. This concept is familiar to many European lawyers, for example in France and Germany, and to United Kingdom lawyers in Scotland. It has not, however, previously received much legal attention in England and Wales.[50] A new era in contract law began for all UK consumers on 1 July 1995.

Implied terms and guarantees

A Directive on certain aspects of the sale of consumer goods and associated guarantees was adopted on 25 May1999.[51] Some modification of UK statutory

[46] Reg 5 (1).
[47] Reg 7.
[48] Reg 6.
[49] (1998) 17 Tr LR 526.
[50] For further reading on good faith see, *inter alia*, J. Beatson and D. Freidmann (eds) *Good Faith and Fault in Contract Law* (Oxford, Clarendon Press, 1995); R. Harrison *Good Faith in Sales* (London, Sweet & Maxwell, 1997); R. Brownsword, N. J. Hird and G. Howells (eds) *Good Faith in Contracts: Concept and Context* (Aldershot, Ashgate, 1999).
[51] Directive 1999/44/EC, OJ 1999 L 171/12.

measures on implied terms in sale and supply contracts is needed by 1 January 2002, to create rights of repair and replacement, make changes to acceptance in sale of goods contracts and extend rights regarding guarantees. It is vital that, where pre-existing provisions are more generous to UK consumers, these are maintained when the Directive is incorporated into UK law, thereby enhancing the position of consumers.

TORT

Product liability has been a focus of attention from the beginning of the European Programme for Consumer Protection. As a result of the Directive on product liability[52] and the initial implementing legislation: the Consumer Protection Act 1987, Part I and the Consumer Protection (Northern Ireland) Order 1987,[53] UK consumers now benefit from a form of strict liability for defective products which cause death, personal injury and certain forms of property damage. Liability is usually placed on the producer, Community importer or own-brander of the goods.

Looking at the impact on UK consumers, at a simple practical level it can be argued that their position has been improved. Whereas prior to the Act fault on the part of the producer had to be proved by the injured victim, in the absence of a contractual relationship, now "fault" per se is not relevant, save for a defence of contributory negligence. The claimant only has to establish a relevant injury caused by a defective product.[54] Injured consumers may now receive prompt offers of compensation from producers of defective products, instead of long protracted denials of liability.[55]

Sometimes, instead of using the tort of negligence to sue the user of a defective product that harms another, action may be taken by the victim, under the Part I of the 1987 Act, directly against the producer of the defective product. For example, a manufacturer settled a claim for personal injury caused when a defective surgical instrument broke and was left inside a patient during an operation.[56] Prior to implementation of the Directive a protracted negligence claim

[52] Council Directive on the approximation of the laws, regulations and administrative provisions for the Member States concerning liability for defective products, 85/374/EEC, OJ 1985 L 210/29, as amended by Directive 1999/34/EC, OJ 1999 L 141/20.

[53] SI 1987/2049 (NI 20).

[54] It is, however, the case that establishing that a product is "defective" raises many issues also relevant to proving fault. See further C. Newdick, "The Future of Negligence in Product Liability" (1987) 104 LQR 288.

[55] This has been the author's experience when advising on a claim for burns and shock from a faulty coffee machine. See also M. Mildred, "The Impact of the Directive in the United Kingdom" in M. Goyens (ed.), *Directive 85/374/EEC on Product Liability: Ten Years After* (Louvain-la-Neuve, CDC, 1996). The National Consumer Council, however, produced a critical report on the apparent lack of use of the Act, see *Unsafe products*, NCC, November 1995.

[56] *Which?* February 1993, p 5.

against the surgeon and hospital authorities would have been a much more likely action.

These developments signify changes in approach on the part of both producers and consumers in the light of the legislation. It could also be suggested that producers might be more willing to countenance claims for compensation, being mindful of similar statutory provisions creating criminal liability, formerly under section 10 of the Consumer Protection Act 1987 and now under the General Product Safety Regulations 1994.[57] A consumer, whose civil complaint has been dealt with promptly and with some generosity, is less likely to report the existence of a defective product to the enforcement authorities.

It is also interesting to consider, first, whether the European model was the best model of strict liability to adopt, given that there were other alternatives already "on the table" in the UK.[58] Second, could the Directive preclude the UK from, unilaterally, providing greater protection to its consumers at some future time? Third, does European intervention on product liability create a barrier to more widespread UK reforms to provide compensation for personal injuries regardless of the way they are caused or on a no-fault basis?[59] It is important, in identifying immediate improvements for consumers, not to lose sight of the possible long-term implications of changes adopted on the basis of compromises between a large number of differing approaches, attitudes and pre-existing regimes, where not only consumer protection is the aim but also free movement of goods. The derogations permitted under the Directive[60] have resulted in inconsistent implementation throughout the Community, thereby hampering the free movement aims and it is not entirely apparent that the "level playing field" of Europe is better than any national "playing field". Further evidence is required before a proper conclusion can be drawn on the effects of the Directive.

CRIMINAL LAW

It is suggested that the greatest impact the European Union has made on UK consumer protection is within the criminal sphere. Several aspects will be examined briefly[61] to illustrate developments and the effects of European activity. Entire areas of criminal control have been subject to "Europeanisation", with

[57] SI 1994/2328, see further *infra*.

[58] *Liability for Defective Products*, Law Com. No. 82, Scot Law Com. No 45, 1977, Cmnd. 6831; Council of Europe Convention on Products Liability in regard to Personal Injury and Death (the Strasbourg Convention), January 1977; Royal Commission on Civil Liability and Compensation for Personal Injury and Death, 1978, Cmnd. 7054, (the Pearson Report).

[59] For an interesting discussion of these issues see Stapleton *Product Liability*, (London, Butterworths, 1994) pp. 52–64.

[60] The permitted exclusion of primary agricultural products and game has been curtailed by Directive 1999/34/EC amending Directive 85/374/EEC. Implementation of the change has to be made by Member States by 4 December 2000.

[61] Detailed discussion of the affected areas can be found in consumer textbooks and practitioner works.

new approaches and regimes introduced; often as much to aid competition and free movement as to provide direct protection/information for consumers.

Members of the public, when asked about the impact of Europe on consumers might mention metrication affecting food, drink and petrol, the destruction of "wrong sized" fruit and vegetables, and threats to the British "pinta" and the names of products such as "Bath" buns, "ice-cream" and "Cheddar" cheese. Is this, often rather negative, impression the right one for consumers to possess? The actual effects of European measures on criminal law can be analysed under a number of headings.

1) Expansion

European measures have led to the creation of many new offences, both covering areas already regulated by UK laws, such as labelling of foodstuffs, and new areas, for example package holidays.[62] On the face of it consumers gain from this in that public enforcement, usually by local authorities, of new protective measures appears only to be advantageous.

There can, however, be hidden disadvantages if the legal requirements become very extensive and complicated. New entrants to a particular trading activity might be deterred from commencing business (thus restricting competition), and/or existing traders could find the demands made on them are so onerous that it is not financially viable to continue. These concerns have been to the fore-front of British Government thinking since the mid 1980s with a number of reports published,[63] notably the former Conservative Government's Deregulation Initiative and introduction of the Deregulation and Contracting Out Act 1994 and the current Labour Government's Better Regulation Initiative. A common theme is the desire to limit additional regulatory requirements and associated offences and to streamline and, preferably, reduce existing measures, an aim not always compatible with European objectives.

2) Alteration

A second effect of European measures has been sometimes to "change the way we do things", usually to ensure compatibility throughout the Community. For example two Council Directives[64] required the introduction of an "average" weight system for pre-packaged goods, in place of the "minimum" weight system previously used in the UK.

[62] See above p 228.

[63] *Lifting the Burden*, Cmnd. 9571, 1985; *Building Business . . . Not Barriers*, Cmnd. 9794, 1986; *Competitiveness: Forging Ahead*, Cm. 2867, 1995; *Better Regulation Task Force Review: Consumer Affairs*, Better Regulation Task Force, May 1998.

[64] 75/106/EEC, OJ 1975 L 42 (as amended) and 76/211/EEC, OJ 1976 L 46.

It is extremely difficult to evaluate whether or not consumers benefit from such changes. Clearly considerable expense can be incurred in changing long-established systems, much confusion may occur during the change-over period (possibly continuing for elderly or less-adaptable consumers) and there will always be traders who profit from taking advantage of consumers' ignorance and gullibility when such changes occur. On the other hand, if a uniform system operates throughout the Community, consumers can make more accurate comparisons between products produced in different countries and suppliers will be encouraged to supply beyond their home market, improving competition, and, in theory, providing more choice and, ultimately, lower prices.

3) Restriction

A third effect, closely linked to the second, concerns the issues raised by requiring free movement of goods between Member States. Care has to be taken to ensure that indirect, as well as direct, trade barriers between Member States are not created by national provisions, thereby breaching Treaty obligations, and that products complying with European requirements can be supplied freely within Member States. Two illustrations of European restrictions on UK activities will be considered.

Origin marking

An example of UK measures in conflict with free movement provisions arose over the Trade Descriptions Act 1972. The Act applied to imported goods carrying an UK name or mark and required an indication of the country of manufacture or production if not produced in the UK. Failure to do so incurred criminal liability. The European Commission considered this requirement breached Article 30 of the Treaty of Rome, as non-UK manufacturers were perceived to be at a disadvantage. This view was supported by the European Court of Justice in *Commission of the European Community* v. *United Kingdom of Great Britain and Northern Ireland*.[65]

Subsequently, the 1972 Act was repealed and replaced by the Trade Descriptions (Place of Production) (Marking) Order 1988,[66] which required goods presented in a way suggesting they were produced somewhere other than where actually produced, to indicate their true place of production. The 1988 Order was revoked in 1996[67] and now there is no mandatory requirement to indicate the origin of goods (nor indeed does any provision prevent the disclosure of origin) but any false indications of origin can give rise to offences under

[65] Case 207/83, [1985] ECR 1202.

[66] SI 1988/1771.

[67] Trade Descriptions (Place of Production) (Marking) (Revocation) Order 1996, SI 1996/2757.

the Trade Descriptions Act 1968, section 1.[68] It can thus be seen that the position has reverted to that in place before the 1972 Act, partially as a result of European requirements.

Origin marking is clearly a problematic area for free movement as revelations that a product is made in a particular Member State or even a Member State other than the UK may deter consumers in the UK from buying it.[69] On the other hand if British producers use German-sounding brand names for electrical goods, to induce consumers to believe they are made outside the UK and meet superior technical specifications, this too can distort trade. It could be argued that the consumer gains most from full, accurate disclosure of information regarding the origin of goods, but this, it appears, is not compatible with Community requirements. In this particular contest between free movement requirements and the protection of consumers, free movement prevailed. Whether this will always be the outcome of such a conflict of interests is not certain.

Safety

Producers wishing to distribute goods in various Member States face difficulties if they have to comply with different safety requirements in each Member State. Likewise consumers purchasing goods need to be assured that the goods available, from whatever source, will be safe to use. Safety has been consistently high on the European agenda and a number of initiatives have been taken.

To overcome restrictions on free movement and, simultaneously, to protect consumers and reputable traders, specific measures, such as the Toy Safety Directive, have been introduced.[70] This Directive was made under the "New Approach"[71] where, instead of detailed, specific requirements being laid down, essential safety requirements are set out in the Directive, and are supported by harmonised European standards[72] providing guidance on compliance. Producers must manufacture in conformity with either these standards or, alternatively, obtain an "EC type-examination certificate", indicating conformity of a model of the product with the essential safety requirements. Manufacturers mark products they believe meet the stipulated essential safety requirements with the European safety mark—the "CE mark", and can then freely supply these throughout the Community. Supply in the absence of the CE mark, where

[68] See also "Trade Descriptions Act 1968—Origin Marking Guidance Notes" DTI, December 1996.

[69] An example given by R. Bragg is a souvenir of the Tower of London made in France, *Trade Descriptions*, (Oxford, Clarendon Press, 1991) pp 226–7.

[70] Council Directive on the approximation of the laws of the Member States concerning the safety of toys, 88/378/EEC, OJ 1988 L 187/1, as amended by 93/68/EEC, OJ 1993 L 220/1. The Toys (Safety) Regulations 1989, SI 1989/1275 implemented the Directive in UK law, see now the Toys (Safety) Regulations 1995, SI 1995/204.

[71] OJ 1985 C 136/1, COM (85) 19.

[72] Produced by the European Committee for Standardisation, CEN and the European Committee for Electrotechnical Standardisation, CENELEC.

required, is an offence in the UK, under section 12 of the Consumer Protection Act 1987, and application of the CE mark to a product which does not meet the required standards is similarly illegal.

Such harmonisation measures have caused some concern to consumer organisations. There are fears that in setting standards a "lowest common denominator" approach could be adopted, instead of a "highest common factor". It is believed by many, though not always correctly, that the pre-existing standards applicable in the UK were amongst the highest in Europe and there are concerns[73] in case European standards are lowered to achieve harmonisation, in particular as the number of Member States increases. The use of the CE mark and self-certification is also open to potential abuse by producers. It is not until an enforcement authority tests a product that any incorrect application of approval marks can be detected, and this may occur only after consumers have been harmed by the product. It is also essential that there is confidence in testing and certification occurring in each Member State, otherwise it is not possible to harmonise the standards and, at the same time, guarantee protection of consumers.

In addition to many Directives concerning specific products, the General Product Safety Directive[74] seeks to ensure that products, placed on the market for use by consumers, satisfy the general product safety requirement, regardless of whether or not specific regulations apply to those goods. The General Product Safety Regulations 1994[75] incorporate the Directive into UK law, largely replacing the provisions of section 10 of the Consumer Protection Act 1987. The 1994 Regulations have been analysed and the protection provided contrasted with that previously available.[76] Since the Directive largely reflects the pre-existing British safety model and has extended protection to such items as second-hand goods, it could be said to have done little harm[77] and probably some good.

In conclusion, European measures relating to product safety have restricted the scope for independent action in the UK and require acceptance of European standards, self-certification by producers and testing undertaken in other Member States, with their associated dangers and concerns for consumers.

[73] See V. Graham, Head of Communications, BEUC, "The single market—myth or reality?" (1994) Consumer Policy Review 11.

[74] 92/59/EEC, (1992) OJ 1992 L 228/24.

[75] SI 1994/2328.

[76] See further P. Cartwright, "Product Safety and Consumer Protection" (1995) 58 MLR 222; D. Clarke, "The General Product Safety Regulations", (1995) 103 Trading Standards Review, February, 16; G. Howells "The General Duty to Market Safe Products in the United Kingdom", [1994] LMCLQ 479; D. L. Parry, "Product safety: European Style—an Appraisal" [1995] JBL 268.

[77] Eg maximum imprisonment is only three months, instead of six months under previous legislation.

4) Information

In considering the European impact on criminal law, a fourth and final effect has been to increase information provided, both for individual consumers and for enforcement purposes. Consumers must now receive more information about such matters as product contents, for example cosmetics[78] and the price of products.[79] It is likely, however, that many consumers are ill-equipped to make beneficial use of much of the information provided. On the enforcement side, the Rapid Exchange of Information on Dangers Arising from the Use of Consumer Products System (RAPEX) was introduced,[80] requiring the Commission to be informed when Member States take urgent measures concerning dangerous products, to enable the information to be passed to other Member States. More recently there has been the introduction of a Community system for information on home and leisure accidents (EHLASS).[81] Reporting systems can only provide consumer benefits when immediate positive action is initiated in response to identified hazards and it is apparent that improvements are needed to make these systems effective.[82]

ADMINISTRATIVE REGULATION

One of the growth areas stimulated by European measures has been in the field of what might be called "administrative regulation". This refers to the use of administrative bodies to support, enforce, supervise and regulate measures introduced to protect consumers. Although administrative regulation has been used to implement domestic measures, for example licensing under the Consumer Credit Act 1974 and assurances under Part III of the Fair Trading Act 1973, there has been a considerable expansion under the influence of Europe. The primary body which has received noticeable support in the UK implementation of Directives is the Office of Fair Trading, through the Director General of Fair Trading, in particular with the introduction of new assurance and injunctive procedures. An examination will now be made of the effects of these Directives for UK consumers.

[78] Cosmetic Products Directive 1976, 76/768/EEC, (1976) OJ 1976 L 262/169, as amended.

[79] Council Directive on consumer protection in the indication of the prices of foodstuffs, 79/581/EEC, OJ 1979 L 158/19; Council Directive on consumer protection in the indication of the prices of non-food products, 88/314/EEC, OJ 1988 L 142/19; replaced, from March 2000, by Council Directive on consumer protection in the indication of the prices of products offered to consumers, 98/6/EC, OJ 1998 L 80/27.

[80] Council Decision 84/133/EEC, OJ 1984 L 70/16, now incorporated in art 8 of Directive 92/59/EEC.

[81] EC Parliament and Council Decision 3092/94/EC of 7 December 1994, as amended by Council Decision 95/184/EC.

[82] *Consumer Policy: Past Achievements*, Commission staff paper, SEC (1998) 564.

Credit

The Consumer Credit Directive[83] of 1986 was based largely on the British model of credit control: the Consumer Credit Act 1974. Part III of the 1974 Act established a licensing system under the auspices of the Office of Fair Trading. The Directive, under Article 12(1), has endorsed such a system of licensing, making it a requirement for all Member States. No changes to the pre-existing licensing controls have been required in implementing the Directive in the United Kingdom.[84]

Advertising

In the 1970s, both Europe and the United Kingdom turned attention to the control of misleading and deceptive advertising. To safeguard consumers' economic interests the Commission planned to make proposals "to protect the consumer by appropriate measures against false or misleading advertising".[85] At the same time the Director General of Fair Trading recommended the introduction of an injunctive power, operated by himself, to supplement the existing voluntary control system.[86] Ultimately the Commission's deliberations resulted in a Directive,[87] which, under Article 4, required consumers to be able to bring misleading advertising "before an administrative authority competent either to decide on complaints or to initiate appropriate legal proceedings". In implementing the Directive in the UK, the Director General of Fair Trading has been given powers,[88] where existing voluntary controls are inadequate or unavailable, to seek injunctions to prohibit misleading advertisements (excluding television and radio advertising). It appears here that the UK consumer has thus benefited from the combined approaches of Europe and the UK in the creation of this new weapon against misleading advertising.

[83] Council Directive for the approximation of the laws, regulations and administrative provisions of the Member States concerning consumer credit (87/102/EEC), OJ 1987 L42/48. Subsequent amendments to the Directive have not affected art 12(1).

[84] It is to be noted that the Banking Co-ordination (Second Council Directive) Regulations 1992 (SI 1992/3218) do remove certain "European institutions" and "quasi-European institutions" from UK licence controls when conducting activities which the institution also carries on in its "home" State; control, instead, is operated by the "home" State.

[85] Preliminary Programme, paras 22–23, OJ 1975 C 92/1.

[86] Review of the UK self-regulatory system of advertising control—a report by the Director General of Fair Trading, November 1978, para 6.10. A similar view was reflected in the Report of the Working Party of the Department of Trade, 1980, para 33.

[87] Council Directive of 10 September 1984 relating to the approximation of the laws, regulations and administrative provisions of the Member States concerning misleading advertising (84/450/EEC), O J 1984 L 250/17.

[88] Under the Control of Misleading Advertisements Regulations 1988, SI 1988/915, reg 5.

However, it important to remember that, in addition to there being a number of restrictions over what qualifies as a "misleading advertisement",[89] the injunctive procedure is seen as a "long-stop" for use only when the voluntary control system, operated by the Advertising Standards Authority, is unable to deal satisfactorily with the complaint. As was noted by C Sandford, Chairman of the Code of Advertising Practice Committee of the Advertising Standards Authority:

> "The EEC Directive, which has for many years been something of a Sword of Damocles over the British system of self regulation, in the end leaves the system largely unscathed."[90]

It is very difficult to assess whether British consumers have gained much *real* benefit from the injunctive power. Little use has been made of it since 1988: only ten interim injunctions have been sought. The Director General has also obtained thirty-nine "undertakings", similar to those used for restrictive trade practices and under the assurance procedure under Part III of the Fair Trading Act 1973.

The small number of injunctions/undertakings may, of course, reflect the hopes of Hoffman J in *Director General of Fair Trading* v. *Tobyward Ltd*:[91]

> "that advertisers would be more inclined to accept the rulings of their self-regulatory bodies if it were generally known that in cases in which their procedures had been exhausted and the advertiser was still publishing an advertisement which appeared to the court to be prima facie misleading an injunction would ordinarily be granted."

It may, indeed, indicate that there are very few "misleading" advertisements in need of control by administrative or court proceedings. A total of two thousand three hundred and eleven complaints had been referred to the Director General by the end of 1999, many of which were passed on to other agencies for first comment. Very few complaints submitted by members of the public actually fall within the scope of the Director's powers.

Further changes to the 1988 Regulations were implemented in April 2000, to comply with Directive 97/55/EC,[92] which amends the 1984 Directive to include measures on comparative advertising. No alteration to the existing procedures were necessary, but UK consumers will benefit from the extended scope of the provisions.

[89] See, in particular, the definition of "misleading" under reg 2 (2) and the ruling of the European Court in *Procureur de la République* v. X Case C-373/90 [1992] ECR I-131 where a significant numbers of consumers needed to be confused for the Directive to operate.

[90] Annual Report 1984–85 of the Advertising Standards Authority, p 8.

[91] [1989] 1 WLR 517 at p 522.

[92] Directive amending Directive 84/450/EEC concerning misleading advertising so as to include comparative advertising, OJ 1997 L 290/18; see SI 2000/914.

Unfair Terms

Article 7 of the Directive on unfair terms in consumer contracts[93] requires the provision of adequate and effective means to prevent the continued use of unfair terms in contracts made between consumers and suppliers. This includes enabling persons or organisations "having a legitimate interest under national law in protecting consumers" to take action in court or before administrative bodies to see if contractual terms drawn up for general use are unfair. In implementing the Directive in UK law,[94] the Conservative Government, somewhat reluctantly, gave powers to the Director General to seek an injunction or to accept undertakings to prevent continued use of unfair terms.

The Consumers' Association was granted leave, by the High Court, to apply for judicial review of the provisions, arguing that other bodies, such as themselves, should also be able to challenge contractual terms drawn up for general use. Proceedings were commenced before the European Court of Justice[95] but in June 1997 the newly elected Labour Government announced[96] an intention to widen access to the injunctive process. This has been implemented, as of 1 October 1999, in the Unfair Terms in Consumer Contracts Regulations 1999.[97] Powers, similar to those provided for the Director General of Fair Trading, are granted[98] to the bodies specified in Part One of Schedule 1. These bodies include the statutory regulators, weights and measures authorities and the Department of Economic Development in Northern Ireland. The Consumers' Association is granted a more limited power, solely to seek injunctions, under regulation 12.

The 1994 Regulations came into force on 1 July 1995, and it is possible to provide an assessment of the impact Regulation 8[99] has already made. The most recent Bulletin of the Office of Fair Trading, *Unfair Contract Terms*,[100] shows that four thousand, one hundred and forty three cases had been examined between 1 July 1995 and 30 June 1999 and of these two thousand, nine hundred and twenty two had action taken under the Regulations. In four hundred and ten cases unfair terms were revised or discontinued without formal undertakings, in eight cases formal undertakings were given and eight hundred cases were still in hand. In many instances potentially unfair terms have been removed voluntarily by traders, on a number of occasions when court action was threatened and in some cases where the issue of court proceedings was imminent.

93 93/31/EEC, OJ 1993 L 95/29.

94 The Unfair Terms in Consumer Contracts Regulations 1994, SI 1994/3159, reg 8.

95 *R v. Secretary of State for Trade and Industry, ex p Consumers Association* case C-82/96, 96/C 145/05; A. Wilson and R. MacArthur, "Unfair Contract Terms: CA's Challenge", (1997) 7 Consumer Policy Review 47.

96 DTI Press Release No P/97/376, 6.6.97.

97 SI 1999/2083.

98 By regs 11–13.

99 Now in more extensive form in reg 12 of the 1999 Regulations.

100 Bulletin No 8, OFT, December 1999.

The first court proceedings seeking an injunction were brought in *Director General of Fair Trading* v. *First National Bank plc*.[101] The case concerned a term whereby the lender reserved the right to charge its borrowers interest even if a court had agreed a sum for a borrower to pay off the outstanding debt. The Director, on appeal, established that the provision was unfair in causing an unfair surprise to the borrower and did not satisfy the requirement of good faith. The court decided not to grant an injunction. Instead the lender was permitted to draft an amendment to meet the Director's objections and to provide an undertaking to incorporate the amendment in its standard terms.

The apparent reluctance of the Office of Fair Trading to bring court proceedings has been criticised[102] and suggestions have been made that it is slow to secure the desired changes in contract terms, with large organisations using delaying tactics. It is also accused of being unwilling to take court proceedings against recalcitrant traders. In the light of the successful outcome of the first court case there may now be more enthusiasm for litigation. Although the criticisms may have some validity, if the contracts affected by the Office's activities are examined, it can be seen that many national companies, whose terms affect millions of consumers, have been successfully targeted. For example Northern Rock Building Society (twice, regarding penalties for early redemption of mortgage contracts and variation clauses in financial service contracts), J Sainsbury plc ("no liability" clauses in supermarket car parks), nine mobile phone companies (high disconnection charges and long periods of notice in particular), BSkyB (changing programming, price variations, unilateral changes of terms, exclusion of liability inter alia) and City Mortgage Corporation (unfair penalties for early redemption of loans) have all ultimately agreed to modifications requested by the Office.

In addition to dealing with contracts of individual companies, the model terms of several trade associations have been subject to consultation and modification, for example the Plastics Window Federation, the Auto Cycle Union and the British Vehicle Rental and Leasing Association. Sectoral guidance has also been issued on home improvement contracts.[103] The Bulletins have, in addition, provided valuable guidance on terms regarded as unfair and illustrations of how more balanced and acceptable provisions may be drafted. It is intended to publish a separate "directory" of specimen terms considered to be potentially unfair, in addition to regular reports on the Office's monitoring and enforcement activities.

In analysing the impact of the use of the Director's powers the following comments can be made. First, it is significant that, unlike the use of the assurance procedures under the Fair Trading Act 1973, Part III, activity is not largely confined to smaller, less well-known businesses where defensive legal advice might

101 [2000] 1 All ER 240, ChD; rvsd: [2000] 2 All ER 759, CA.

102 R. Colbey, "Unfair Terms and the Office of Fair Trading" (1998) 148 NLJ 46.

103 *Unfair Contract Terms*, Bulletin No 3, March 1997, p 7, updated January 1998. This has resulted in some companies subsequently changing their terms.

be lacking. Contracts of small local traders to multi-national companies have been dealt with. Second, the powers exercised by the Director have meant innumerable consumers have benefited from contractual changes over which they have had to take no action. In most cases, the consumer would be completely unaware of the imbalance in the contract until a problem arose where the term would adversely affect them. Although consumers could use the Regulations to challenge terms, as discussed earlier, it is rare for consumers to be aware of such rights and even rarer for them to exercise them on an individual basis. The Director's powers, now extended to further bodies, supplement those of the individual contracting consumer, often obviating the need for such action and making further very substantial inroads into the notion of "freedom of contract". Finally, it is particularly interesting to see use being made of these powers where other measures, such as provisions for early settlement of long term consumer credit contracts,[104] have not achieved fair results or where a combined approach, for example in conjunction with the misleading advertisements provisions,[105] can prove successful.

It must be concluded from the above discussion that the unfair terms Directive has had a very considerable, beneficial impact on the position of UK consumers. This could, perhaps, be further enhanced by more vigorous enforcement by the Office of Fair Trading. It is hoped that the enforcement powers now granted to additional consumer bodies, with their own particular areas of expertise and knowledge, will be energetically adopted to the benefit of consumers.

Future Developments

The implementation of the Directive on injunctions for the protection of consumers' interests,[106] required by November 2000, will increase both the range of Directives subject to this form of enforcement and is also likely to expand the range of bodies entitled to seek injunctions. The protection afforded to consumers will be further extended without the need for individual action.

CONCLUSIONS

It is very difficult to provide a set of coherent and comprehensive conclusions regarding the impact of the European Union on the UK consumer. Considering

[104] Under the Consumer Credit Act 1974, s 95 and the Consumer Credit (Rebate on Early Settlement) Regulations 1983 (SI 1983/1561), see commentary on City Mortgage Corporation and the discontinuation of its use of the "Rule of 78" in *Unfair Contract Terms* Bulletin No 5, OFT, October 1998, at pp 8–9. See also supra n 47.

[105] For example County Holidays, *Unfair Contract Terms* Bulletin No 3, March 1997, pp 28–29.

[106] (98/27/EC) OJ 1998 L 166/51.

first European consumer protection policy, throughout the 25 years of Community involvement there has been a noticeable improvement in the efforts and attention devoted to it. "[A] contribution to the strengthening of consumer protection" has become a stated objective of Community action,[107] there is now a separate Treaty title devoted to it and detailed three-year action plans appear the norm. Considerable slippage occurs, however, with all the plans and targets. Comparatively little progress has been made on the rights of redress and consumer education, with much more action concerning the protection of health, safety and economic interests. Whilst enormous numbers of detailed Directives have been made on labelling, weights and measures, safety of products etc, these are not always promptly, nor uniformly, incorporated into the laws of Member States. Increased membership of the European Union results in the need for transitional provisions, thereby compounding differences. It is clear there is by no means a "level playing field" in practice.

Focusing now on the UK position, it may be useful to consider the words of the Commission:[108]

> "Advances in consumer protection are measured not only in terms of the number of texts adopted or in the process of being adopted. It is also imperative that the measures taken at Community level be perceived by consumers as providing new and effective protection. Consequently, it is important that consumer rights deriving from the Community measures are actually conferred to consumers at national level and that consumers are able to make full use of them."

Compared with other Member States the UK has a good record regarding implementation of Community measures in terms both of promptness and complying with the intentions and spirit of the measures.[109] The issue of whether UK consumers are "able to make full use of them" is more open to debate. Those seeking to discover the law on a given area have been hindered by the manner in which many European measures have been implemented into UK law. Often no attempt is made at integration with, or rationalisation of, the pre-existing law. Examples of such unnecessary complication are the Unfair Terms in Consumer Contracts Regulations 1999[110] and the General Product Safety Regulations 1994.[111] Such problems compound the usual difficulties in informing the consuming public of their rights and how to go about ensuring that these are respected.

It has been seen that contractual, tortious and criminal laws have all been affected by European developments, coupled with considerable expansion in administrative measures. Some commentators have considered that European

[107] Article 3(t) Treaty of Rome, as amended.

[108] Second Three-year Action Plan, COM (93) 378.

[109] This is not to say there are never problems, for example regarding s 4(1)(e) of the Consumer Protection Act 1987 and the development risk defence, see *Commission of the European Communities* v. *United Kingdom* C 300/95.

[110] SI 1999/2083.

[111] SI 1994/2328.

intervention has, at times, been misconceived. For example Sir Gordon Borrie,[112] when Director General of Fair Trading, having welcomed the harmonisation of measures concerning safety, quality standards and weights and measures, criticised measures proposed or implemented concerning economic interests of consumers. He considered some, such as the consumer credit Directive as "irrelevant and irritating", some "retrograde", such as proposals on insurance contracts and others "well-intentioned but damaging to national initiatives", for example the product liability Directive. The Better Regulation Task Force considered that the original proposal for the consumer guarantees Directive did not satisfy the principles of good regulation of being targeted and proportionate.[113] Many would have some sympathy with these views.

Measures passed for the sake of harmonisation often provide little direct benefit to consumers. For there to be a true *benefit* the consumer must achieve *better protection* from the changes introduced. If one is starting from a low base-line of protection then benefits will frequently arise. If, however, there is a reasonable or extensive level of protection already in existence as, it could be said, is the case in the UK, minor additional improvements, which at the same time may involve major changes in how things are regulated, are of dubious benefit. Clearly some measures, like the unfair terms Directive, are producing considerable benefits for UK consumers. This is particularly due to the introduction of administrative regulation; if dependent solely on consumer-initiated action, gains would be much more limited. Many other measures, like the credit directive, produce few additional benefits.

On balance it can be concluded that the European influence has benefited consumers in the UK but at some financial cost to those consumers and to manufacturers, retailers and enforcement agencies. For the future, care must be taken to ensure that European involvement does not stifle or delay national developments, place unwarranted burdens on business nor provide benefits only for well-informed and economically strong consumers. Attempts should also be made to create a better public image of the advantages that consumers gain from European initiatives in the field of consumer protection.

[112] *The Development of Consumer Law and Policy—Bold Sprits and Timorous Souls*, (London, Stevens, 1984) Ch V.

[113] *Better Regulation Task Force Review: Consumer Affairs*, Better Regulation Task Force, May 1998, p 5.

11

Consumer Protection in Private International Law

JONATHAN HARRIS

UNTIL COMPARATIVELY RECENTLY in the development of English Private International Law, consumer protection could not coherently be addressed as a distinct topic. Whether an English court had jurisdiction in transnational litigation would be determined ordinarily by the principles of *forum non conveniens*. These involved primarily an assessment of the centre of gravity of the litigation. The fact that a consumer might be forced to litigate away from home, confronting an unfamiliar legal system, was of no especial significance.[1] Furthermore, if the parties had contractually agreed upon a forum in which to sue, this would be highly conclusive as to where litigation ought to occur. It mattered not that the consumer might have had no effective say on the matter.[2]

When it came to the law applicable on the merits in an English court, matters differed little. The applicable law of an international contract would be that expressly or impliedly chosen by the parties, or, in default, the law of closest connection (objective proper law).[3] Once again, the consumer would be unlikely to have an effective choice in the matter. True, the consumer's position might in part be ameliorated by the application of mandatory rules of law superimposed onto the law governing the contract. Such rules are essentially ones which cannot be derogated from by the parties through the simple expedient of choosing another law to govern the contract. Moreover, it was always open to an English court to find that the application of the governing law of the contract would, on the facts, offend English public policy and should hence be disapplied, in whole or in part. However, these limited protections were always

[1] Although once the defendant had shown that the natural forum lay overseas, the claimant could still resist a stay of English proceedings if he could show that it would be unjust to confine him to his remedies overseas: see *Spiliada Maritime Corp.* v. *Cansulex* [1987] AC 460. His particular vulnerability as a consumer might conceivably be introduced by him at this stage.

[2] See e.g. *The Elefthria* [1970] P 94; *The El Amria* [1981] 2 Lloyd's Rep 119; *The Sennar (no. 2)* [1985] 1 WLR 490; *The Pioneer Container* [1994] 2 AC 324; *Citi-March* v. *Neptune Orient Lines Ltd* [1996] 2 All ER 545.

[3] See e.g. *Vita Food Products Inc.* v. *Unus Shipping Co. Ltd* [1939] AC 277; *Compagnie Tunisienne de Navigation SA* v. *Compagnie d'Armement Maritime SA* [1971] AC 572; *Amin Rasheed Shipping Corp.* v. *Kuwait Insurance Co.* [1984] AC 50.

available as a matter of the English Private International Law of contract.[4] They did not constitute a specific body of legal protection for the consumer.

The accession of the United Kingdom to European Conventions on Private International Law has altered the position. In particular, both the Brussels Convention on Jurisdiction and Judgments[5] and the Rome Convention on the Law Applicable to Contractual Obligations[6] contain specific provisions designed to afford a measure of protection to the consumer. This chapter examines the nature and scope of these provisions[7] and possible reforms thereof.[8]

1. BRUSSELS CONVENTION

The general rule of the Brussels Convention is that a defendant is entitled to be sued in the courts of his or her domicile.[9] There is a feeling that, in international litigation, it is the claimant who holds most of the cards, in that he can choose to commence litigation in the courts of the country where the most advantageous procedural and substantive rules will be applied. The Court of Justice has sought to ensure that any exceptions to the "defendant domicile" rule are construed narrowly.[10] However, exceptions are permitted by the Convention, e.g. where the parties had contractually chosen the courts of another Contracting State as having exclusive jurisdiction over the matter.[11]

Nonetheless, the consumer contract is thought to raise particular problems within the general Convention rules. In the first place, application of the defendant domicile rule would mean that the consumer claimant, already faced with the prospect of suing a company likely to have far greater resources, would have

[4] See e.g. *Ralli Bros.* v. *Compania Naviera Sota y* Aznar [1920] 1 KB 614; *Foster* v. *Driscoll* [1929] 1 KB 479; *Regazzoni* v. *K.C. Sethia Ltd.* [1956] 2 QB 490; *English* v. *Donnelly* 1958 SC 494; *Lemenda Trading Co. Ltd* v. *African Middle East Petroleum Co. Ltd* [1988] QB 448.

[5] Enacted in the UK by the Civil Jurisdiction and Judgments Act 1982, as amended. It came into force in the UK on 1 January 1987.

[6] Enacted in the UK by the Contracts (Applicable Law) Act 1990. It came into force in the UK on 1 April 1991.

[7] An interesting recent discussion of the questions raised by consumer contracts can be found in P. Nygh, *Autonomy in International Contracts* (Oxford: Clarendon Press, 1999), chapter 7.

[8] The Commission has recently issued a Proposal for a Council Regulation on Jurisdiction and the Recognition and Enforcement of Judgments in Civil and Commercial Matters (COM (1999) 348 Final), to replace the Brussels Convention. This has been made possible by Article 65 of the Treaty of Amsterdam, which has brought judicial co-operation in civil matters having cross-border implications within the scope of the first pillar of European Law, insofar as it is necessary for the completion of the internal market. This means that future European initiatives in the field can take the form of a Directive or Regulation (see Beaumont, (1999) 48 ICLQ 225). The United Kingdom has an opt-out from Article 65, but may opt back in to initiatives introduced thereunder. The Commission's proposal would make significant substantive changes to the jurisdiction provisions and would liberalise still further the rules on recognition of foreign judgments. However, proposed reforms to the consumer contract provisions are relatively modest.

[9] Article 2.

[10] See e.g. Case 180/87 *Kalfelis* v. *Schroeder* [1988] ECR 5565; Case C-115/88 *Reichert* v. *Dresdner Bank* [1990] ECR 1–27; Case C-364/93 *Marinari* v. *Lloyds Bank plc* [1995] ECR 1–2719.

[11] Article 17.

to do so on the latter's home ground. The image of the defendant in need of the protection of his own courts hardly seemed apt in such circumstances. Secondly, where the defendant domicile rule was ousted by a choice of court agreement, the inferior bargaining position of the consumer raised the risk that he would effectively have no choice but to consent to an exclusive jurisdiction clause in favour of the courts of the company's home state. This would have the result of depriving the consumer defendant of the right to be sued at home. In other words, the consumer, unable to negotiate favourable jurisdictional terms, would be peculiarly disadvantaged by the operation of the Brussels Convention.

(i) The consumer provisions

The consumer provisions are contained in Articles 13–15 of the Convention. The main provisions of Article 14 are as follows:

> "A consumer may bring proceedings against the other party to a contract either in the courts of the Contracting State in which that party is domiciled or in the courts of the Contracting State in which he is himself domiciled.
> Proceedings may be brought against a consumer by the other party to the contract only in the courts of the Contracting State in which the consumer is domiciled."

In order for these provisions to apply, the defendant must be domiciled in a Contracting State to the Convention.[12] However, it will suffice for these purposes if a company domiciled elsewhere has a branch, agency or other establishment in a Contracting State, if the dispute arises from the operation of that office.[13]

The consumer provisions are not merely a derogation from the defendant domicile rule, but the converse thereof, in that they allow the consumer claimant to sue in his own courts. The Court of Justice has wrestled with two directly competing policies when interpreting them. On the one hand, it has remarked that:

> ". . . the special system established by Article 13 et seq. of the Convention is inspired by the concern to protect the consumer as the party deemed to be economically weaker and less experienced in legal matters than the other party to the contract, and the consumer must not therefore be discouraged from suing by being compelled to bring his action before the courts in the Contracting State in which the other party to the contract is domiciled."[14]

On the other hand:

[12] Jurisdiction will otherwise normally be determined by a State's own national jurisdictional rules, pursuant to Article 4.

[13] Article 13(2).

[14] Case C-89/91 *Shearson Lehman Hutton* v. *TVB* [1993]-I ECR 139, para. 18 of the Judgment.

> "... the rules of jurisdiction which derogate from ... [the defendant domicile] principle cannot give rise to an interpretation going beyond the cases envisaged by the Convention. Such an interpretation must apply *a fortiori* with respect to a rule of jurisdiction such as that contained in Article 14 ... [since] the Convention appears clearly hostile to the attribution of jurisdiction to the courts of the claimant's domicile."[15]

Some form of balance is maintained between these conflicting goals by the fairly restrictive scope of the consumer provisions and by the many pre-conditions for their application which exist. A number of issues need consideration.

(ii) Who is a "consumer"?

In order to ensure the uniform application of the Convention provisions throughout the Contracting States,[16] the definition of "consumer" must be a European autonomous one.[17] Accordingly, an English court is not entitled to apply its own domestic law understanding of the word. However, there is only limited help on the correct interpretation in the Convention itself. Article 13 refers to a person concluding a contract "for a purpose which can be regarded as being outside his trade or profession". However, it does not go on to say that the other contracting party must have acted *within* their trade or profession. This is rather curious, since it is the inequality of bargaining power which justifies the special protection of the consumer. Yet, as a result of this omission, "It would follow that if a student in Oxford buys a second-hand bicycle from another student who is about to return home to Germany, and agrees to pay £30 a month for three months, the buyer is a consumer".[18] However, such a contract would not normally be considered worthy of special protection in domestic legal systems and it would be most surprising if the Convention definition were broader than that commonly found in national law. Although it would not be unreasonable for the Court of Justice to read into Article 13 a requirement that the other party must act in the course of business, the current version of the Convention is an unhelpful source of uncertainty.

Two Court of Justice cases will be considered on the "consumer" definition. In the first, *Shearson Lehman Hutton*, a German consumer had entered into contracts with Hutton Inc (US brokers), to speculate on futures. He apparently had a claim against Hutton Inc for losses caused by their investments, alleging breach of contract, liability in tort and entitlement to restitution for unjust enrichment. Advocate General Darmon considered whether such an agreement could be a "consumer" contract. On one view, those who speculate in futures

[15] Case C-89/91 *Shearson Lehman Hutton* v. *TVB* [1993]-I ECR 139, paras 16–17 of the Judgment.

[16] And hence to facilitate the free movement of judgments.

[17] Case C-89/91 *Shearson Lehman Hutton* [1993]-I ECR 139, para. 13 of the Judgment.

[18] A. Briggs and P. Rees, *Civil Jurisdiction and Judgments*, (Lloyd's of London Press, 2nd ed 1997), 60.

are hardly the paradigm consumers in need of special protection. However, there is no indication in the Convention itself that the type of product to be purchased and the purpose of the purchase are relevant, once it is established that it is not for business purposes. The Advocate General noted that, under the consumer provisions of the Rome Convention, sales of securities are arguably excluded.[19] However, three reasons prevented the adoption of such a view for Brussels Convention purposes. First, as a matter of statutory construction, no restriction as to the product purchased or the degree of sophistication of the transaction is stated. It would be an excessively teleological construction so to construe the provisions. Second, even if futures speculators were not "paradigms for consumers deserving of protection", the Advocate General saw the undesirability in attempting to distinguish between parties on the basis of the object of entering into a particular transaction: "could it be argued that an agency contract concluded in order to manage one's assets prudently would fall within the scope of Article 13 whereas an agency contract concluded for purposes purely speculative would not?".[20] On one view, this objection seems correct. It should be possible objectively to determine in advance which courts have jurisdiction under the Convention. A subjective interpretation of the provisions creates uncertainty and the risk of litigation solely to decide where the parties may litigate on the merits. On the other hand, subjectivity already exists, in that the purpose of the purchaser's activity must be investigated in order to determine whether it is outside his trade or profession. Indeed, the status of consumer cannot easily be determined objectively. But once the reasons for the purchaser's conduct become relevant, and the policy of protection for those who need it is addressed, it is not obvious that the sophistication of the transaction should be ignored, when seeking to determine whether that inequality existed and whether the purchaser's dealings were "normal" consumer behaviour. Against this, such an approach could be the thin end of the wedge, if it allowed consideration of the sophistication not only of the transaction, but also of the consumer himself, and of whether the purchase might be said to be a reasonable management of his assets.

In any event, the Court did not need to address these issues, since the purchaser then assigned his right to sue to a German organisation, TVB. Hutton Inc had since merged with other US brokers to form Shearson Lehman Hutton Inc. TVB commenced litigation in Germany against this company. The issue arose as to whether TVB, as assignee, could benefit from the consumer provisions. The Court held that it could not, as the word "consumer" referred to "a private final consumer, not engaged in trade or professional activities."[21] In other

[19] Giuliano-Lagarde Report OJ 1980 C282/1, 23; Case C-89/91 *Shearson Lehman Hutton* v. *TVB* [1993]-I ECR 139, para. 75 of the Opinion.

[20] *Ibid.*, para. 75 of the Opinion.

[21] Giuliano-Lagarde Report OJ 1980 C282/1, 23; Case C-89/91 *Shearson Lehman Hutton* v. *TVB* [1993]-I ECR 139, para. 22 of the Judgment. This accords with the statement in the Schlosser Report OJ 1979 C59/71, para. 153.

words, the rules apply to those who contract *and sue* outside their trade and profession. This seems instinctively correct: TVB, a corporate entity, did not need, still less deserve, the degree of protection which the archetypal consumer might. However, the counter-argument would be that the contract was concluded outside the initial purchaser's profession, as required by Article 13. It was the right to sue under that initial *consumer* contract which was assigned. It could be said that assignment of contractual rights cannot alter the character of the initial contract, the rights under which are sought to be enforced. Nonetheless, it must be conceded that this view would be most unattractive, since it would mean that the origin of a contract would be all-important, to the exclusion of considering whether the litigant, who is, after all, the focus of the Convention's protective provisions, merits special protection. It follows that the Court's decision, whilst arguably insufficiently reasoned, should nonetheless be welcomed in principle.

In *Francesco Benincasa* v. *Dentalkit Srl*,[22] Dentalkit Srl, a company registered in Florence specialising in the sale of dental hygiene products, purported to enter into a franchise agreement with Benincasa, an Italian national, for the opening of a shop in Munich, where Benincasa stated that he resided. He opened the shop and paid some 8 million lire for Dentalkit's advice and assistance in setting up the business. Subsequently, he made several purchases from Dentalkit pursuant to the franchising arrangement, for which he did not pay. He then ceased trading and sued in Germany to recover the 8 million lire and to obtain a declaration that the franchise agreement was void and that accordingly the subsequent contracts of sale were also void. To Dentalkit's argument that the German court had no jurisdiction to hear the case, Benincasa responded that the contract fell within Article 13.

The argument was rejected by the Court of Justice. Influenced by *Shearson Lehman* and the need for Benincasa to be a private final consumer, it was possible to distinguish Benincasa's status at the time of contracting from the purpose of his activities. At that point, he may not have been in business, [23] but once he had signed the franchising contract, it would be difficult to describe him as operating outside a business context. Moreover, the purpose of the transaction was clearly to help establish a business venture and it is to the purpose of the contract that Article 13 refers. The Court of Justice accordingly held that "only contracts concluded for the purpose of satisfying an individual's needs in terms of private consumption come under the provisions designed to protect the consumer as the party deemed to be the weaker economically".[24]

To focus on the purpose, rather than contracting status, of Benincasa undoubtedly accorded with the literal construction of Article 13 and with the need to construe the consumer provisions narrowly. But insofar as the pro-

[22] Case C-269/95, [1997] ECR I-3767.

[23] Although paradoxically, Benincasa alleged that the consumer contract provisions applied, even though his argument, both to defeat the jurisdiction clause and on the merits, was that no contract existed between the parties.

[24] *Ibid.*, para. 17 of the Judgment.

visions exist to protect a contracting party's weaker bargaining position, the result is not self-evidently to be welcomed. Whatever Benincasa's goals, the would-be entrepreneur is manifestly in much the weaker bargaining position at the time when he concludes the contract. True, at the time of litigation, the disparity might be much reduced; but that litigation may be founded on contractual terms which the purchaser was unable effectively to negotiate. In particular, if he agreed to an exclusive jurisdiction clause at the time of contracting, instigated at the seller's insistence, it is not obvious that he should be denied the protection of the consumer provisions limiting the effect of such clauses.[25] In other words, whatever the relative economic positions of the parties at the time of litigation, there may have been considerable inequality between them at the time when the contract, upon which the litigation is now founded, was concluded.[26] The result of *Shearson* and *Benincasa* is that a person speculating in futures may gain the protection of the consumer provisions, whereas one seeking to make a living by setting up a business will not gain such assistance.

(iii) **What is a "contract"?**

It will not suffice that the claimant is a consumer, if his claim is not treated as contractual within the meaning of the Convention. It has been stressed that, in order to ensure the uniform application of the Convention, "contract" must bear a European autonomous meaning. In *Peters* v. *Zuid Nedelandse Aannermers Vereniging*,[27] a dispute between members of a trade association and the association itself was held to fall within this autonomous definition, even though the Dutch court before which the claim was brought did not think this a contractual claim. In *Handte* v. *Traitements Mécano-chimiques des Surfaces*, it was explained that a matter could not relate to contract where "there does not exist an obligation freely entered into by one party in relation to another".[28] On the facts, this excluded a claim by a sub-buyer of a chattel against its manufacturer pursuant to French law, under which the buyer's rights were assigned to the sub-buyer. The manufacturer had not knowingly entered into a contractual relationship with the sub-buyer. Hence assignments will not normally create contractual relationships for Convention purposes between the manufacturer and the assignee. Privity of obligation is insufficient without the consent of the defendant to the existence of the obligation to the claimant. On the other hand, claims which would be treated as tortious in English domestic law may fall within the *Handte* definition. Most notably, actions based on

[25] See sub-section (v) below.

[26] This position could have been ameliorated if the Court of Justice had allowed Benincasa to argue that, according to the substantive law of the contract, he did not freely consent to all the terms thereof.

[27] Case 34/82, [1983] ECR 987.

[28] Case C-280/90, [1992] ECR 3967, para. 15 of the Judgment.

pre-contractual misrepresentations give rise to voluntarily incurred obligations towards the promisee and would appear to fall within the definition of "contract".[29]

However, claims falling outside the definition of "contract" which a consumer might bring gain no special protection in the Convention. Problems arise where a consumer brings a number of claims falling within and outside Article 13. In *Shearson Lehmann*, the consumer also sued for restitution in respect of unjust enrichment and tortious damages. It might be thought that, if a court has jurisdiction pursuant to Article 13 over a contractual claim, it should also be permitted to take jurisdiction over related non-contractual claims. However, the ECJ ruled in *Kalfelis* v. *Schroeder* that a court could not take jurisdiction over a matter which it would not otherwise be competent to hear solely on the basis that it had jurisdiction over a related claim. This rather literalistic approach can lead to a fragmentation of related claims. Whilst a claimant can always bring the entire claim before the courts of the defendant's domicile under the general Convention rules, this is unlikely greatly to assist the consumer, who will normally want to sue in the courts of his own domicile pursuant to Article 14. The result is that only "pure" contractual claims will benefit from the consumer provisions. A consumer's claim in tort or unjust enrichment will not fall within the special provisions, even if combined with a contractual claim.

(iv) The relevant types of consumer contract

Consumer contracts must also be of a specific type to come within the Convention rules. By Article 13, these require a contract either (1) for the sale of goods on instalment credit terms; or (2) for a loan repayable by instalments, or for any other form of credit, made to finance the sale of goods; or (3) any other contract for the supply of goods or services where (a) in the State of the consumer's domicile the conclusion of the contract was preceded by a specific invitation addressed to him or by advertising and (b) the consumer took in that State the steps necessary for the conclusion of the contract. Contracts of transport are specifically excluded from the consumer provisions.[30]

These provisions draw heavily on the consumer provisions of the Rome Convention, [31] though differ on points of detail. "Instalment credit" has a European autonomous meaning.[32] Hence the first pre-condition would include e.g. hire purchase agreements, even if not treated as sale of goods contracts in domestic law. It is essential, however, that a purchase by instalments be made on credit. In *Mietz* v. *Intership Yachting Sneek BV*,[33] a purchaser was to pay for

[29] *Agnew* v. *Lansförsäkringsbflangens* [2000] 2 WLR 497.
[30] By Article 13(4).
[31] It is so stated by Schlosser, OJ 1979 C59/71, para. 153.
[32] Case 150/77 *Société Bertrand* v. *Ott* [1978] ECR 1431.
[33] Case C-99/96, (1999) ECR I-2277.

a yacht by a series of instalments. However, the final instalment was payable at the time of the trial voyage, i.e. before possession of the yacht passed to him. The ECJ ruled that Article 13(1) would only apply if possession had passed before the price was paid in full, as otherwise no credit was provided. In a genuine credit case, "the purchaser may, when the contract is concluded, be misled as to the real amount which he owes, and . . . he will bear the risk of loss of those goods while remaining obliged to pay any outstanding instalments. Such considerations do not, however, apply where the price must be paid in full before transfer or possession takes place".[34] In *Société Bertrand* v. *Ott*,[35] the ECJ also ruled that the provision excluded payment by bills of exchange. Those paying by such a sophisticated method were thought outside the mischief of the provisions. Yet if the fact that a person deals in futures does not prevent him from being a "consumer",[36] it is difficult to see why the means of payment should be relevant, if it demonstrates the features of instalment credit. Moreover, it has been noted that it would be extraordinary if the decision excluded payment by a series of cheques.[37]

The second alternative pre-condition deals with credit provision, and applies even if the loan itself to finance a sale of goods is not repayable by instalments.[38] It is not expressly stated whether the provision is confined to cases where the purpose of the credit was to purchase goods, or if it also extends to any case where goods are subsequently purchased with that loan money. However, Briggs and Rees convincingly argue that the purpose of the original loan should be the critical factor, since a lender might otherwise have no idea at the time of conclusion that he faced the prospect of being sued in the borrower's own domicile under the consumer provisions.[39]

The third pre-condition is much more general. However, it raises a number of questions. Whilst it is not difficult to determine whether a specific invitation has been made to a purchaser, it can be much harder to decide whether advertising preceded the conclusion of a contract. This is especially so when the advertisement was not directed primarily at the state of the consumer's domicile. In particular, what if a French supplier were to argue that, even though the purchaser responded to an advertisement in Germany, he had not intended to advertise in Germany? Although the Convention nowhere states that the intent of the supplier is relevant, support can be found from an identical provision of the Rome Convention, as interpreted in the Official Report of that latter Convention:

> "Thus the trader must have done certain acts . . . aimed specifically at that country. If, for example, a German makes a contract in response to an advertisement published by

[34] *Ibid.*, para. 31 of the Judgment.
[35] Case 150/77, [1978] ECR 1431.
[36] Case C-89/91 *Shearson Lehman Hutton* v *TVB* [1993]-I ECR 139, discussed above.
[37] A. Briggs and P. Rees, *Civil Jurisdiction and Judgments*, 61.
[38] Schlosser Report OJ 1979 C59/71, para. 156.
[39] A. Briggs and P. Rees, *Civil Jurisdiction and Judgments*, 61.

> a French company in a German publication, the contract is governed by the special rule. If, on the other hand, the German replies to an advertisement in American publications, even if they are sold in Germany, the rule does not apply unless the advertisement appeared in special editions of the publication intended for European countries".[40]

This interpretation is not without difficulty.[41] It is not obvious that the primary destination of the publication should be conclusive, in the absence of a special European edition. A supplier may intend that his advertisement should reach European consumers when advertising in an American publication sold worldwide, or at least have actual or constructive notice that the advert is likely to be seen by European consumers. It might be argued that, with the benefit of any incidental European trade generated by such an advertisement should pass the burden of the consumer contract provisions. A preferable test might accordingly be to ask whether the supplier might reasonably have expected its advertisement to induce a European consumer to contract. Within that test, the primary destination of the publication would be the greatest, but not a conclusive factor.

A further problem arises in determining whether the advertising *preceded* the contract. In *Shearson Lehman*, it was unclear whether the advertisement had caused the consumer to enter into the contract. Advocate General Darmon thought this immaterial, provided that the contract was entered into within a reasonable time after the advertising, both because of the lack of a causation requirement in the Article itself and because of the difficulties of proof.[42] The presumption of causation between the advertisement and conclusion of the contract was "irrebuttable".[43] Yet, it has been noted that an advertisement proven not to have been read by a consumer cannot have *preceded* a contract and hence no case for application of Article 13 exists.[44] Moreover, the Advocate General's approach hardly promotes the supposed narrow interpretation of the consumer provisions. For these reasons, it would be better for causation to be regarded as a requirement of this provision, albeit one rebuttably presumed to exist.

As to the additional need under the third pre-condition to identify the steps necessary by the consumer for conclusion of the contract, the wording is designed to alleviate the need to determine where the contract itself was formed, a question on which different legal systems may take differing views. However, it is reasonable to suppose that different national laws may equally take diverging views as to the essential requirements of the consumer in order to complete the contract. This is particularly likely in relation to contracts concluded via an interactive website. In such a case, it might still be necessary to refer to the law applicable to the contract on the merits in order to ascertain whether, by that

[40] Giuliano and Lagarde Report, 1980 OJ C282/1, 24.

[41] See C. Morse, "Consumer Contracts, Employment Contracts and the Rome Convention" (1992) 41 ICLQ 1, 7. It is now likely to cause particular problems in relation to internet transactions.

[42] Case C-89/91, [1993]-I ECR 139, paras 84 and 85 of the Opinion.

[43] *Ibid.*, para. 85 of the Opinion.

[44] A. Briggs, (1993) 13 Y.E.L. 511, 515.

law, the consumer took all necessary steps for completion of the contract in his state of domicile. Such a test is hardly a convenient one at the jurisdiction stage.

The Commission's recent Proposal for a Council Regulation on Jurisdiction and the Recognition and Enforcement of Judgments in Civil and Commercial Matters,[45] which is intended to replace the Brussels Convention, makes its only major proposed change to the consumer contract provisions in relation to this third pre-condition.[46] It would apply to all contracts not caught by either of the first two pre-conditions if;

> "the contract has been concluded with a person who pursues commercial or professional activities in the Member State of the consumer's domicile or, by any means, directs such activities to that Member State or to several countries including that Member State, and the contract falls with the scope of such activities".

There are a number of significant points to note about this. First, it is expressly stated that the other party must be acting in the course of his trade or profession.[47] Secondly, there is no longer any requirement that the contract be for the supply of goods or services. Any contract,[48] may fall within this provision. Thirdly, it appears that the provision would apply if the other party pursues activities in the State of the consumer's domicile, even if the consumer was in no way induced to contract and the other party primarily operates in another State. It is not obvious that there is a justification for extending the provision so widely. Fourthly, there is no longer a requirement that the consumer should have taken the necessary steps to conclude the contract in the state of his domicile. This should be welcomed, since it eliminates the technical difficulties considered in the previous paragraph and "removes a perceived deficiency in the text of old Article 13, namely that the consumer could not rely on this protective jurisdiction when he had been induced, at the co-contractor's instigation, to leave his home State to conclude the contract".[49] Fifthly, the references to "specific invitation" and "advertising" have been removed. Instead, activities "directed" to the State of the consumer's domicile are caught by the new provision. In this respect, it matters not that they are also directed to other Member States and it is not necessary that they are primarily directed to the consumer's home State. Nevertheless, the word "directs" is highly problematic. It remains unclear to what extent information which is primarily destined for one State, but which will forseeably be received in another State, can be said to be directed at the latter. Moreover, the commentary to the draft Regulation points out that the concept is especially difficult to apply to internet contracts, since "companies engaging in electronic commerce will have to contend with potential litigation in every Member State, or will have to specify that their products or services

[45] COM (1999) 348 Final; see footnote 8 above.

[46] *Ibid.*, Article 15(3).

[47] See section (ii) above.

[48] Other than a contract of transport. Such contracts remain excluded from the consumer provisions in the proposed Article 15.

[49] See commentary to Article 15 in COM (1999) 348 Final.

are not intended for consumers domiciled in certain Member States".[50] Although the Commission suggests that "the fact that a consumer simply had knowledge of a service or possibility of buying goods via a passive website accessible in his country of domicile will not trigger the protective jurisdiction",[51] it is far from clear where the line should be drawn. It appears that, in removing a number of problems, the Commission's proposal would replace them with them with another set.

(v) Choice of court clauses

Article 15 provides:

> "The provisions of this Section may be departed from only by an agreement:
> (1) which is entered into after the dispute has arisen, or
> (2) which allows the consumer to bring proceedings in courts other than those indicated in this Section, or
> (3) which is entered into by the consumer and the other party to the contract, both of whom are at the time domiciled or habitually resident in the same Contracting State, and which confers jurisdiction on the courts of that State, provided that such an agreement is not contrary to the law of the State."

Ordinarily, parties are free to chose the courts of a Contracting State which they wish to have exclusive jurisdiction over a dispute under Article 17,[52] provided that the formality requirements thereof are satisfied.[53] Such an agreement has the effect of ousting the defendant domicile rule. The perceived danger in consumer contracts is that a choice of court clause might be inserted at the instigation of the trader, which not only deprives the consumer of the right under Article 14 to sue either in the courts of his domicile or those of the trader, but also means that the consumer himself could be sued in the trader's home courts. Such a situation might happen e.g. if a French trader and a German consumer contractually agree that all disputes arising between them shall be heard exclusively in the courts of France.

Article 15 accordingly seeks to provide extra protection for the consumer. A jurisdiction clause must still satisfy the formal requirements of Article 17,[54] which lays down the "general" rules for jurisdiction clauses. But a consumer would not ordinarily be bound by a clause inserted at the time of conclusion of the contract or before a dispute arose. However, the unfortunate effect is that

[50] *Ibid.* The Commission is currently considering the specific Private International Law problems caused by electronic commerce.

[51] *Ibid.*

[52] Unless the matter falls within the exclusive jurisdiction provisions of Article 16, or the consumer of insurance provisions.

[53] Namely, that the clause was either: (i) made or evidenced in writing; or (ii) was in a form according with previous business practice between the parties; or (iii) that it was in a form widely used in international trade or commerce, of which the parties were or ought to have been aware.

two parties willing to agree to an exclusive jurisdiction clause in a consumer contract may not do so conclusively at the time of contracting, unless they are domiciled or habitually resident in the same State and choose the courts thereof. Moreover, it may be difficult to determine when a dispute has arisen between the parties. Jenard speaks of the time when legal proceedings are imminent.[55] But this is scarcely more illuminating, focusing neither on the time at which the facts arose provoking litigation, nor on the time when proceedings were commenced.

It is also unclear whether Article 15 is limited to exclusive jurisdiction clauses. Such clauses narrow the consumer's choice. But what if, instead of agreeing that the courts of France exclusively have jurisdiction, the parties were to state that "in addition to those courts specified by the Convention, the courts of France shall also be jurisdictionally competent"? Such a non-exclusive jurisdiction clause is not obviously one from which the consumer needs protection as a claimant, since it will not deprive him of his rights under the Convention. Against this, such a clause could still deprive him of his rights as a defendant to be sued in his home courts. It appears that Article 15(2) envisages that a clause allowing the consumer to sue in courts other than those indicated in the Section will be valid. Briggs and Rees convincingly argue that this provisions should be regarded as giving effect to jurisdiction clauses made solely for the benefit of the consumer, i.e. which open another forum to him, without giving the trader another place to sue.[56] In other words, non-exclusive jurisdiction clauses would only be valid when Article 15(2) applies and the consumer's choice of forum to sue or be sued is not narrowed or compromised; exclusive jurisdiction clauses, which necessarily limit the consumer's choice, will be valid only if the pre-conditions of Article 15(1) or (3) are satisfied.

(vi) Conclusion

The consumer provisions of the Brussels Convention are a significant initial step towards effective jurisdictional protection of the consumer. The right of a consumer to sue at home, even if the natural forum lies elsewhere, is quite new to English law. However, the effectiveness of the provisions is compromised by the narrow definition of "consumer contract" and by the difficulty in applying the provisions. Nor are they always sensitive enough to the differing needs of the consumer at the time of contracting and at the time of litigation. It is also notable that consumer protection has not yet extended beyond the realms of purely contractual disputes. In consequence, consumer protection at the jurisdiction stage is still somewhat piecemeal.

54 Schlosser Report, OJ 1979 C59/71, para. 161.

55 Jenard Report, 1979 OJ C59/1, 33.

56 A. Briggs and P. Rees, *Civil Jurisdiction and Judgments*, 62.

Whilst the Commission's proposed Regulation would broaden the range of contracts caught by the consumer provisions and remove a number of technical difficulties, it is itself likely to cause uncertainty in determining to which States activities are "directed". It is also disappointingly conservative in many respects. It does not attempt any further definition of the word "consumer" and continues to exclude non-contractual claims. To a considerable extent, one must conclude that, if adopted by the Council in this form, it would represent an opportunity missed.

2. ROME CONVENTION

The Rome Convention on the Law Applicable to Contractual Obligations contains a set of harmonised choice of law rules to determine which law ought to be applied on the merits in a transnational contractual dispute. The Convention affords considerable freedom to the parties to choose the applicable law and respects any such choice, if either express of implied with reasonable certainty from the terms of the contract or the circumstances of the case.[57] The danger of applying this provision to consumers is apparent: the trader, using its superior bargaining position, could insist on the application of either its own legal system or of one particularly favourable to it.

In the absence of choice, the applicable law is determined by Article 4, which states that "the contract shall be governed by the law of the country with which it is most closely connected".[58] However, this rather vague statement is qualified by a rebuttable presumption[59] in Article 4(2) as to which law this will ordinarily be. It provides "it shall be presumed that the contract is most closely connected with the country where the party who is to effect the performance which is characteristic of the contract has, at the time of conclusion of the contract, his habitual residence, or, in the case of a body corporate, its central administration". This notion of characteristic performance is itself in need of further explanation. The Official Report by Giuliano and Lagarde states that, in a bilateral contract, characteristic performance is not the payment of money but "the performance for which the payment is due".[60] In a simple contract of sale between retailer and purchaser, it would thus be the law of the retailer's habitual residence which would be applied. Once again, the need for special consumer provisions is obvious. In the absence of choice, a contract would, by virtue of Article 4(2), be governed by the law of the stronger party and not by the law of the consumer.

[57] Article 3.

[58] Article 4(1).

[59] Article 4(5) allows the presumption to be rebutted where it is shown that the contract is more closely connected with another country, or if the characteristic performance cannot be ascertained.

[60] 1980 OJ C282/1, 20.